SHAW'S ACADEMICAL DRESS

of Great Britain and Ireland

Third edition

edited by Nicholas Groves

assisted by
Bruce Christianson, Colin Fleming, William Gibson,
Nicholas Jackson, and Alex Kerr
Diagrams by Kate Douglas

2011

Published by the Burgon Society (registered charity no 1137522); www.burgon.org.uk

ISBN: 978-0-95612723-5

Printed and bound by Lulu.com

The cover picture shows some University of Wales higher doctors' robes.

3.1.1

ABOUT THE EDITORS

Nicholas Groves has been fascinated by academic dress since first his first sightings of it at school, an interest strengthened by being given a copy of the first edition of this book by George Shaw. A varied academic career has entitled him to wear the robes of three universities: Wales (MA, BMus, PhD), London (BA) and East Anglia (MA), as well as of a number of learned societies and colleges, which naturally include the Burgon Society. He has designed or revised the robes for a number of institutions, including the University of Malta, and has published widely on the subject.

Bruce Christianson is from New Zealand, where he first encountered academic dress at the age of four and was instantly hooked. Eight years later he found the first edition of Shaw in the reference section of the Auckland Public Library, next to Hargreaves-Mawdsley, and realised that his peculiar interest placed him in august company. His own robes are from the Victoria University of Wellington (MSc), the University of Oxford (DPhil), and the Burgon Society (FBS). Bruce is Professor of Informatics at the University of Hertfordshire, where he has taught for twenty-five years.

Colin Fleming was born in Bermuda and was attending Stirling University when he first encountered Dr Charles Franklyn's scathing criticisms of the University's academic dress. This ultimately inspired him to enquire more deeply and critically into the topic, and was awarded the FBS for his research into the Stirling robes. He is also an MA of London, and has been chair of the Burgon Society since 2010.

William Gibson is Professor of Ecclesiastical History and Director of the Oxford Centre for Methodism and Church History at Oxford Brookes University. He was chair of the Burgon Society between 2008 and 2010. His interest in academic dress was a result of his study of universities in the eighteenth century and of his admiration for the shot silks of the University of Wales academic dress, and is entitled to wear those of the MA and DLitt, as well as the PhD robes of Middlesex.

Nicholas Jackson first became curious about academic dress while at school, having noticed the interesting robes that the teachers wore during the annual Speech Day and Founder's Day ceremonies. He began to investigate further some years later, as a much-needed distraction from his software engineering career and graduate studies in mathematics. He is a BA of York, an MSc and PhD of Warwick, and a Fellow of the Burgon Society. He teaches mathematics at the University of Warwick.

Alex Kerr was intrigued by the various gowns and hoods worn by masters at his grammar school, where (he learned only a few years ago) George Shaw himself had been a pupil in the 1940s. However, his enthusiasm for the subject took off at university, where a fellow student gave him a copy of Shaw's 1966 book, which had been an unwanted present. Then he discovered early engravings of academic dress gathering dust in Oxford print sellers' shops and started to make a collection. There was no turning back. He is an MA(Oxon), and MA and PhD (Reading).

Kate Douglas was born and bred in Hertfordshire, and worked as a graphic designer and studio manager for twenty years before setting up her own company. She was artist and designer for the booklet illustrating the Academic Dress of the University of Hertfordshire, having previously designed the programmes for nearly a hundred of their awards ceremonies, and now finds herself following in the footsteps of Lt-Col A. J. Hannah. Her HND hood is often mistaken for a DPhil by those who don't know their [f5] from their [a1].

LIST OF CONTENTS

PREFACE

George Shaw first published his *Academical Dress of British Universities* in 1966, and it included just twenty-eight universities, the latest of which was Sussex, chartered in 1961. A further twenty-four, and the Council for National Academic Awards (CNAA), had been chartered before 1966, but their schemes of academic dress had not been finalized when the book went to press. A few new institutions appeared in succeeding years – *e.g.* Cranfield – but the 1992 conversion of polytechnics into universities led to a second edition, in 1995, which contained ninety-six universities and degree-awarding bodies. In October 2000, the Burgon Society was founded, and in the ten years of its existence, it has undertaken much research on the history and developments of academic robes, as well as taking interest in the new schemes and additions. Before his death in 2006, Dr Shaw assigned the copyright of this book to the Society, with the intention that it should undertake future revisions.

As is the nature of such publications, both editions of Shaw's books were out-of-date as soon as they appeared (as indeed this edition will be), as universities added new degrees, and thus new robes, and withdrew others. Since 1995, there has been a further increase in the number of universities, another fourteen institutions, including many of the colleges of the Universities of London and Wales, having been upgraded to university status. (It is interesting that, with the exception of the privately-run Buckingham, there have been no new *ab initio* foundations since the 1960s.) This third edition contains details for 158 degree-awarding bodies, some of which are not strictly universities, but nonetheless can award their own degrees, which has been taken as the criterion for inclusion. Thus, for example, the Royal Colleges of Art (RCA) and of Music (RCM) appear for the first time, although they have been awarding their own degrees for many years. This third edition builds on both its predecessors, and attempts to be as comprehensive as possible, by including disused and superseded robes, as well as those still current.

Another development is the increase of degrees awarded jointly by two universities. These degrees always have their own robes, and such graduates may not wear the robes of either parent university. In some cases, it is just a single degree, such as the MSc in Crop Breeding and Improvement of Birmingham and Reading: in these cases, the degree is listed under both the relevant universities. In other cases, universities have combined to set up a fresh institution, awarding several degrees, such as the Hull-York Medical School, or University Campus Suffolk (a joint venture of East Anglia and Essex); in these cases the new institution has its own entry. There are also a few institutions which, while awarding degrees of a university, have their own robes, such as Henley Business School, which awards Reading degrees. These are listed under the relevant university.

ACKNOWLEDGMENTS

I am extremely grateful to a number of people for their assistance in compiling and updating the information in this work.

- Dr Richard Baker, FBS, for information on the University of Hull.
- Michael Brewer, MPhil, FBS, for information on University of Kent and Christ Church Canterbury University.
- Dr Giles Brightwell, FBS, for information on the University of Durham.
- Tony Chamberlain, of Ryder and Amies, Cambridge, for information on the University of Cambridge, and the Royal College of Art.
- Professor Bruce Christianson, FBS, for information on the University of Hertfordshire, and for overseeing the production of the line-drawings.
- Stephen Coombe, BA, and Dr Wayne Campbell, for information on the University of Essex.
- Dr Paul Coxon, for information on the University of Newcastle-upon-Tyne.
- Kate Douglas, FBS, for the drawings of gowns, hoods and hats, and for the cover design.
- Clifford Dunkley, MA, FBS, for information on the University of Leicester.
- Colin Fleming, MA, FBS, for revising all the Scottish entries.
- Professor William Gibson, FBS, for information on Oxford Brookes University, the University of Wales, and St David's College, Lampeter.
- The Rev'd Philip Goff, BD, FBS, FSA, for information on King's, Imperial, LSE, University of the Arts, the Institute of Education, the University for the Creative Arts, and the University of London.
- Peter Henry, MA, for information on the University of Dublin.
- Dr John Horton, FBS, for information on the University of Nottingham, and the University of Cambridge.
- Dr Nicholas Jackson, FBS, for information on the Universities of Warwick and of York, and overseeing the final stages of production.
- Dr Alex Kerr, FBS, for historical information on the Universities of Oxford and Cambridge, and for overseeing the proof-reading and copy-editing.
- M Perkins and Son, Ltd, for the reproductions of the brocade patterns and the St Benet braid.
- Dr Les Robarts, FBS, for assisting with the proof-reading and copy-editing.
- Elizabeth Scott, MSc, FBS, for information on the Universities of Salford and Nottingham Trent.
- Robin Richardson, of J Wippell & Co, for answering many questions, and sending a number of robes for inspection.
- Nick Shipp, FBS, of Ede & Ravenscroft at Waterbeach, for much helpful information, and making time for me to inspect robes.
- Kim Smith, MSc, CChem, MRSC, for information on the Royal Society of Chemistry.
- The Rev'd Peter Thompson, BA, MPhil, for information on Queen's University, Belfast.
- Charles Rupert Tsua, BA, FBS, for scans of various gimps and laces.

NWG

GEORGE SHAW, MA, MSc, DPhil, DSc, FIBiol, FBS

Dr George Shaw was an acknowledged authority on academic dress, and published several works on the subject, including the two books which were the predecessors of this one: *Academical Dress of British Universities* (1966), and *Academical Dress of British and Irish Universities* (1995). He was one of the first Fellows *honoris causa* of the Burgon Society, and latterly one of its Patrons; in 2005 he announced at a meeting of the Society that he had decided to pass the copyright of these works to the Society, with the intention that a third edition would be produced. The present volume is that third edition, and the Publications Committee of the Society felt it right that it, and subsequent editions, should bear his name in the title, hence *Shaw's Academical Dress: third edition* (already known familiarly as 'Shaw III').

George was born in 1928 at Stalybridge in Cheshire, and died in 2006 at Grantchester. As has so often been the case, his interest in the subject was sparked while at school, observing the masters' gowns. He went to the University College of North Wales at Bangor (now Bangor University), where he gained a BSc in biology, and later completed an MSc while in his first teaching post. In 1956 he was awarded a grant by the Department for Scientific and Industrial Research, which enabled him to go up to Wadham College, Oxford, to read for a DPhil, which was awarded in 1958. He then took a post at Lancing College, where he remained until he retired. Further awards included the Fellowship of the Institute of Biology (FIBiol), and a DSc awarded by the University of Hong Kong, which had invited him to submit his published work in biology for the degree. He also became a Fellow-Commoner of Girton College, Cambridge. A final honorary award was an MA from the University of Bath, for which George had been invited to design the robes.

In addition to the robes for Bath, George designed schemes for the Institute of Biology; the Simon Bolivar University in Caracas; Trent University in Peterborough, Ontario; and he proposed several modifications, which were adopted, to the scheme already in use at Strathclyde. He also drew up a scheme for Sussex, which was not accepted. His publications in the field, besides the 1966 and 1995 books, include a booklet *Cambridge University Academical Dress* (1992), and he was one of the four editors of the 1972 revision of Haycraft, to which he contributed a good deal of material.

NWG

INTRODUCTION

When George Shaw published his first edition of this work in 1966, academic dress was still a familiar part of everyday life in many schools and at most universities. Since then, its use on a daily basis has diminished, even in Oxford and Cambridge. Nonetheless, it is instructive that every new university has introduced a scheme of academic dress. It is true that, in many cases, the robes are worn now but once a year, at graduation ceremonies[1] – indeed, often being referred to as 'graduation robes', implying they are not worn at other times – and even the full-time teaching staff do not, as a rule, now own their robes, but tend to hire them. Following some notable experiments in the 1960s – Sussex, East Anglia, and Kent – the new schemes have, on the whole, been very conservative, making use of pre-existing patterns and styles of trimming. New designs, either new schemes, or additions to existing ones, are more likely these days to emanate from robemakers than from universities or individual designers, and this may well dictate this conservative trend: they are able to use what they already have in stock.

NEW DESIGNS

For the most part, new universities' robes are founded on pre-existing exemplars. Leicester (1957) experimented with recut versions of existing hood shapes, but there were three universities, all new foundations of the 1960s, which tried to break the mould. The first was Sussex (1961), which had its bachelors' hood lined with grey nylon fur, arranged in five-inch squares with a half-inch gap between them, and which did not have any hoods at all for its doctors to start with. The next was East Anglia (1963), whose scheme was designed by Cecil Beaton. This scheme is notable for having replaced the standard black gowns by dark blue ones, and for having hoods that are effectively worn inside-out. It also had some unique hats, which had been replaced by standard squares by 1980. Despite East Anglia's desire not to have robes which were 'another variant on eighteenth-century Oxbridge', it appears that Beaton in fact modelled his robes on late seventeenth-century prints of Oxford robes.[2] Kent (1967) has a scheme which is very traditional save for the hoods, which are simply flat panels,[3] held together in front by cords. Following these very unusual (and not universally loved) designs, universities kept to traditional styles until 2008, when King's College, London, employed Vivienne Westwood to design its robes. Compared with UEA and Kent, they are comparatively conservative, the sole criticism being that the hoods do not have neckbands, but are buttoned onto the shoulders of the gowns, and are thus difficult to wear without the gown – *e.g.*, over a surplice.[4]

---

[1] In many cases, what is referred to as the 'graduation ceremony' is not. Some universities follow the protocol of admitting all candidates *in absentia*, and then later holding what are more correctly called 'presentation ceremonies', as the new graduates are presented to the assembled university.

[2] NW Groves, *The Academical Dress of the University of East Anglia*; Burgon Society, 2005, p 7.

[3] Shaw's 1995 statement that they were designed by Hardy Amies is now known to be false. I am grateful to Michael Brewer, FBS, for this information.

[4] It appears that a version of the hood with neckband has now been sanctioned for ecclesiastical use.

DISUSE OF FUR

One development, noted by Shaw in 1995, is the disuse of fur in new schemes: 'It is also remarkable that none of the new universities has used fur in their hoods, no doubt fearing the wrath of the so-called 'animal rights activists'.'[5] This is partly true: at least one robemaker refuses to make hoods with real fur at all, and several universities which do include fur in their hoods now specify that artificial fur must be used. There is also the cost: a Cambridge BA made with artificial fur can be had for about £60, while one with real fur costs over £200. It is true that over the years the quality of artificial fur has improved, and some very high quality products now available can pass for the real thing, but cheaper versions and those used until recently do not hang well, as the backing material is too inflexible. The last university to specify fur as part of its original scheme was Dundee (chartered 1967). Before that, Stirling did so (1967), and also Sussex (1961), with its grey nylon fur squares, which earned a certain notoriety among specialist observers. Newcastle (1961) inherited it from Durham, and Strathclyde, oddly, introduced it as a faculty edging for its engineering degrees when they were instituted in 1978.[6] Even though it is the marker of bachelors' degree at Liverpool, some of the recently-introduced degrees (BNurs, BClinSc, BMedSc) do not have a fur binding. Most recently, the cape used for the post-PhD diploma of LicDD at Lampeter, instituted in 2008, is trimmed with fur.

COLOURS

Another casualty has been the range of colours used. It is no longer economic to carry stocks of many slightly different shades of silk, and so they tend to fall together: Liverpool's 'apple blossom', used for the Faculty of Arts, was originally a slightly different colour from Manchester's 'salmon pink',[7] used for the Faculty of Science, but for many years the same silk has been used for both. The actual shades also tend to shift over the years, usually getting lighter. The best-known example of this is the Oxford DPhil blue, which started as a deep navy blue, but current robes and hoods are trimmed with a royal blue silk. Another notoriously fluid shade is Durham's 'palatinate purple'. This is usually explained as 'a soft mauve', but may vary from a rich lavender to almost silver-grey. Lack of stability of the dye as the garments age over the years is also a problem, particularly with shades of blue: these tend to turn pink, crimson, or purple, and so one may, albeit unintentionally, appear to hold a degree one does not.

Colours come in variety of shades. One which has a very wide variety of interpretations is 'gold'. This can range from a very pale yellow (London, science) through a rich yellow (Southampton, science) to a deep ochre (Leeds Metropolitan). Wherever possible in this volume, an ambiguous colour name is defined, especially where the university describes it as 'university red/blue/green/…', which is less than helpful.

Until the end of the nineteenth century, the colours of the shells of hoods were very restricted, and easily interpreted. Bachelors and masters wore black hoods, and

---

[5] Shaw, *Academical Dress* 1995, p 3. One hears the voice of the biologist. In fact the real fur, when used, is a by-product of the restaurant trade, and the rabbits are not specially bred for their fur.

[6] The other faculty edgings are coloured cords.

[7] Itself originally described as 'pale red'.

doctors scarlet.[8] The few exceptions were the higher bachelors at Oxford and to an extent Durham, which had coloured hoods but with fur trim, and Doctors of Music, who wore white or cream brocade hoods. This convention was first broken by Leeds (1903) and Sheffield (1904), which use green hoods, and perhaps more seriously Bristol (1909), which uses red shells for all degrees, red hoods having until then been the prerogative of doctors. Since then, a variety of colours has been introduced, and it is now almost impossible to say at a glance what level of degree is represented by any given hood.

ABANDONMENT OF FACULTY COLOURS

One development probably to be welcomed, although started so early as 1909 at Bristol, is the abandonment of faculty colours. It would appear that the notion of rigid 'faculty colours' is a nineteenth-century development in any case; hoods originally indicated status, not faculty. Although their use adds to the interest of a scheme, with the plethora of specially-named degrees that universities seem to find it necessary to grant these days,[9] the systems that use faculty colours are in danger of breaking down: see especially, for example, Liverpool and Birmingham. In the latter case, bindings which have little relevance have been added to the hoods: silver-grey is the Science colour; the MSci has a hood with a silver grey border – and a tangerine binding to difference it from the BSc hood: but tangerine is the Music faculty colour. An even worse case is Leeds, which tries to confine itself to three shades of green, with the addition of white for masters and scarlet for doctors; the newer combinations are far from memorable. Systems which have one hood per grade of degree (the 'grade hood system') are very flexible: any number of named bachelors can be accommodated in a scheme that has a common hood for them all. Taking this to an extreme are the Universities of Kingston and of Teesside, which each have a single 'university' hood, the differences in degree being marked by the gowns. (This of course poses a problem when the hood is worn without the gown – *e.g.*, over a surplice.) The extreme example in the other direction was the National University of Ireland (NUI), which had, when Shaw compiled his 1995 edition, over sixty-six different hoods, each specific to a particular degree, and many of which were so similar it was impossible to tell them apart without the aid of a tape-measure: for example, the MPA was lined white, with two two-inch bands of strawberry set two inches apart, while the MEconSc had two one-and-a-half inch bands, set one and a half inches apart. This scheme has now been rationalized to a great extent, so that all masters in any given faculty wear the same hood.

MATERIALS

Universities usually specify the materials from which the robes are to be made, and they are usually of three kinds: silk, stuff, or cloth. Real silk tends not be used these days, on account of the cost: a standard BA or MA gown made of real corded Ottoman silk

[8] This was before the PhD was introduced.

[9] *E.g.*, BAdmin, Agr(Forest)B, MFA, MBioTech – and maybe the worst example, the now-defunct BBroadcasting(Leeds), which had no abbreviated form. It is not clear why these cannot be awarded a BA, BSc, MA or MSc. The NUI awards an MAgrSc and an MSc(Agr): the difference is far from obvious.

would cost (in 2008) about £925; one made from Russell cord would cost about £220, and one in polyester about £170.[10] For the shell of hoods, and for gowns, silk is usually replaced by a corded or ribbed rayon, which gives much the same appearance, and also has the merit of lasting longer. For hood and robe linings, a taffeta is generally used, as they have the required shiny surface. 'Cloth' strictly means a fabric made from wool, and has historically been restricted to doctors' robes, although it is used for lower degrees in some places: *e.g.*, Sheffield bachelors' hoods are made of dark green cloth. For doctoral robes, it is usually either superfine cloth, which has a slightly felt-like appearance, or wool panama, which is a plain weave material.

'Stuff' is most commonly specified for black gowns (or, for some universities, blue or grey ones). It was until recently usually Russell cord, which is a slightly ribbed material. It is an excellent choice, as it hangs well – and, if of good quality, will last for years of daily wear. Some gowns were made from spun rayon, of which the only things to be said in its favour were its cheapness, and the fact that if creased it hung out easily; but it does not hold its shape, and has no body. Ribbed rayon resembles corded silk, and is much stouter. Of recent years, a move has been made to polyester of varying qualities. Again, it has the merit of cheapness – as noted above, a polyester gown costs significantly less than a Russell cord one – but, unless the fabric is of a very high quality, it retains a stiffness, and does not hang well. Its use in hoods is to be avoided for this reason.

'Lace' is often specified as a trim to gowns; the term 'gimp' is used at Oxford, and occasionally the term 'braid' is used, which is possibly more accurate. There are at least seven types of lace and braid in use:

(a) Oxford gimp: also used at Durham and Hull for music degrees;
(b) Cambridge lace: also used at Exeter and Bath;
(c) Leeds lace: also used at Hull;
(d) Birmingham lace: also used at Nottingham and Leicester;
(e) Durham MB lace: used at Newcastle on the MB, BCh, BHy, and BDS gowns;[11]
(f) Durham MD lace: a 'Greek key' pattern braid used at Newcastle on the MD, DCh, DHy and DDS undress gowns;
(g) St Benet braid: an ecclesiastical braid used on some gowns and hoods at Portsmouth.

Photographs of these are shown on page 42.

Each university tries to have some diagnostic feature by which its hoods can be recognized. For example, of the older ones, Wales (1893) adopted shot silks; Birmingham (1900), watered silks; while Belfast (1909) added a binding of pale blue watered silk to the old Royal University of Ireland (RUI) hoods. A new concept was introduced by Aston (1963): the lining of all its hoods, and the trim on the doctors' robes, has the shield of the university arms woven in. Aston remained the only example of this until 1992, when several of the new universities took up the idea, using either the coat of arms or some

[10] I am grateful to Nick Shipp, FBS, of Ede & Ravenscroft for these costings. Costs change, of course: in the 1966 edition, Shaw said a silk gown cost £40, and one made from 'artificial fibres' about £5.

[11] It appears that the standard BA gown is currently being supplied for medical and dental graduates (personal communication from Dr Paul Coxon).

other symbol; it is a matter of taste as to whether these garments are æsthetically pleasing. Surrey introduced the idea of using brocade as a lining for all hoods, and this is another idea which has been taken up by several of the post-1992 foundations. Some specify which pattern of brocade is to be used, some do not. Where possible, the pattern normally used has been stated in the specifications. The six commonest patterns are illustrated on page 41, although some universities have their own: for example, Brighton has a special damask with the university's elm-leaf logo as the pattern, and York St John's is based on the rose window of York Minster.

DEGREES

Shaw's original 1966 book noted just three levels of degree: bachelor, master, and doctor. While these titles remain the basis of degree nomenclature, a variety of levels within them has evolved. This is particularly the case with masters' degrees. The MPhil, which is a two-year research-based degree,[12] frequently has some special method of distinguishing it from the taught masters (MA, MSc, *etc*), such as coloured facings on the gown, or a distinctive hood. A recent development is the concept of 'first-degree masters',[13] such as MSci, MMath and MPhys.[14] These are awarded after four years' study, rather than the usual three. There has long been a distinction between the robes of the PhD and the higher doctors (DD, DLitt, *etc*), but a new class of doctorate, variously called 'professional', 'specialist', or 'taught', has recently appeared: such are DBA, and DClinPsy. These degrees often include a significant taught element, where the PhD is based solely on research, and their robes are, in most cases, differentiated from those of the purely research-based PhD. The final addition has been the Foundation Degree, which is the equivalent of the first two years of a standard bachelor's degree. They are designated 'Fd' followed by the faculty: thus FdA for Arts, FdSc for Science, FdEng for Engineering. (In the USA these are called Associate Degrees, and are designated AA, AS, *etc*).

Thus the simple threefold listing in the first edition of Bachelor, Master, Doctor has now given place to (at its fullest extent): Foundation Degree, Bachelor, First-Degree Master, Master, Master of Philosophy, Professional Doctor, Doctor of Philosophy, Higher Doctor. In some cases these divisions can be conflated, *e.g.*, at Reading the Masters and MPhils wear the same robes. In many cases, further non-degree awards have had to be included, as the universities are increasingly permitting holders of diplomas and certificates to wear robes. These are slotted into the above scheme at the appropriate point – *e.g.*, postgraduate certificates between First-Degree Master and Master.

CONCLUSION

When George Shaw compiled his first edition at the beginning of the nineteen-sixties, the situation was still relatively straightforward. Apart from the ancient universities,[15] the different systems in use could still, for the most part, be regarded as

---

[12] Except at Oxford, Cambridge, and Dublin, where it is the taught master's degree.

[13] Sometimes called 'enhanced masters', which is nonsense, as they are really enhanced bachelors' degrees.

[14] A number of degrees which were formerly 'full' masters have now become 'first-degree' masters – notably the MEng and MPharm.

variations on a single basic theme, albeit with a large number of exceptions. This basic scheme was as follows:

Bachelors wore a black gown with open pointed sleeves, with the front of the sleeve usually modified in some way distinctive to the university, and a black hood lined with silk of a colour distinctive of the particular degree. The bachelor's hood was frequently trimmed with fur. Masters wore a black gown with a long closed sleeve, usually having a university-specific shape cut out of the side at the boot, and a black hood lined with the appropriate degree colour. Doctors in undress generally wore the masters' gown, often with a form of lace sewn over the armhole of the sleeve or sometimes along the facings, and in full dress wore a coloured robe, usually scarlet or crimson, with wide sleeves and facings trimmed with silk of the degree colour. The doctors' hood was usually made of, and lined with, the same materials as the full dress robe. Undergraduates wore a cut-down version of the bachelors' gown. Doctors in full dress usually wore a Tudor bonnet, often with a coloured cord, while everybody else wore the black cloth square cap.

This simple system has been elaborated as more universities have been designated, and as the various levels of degree have proliferated.

[15] *I.e.*, Oxford, Cambridge, and Dublin – and the four Scottish universities (St Andrews, Glasgow, Aberdeen, and Edinburgh). Durham may be disregarded too, as it follows Oxford use very closely.

ACADEMIC DRESS: A BASIC INTRODUCTION

GOWNS

These are the basic item of academic dress, and until the 1960s, were invariably made in black, either stuff or silk. The University of East Anglia (1963) specified blue gowns (indigo); and the University of York (1963) chose grey ones. These, together with the Open University and its dark blue gowns, remained the sole exceptions until the 1992 foundations, several of which have chosen to have dark blue gowns.

At the back of most gowns, the fullness of the body is gathered in to a yoke by means of 'organ-pipe' pleats. These yokes were until recently fairly small, some being no more than two inches deep, and have an arched base (see page 20). With the advent of mass-production, very large, deep yokes (as much as seven or eight inches) with straight bases became the norm, as they are easier to produce (see page 21). The fronts of the gown are turned back to form facings, usually about two inches wide, which in some cases are of a differently-coloured material.

BACHELORS AND MASTERS

There are two basic sleeve patterns for the black gown: the open style, which is associated with bachelors' degrees; and the closed, associated with masters. Both have their origin in the same style: the bell-sleeve. In the case of the open (BA) sleeve, it became wider, and longer at the back, eventually developing a definite point, which reaches at least to the knee, and sometimes to the hem.

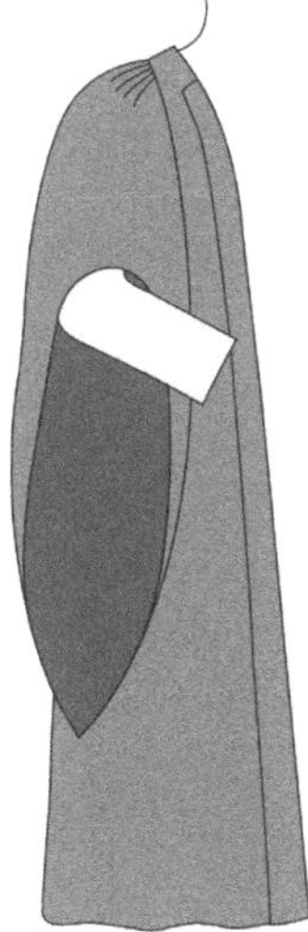

Basic bachelor's gown [b1]

The 'basic bachelor' gown [b1], is of this pattern: the forearm reaches to the elbow, and the point to the knee, or lower, and it is used by the vast majority of universities. Others vary the sleeve in different ways, of which the most common are the slit in the forearm seam (Cambridge BA [b2]); and pleats held by a cord and button (London BA [b4]).

The closed-sleeve[16] (MA) gown came from the original bell-sleeve becoming longer and narrower, until it reached well beyond the ends of the fingers, which necessitated an opening at elbow-level to free the arm. In course of time, the end of the sleeve was sewn shut, forming a bag. The sleeve-end, or 'boot', usually has a crescent cut in it, and the shape of the cut can be diagnostic of the university, but the basic form [m10], has no cut. The armhole is generally a horizontal slit, but in some cases has also an upright cut, forming an inverted T shape. This style of gown is occasionally varied with cords and buttons on the sleeves,[17] or, when used for doctors' undress gowns, with lace or velvet.

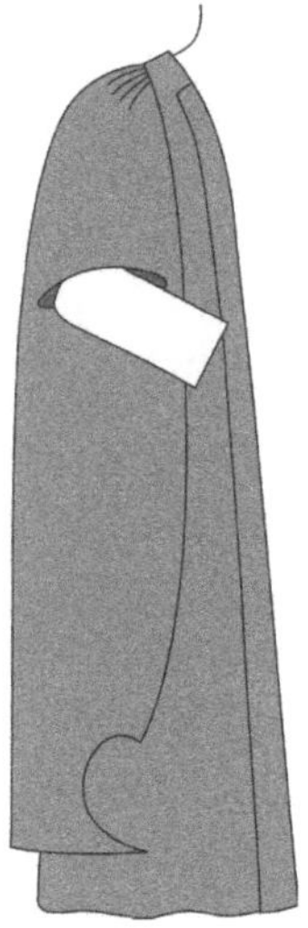

Oxford MA gown [m1]

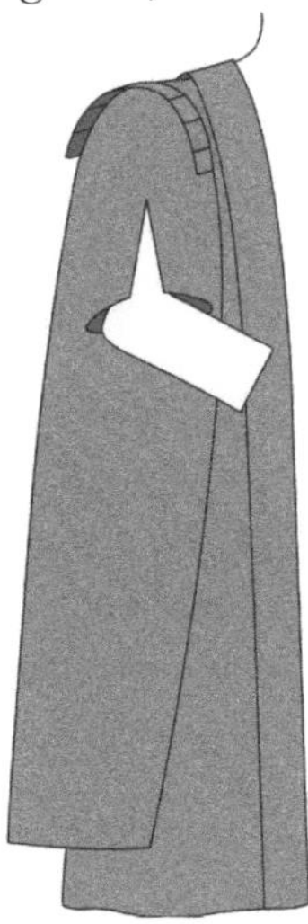

Flap-collar gown [d4]

Both these styles of gown may have a cord and button on the yoke. This was originally a practical addition, as it anchored the black scarf worn by Doctors of Divinity, but now is merely a decorative addition, which in some cases serves to differentiate between two degrees or universities. These cords and buttons, whether on the yoke or the sleeves, are usually black, but in some cases are coloured.

A third style of gown is the flap-collar gown [d4]. This is perhaps more familiar as the verger's or QC gown, and is also the style usually used for Chancellors' and other official robes. It is less full than other two, and has flat pleats at the back instead of gathers. It has wide facings (five inches or so) which continue to form a flap collar, covering the pleating. The sleeves resemble those on the closed-sleeve gown, but they are sewn shut immediately below the armhole (which is always an inverted-T), and thus form panels rather than bags. The sleeve boot is cut square (with the exception of the medical and music gowns at London). It may be plain, or be decorated with various forms of lace or velvet.

[16] Also 'glove-sleeve' or 'bag-sleeve'.

[17] See especially the Cambridge masters' gowns.

'FIRST-DEGREE' MASTERS

Universities have various ways of dealing with these: some allow them the masters' gown with bachelors' hood; some the bachelors' gown with masters' hood; others have special hoods, with either the masters' or the bachelors' gown. It is unclear why this should be, as the four 'ancient' Scottish universities have awarded the MA on this basis for many years, and treat it (so far as robes are concerned) as a full master.[18]

DOCTORS' DRESS ROBES

There are two principal patterns for dress robes: the Oxford [d2], which has bell-sleeves, and the Cambridge [d1], which has sleeves resembling a BA gown.[19] As with other aspects of academic dress, these are local variants on a common original. This original had bell-sleeves, like the other graduates' gowns; at Oxford they became rather fuller, while at Cambridge they developed along the same lines as the bachelors' gown. They are usually lined or faced with a contrasting colour: both have the facings covered with it. On the Oxford form, the sleeves are covered to about eight inches below the shoulder, while on the Cambridge form the sleeves are lined with it. This is the remnant of the historical form, in which the whole robe was lined with the contrasting colour. At Oxford the sleeve lining gradually crept up the outside of the sleeves; sixteenth- and seventeenth-century pictures show the robe with only a seven or eight inch turned back cuff, and this style has been revived by several new universities. The original form, with narrower sleeves and four-inch cuff, is still used by the Cambridge MusD.

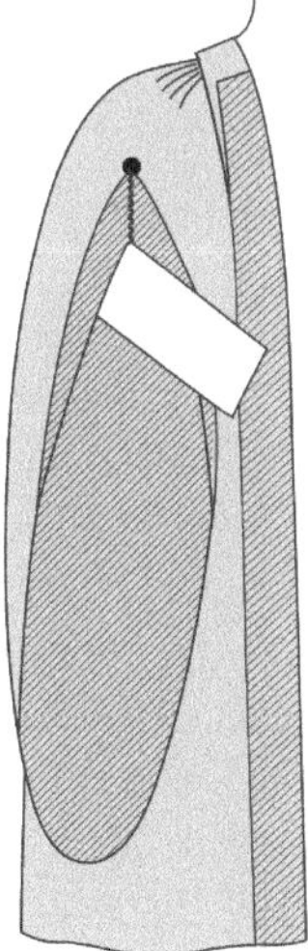

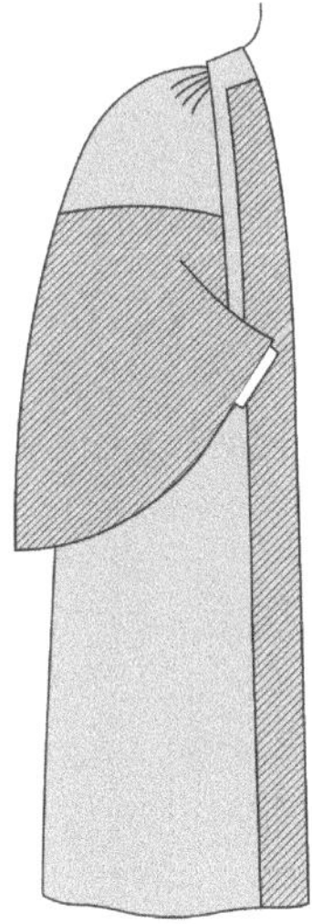

Cambridge pattern robe [d1]

Oxford pattern robe [d2]

[18] The same may be said about the PhD: either one is a doctor or one is not.

[19] In the second edition, Shaw differentiated between a Cambridge and a London version of this robe, based on minor differences in cut, principally the London version having pointed sleeves, while the Cambridge had rounded ones. As plenty of robes can be found with the 'wrong' style of sleeve, the present editors do not see the need for this distinction. It may well have its origins in the 'house-styles' of the different robemakers.

By the seventeenth century, doctors' robes were of scarlet cloth, with the exception of Doctors of Music, whose robes were of cream brocade. This seems to have come about owing to the ambiguous standing of music graduates: they were graduates, but not members, of their university, as the BMus and DMus could be taken without first holding a BA or MA. Initially, Doctors of Music wore the same robes as Doctors of Medicine, and it is unclear exactly when the change to brocade happened, and even less clear why cream brocade was chosen. This use was retained by Dublin, and also by Durham; Charles Franklyn revived it for Hull and George Shaw for Bath, but otherwise Doctors of Music wear scarlet (or the equivalent), though some (*e.g.*, Sheffield, Leicester) incorporate cream brocade as a lining.

Doctoral robes of colours other than scarlet or red are very common now, and there is ample historical precedent for them.[20] St Andrews may have started this trend with its revived French-inspired robes of the 1860s, where the whole robe is made in the faculty colour. Leeds gave its PhD a green robe, and Keele caused some comment in 1962 with its purple robe for higher doctors, as did Sussex with its yellow ones (and blue for DPhil).

DOCTORS' UNDRESS

In the days when gowns were worn daily for lecturing, *etc*, doctors had an undress gown which was worn for such occasions. This was in many cases the masters' gown, with or without some extra trim,[21] but at some universities special undress gowns are specified. Few universities founded after 1960 have made this provision, thus tacitly acknowledging that the daily use of the gown is not expected. When one is required, it is suggested that the MA gown be used, as this follows the majority practice.

CONVOCATION HABITS

Doctors at Oxford (except the DMus and the new professional doctors) have a 'semi-dress' robe: the convocation habit [d5]. This resembles the dress robe, but with the sleeves removed, and made so that it buttons at the throat. It is worn over the undress gown, with the sleeves pulled through the armholes. The Cambridge version fell out of general use by the late nineteenth century, and survives now solely in the so-called 'cope' which the Vice-Chancellor and certain other officials wear at degree ceremonies: it is in fact the DD convocation habit. Durham doctors did have habits, of the Oxford style, but they were obsolete by the start of the twentieth century. No other university has ever specified them, and it is a moot point whether their doctors are entitled to use them.[22]

---

[20] See B Christianson, 'Doctors' Greens', *Transactions of the Burgon Society* 6 (2006), pp 44-48.

[21] Usually some form of 'lace' sewn on the gown.

[22] Charles Franklyn was adamant that they are, and that they should be made like the dress robe, but without sleeves, and faced inside with six to eight inches of lining colour. So a Wales PhD would have one in crimson, faced with faculty shot silk; a Leeds PhD a green one; but what of the Cambridge or Glasgow PhD? Franklyn is silent at this point.

DOCTORS OF PHILOSOPHY

The degree of Doctor of Philosophy was introduced as a research degree from Germany *via* America in the early twentieth century. Historically, it was an alternative title for Master of Arts, and this explains why there is such a wide variety of robes for this degree. At some (*e.g.*, Oxford, Durham) it is ranked alongside other doctors, and given scarlet robes; at others (*e.g.*, London, Wales) it ranks as a 'lower' doctorate, and is given robes of a darker shade of red – usually crimson or claret; and a third group (*e.g.*, Cambridge, Keele) treats it as an 'enhanced master', and allows it only the black MA gown with coloured facings.[23] Unfortunately, some newer universities allow the black gown with coloured facings to their MPhil graduates, while the PhD has a coloured robe, and some are allowing coloured facings to MAs and other 'taught masters', so the black gown with coloured facings is not at all diagnostic of its wearer's academic standing. At least one university has upgraded its PhD robes: Surrey, which initially gave its PhD a black MA gown with blue brocade facings, now allows it a crimson robe with brocade facings. This is one area of academic dress where some kind of standardization is much to be desired if the robes are to mean anything. A suggestion would be that all PhDs should be allowed a coloured robe, while the MPhils should have a black gown with coloured facings, leaving the plain black gown to the MA, MSc, *etc.*

TAUGHT, VOCATIONAL, OR PROFESSIONAL DOCTORS

A new development is the 'taught', 'vocational', or 'professional' doctorate (the terminology varies from university to university), which may be assessed by means of coursework and dissertation: the better-known examples are Doctor of Education (EdD), of Engineering (EngD), and of Clinical Psychology (ClinPsyD). These are generally ranked with the PhD, and are thus given PhD-style robes: a notable exception is de Montfort, where they wear the same as the higher doctors, presumably because the regulations, drawn up before these degrees were introduced, give the PhD as an exception to the doctoral robes.[24] An exception at the other extreme is Oxford, which allows its DEng and DClinPsy only a master's gown, and master's-style hoods. Some universities[25] have now 'downgraded' the Doctor of Medicine (MD) to the status of professional doctor, and no longer allow it full doctoral robes, which recognizes that the degree has always been awarded on the basis of experience and a dissertation, rather than for major published work.

UNDERGRADUATES

Until the 1960s, all university undergraduates, and students at some non-university institutions, expected to wear a gown. With the advent of greater informality, their use has decreased significantly in the last forty years, although they are still regularly worn at Oxford, Cambridge, and St Andrews, and some Durham colleges require them, but

---

[23] Two, Edinburgh and Dundee, did not even allow that, but merely the black MA gown. Both have recently granted them coloured facings (scarlet at Edinburgh, and blue at Dundee).

[24] The same is true of Wales. See its entry.

[25] *E.g.*, Glasgow. The NUI has also done so, instituting the DMed in its place as a higher doctorate. Others which have recently instituted the MD (East Anglia, Bath, Keele) gave it PhD-style robes from the start.

elsewhere they have effectively vanished. It is interesting that some of the universities founded in the 1960s, such as Lancaster, UEA, and Sussex, made provision for undergraduate gowns, although they were never worn on a daily basis, and one suspects that most undergraduates passed their three years unaware of their existence. Few, if any, of the post-1992 universities have made any provision for undergraduates, although some do specify that 'when needed' undergraduates may wear the bachelors' gown without a hood. A few older universities never did have undergraduate gowns: Belfast is a noted example.

Undergraduate gowns[26] are of knee-length, and generally resemble a small version of a BA gown. However, there are grounds (principally pictorial) for believing that historically they ought to be full-length, but that the sleeves should not hang lower than the knee. The reduction in overall length would appear to be partly a matter of practicality, and also partly a matter of fashion. This is especially so in the case of the Oxford commoners' gown, which as made reaches to the hips, whereas the statutes still require it to be ankle length.[27] What happened was that as the student went through his daily life, the gown became ripped and torn, and to wear such a gown indicated that one was not a freshman. Eventually, during the later nineteenth century, tailors started to make them in this abbreviated form.[28]

HOODS

Hoods descend from the mediæval head covering, and have come to be the mark of the graduate, although Arts undergraduates at Oxford wore a plain black hood as late as the nineteenth century, and this practice seems to have been copied for a time at Durham.[29] All institutions granted university status since 1992 have included in their schemes provision for undergraduate and postgraduate diplomas, and many of the older ones have also now specified robes (usually a special hood with the bachelor's or master's gown) for these awards,[30] so that a university hood no longer necessarily represents a degree. There have been diploma hoods, principally for theological and musical college diplomas, since the late nineteenth century.

---

[26] There is a distressing trend to refer to first degrees (BA, BSc, LL.B) as 'undergraduate degrees', (*i.e.*, 'a degree for which an undergraduate may read') and thus the gown as the 'undergraduate gown', which is clearly nonsensical, and can lead to serious misinterpretation of regulations.

[27] Recent examples of the commoners' gown suggest that it is regaining a little of its lost length.

[28] Modern parallels may be drawn with 'distressed' denim jeans, sold with ready-made tears and holes …

[29] Whether this at least partly gave rise to that highly contentious garment, 'the literate's hood', is a moot point.

[30] Durham had allowed them to its long-defunct diplomas of ATh, LTh, LSSc, and ASc.

The original hood had three parts – a cape, a cowl, and a liripipe:

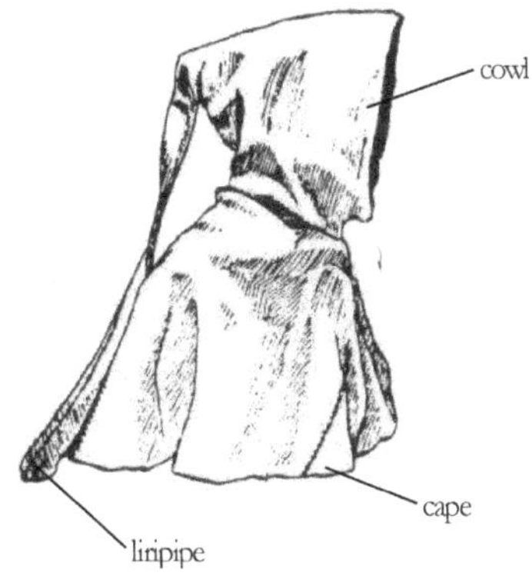

The mediæval hood

From the seventeenth century onwards, the hood came to be split along the front of the cape, probably so as to free the arms from it,[31] and the hood thus came to hang down the wearers' back; the two sides eventually parted company completely at the front, and, except for some simple shapes and all [a] shapes, are held together by an inserted neck-band.[32] The neck-band is not usually described in the specification of a hood, unless it is important in differentiating one hood from another. The best-known case was City University, where the neck-band indicated the faculty colour, although this has been changed in recent years.

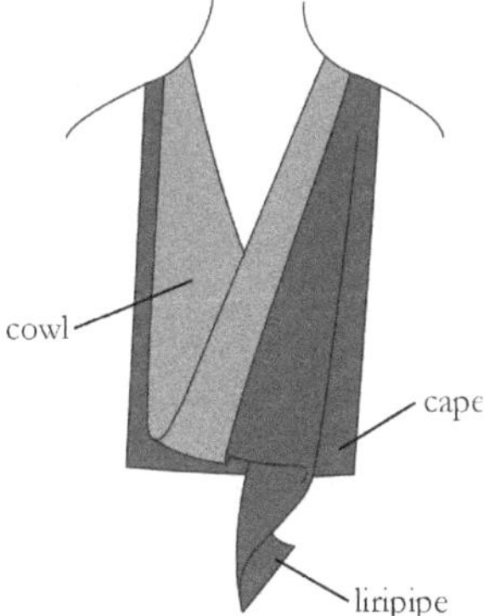

Cambridge full shape hood [f1]

The full-shaped hoods still retain all three of these parts: some have the rounded cape, some have it with square corners. By pulling the hood forwards on the shoulders, it starts to return to its original shape.

[31] This is about the same time as the gown came to worn open in front. The splitting of the hood is often stated to be due to the introduction of periwigs, which made it difficult to put the hood on without removing the wig, but wigs did not become fashionable until well after the hood started to hang down the back.

[32] This has been reversed at St Mary's UC, Twickenham, where the neckband is omitted, and the two sides are sewn together.

At Oxford, but not at Cambridge, a development came about whereby the capes of the hoods of the MA and all bachelors except BD were cut away, leaving merely the cowl and liripipe: these are known as 'simple' hoods. The basic simple cut, with cape removed, is most easily seen in what is now known as the Belfast or Irish shape [s3]. Somehow, the Oxford version [s1] (now known as the 'Oxford plain' or 'Oxford simple' shape) came to be worn backwards, in the process losing much of the original cowl as well. Nearly all of the later simple styles derive from this form. The so-called 'Burgon' shape[33] [s2] turned it the right way round again, and restored the cowl.

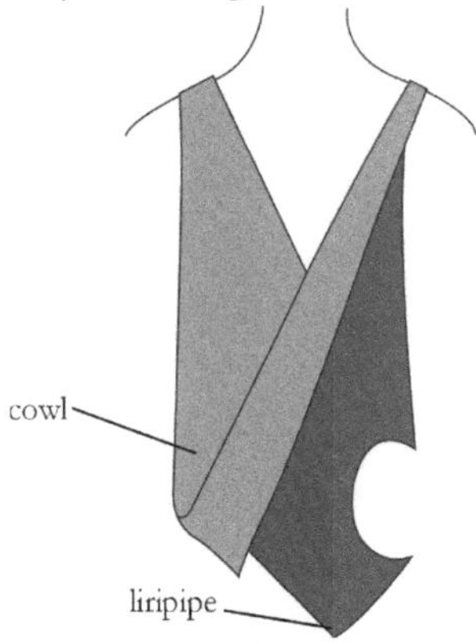

Burgon simple shape hood [s2]

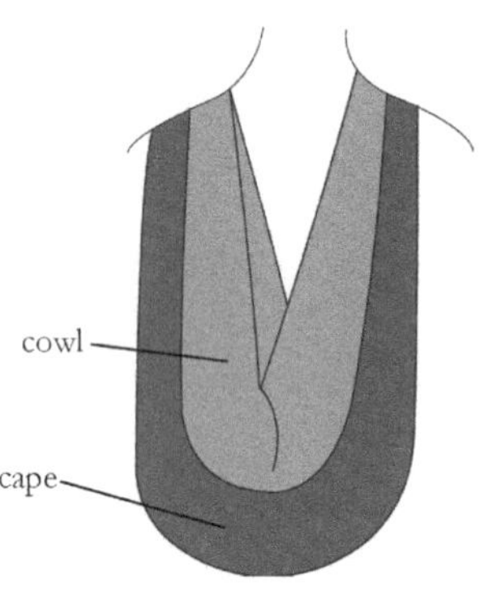

CNAA shape hood [a1]

A third form of hood is known as the 'Aberdeen' shape. This has a cape, a vestigial cowl, and no liripipe. It seems to have been invented at the University of Aberdeen when academic dress was reintroduced there in the later nineteenth century, although it is unclear how this variant arose.[34] It remained peculiar to Aberdeen until 1964, when it was adopted by the Council for National Academic Awards (CNAA), which used a form with a slightly larger cowl; its use in many of the post-1992 universities may stem from this, as they were familiar with it while they were polytechnics. Leicester had invented its own forms of this shape for the masters' and doctors' hoods in 1957, and it appeared also at a number of the 1960s foundations – including East Anglia, which has its own very distinctive form.

In the USA, there is a single relatively simple scheme of hoods,[35] in which a black hood is lined with silk of the university's colours, and bordered with velvet of the faculty colour; the difference in grade is marked by the length of the hood and the width of the velvet border.[36] This uniformity has never obtained in the UK, and without a knowledge

[33] So called after Dean John Burgon (1813-88), who is supposed to have either invented it or discovered an old hood of this shape. Solid documentary evidence is so far lacking, however. See C Dunkley, 'JW Burgon and the eponymous hood: a trawl through Oxford University archives', *Transactions of the Burgon Society* 3, pp 32–33, and B Christianson, 'The evolution of the Oxford simple shape', *Transactions of the Burgon Society* 2, 30–36.

[34] There is a possibility that it is based on a form of hood in use at Cambridge at this time.

[35] There are some noted exceptions to this.

[36] The doctoral hood is further distinguished by being of a full shape, while the others are simple.

of the various schemes, it is almost impossible to say at first glance exactly what level of award is signified by a given hood. A crimson or red hood does not necessarily indicate a doctoral degree (see Leicester, Bristol, Bolton), while not all doctors wear a shade of red (see Leeds, Brunel, CNAA). A part-lining or border generally indicates a bachelor, but the Aston PhD and Aberystwyth MPhil are only bordered, while many bachelors have fully-lined hoods. Even the restriction of fur to bachelors was overturned by the Royal College of Art and by Stirling, which both use it on their masters' hoods instead.

Hoods are generally of two or more colours, and there are various methods of arranging the colours.

1. *Lining.* This is where the whole hood is fully lined with a colour. In some cases the lining finishes flush with the edge, but in others it is carried over as a binding. Sometimes the binding is unimportant, but in others it can make the difference between two hoods. For example, the Oxford MA is black lined crimson, and the London MA black lined brown, and although they are generally made lined and bound, the binding is not an important part of the design, and so both hoods can be described as 'lined'. At Loughborough, on the other hand, the BA is purple lined green, while the MA is purple lined and bound green: here the binding is important. In the following specifications, 'lined' means flush ('edge-to-edge'), while 'lined and bound' means the lining is brought over the edge, either cape, or cowl, or both ('all edges')
2. *Bordered.* This is where the hood is part-lined only – usually to a depth of three or four inches. Again, the border is sometimes brought over the edge as a binding, but there is no case where this makes any difference, and so it is not referred to. Occasionally, the border is placed on the outside of the hood: in all cases, it is clearly specified where the border is placed – inside the cowl, outside the cape, *etc.*
3. *Binding.* This is a narrow strip of material placed over the edge of a hood, generally, but not always, of equal width on either side, and rarely more than two inches wide. The width specified is the width seen: this a hood 'bound one inch green' will show one inch inside and one inch outside, while one 'bound green, one inch inside and half-an-inch outside' is self-explanatory.[37]
4. *Tipping.* This is a comparatively new method, and is, so far, confined to CNAA-shape hoods [a1]. The hood is lined with two colours, divided along a V-shaped line when worn; the upper colour occupies about two-thirds of the hood. Thus the upper colour is regarded as the main colour: 'lined green, tipped red' means that the main lining colour is green, while the lower end of the cowl is red.
5. *Piping.* This is usually done with a cord, and usually placed right on one or more edges of a hood. Formerly quite rare, it is now becoming more common.
6. *Split linings.* There are a few cases where the lining is split equally – usually vertically when the hood is worn. In these cases, the colours are described as worn: *e.g.*, 'red on the left shoulder, blue on the right' for a vertical split, or 'white over blue' for a horizontal one.

---

[37] Some earlier writers (notably Hugh Smith) confusingly regarded a hood with a three inch inside border, brought out for quarter of an inch (as, *e.g.*, the BA Wales) as 'bound'. This is described here as 'bordered inside and bound on the cowl'.

Combinations of these methods are easily worked out: the London BA, for example, is 'black, lined white, bordered inside the cowl 3″ brown': a black hood, fully lined white, with a 3″ brown strip inside the cowl edge. The Nottingham MA is 'black, lined light blue, the cowl bound cherry, 1″ inside and ½″ outside', while the former Arts MPhil is 'black, lined light blue, bound on all edges cherry, 1″ inside and ½″ outside'.

EPITOGES

The epitoge is increasingly used by some universities instead of a hood, especially in the Irish Republic, to indicate diplomas. The epitoge has its roots in the hood, but has followed a different development. By about 1450, there was a fashion for wearing the hood with head inserted into the cowl, leaving the cape and the liripipe to hang to either side – a hat known as the *chaperon.* The liripipe became very long, and was wound round the neck like a scarf, while the cape became a mere flap of material, and the edge of the cowl was rolled up to make a solid roundel.

Hood (chaperon) worn on head

Chaperon on civic robe

It then became the fashion to wear this garment with the roundel on the left shoulder, the liripipe hanging in front, and the reduced cape behind. Over time, it became reduced to a single piece of material, cut in the shape shown below.

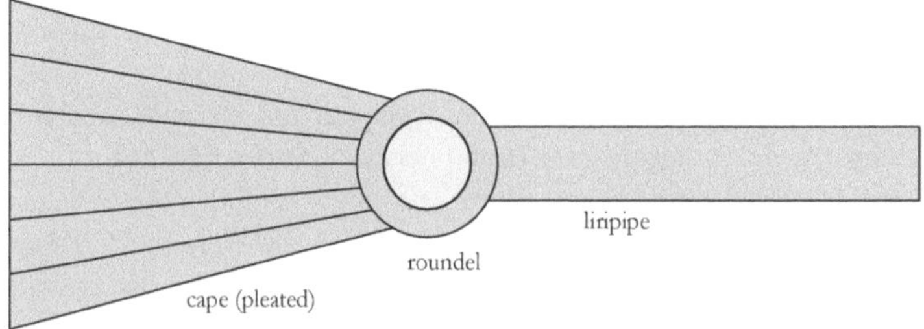

Modern epitoge

In this form it is still used in French universities. It is trimmed with bands of ermine, which denote the level of the degree: one for bachelors, two for *licenciés* (masters), and three for doctors. Although the two English universities[38] insisted on the hood being worn in its original form, the epitoge can be found as part of the robes of some orders of chivalry, and in a very residual form on the barrister's gown. Epitoges are always worn on the left shoulder, with the narrow portion (the liripipe) hanging in front.

Those now used in Ireland have undergone a further simplification: the roundel is no longer present, and the 'cape' portion is not pleated, so they consist of a single long, narrow, piece of material (liripipe) broadening into a triangular (cape) portion. See page 39. They are usually constructed of a stout backing material, to which the silk or velvet facing is applied. St Patrick's College, Maynooth, as a pontifical university, uses epitoges for all awards. They are of two colours of velvet, divided along the length of the epitoge, and trimmed with bands of white fur, which are three inches wide for degrees, and one inch for diplomas. Other Irish universities use bands of coloured silk instead of fur, and there may be up to four of them.

'SCARVES' OR 'STOLES'

These have been used by some universities for non-degree awards, notably Leeds (which has now replaced them with hoods) and de Montfort. They usually take the form of a piece of silk, about seven or eight inches wide, worn over both shoulders, and which hang to about waist level in front. The ends are usually 'mitred' – cut to a point – and the middle, which lies against the neck, is usually pleated to help shape it, so that the scarf lies flat. However, the black scarves (white at Newcastle) used by Doctors of Divinity at some universities take the form of the traditional 'preaching scarf', of full length, with square ends.

HATS

There are very few types of academic hat in use. Without question, the best-known is the square cap ('mortar-board', trencher), which remains the universal icon of scholarship. It consists of a skull-cap, on which is fixed a square board, from the centre of which issues a tassel. Following the demise of the peculiar hats designed for UEA, it is the hat now used by all masters, bachelors, and diploma-holders in Great Britain and Ireland. It is generally covered in black cloth, although some universities specify dark blue (grey in the case of York) to match the gowns. Some specify it for their doctors, in which case it is usually covered in black velvet.

Most universities prescribe a Tudor bonnet for their doctors, usually in black velvet or black cloth, although some newer creations specify other colours. It is generally encircled by a cord with tassels, which may be of metallic gold (as Cambridge) or coloured silk (as London), while Oxford uses a black silk ribbon.

Other hats are rare. The 'John Knox' hat is used by several Scottish universities for their doctors, and a version of it is used at Durham. The 'Oxford ladies' soft cap', which was used by women at a number of places, is gradually being replaced by the square.

[38] Hoods at the three Scottish universities fell into disuse around the time of this development. Dublin, founded 1591, followed the English use.

Others, such as the Sussex and the Leicester doctors' hats, are confined to a single institution.

The sole recent development has been that, for various reasons, universities are increasingly specifying that hats shall not be worn at graduation ceremonies,[39] which has led to the myth that 'hats do not form part of the academic dress'. The only cases where this is in fact so are Stirling, where the regulations specifically state that hats do not form part of the dress; and King's College London, where Vivienne Westwood specified that hats do not form part of the scheme, although student pressure there led to a compromise whereby they are not worn during the ceremony, but may be used for photographs afterwards.

ROBES NOT INCLUDED

Following the practice of earlier editions, the robes for awards such as honorary fellowships have not been included, nor the robes for officers.

OBSOLETE ROBES

In previous editions, hoods that were no longer current were not listed. However, as they may still be seen for a good while after the degree is withdrawn, they have been included in this edition; and it has thus seemed sensible to include also all obsolete robes, however long they may have been disused,[40] as this will enable the book to be a full historical record, and also to show how an institution's scheme has expanded and developed. Thus the specification of the hood for that doubtless much-prized diploma, the Licence in Sanitary Science (LSSc) of Durham, has been resurrected.

UPDATES

Obviously, a book of this nature is out of date as soon as it is published. The editorial team is keeping records of new robes, *etc*, for future editions, and will be pleased to learn of any developments, and indeed of corrections to this edition. Such information should be communicated via the dedicated e-mail address, shaw@burgon.org.uk.

---

[39] Whether this has anything to do with the general disuse of hats in daily life is a moot point. It may also have to do with the increasingly fashionable practice of groups of graduates throwing their hats in the air after the ceremony. Apart from the damage done to the hats when they return to earth, they can also cause serious damage to anyone who gets in their way.

[40] Such robes are clearly indicated in the entries, usually by being placed in brackets.

GOWN, HOOD AND HAT PATTERNS

A new feature is the addition of a two-character code enabling the pattern of gown or hood to be identified. It covers the majority of the patterns used, and any departures are easily understood. This is particularly the case with [m]-style gowns, some of which have an inverted-T armhole, which is always noted if present – *e.g.*, the Cambridge MA is just '[m2]', but the Birmingham MA is '[m2] with inverted-T armhole'. The diagrams of patterns are arranged according to this classification.

Each code, contained in square brackets, consists of a letter and a number, thus: [f3], [b4]. The letter refers to the basic style of hood or gown, while the number refers to a version within that basic style. BA-style gown are designated [b], MA-style ones [m], and doctors' robes [d].[41] Full hoods are [f], simple [s], and 'Aberdeen' ones (*i.e.*, cape and residual cowl) are [a].

A full list of these pattern codes is given on page 24.

NOTE

There can be wide variations in the cut and dimensions of the same pattern, depending on when a hood was made, and by whom. This is especially the case with the 'Cambridge' shape [f1], where there are wide discrepancies in the length of the cowl in relation to the length of the cape, and in the length and width of the liripipe. Some universities have their own versions of this shape (*e.g.*, Wales, Leeds), but virtually all say it is 'Cambridge shape'. The designation [f1] is thus used in this book to mean a full-shaped hood with square corners to its cape. Such hoods may therefore not conform exactly to the [f1] pattern given here. The sole exception is the Glasgow version [f9], as it is a very distinctive variation.

[41] [d] also includes the flap-collar gown.

Parts of **Gowns**

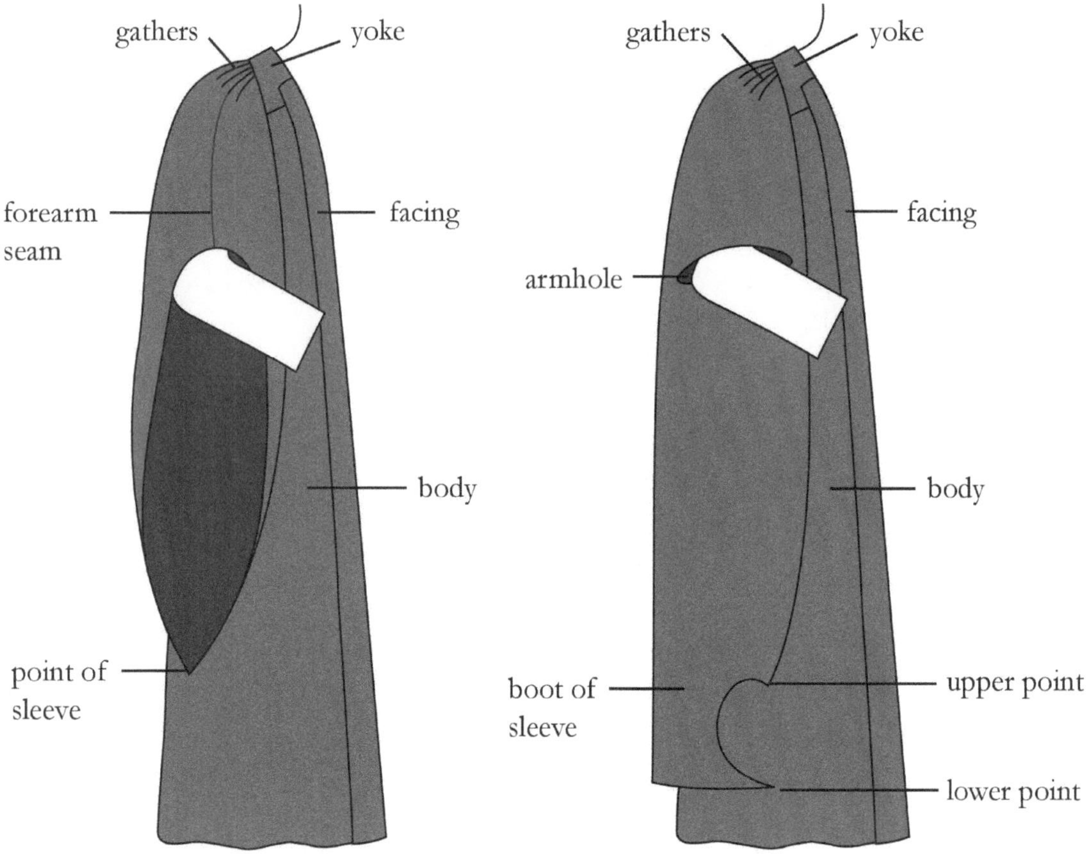

gathers
yoke
forearm seam
facing
body
point of sleeve
gathers
yoke
facing
armhole
body
boot of sleeve
upper point
lower point

cord and button (where present)
yoke
gathers (pencil pleats)

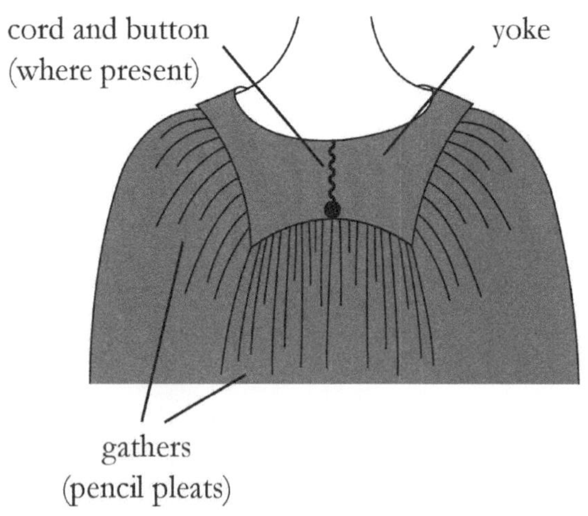

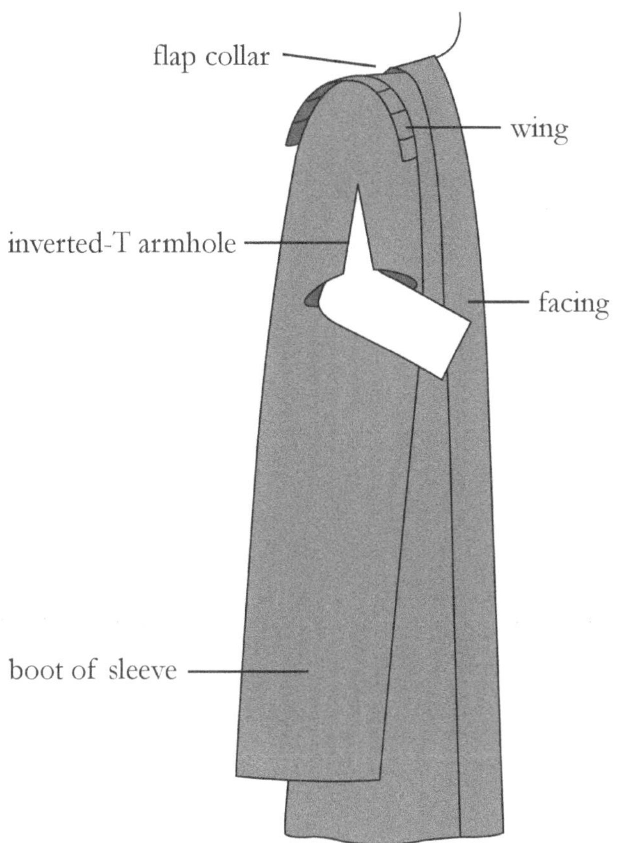
flap collar
wing
inverted-T armhole
facing
boot of sleeve

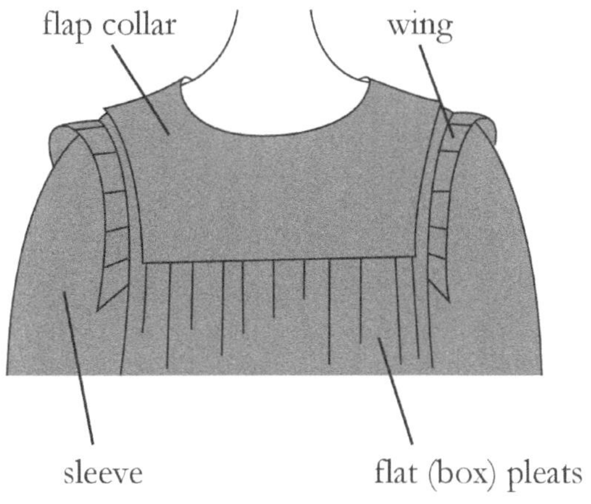
flap collar
wing
sleeve
flat (box) pleats

Parts of
Hoods

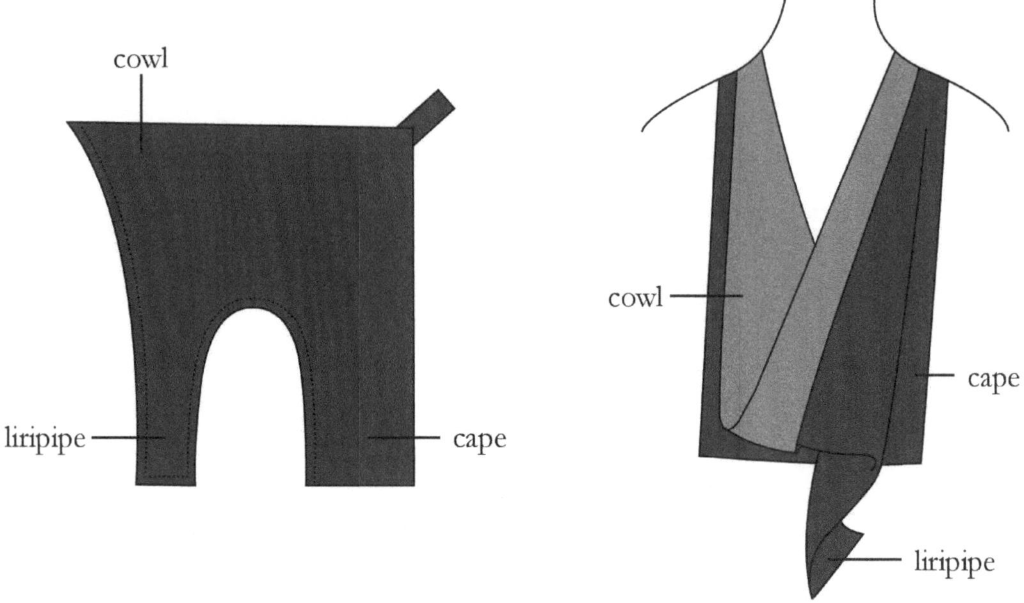

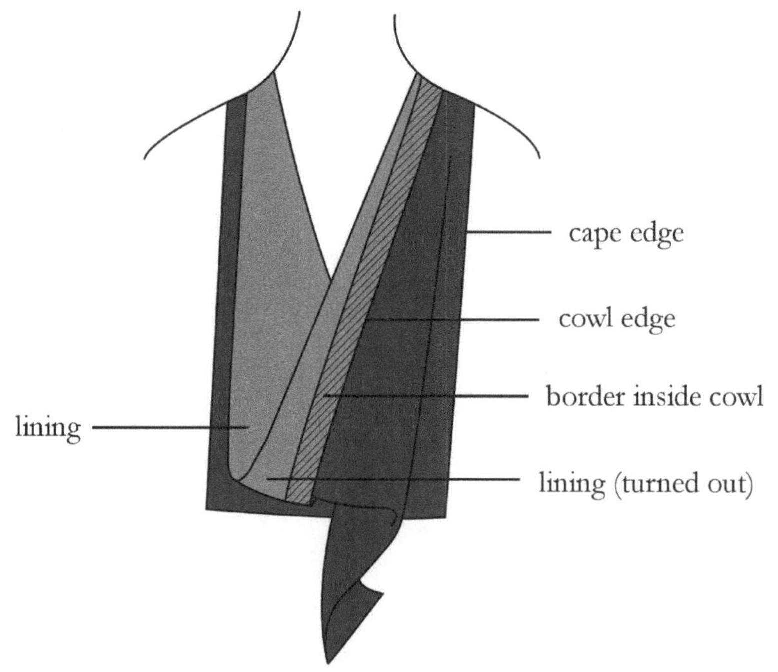

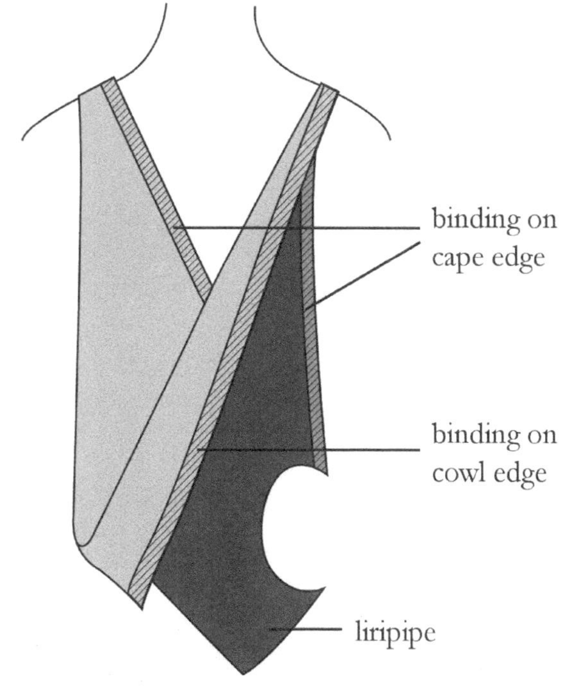
binding on
cape edge
binding on
cowl edge
liripipe

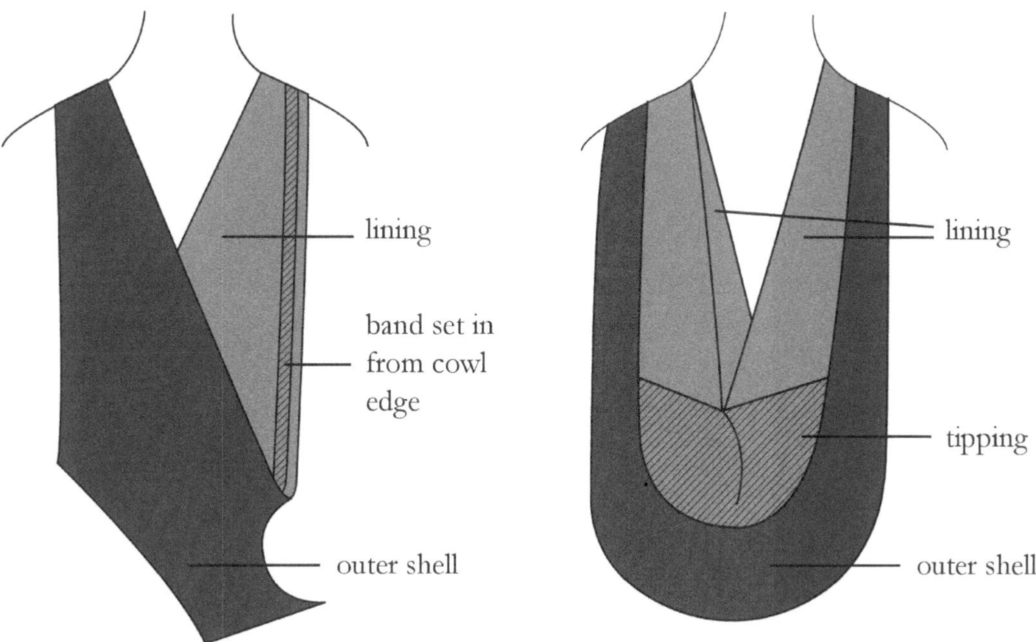
lining
band set in
from cowl
edge
outer shell
lining
tipping
outer shell

UNDERGRADUATE GOWNS

[u1] Cambridge basic
[u2] Oxford scholar
[u3] London
[u4] Durham
[u5] Oxford commoner
[u6] Sussex.
[u7] East Anglia
[u8] Trinity College Dublin
[u9] St Andrews

Other Cambridge undergraduate gowns are described as being variants on [u1] or [u3].

BACHELORS' GOWNS

[b1] Basic bachelor
[b2] Cambridge BA
[b3] Cambridge MB
[b4] London BA
[b5] Durham BA
[b6] Wales BA
[b7] Bath BA
[b8] Oxford BA
[b9] Belfast BA
[b10] Dublin BA
[b11] Reading BA
[b12] Sussex BA

MASTERS' GOWNS

[m1] Oxford MA
[m2] Cambridge MA
[m3] Dublin MA
[m4] Wales MA
[m5] London MA
[m6] Victoria MA
[m7] Lampeter BD
[m8] Leicester MA
[m9] Bristol MA
[m10] Basic master
[m11] Lancaster MA
[m12] Scottish MA
[m13] (not used)
[m14] Open (all degrees)
[m15] Warwick MA
[m16] Bath MA
[m17] Sussex MA
[m18] Manchester new
[m19] King's MA

DOCTORS' GOWNS

[d1] Cambridge doctors
[d2] Oxford doctors
[d3] Cambridge MusD
[d4] Cambridge LLD undress
[d5] Oxford convocation habit
[d6] Sussex doctors
[d7] Aston (all degrees)
[d8] Cambridge DD undress.
[d9] St Andrews honorary doctors

FULL HOODS

[f1] Cambridge
[f2] Dublin
[f3] London
[f4] Durham doctors
[f5] Oxford full
[f6] Durham BA
[f7] Durham BSc
[f8] Edinburgh full
[f9] Glasgow
[f10] St Andrews
[f11] Warham Guild*
[f12] King's full
[f13] UMIST doctors
[f14] AIC doctors*
[f15] Toronto full*

SIMPLE HOODS

[s1] Oxford simple
[s2] Burgon
[s3] Belfast
[s4] Edinburgh simple
[s5] Wales simple
[s6] Leicester bachelors
[s7] Leeds
[s8] Sussex
[s9] Victoria
[s10] Aston
[s11] Glasgow Caledonian
[s12] King's simple

ABERDEEN HOODS

[a1] CNAA
[a2] Leicester masters
[a3] Kent
[a4] East Anglia
[a5] Leicester doctors
[a6] Dundee
[a7] Aberdeen

EPITOGES

[e1] Irish epitoge

HATS

[h1] Square cap
[h2] Doctors' bonnet
[h3] John Knox cap
[h4] Bishop Andrewes' cap
[h5] Oxford ladies' cap
[h6] Sussex pileus
[h7] Leicester doctors' hat*
[h8] old UEA BA hat*
[h9] old UEA MA hat*

* *not illustrated*

Gowns

UNDERGRADUATE GOWNS

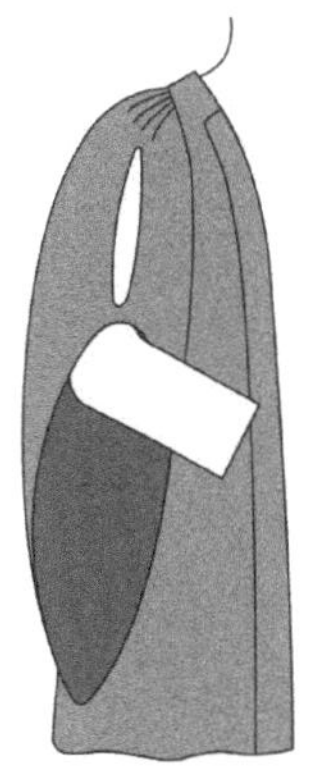

[u1]
Cambridge Basic

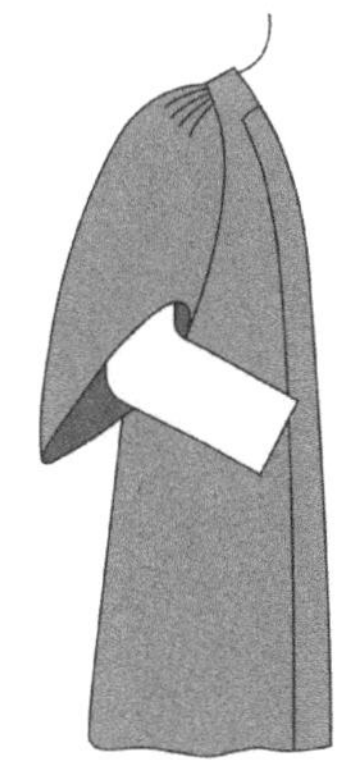

[u2]
Oxford Scholar

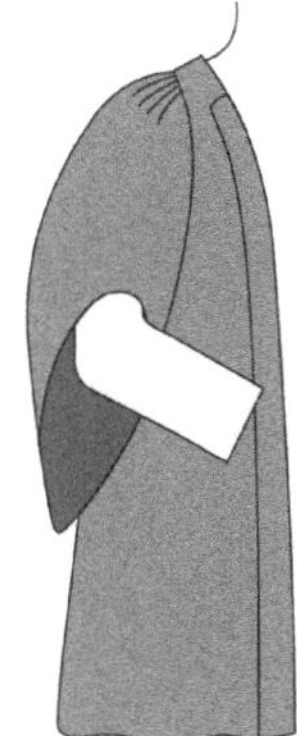

[u3]
London

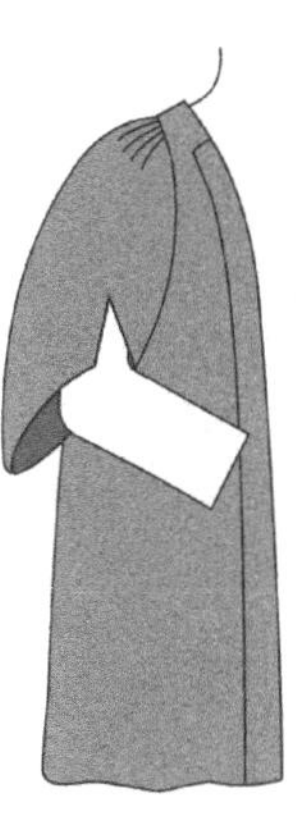

[u4]
Durham

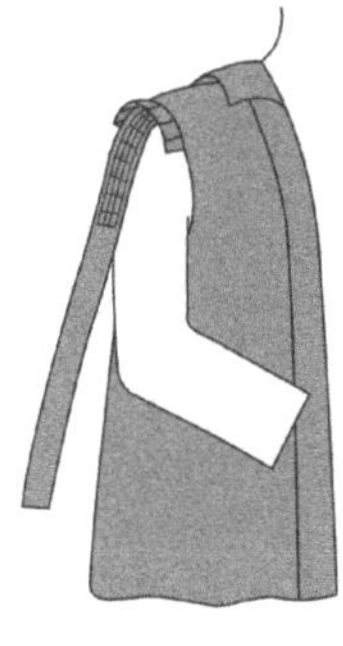

[u5]
Oxford Commoner

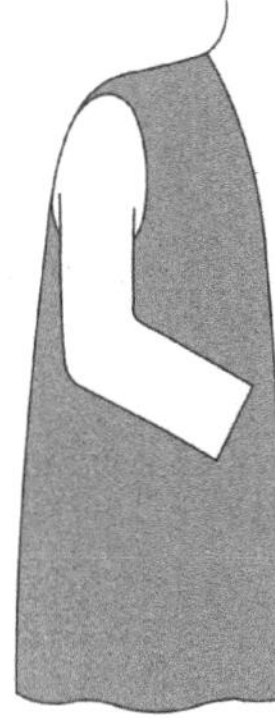

[u6]
Sussex

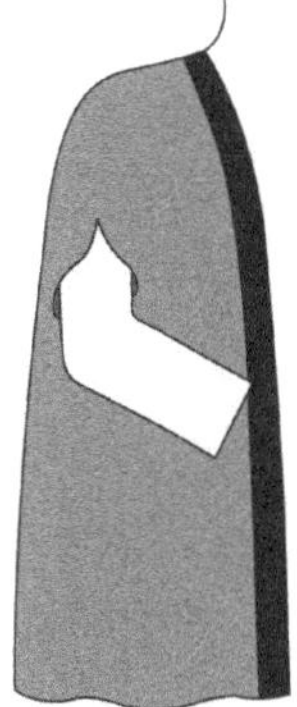

[u7]
East Anglia

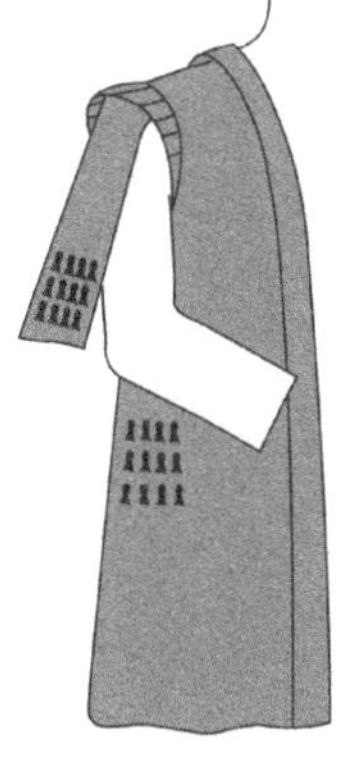

[u8]
Trinity College Dublin

[u9]
St Andrews

Gowns

BACHELORS' GOWNS

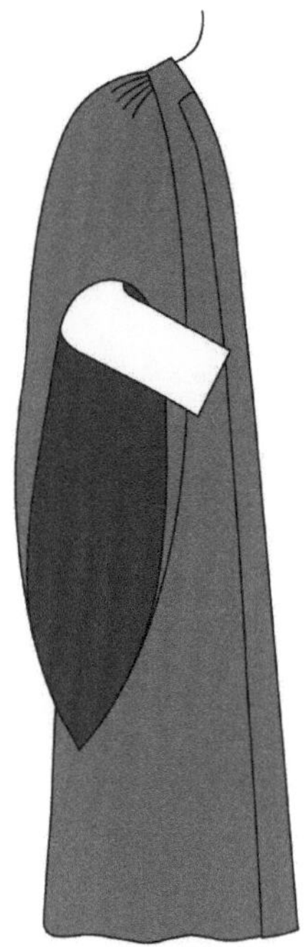

[b1]
Basic Bachelor

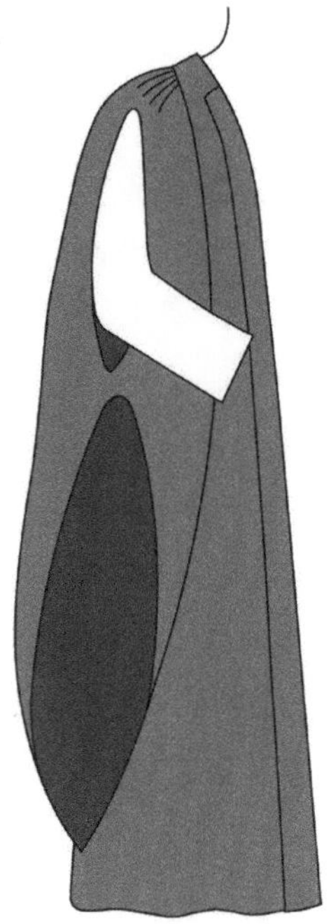

[b2]
Cambridge BA

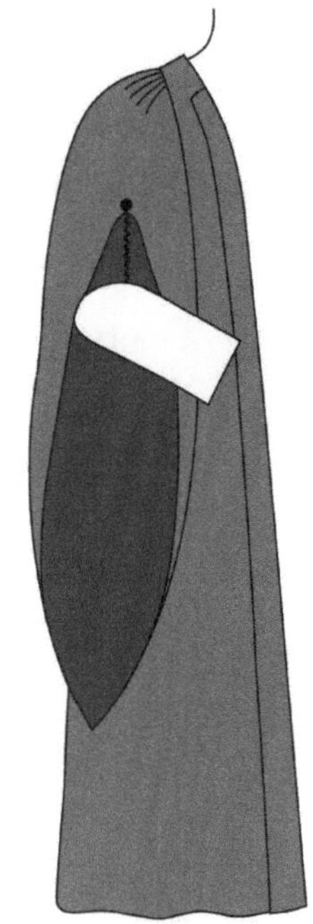

[b3]
Cambridge MB

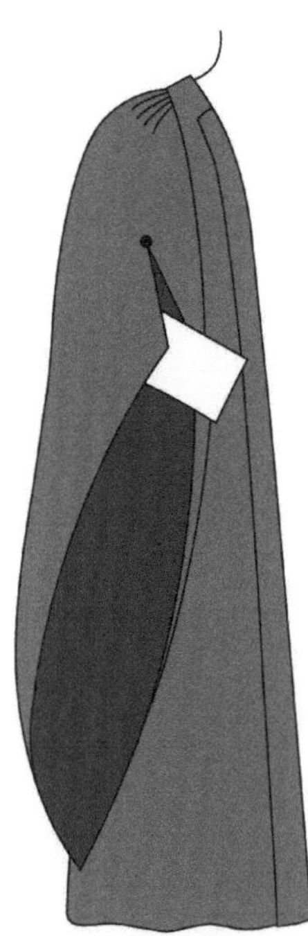

[b7]
Bath BA

[b8]
Oxford BA

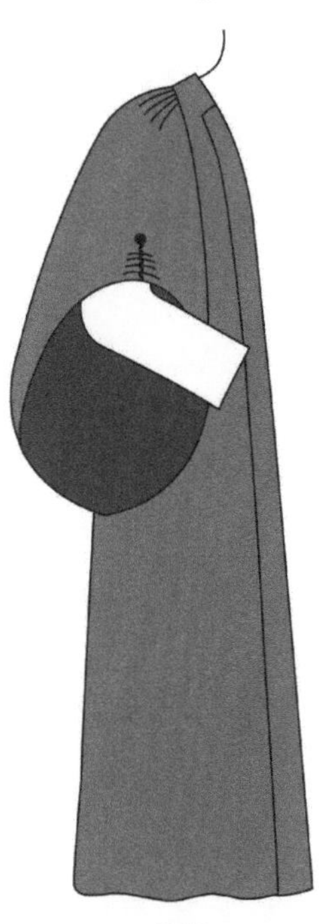

[b9]
Belfast BA

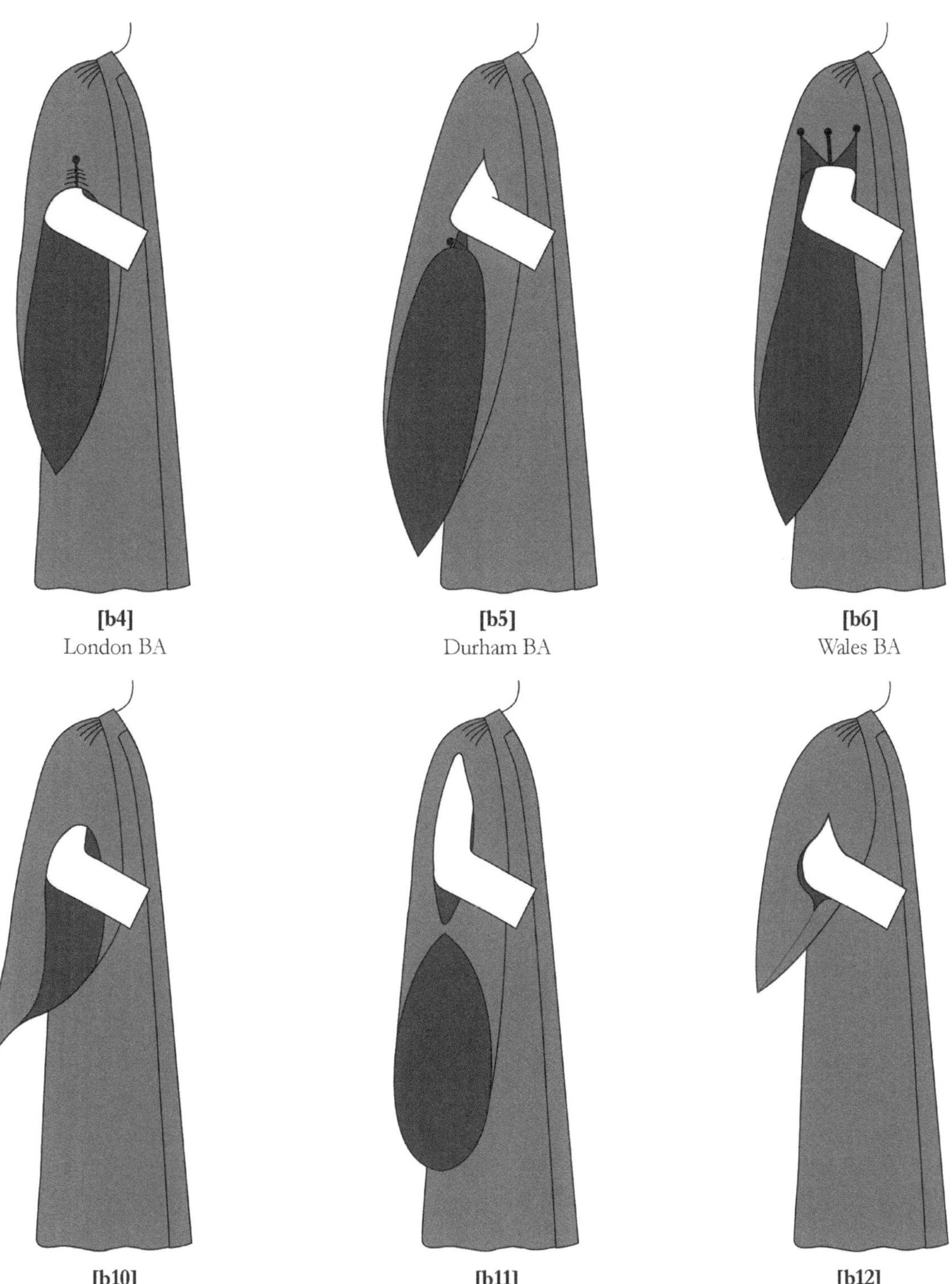

[b4] London BA

[b5] Durham BA

[b6] Wales BA

[b10] Dublin BA

[b11] Reading BA

[b12] Sussex BA

Gowns

MASTERS' GOWNS

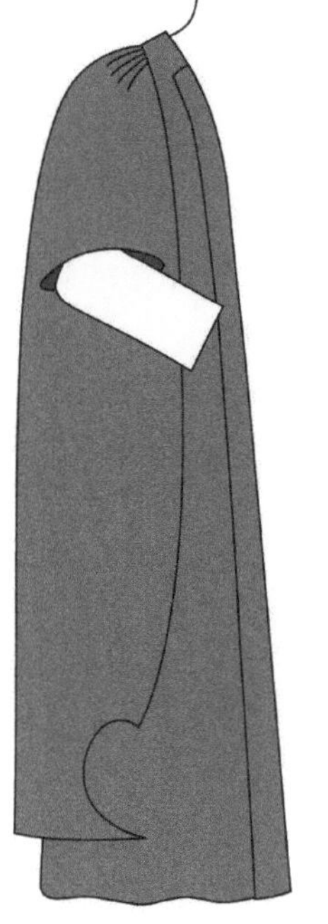

[m1]
Oxford MA

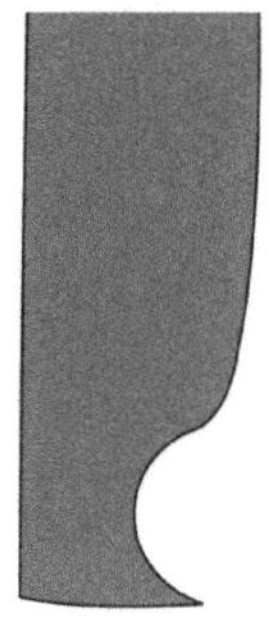

[m2]
Cambridge MA

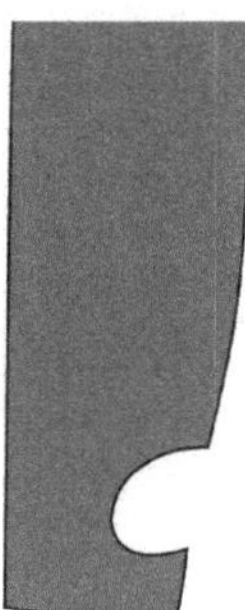

[m3]
Dublin MA

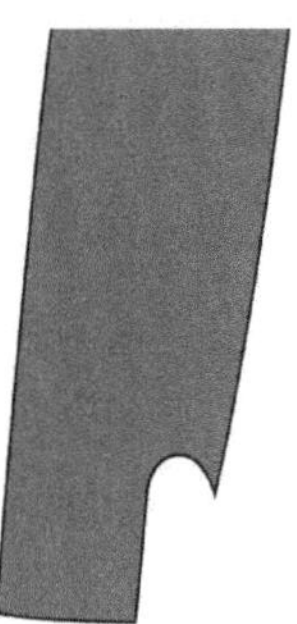

[m4]
Wales MA

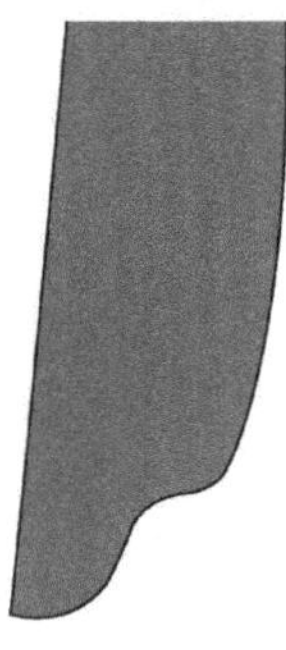

[m5]
London MA

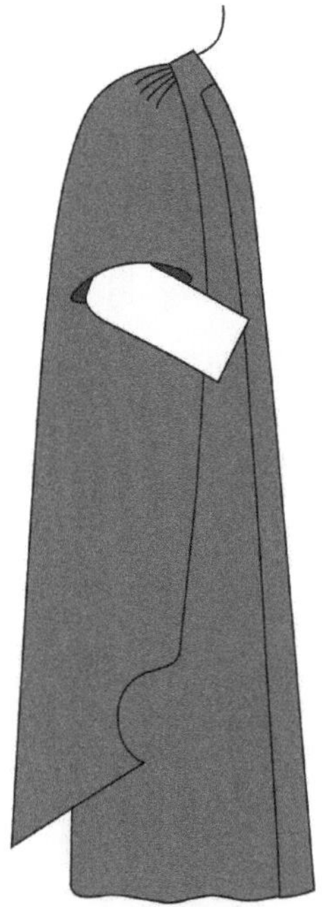

[m11]
Lancaster MA

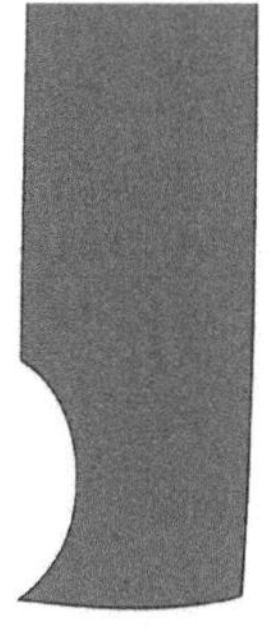

[m12]
Scottish MA

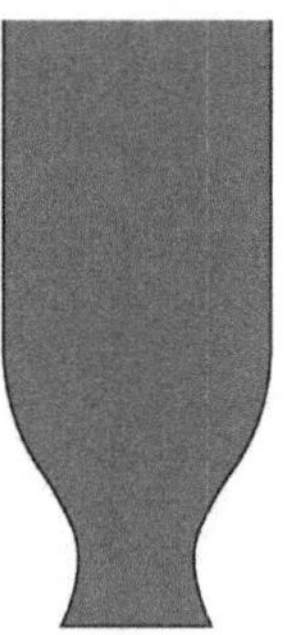

[m15]
Warwick MA

[m16]
Bath MA

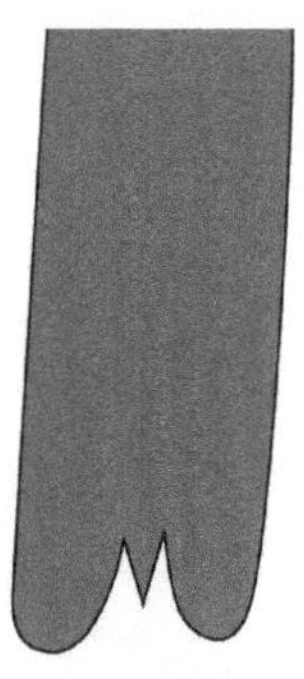

[m18]
Manchester MA

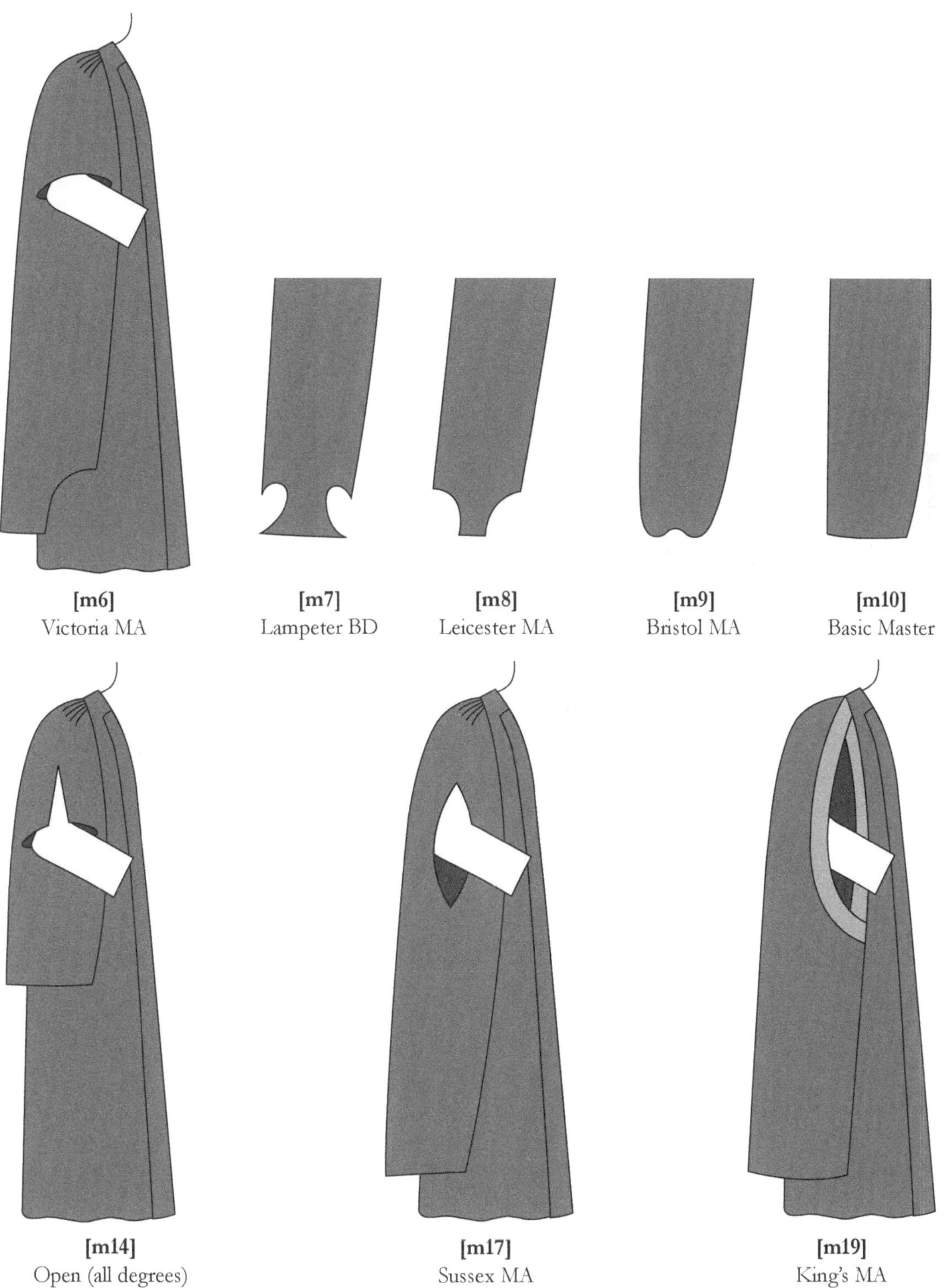

[m6] Victoria MA

[m7] Lampeter BD

[m8] Leicester MA

[m9] Bristol MA

[m10] Basic Master

[m14] Open (all degrees)

[m17] Sussex MA

[m19] King's MA

Gowns

DOCTORS' UNDRESS GOWNS

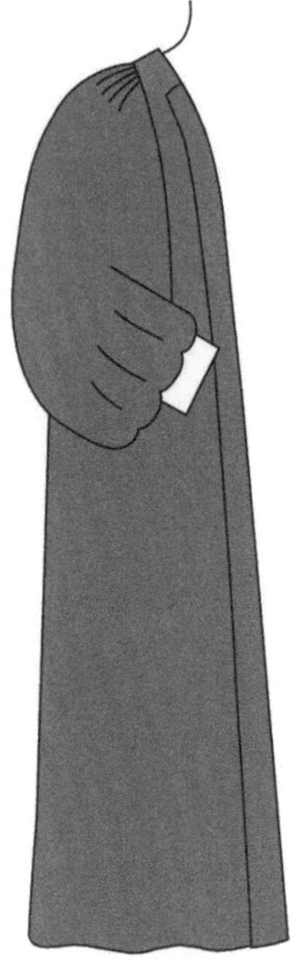

[d8]
Cambridge DD

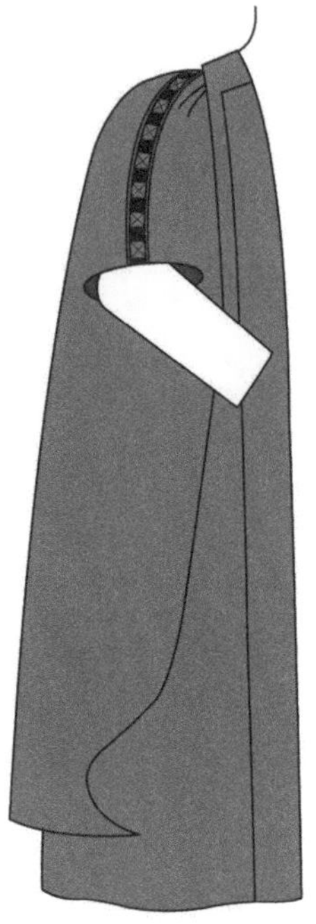

[m2] with lace
Cambridge LittD

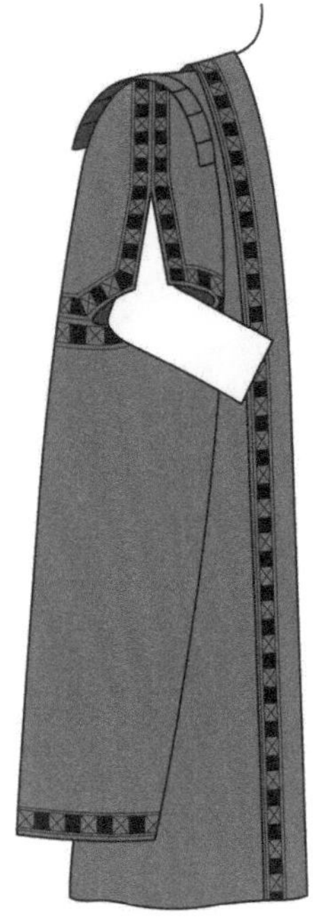

[d4] with lace
Cambridge MD

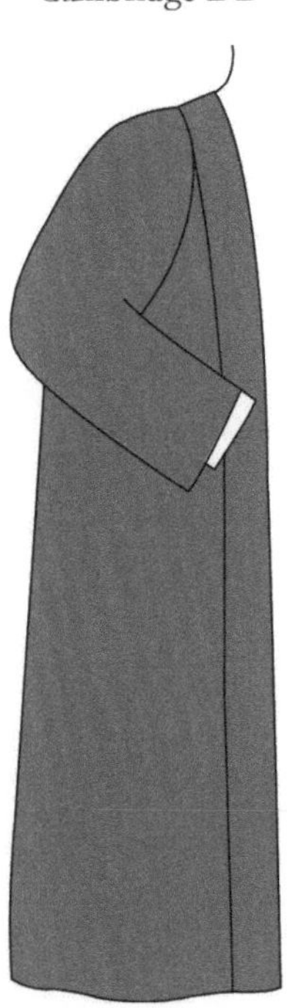

[d7]
Aston (all degrees)

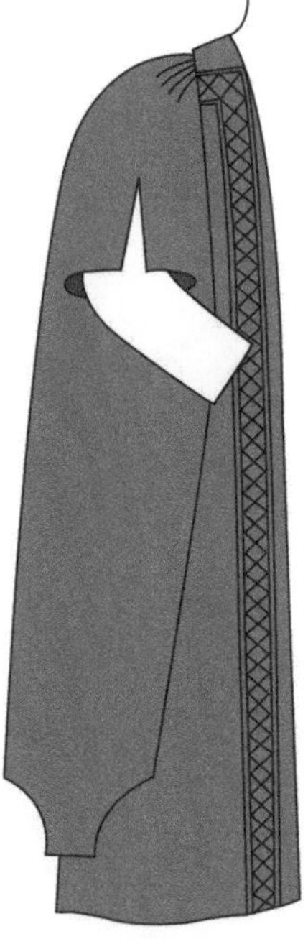

[m8] with lace
Leicester PhD

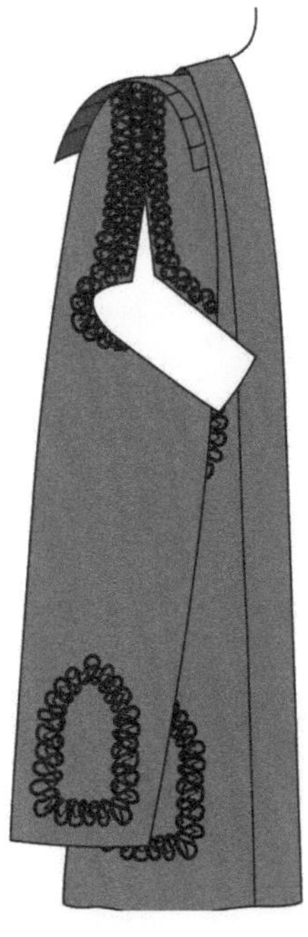

[d4] with lace
Oxford Lay Doctors

DOCTORS' FULL-DRESS ROBES

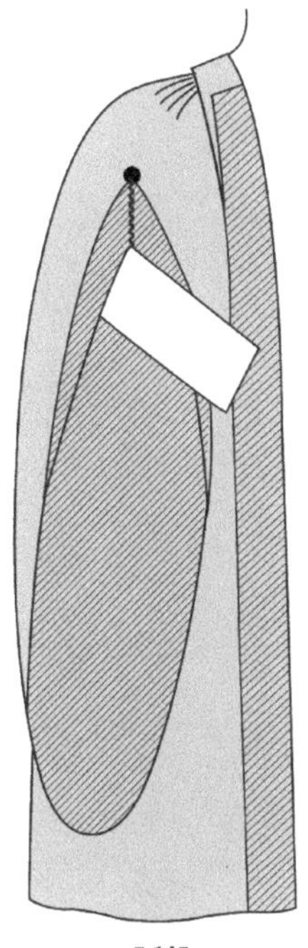

[d1]
Cambridge Doctors

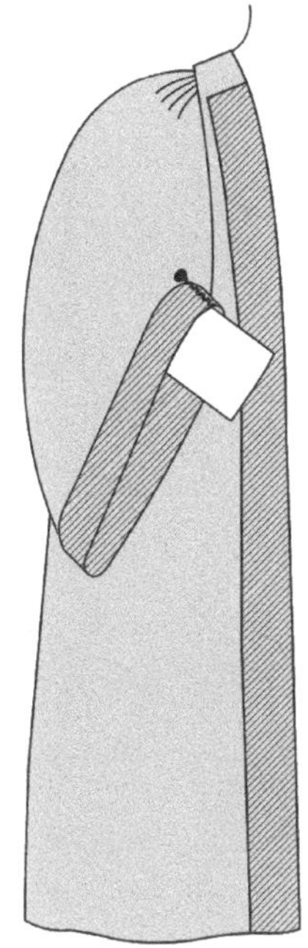

[d3]
Cambridge MusD

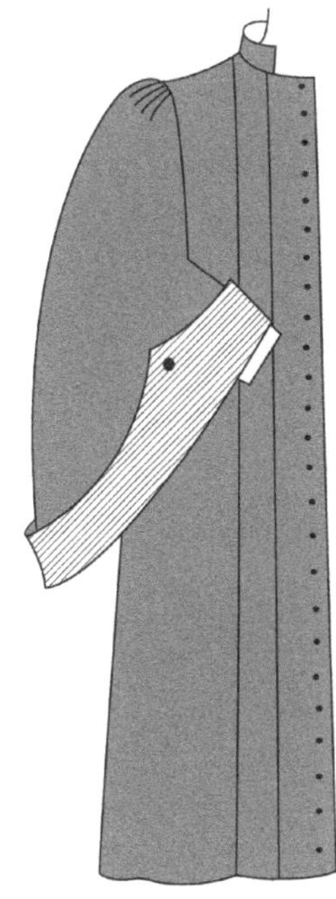

[d9]
St Andrews Honorary Doctors

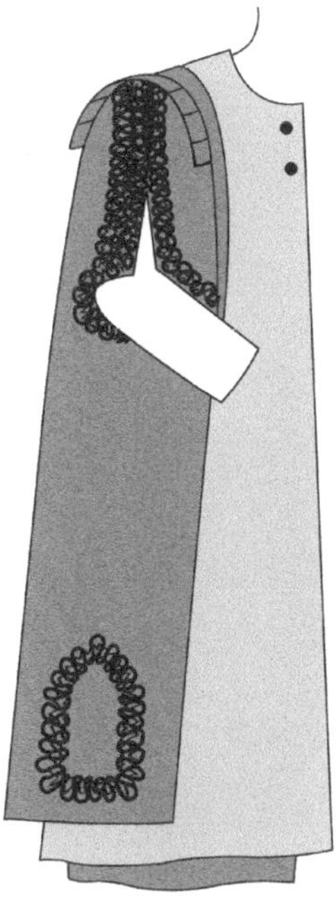

[d5] over lay gown
Oxford Convocation Habit

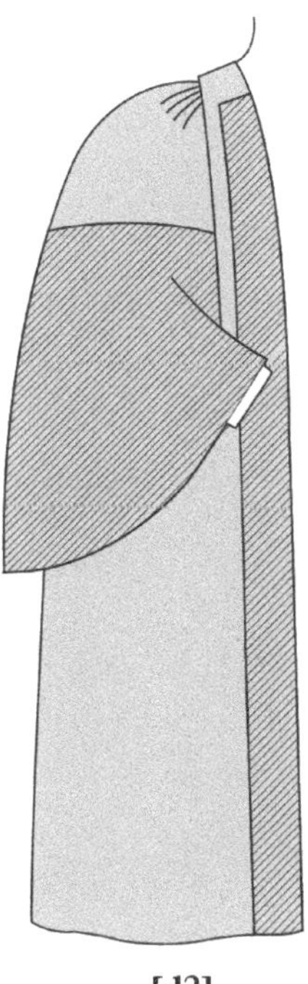

[d2]
Oxford Doctors

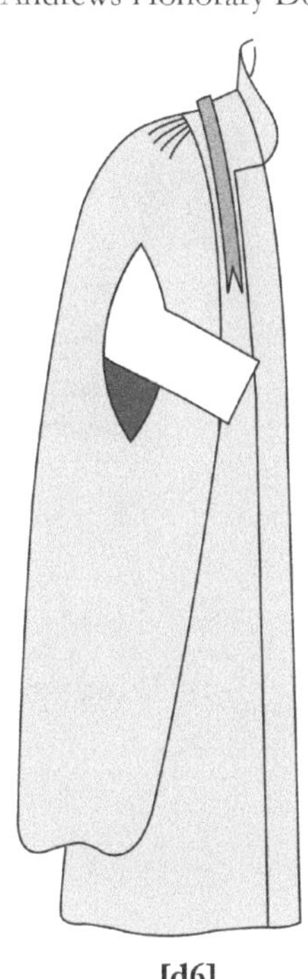

[d6]
Sussex Doctors

Hoods

FULL HOODS

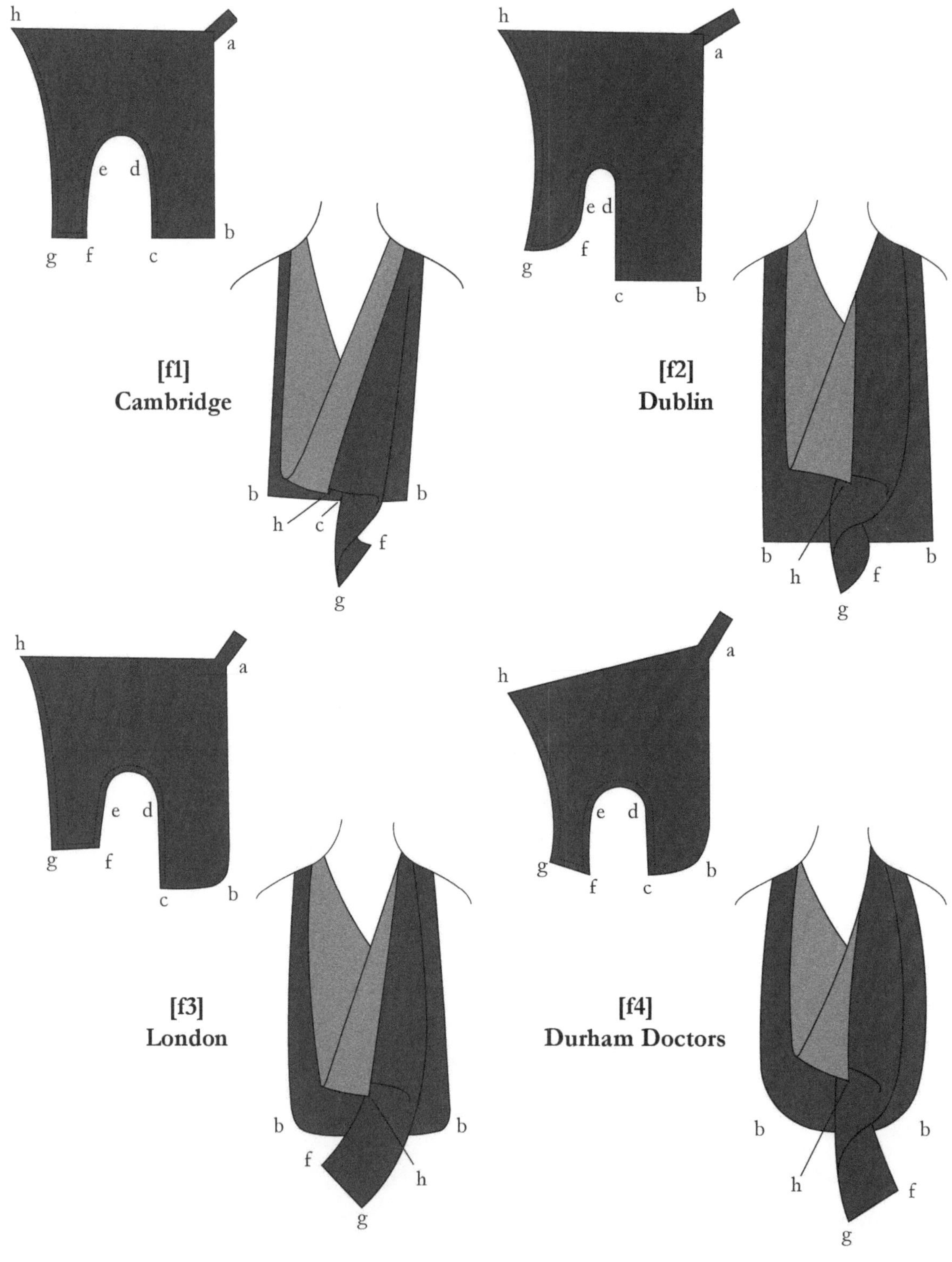

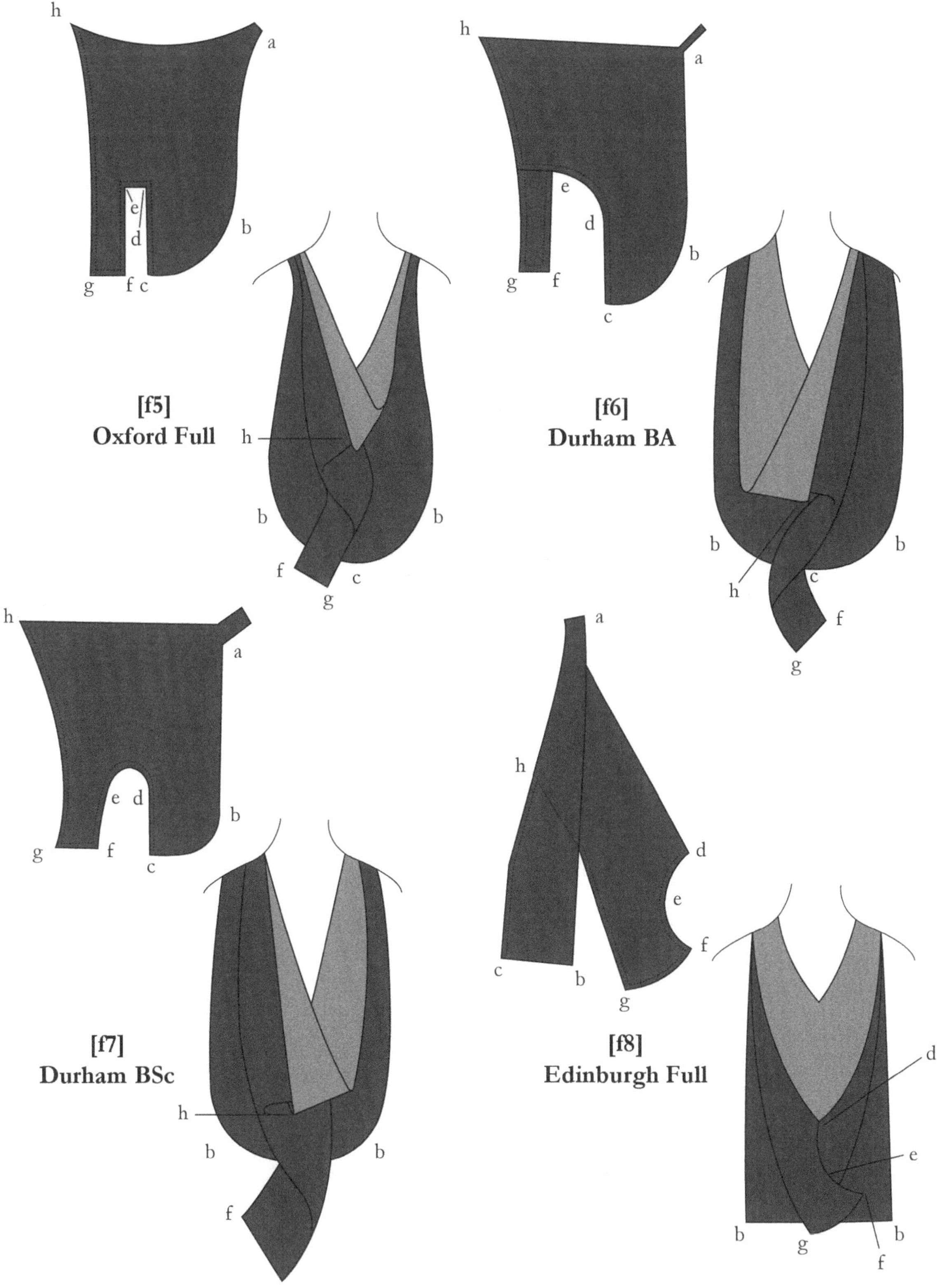

[f5]
Oxford Full

[f6]
Durham BA

[f7]
Durham BSc

[f8]
Edinburgh Full

Hoods

FULL HOODS (ctd)

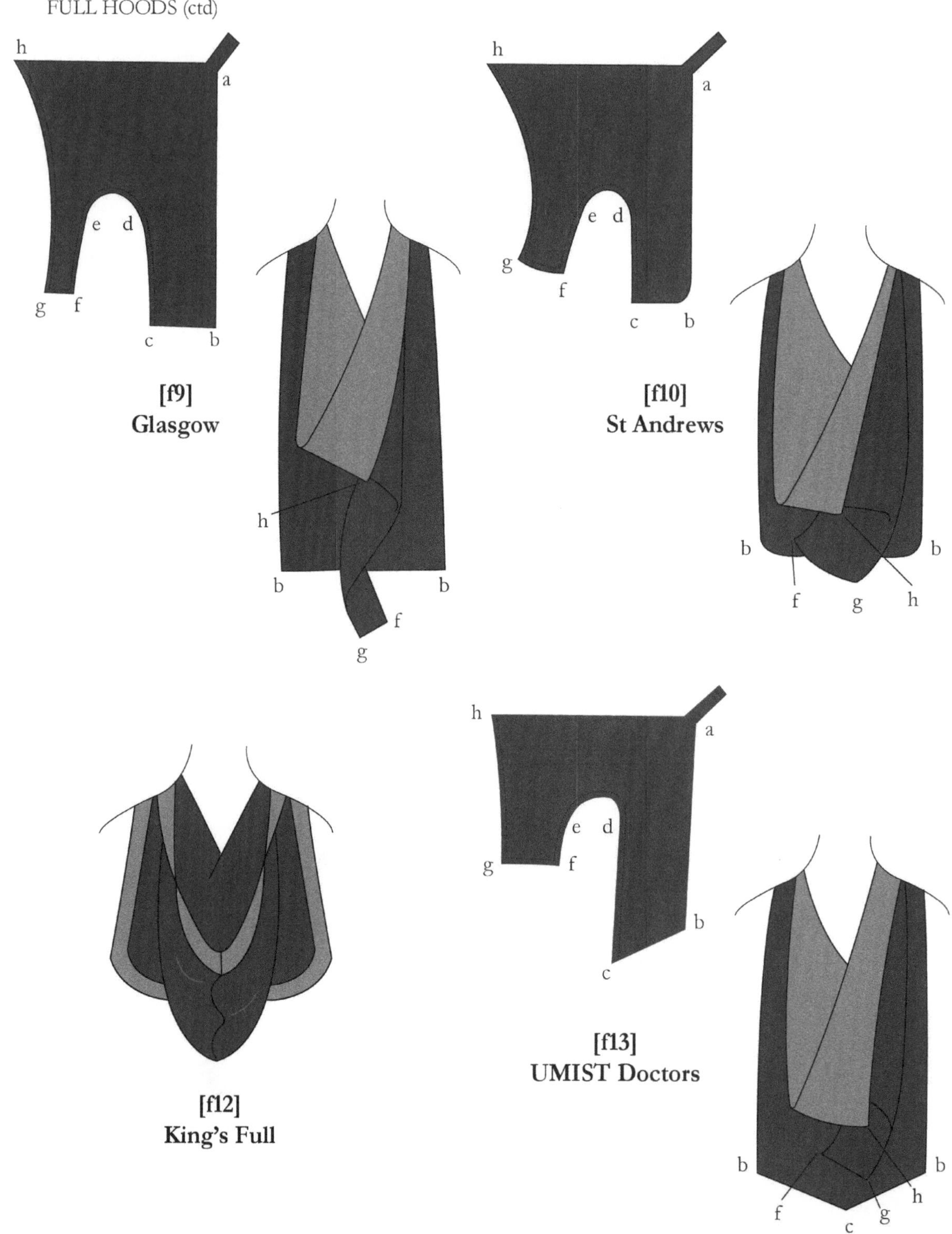

[f9] Glasgow

[f10] St Andrews

[f12] King's Full

[f13] UMIST Doctors

Hoods

SIMPLE HOODS

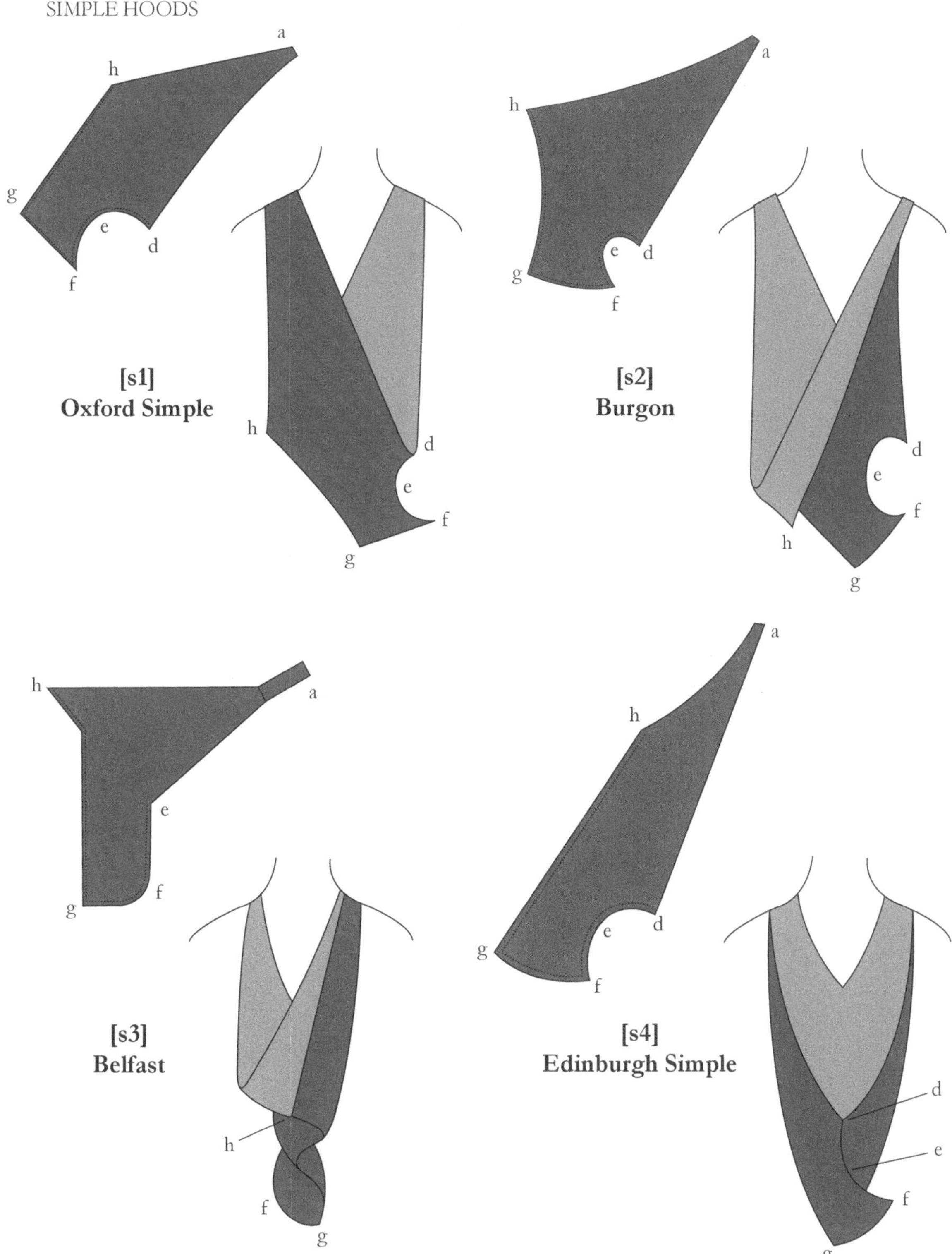

Hoods

SIMPLE HOODS (ctd)

[s5]
Wales Simple

[s6]
Leicester Bachelors

[s7]
Leeds

[s8]
Sussex

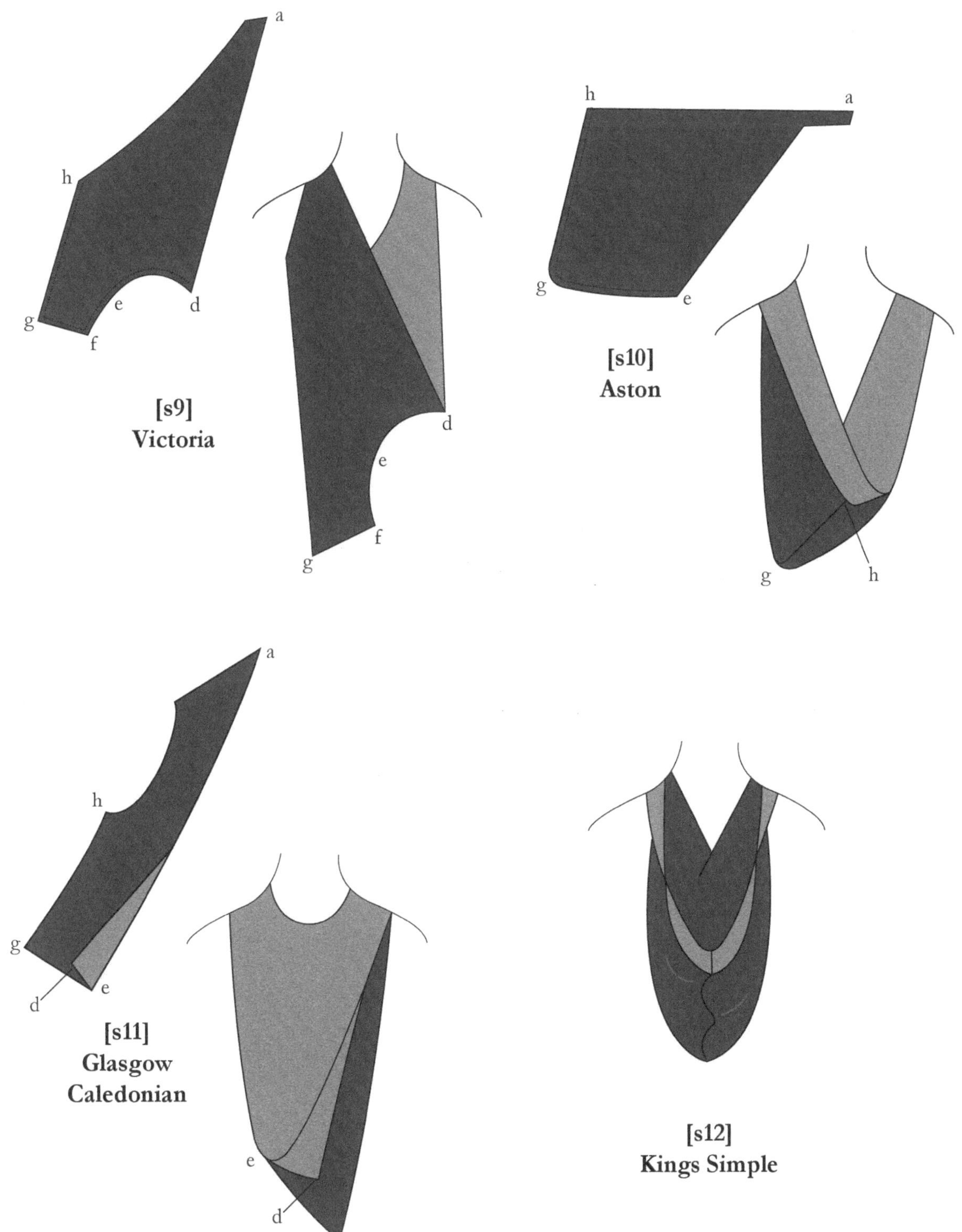

[s9]
Victoria

[s10]
Aston

[s11]
Glasgow Caledonian

[s12]
Kings Simple

Hoods

ABERDEEN HOODS

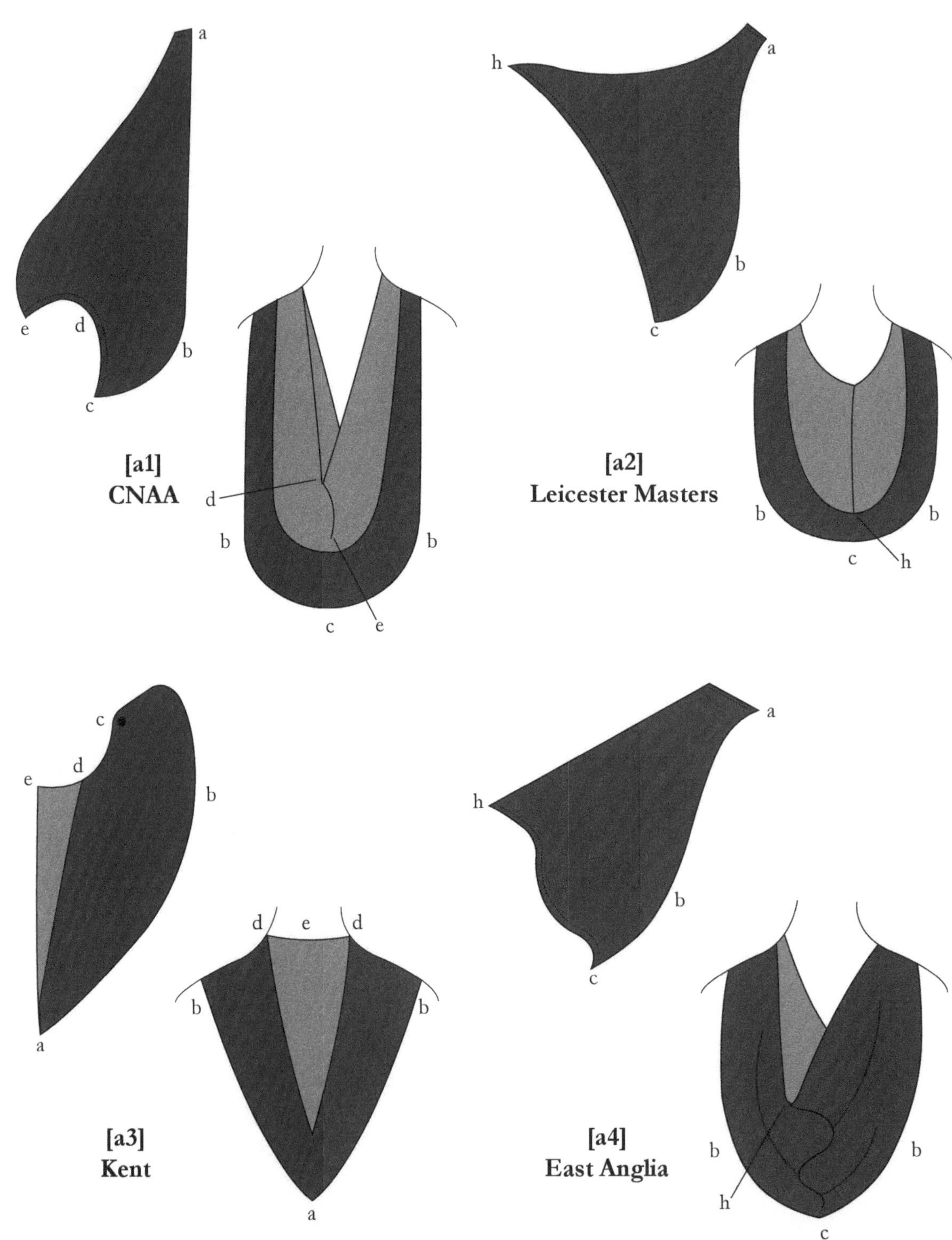

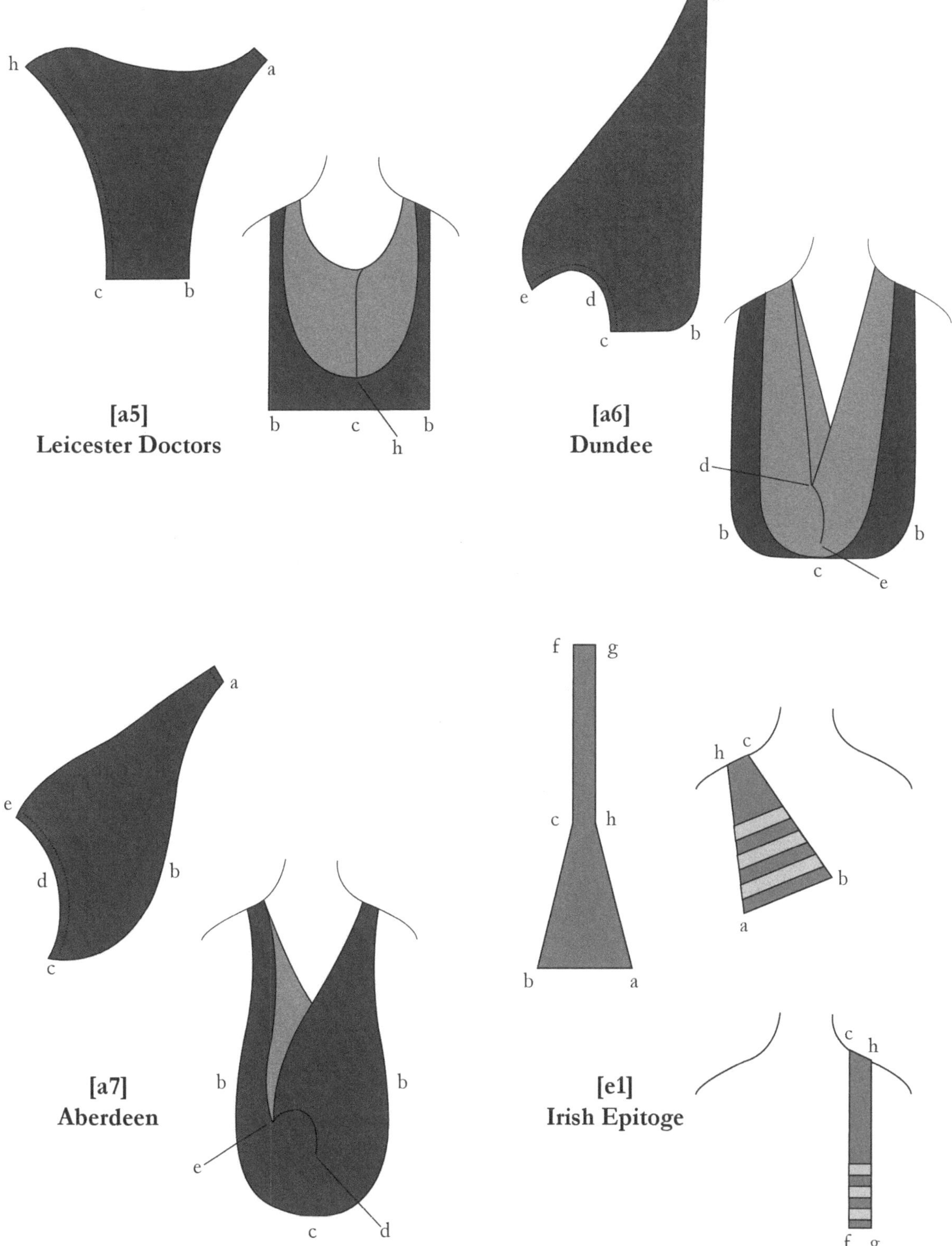

[a5]
Leicester Doctors

[a6]
Dundee

[a7]
Aberdeen

[e1]
Irish Epitoge

Hats

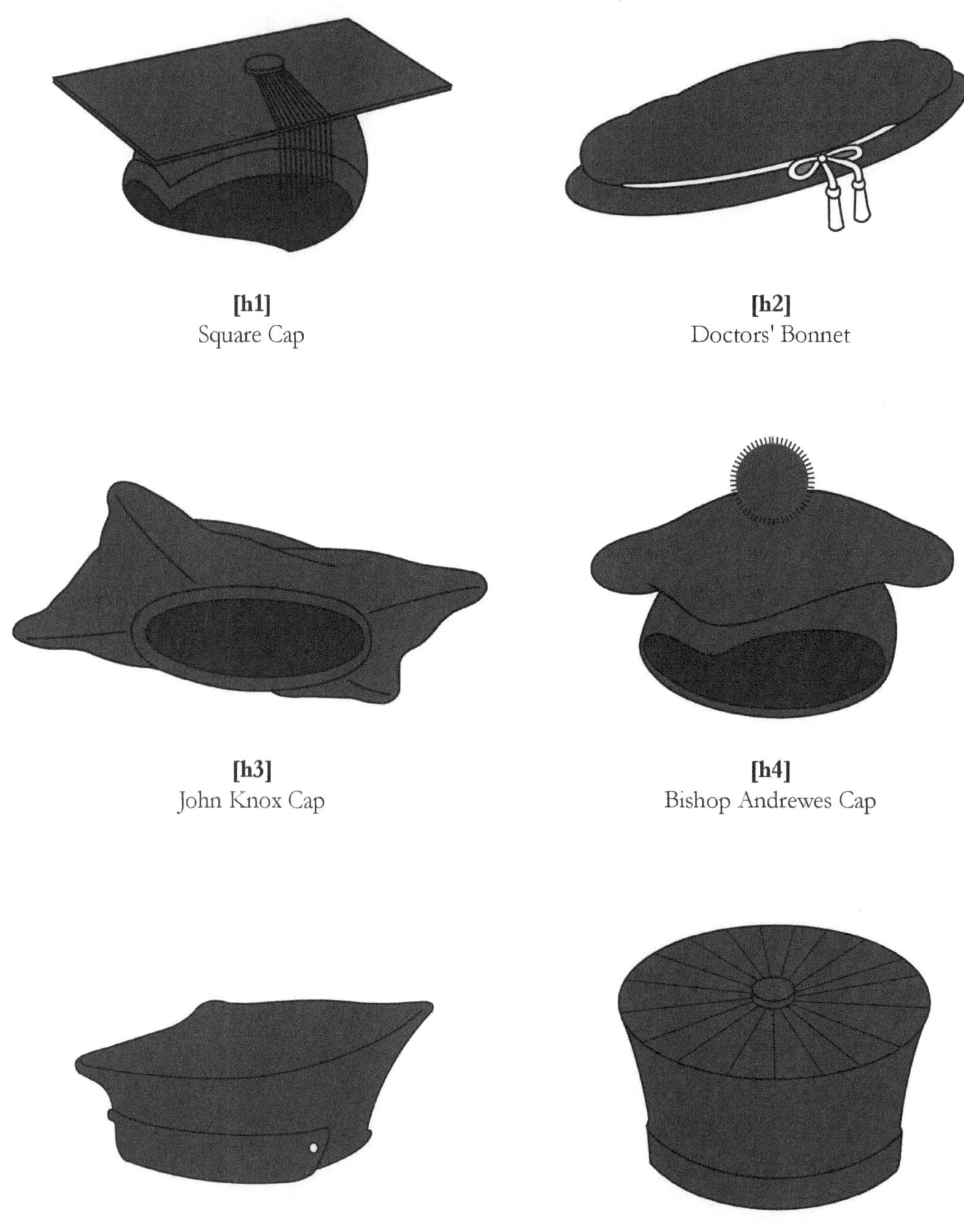

[h1]
Square Cap

[h2]
Doctors' Bonnet

[h3]
John Knox Cap

[h4]
Bishop Andrewes Cap

[h5]
Oxford Ladies' Cap

[h6]
Sussex Pileus

Cloister

Fairford

Lichfield

St Aidan

Tudor Rose

Winchester

Six of the more commonly used brocade patterns

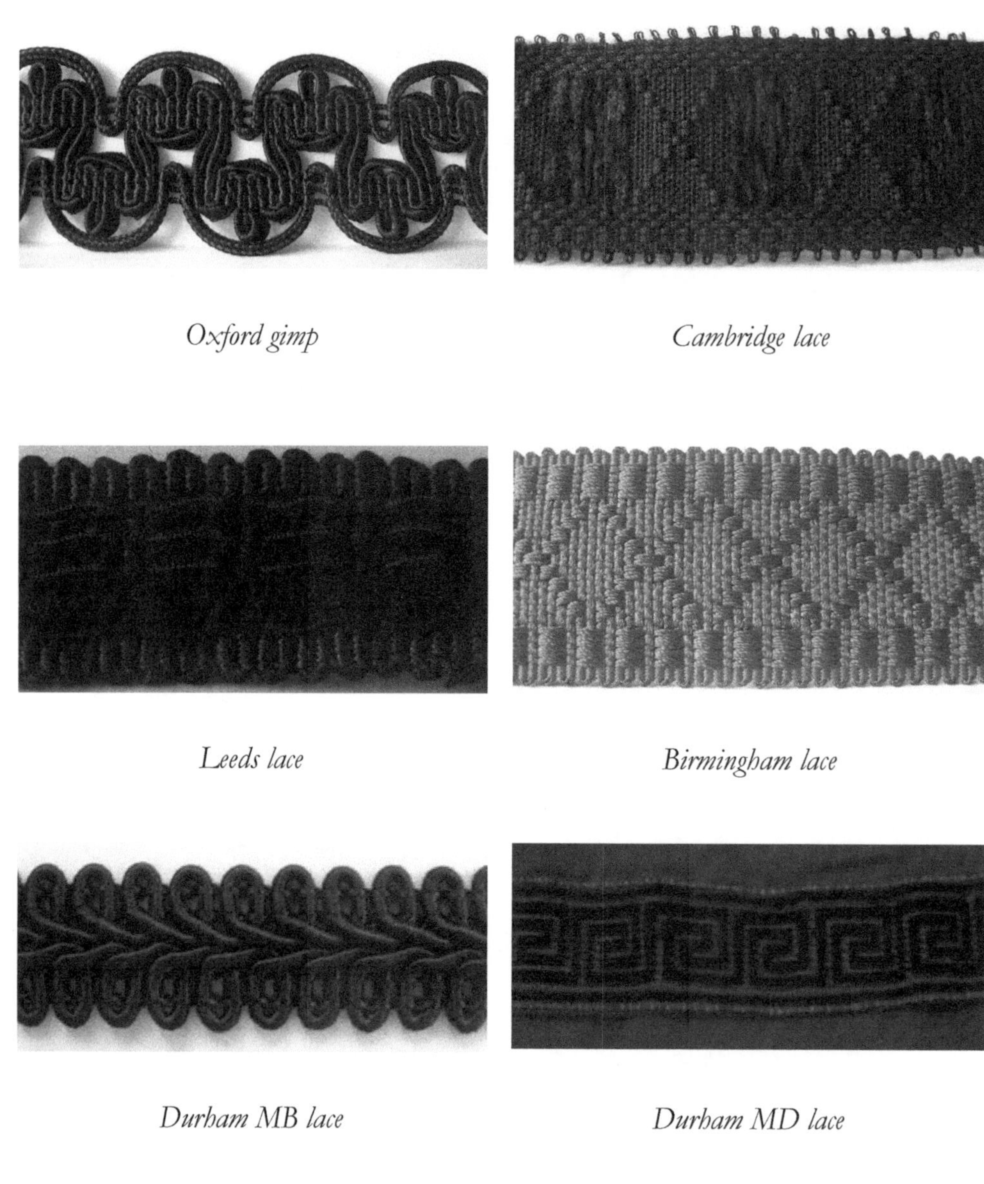

Oxford gimp

Cambridge lace

Leeds lace

Birmingham lace

Durham MB lace

Durham MD lace

St Benet braid

Triple cord with flange

Some examples of lace, gimp and braid

DEGREE AND DIPLOMA ABBREVIATIONS

This list is not, and cannot be, exhaustive. It contains the majority of degrees and diplomas granted by the various universities, even when awarded by only one institution, so that an unfamiliar designation in the specifications may be elucidated here.

Most designations have the grade first (bachelor, master, doctor) and the faculty second. There are a few which reverse the order – *e.g.*, ScD instead of DSc, because the full version is in Latin: thus ScD = *Scientiæ Doctor*. The best-known of these are the MD (*Medicinæ Doctor*) and the PhD (*Philosophiæ Doctor*), and only two universities (Oxford and Sussex) award the latter as DPhil.[42] However, as the Bachelor of Philosophy was invented at Oxford, and the Master of Philosophy at Sussex, this probably explains why they are BPhil and MPhil, and not PhB and PhM.[43] Unfortunately, there seems now to be a perception, probably based on the PhD, that the 'reversed' form is the correct one for 'lower' doctors, and thus the forms EdD, EngD, and ClinPsyD occur. These are then explained as 'Engineering Doctorate' or 'Education Doctorate', *etc*, as the Latin basis has been forgotten.[44] To be consistent, the Doctor of Engineering should be ScMechD = *Scientiæ Mechanicæ Doctor*.

The BA/MA and BSc/MSc are often awarded with other letters appended, sometimes in parentheses. Such are BA(Soc) and BSc(Econ)/BScEcon. The majority of these have been listed below, but others will usually be easily understood. The form 'Bachelor/Master/Doctor *of* …' has been adopted below, as this is the commonly-used form; some writers have insisted on 'Bachelor (etc) *in* …', and this stems also from the Latin forms: *Bacclaureus in Artibus*, *Magister in Scientia*. It is arguable that the full form is 'Master in the Faculty of Arts', and so either is correct. The in/of distinction has also, somewhat ineffectually, been used to differentiate between the MSc (postgraduate taught degree, Master *of* Science) and the MSci (four-year first degree, Master *in* Science).

[42] York did until the early twenty-first century, when it changed to PhD.

[43] Both abbreviations are found in the USA, which has never used DPhil.

[44] It is further complicated as several universities retain the DEng as a higher degree, and some of the professional doctorates retain the initial D: Dublin's Doctor of Education is DEd.

AdminD – Doctor of Administration
AdvDip – Advanced Diploma
AEng – Associate in Engineering
AgrB – Bachelor of Agriculture
AgrM – Master of Agriculture
Agr(Forest)B – Bachelor of Agriculture in Forestry
Agr(Forest)M – Master of Agriculture in Forestry
AMD – Art Masters' Diploma
AMet – Associate in Metallurgy
AMusD – Doctor of Musical Arts
AMusM – Master of Musical Arts
ASc – Associate in Science
ATh – Associate in Theology

BA – Bachelor of Arts
BA(Admin) – Bachelor of Arts in Administration
BACom – Bachelor of Arts in Commerce
BAEcon – Bachelor of Arts in Economics
BA(Ed) – Bachelor of Arts in Education
BA(FS) – Bachelor of Arts in Financial Studies
BALaw – Bachelor of Arts in Law
BA(RelSt) – Bachelor of Arts in Religious Studies
BASoc - Bachelor of Arts in Sociology
BATheol - Bachelor of Arts in Theology
BAcc - Bachelor of Accountancy
BAdmin - Bachelor of Administration
BAgr - Bachelor of Agriculture
BArch - Bachelor of Architecture
BArchSc – Bachelor of Architectural Science
BAH – Bachelor of Animal Health
BAI - Bachelor of Engineering (*Baccalaureus in Arte Ingeniaria*)
BAI(Elect) - Bachelor of Electrical Engineering
BAI(Mech) - Bachelor of Mechanical Engineering
BAO – Bachelor of Obstetrics(*Baccalaureus in Arte Obstetricia)*
BBA – Bachelor of Business Administration
BBLS – Bachelor of Business and Legal Studies
BBS – Bachelor of Business Studies
BBus – Bachelor of Business
BCh – Bachelor of Surgery
BChir – Bachelor of Surgery
BChD - Bachelor of Dental Surgery
BCL –Bachelor of Civil Law
BCLD(SocSc) – Bachelor of Community Learning and Development in Social Science.
BClinSci - Bachelor of Clinical Sciences
BCom – Bachelor of Commerce
BCombStud – Bachelor of Combined Studies
BCommEdCommDev – Bachelor of Community Education and Community Development.
BComSc – Bachelor of Commercial Science
BD – Bachelor of Divinity
BDS - Bachelor of Dental Surgery
BDentSc - Bachelor of Dental Science
BDes – Bachelor of Design
BEd – Bachelor of Education
BEng - Bachelor of Engineering
BEng(Tech) – Bachelor of Engineering in Technology
BES – Bachelor of Engineering Studies
BFA –Bachelor of Fine Art
BFin – Bachelor of Finance
BFLS – Bachelor of Financial and Legal Studies
BFST – Bachelor of Food Science and Technology
BH – Bachelor of Humanities
BHealthSc – Bachelor of Health Sciences
BHy – Bachelor of Hygiene
BIBA – Bachelor of International Business Administration
BJur – Bachelor of Jurisprudence
BL – Bachelor of Law
BLE – Bachelor of Land Economy
BLegSc – Bachelor of Legal Science
BLib - Bachelor of Librarianship
BLing – Bachelor of Linguistics

BLitt – Bachelor of Letters
BLittCelt – Bachelor of Celtic Letters
BLS – Bachelor of Library Studies
BM – Bachelor of Medicine
BMedSc - Bachelor of Medical Sciences
BMet – Bachelor of Metallurgy
BMid – Bachelor of Midwifery
BMS – Bachelor of Midwifery Studies
BMus –Bachelor of Music
BMusEd – Bachelor of Music Education
BMusPerf – Bachelor of Music Performance
BN – Bachelor of Nursing
BNS – Bachelor of Nursing Studies
BNurs – Bachelor of Nursing
BPA – Bachelor of Public Administration
BPharm – Bachelor of Pharmacy
BPhil – Bachelor of Philosophy
BPhil(Ed) – Bachelor of Philosophy in Education
BPhysio –Bachelor of Physiotherapy
BPl – Bachelor of Planning
BRadiog – Bachelor of Radiography
BS – Bachelor of Surgery
BSc – Bachelor of Science
BScAgr – Bachelor of Science in Agriculture
BSc(Dairy) – Bachelor of Science in Dairying
BSc(DomSc) – Bachelor of Science in Domestic Science
BScEcon – Bachelor of Economic Science
BSc(Econ) – Bachelor of Science in Economics
BSc(Eng)- Bachelor of Science in Engineering
BScFor – Bachelor of Science in Forestry
BSc(HealthSc) – Bachelor of Science in Health Sciences
BSc(Hort) – Bachelor of Science in Horticulture
BSc(MCRM) – Bachelor of Science in Marine and Coastal Reserve Management.
BSc(Med) – Bachelor of Science in Medicine
BSc(Mid) – Bachelor of Science in Midwifery
BSc(Min) – Bachelor of Science in Mining
BScPH – Bachelor of Science in Public Health
BScTech – Bachelor of Science in Technology
BSD – Bachelor of Science in Dentistry
BSocSc – Bachelor of Social Sciences
BSS – Bachelor of Social Studies
BStSu – Bachelor of Deaf Studies
BTCP – Bachelor of Town and County Planning
BTEC – British Technical Education Council award
BTech – Bachelor of Technology
BTechEd – Bachelor of Technological Education
BTechS – Bachelor of Technology Studies
BTh – Bachelor of Theology
BTS – Bachelor of Theatre Studies
BVS – Bachelor of Veterinary Surgery
BVSc – Bachelor of Veterinary Sciences
BVetM – Bachelor of Veterinary Medicine
BVetMed – Bachelor of Veterinary Medicine
BVM&S – Bachelor of Veterinary Medicine and Surgery

CertCE – Certificate in Continuing Education
CertEd - Certificate in Education
CertHE – Certificate in Higher Education
ChB – Bachelor of Surgery
ChM – Master of Surgery
ClinPsyD – Doctor of Clinical Psychology

DAP – Doctor of Academic Practice
DBA – Doctor of Business Administration
DBL – Doctor of Business Leadership
DBS – Doctor of Biomedical Science
DCh – Doctor of Surgery
DCL – Doctor of Civil Law
DClinPrac – Doctor of Clinical Practice
DClinPsy – Doctor of Clinical Psychology
DD – Doctor of Divinity
DDP – Doctor of Design Practice
DDS – Doctor of Dental Surgery

DDSc – Doctor of Dental Science
DEconSc – Doctor of Economic Science
DEd – Doctor of Education
DEdPsy – Doctor of Educational Psychology
DEng – Doctor of Engineering
DFin- Doctor of Finance
DFT – Doctor of Family Therapy
DHC – Doctor of Health Care
DHum – Doctor of Humanities
DHy – Doctor of Hygiene
DipArch – Diploma in Architecture
DipTh – Diploma in Theology
DipHE – Diploma in Higher Education
DLang – Doctor of Languages
DLC – Diploma of Loughborough College
DLit – Doctor of Literature
DLitt – Doctor of Letters
DLittCelt – Doctor of Celtic Letters
DM – Doctor of Medicine
DMA – Doctor of Musical Arts
DMan – Doctor of Management
DMedSc – Doctor of Medical Sciences
DMet – Doctor of Metallurgy
DMin – Doctor of Ministry
DMSc – Doctor of Medical Sciences
DMus – Doctor of Music
DMW – Doctor of Midwifery
DOccTher – Doctor of Occupational Therapy
DPA – Doctor of Public Administration
DPH – Doctor of Public Health
DPhil – Doctor of Philosophy
DProf – Doctor of Professional Studies
DPT – Doctor of Physiotherapy
Dr.h.c. – Doctor *honoris causa*
DSc – Doctor of Science
DSocCare – Doctor of Social Care
for such degrees as DScAgr, etc, see under BScAgr above
DSW – Doctor of Social Work
DTech – Doctor of Technology
DTour – Doctor of Tourism
DUniv – Doctor of the University
DVSc – Doctor of Veterinary Sciences
DVetMed – Doctor of Veterinary Medicine
DVM&S – Doctor of Veterinary Medicine and Surgery

EdB – Bachelor of Education
EdD – Doctor of Education
EdPsychD – Doctor of Educational Psychology
EMBA – Executive Master of Business Administration
EMBS – European Master of Business Studies
EngD – Doctor of Engineering

FdA – Foundation Degree in Arts
FdEng – Foundation Degree in Engineering
FdSc – Foundation Degree in Sciences

GradCert – Graduate Certificate
GradDip – Graduate Diploma

HNC – Higher National Certificate
HND – Higher National Diploma
HScD – Doctor of Health Sciences

LD – Licence in Divinity
LDS – Licence in Dental Surgery
LicDD – Licence in Divinity (Doctoral)
LittM – Master of Letters
LittD – Doctor of Letters
LL.B – Bachelor of Laws
LL.D – Doctor of Laws
LL.M – Master of Laws
LSSc – Licence in Sanitary Science
LTh – Licentiate/Licence in Theology
MA – Master of Arts
for such degrees as MA(Ed), etc, see under BA(Ed) above
MAgr – Master of Agriculture
MAI – Master of Engineering (*see* BAI)
MArAd – Master of Archive Administration
MArch – Master of Architecture
MAO – Master of Obstetrics (*see* BAO)
MAcc – Master of Accountancy
MAppPsy – Master of Applied Psychology

MAppSc – Master of Applied Sciences
MARM – Master of Archive and Record Management
MASt – Master of Advanced Studies
MB – Bachelor of Medicine
MBA – Master of Business Administration
MBAcc – Master of Business Accountancy
MBiochem – Master of Biochemistry
MBiotech – Master of Biotechnology
MBL – Master of Business Law
MBS – Master of Business Studies
MBSc –Master of Business Science
MBus – Master of Business
MCA – Master of Computing Arts
MCC – Master of Community Care
MCD – Master of Civic Design
MCDH – Master of Community Dental Health
MCFS – Master of Child Forensic Studies
MCh – Master of Surgery
MChem – Master of Chemistry
MChir – Master of Surgery
MChD – Master of Dental Surgery
MChOrth – Master of Orthopædic Surgery
MChOtol – Master of Otorhinolaryngological Surgery
MCL – Master of Corporate Law
MClinDent – Master of Clinical Dentistry
MClinEd – Master of Clinical Education
MClinSt –Master of Clinical Studies
MCom/MComm – Master of Commerce
MComp - Master of Computing
MCompSc – Master of Computer Sciences
MComSc – Master of Commercial Science
MCoun/MCouns – Master of Counselling
MD – Doctor of Medicine
MDes – Master of Design
MDS – Master of Dental Surgery
MDentSc - Master of Dental Science
MEarthSci - Master of Earth Sciences
MEBA – Master of European Business Administration
MEconSc – Master of Economic Science
MED – Master of Engineering Design
MEDes – Master of European Design
MEd – Master of Education
MEng – Master of Engineering
MEng&Man – Master of Engineering and Management
MEqSt – Master of Equine Studies
MEqualSt –Master of Equality Studies
MESc – Master of Earth Sciences
MFA – Master of Fine Art
MFin – Master of Finance
MGeol – Master of Geology
MGPrac – Master of Gallery Practice
MHist – Master of History
MHPM – Master of Humanitarian Programme Management
MHPrac – Master of Heritage Practice
MHSc – Master of Health Sciences
MIE – Master of Industrial Engineering
MIHR – Master of International Health Research
MInf - Master of Informatics
MIntHsgSc – Master of International Housing Science
MIPH – Master of International Public Health
MIS – Master of Information Sciences
MJur – Master of Jurisprudence; at Oxford, *Magister Juris* (= Master of Law)
MLArch – Master of Landscape Architecture
MLib – Master of Librarianship
MLA – Master of Landscape Architecture
MLD – Master of Landscape Design
MLIS – Master of Library and Information Science
MLitt – Master of Letters
MLittCelt – Master of Celtic Letters
MLS – Master of Library Studies
MM – Master of Midwifery
MMath – Master of Mathematics
MMEd – Master of Medical Education
MMid – Master of Midwifery
MMin – Master of Ministry
MML – Master of Medical Law
MMLE – Master of Medical Law and Ethics
MMPrac – Master of Museum Practice

MMSc – Master of Medical Sciences
MMet – Master of Metallurgy
MMORSE - Master of Mathematics, Operational Research, Statistics, and Economics
MMus – Master of Music
MN – Master of Nursing
MNatSc – Master of Natural Sciences
MObstGyn – Master of Obstetrics and Gynæcology
MPA – Master of Public Administration
MPC – Master of Primary Care
MPH – Master of Public Health
MPM – Master of Public Management
MPharm – Master of Pharmacy
MPhil – Master of Philosophy
MPhys – Master of Physics
MPl – Master of Planning
MProf – Master of Professional Studies
MPS – Master of Pastoral Studies
MPsych – Master of Psychology
MPsychObs – Master of Psychoanalytical Observation Studies
MPsychother – Master of Psychotherapy
MPsyMed – Master of Psychological Medicine
MPsObSt - Master of Psychoanalytical Observation Studies
MRad – Master of Radiology
MRes – Master of Research
MRUP – Master of Rural and Urban Planning
MRurDev – Master of Rural Devèlopment
MS – Master of Surgery
MSc – Master of Science (*postgraduate degree*)
MSci – Master in Science, or in Natural Science (*a First Master degree.)*
for such degrees as MScAgr, etc, see under BScAgr above
MSSc – Master of Social Science *or* Master of Surgical Science
MSt – Master of Studies
MStat – Master of Statistics
MSW – Master of Social Work

MTCH&CP – Master of Tropical Child Health and Clinical Paediatrics
MTCP – Master of Town and County Planning
MTD _ Master of Transport Design
MTeach – Master of Teaching
MTL – Master of Teaching and Learning
MTh – Master of Theology
MTropID – Master of Tropical and Infectious Dieases
MTropMed – Master of Tropical Medicine
MTropPaed – Master of Tropical Paediatrics
MTP – Master of Town Planning
MUA – Master of University Administration
MUBC – Master of Urban and Building Conservation
MURP – Master of Urban and Rural Planning
MusB – Bachelor of Music
MusD – Doctor of Music
MusM – Master of Music
MUniv – Master of the University (*honorary award)*
MUA – Master of University Administration
MVB – Bachelor of Veterinary Medicine
MVM – Master of Veterinary Medicine
MVPH – Master of Veterinary Public Health
MVSc/MVetSc – Master of Veterinary Science
MVetMed – Master of Veterinary Medicine

PGCE – Postgraduate Certificate in Education
PGCert – Postgraduate Certificate
PGDip – Postgraduate Diploma
PhD – Doctor of Philosophy
PsychD – Doctor of Psychology

ScBTech – Bachelor of Science in Technology
ScD – Doctor of Science
SocSciD – Doctor of Social Sciences
STL – Licence in Sacred Theology.

VetMB – Bachelor of Veterinary Medicine

VetMD – Doctor of Veterinary Medicine

ALPHABETICAL LIST OF INSTITUTIONS AWARDING THEIR OWN DEGREES

Those in brackets are no longer operating.

SPECIFICATIONS

In alphabetical order, from Aberdeen to York St John

UNIVERSITY OF ABERDEEN
1495/1593/1860

The University of Aberdeen is comprised of two colleges: King's, founded in 1495 by William Elphinstone, Bishop of Aberdeen, and Marischal, founded in 1593 by George Keith, the fourth Earl Marischal; they operated as two separate universities until they were united in 1860.

As at St Andrews and Glasgow, academic dress more or less fell out of use at the Reformation, and the scheme now in use was drawn up in the 1870s. The hoods are of a shape which has a rounded cape, a vestigial cowl, and no liripipe. This shape was unique to Aberdeen until the 1960s, when the CNAA adopted it in a modified form. The Aberdeen version [a7] has a curve to the cape, which gives a pear-shape when it is worn, though there are grounds for believing it was originally straight-sided, as the CNAA [a1] version.

When a hood is described as 'lined', it is edge-to-edge. Where a binding is specified, it is placed on all edges; borders are laid inside the cape as well as the cowl, even though they are invisible. The regulations describe some borders as being of 'waved' silk: it means watered, which is the term used here.

UNDERGRADUATES

Gown: There are two versions of the undergraduate gown: men's and women's. The men's version is said to be an amalgam of the gowns of King's and Marischal Colleges, each of which had its own gown until they were united, but in fact it is based on the Marischal gown. The women's gown was introduced in 1894, when women were first admitted. It appears that these days the two versions are worn indifferently by both sexes.

Men's gown: a red stuff gown, with elbow-length bell sleeves. It can be closed with two buttons at the top. There is a flap collar of burgundy velvet.

Women's gown: a red stuff gown, with cape-style sleeves. It is worn open, and the burgundy velvet collar is brought over to form facings, which taper to nothing at chest level.

Hat: a black cloth square cap.

UNDERGRADUATE CERTIFICATES AND DIPLOMAS

none specified

BACHELORS

Gown: a black stuff gown of the Scottish MA pattern [m12], with a cord and button on the yoke.

Hood: a black silk hood of the Aberdeen shape [a7], lined as follows:

BA (in Rural Business Management, at the Scottish Agricultural College): lined russet brown silk.

BA (in Professional Studies in Education): lined black, bound ½″ orange silk, bordered inside ½″ white cloth.
BD: lined violet silk, bordered inside 1″ white cloth.
BDS: lined bold red silk.
BDentSc: lined bold red silk, bound ½″ green silk.
BEd: lined orange silk.
BEng: lined pale yellow silk.
BLE: lined black, bound ½″ pale blue silk, bordered inside ½″ white cloth.
LL.B: lined pale blue silk.
MB,ChB: lined crimson silk.
BMedSc: lined crimson silk, bound ½″ green silk.
BMus: lined light brown (fawn) silk.
BSc: lined green silk.
BSc(Agr): lined black, bound ½″ green silk.
BSc(Biomed): lined green silk, bound ½″ white watered silk.
BSc(Eng): bound green silk, bordered inside ½″ white cloth.
BSc(For): lined black, bound ½″ green watered silk.
BSc(HealthSc): lined black, bound ½″ crimson silk, bordered inside ½″ white cloth.
BSc(MedSc): lined crimson silk, bound ½″ white watered silk.
BSc(MCRM): lined black, bound ½″ pale blue silk.
BSc(Rural Dev): lined white, bound ½″ russet brown.
BTech (Agricultural Business Management): lined russet brown.
BTech (Aquaculture): lined russet brown, bordered inside ½″ white cloth set ½″ in.
BTh: lined violet silk, bound ½″ white watered silk.

Hat: a black cloth square cap.

POSTGRADUATE CERTIFICATES AND DIPLOMAS

none specified

FIRST-DEGREE MASTERS

Gown: as for bachelors.

Hood: a black silk hood of the Aberdeen shape [a7], lined as follows:
MA: lined white silk.
MChem: lined green silk, bordered ½″ white cloth set ½″ in.
MEng: lined pale yellow silk, bordered ½″ white cloth set ½″ in.

Hat: a black cloth square cap.

MASTERS including MASTERS OF PHILOSOPHY

Gown: as for bachelors.

Hood: a white silk hood of the Aberdeen shape [a7], lined as follows:
MBA: lined lilac silk.
ChM: lined crimson silk.
MChOrth: lined crimson silk, bordered ½″ white watered silk.
MEd: lined orange silk.

LL.M: lined pale blue silk.
MLE: lined pale blue silk, bordered ½″ white cloth.
MLitt: lined violet silk.
MMedSc: lined crimson silk, bordered ½″ white cloth.
MMus: lined light brown (fawn) silk.
MPhil: lined black silk, bordered ½″ white cloth.
MRad: lined crimson silk, bound ½″ green silk.
MRes: lined black silk, bordered ½″ scarlet cloth.
MScEcon: lined lilac silk, bordered ½″ white cloth.
MSc(Entrepreneurship): lined lilac silk, bound ½″ white watered silk.
MSc: lined green silk.
MTh: lined purple silk.
MUniv: lined dark blue silk, bound ½″ gold silk.

Hat: a black cloth square cap.

ALL DOCTORS

Undress gown: as for bachelors.

Dress robe: a scarlet robe of the Cambridge pattern [d1], but with a flap collar. The facings and collar are covered and the sleeves lined with silk of the same colour as lines the hood.

Hood: a scarlet cloth hood of the Aberdeen shape [a7] (not worn with the dress robe) lined as follows:
DD: lined purple silk.
EdD: lined orange silk.
EngD: lined pale yellow silk.
LL.D: lined pale blue silk.
DLitt: lined white silk.
MD: lined crimson silk.
DMus: lined light brown (fawn) silk.
PhD: lined black ribbed silk, the ribs to run horizontally.
DSc: lined green silk.
Dr.h.c: lined dark blue silk, bound ½″ gold silk.

Hats: in undress, a black cloth square cap; in full dress, a black velvet 'John Knox' hat.

NOTES

1. Obsolete hoods:
   BCom: black silk, bound lilac silk (1919–1949).
   BD: until 1927 did not have the white cloth border.
   BEd: was originally black silk, bound white silk.
   BL: black silk, bound pale blue silk (now used for BSc(MCRM)).
   MBAcc: used the MScEcon hood.
   DPhil: used the DLitt robes.

LTh: worn over a gown as for bachelors, a black stuff epitoge, edged 1˝ purple silk, with a 1˝ white fringe at each end. It was gathered on the shoulder into a large black button.

2. Under the original nineteenth-century scheme, the shells of the DD, LL.D, and MD hoods were made of purple cloth, and the DD was lined white; these were the only doctors' degrees. They had become scarlet by 1910.

INTERNATIONAL CHRISTIAN COLLEGE

Gown: as for bachelors.

Hood: a black hood of Aberdeen shape [a7], lined as follows:

BA (Theology): lined white silk, the cowl bordered purple silk.

BA (Youth Work and Applied Theology): bound purple silk, bordered inside 1˝ white cloth.

Hat: a black cloth square cap.

UNIVERSITY OF ABERTAY
1994

Abertay University traces its origins to the Dundee Institute of Technology, which was founded in 1888, becoming a Central Institution (a degree-granting body concentrating on teaching rather than research, its degrees validated by the CNAA). It was recognized as an 'industrial university' by the Scottish Office as early as 1902. It gained independent degree-giving authority in the 1970s, and was raised to university status in 1994 under the provisions of the Further and Higher Education Act 1992.

The scheme of robes is simple, and based on a faculty colour system: the lining is determined by the subject of the degree rather than the title.

UNDERGRADUATES
none specified

UNDERGRADUATE CERTIFICATES AND DIPLOMAS
Gown: as for bachelors.
Hood: a blue hood of the CNAA shape [a1], lined red.
Hat: a black cloth square cap.

BACHELORS
Gown: a black stuff gown of the basic pattern [b1], with a cord and button on the yoke.
Hood: a blue hood of Cambridge shape [f1], lined with the degree colour. The neckband is reversed to show the lining colour:
BA (Business; Social and Health Science): white.
BA (Computing): pink.
LL.B: blue.
BSc (Business; Computing; Pure Science): green.
BSc (Civil Engineering; Construction; Engineering): silver.
BSc (Social and Health Science): yellow.
Hat: a black cloth square cap.

POSTGRADUATE CERTIFICATES AND DIPLOMAS
Gown: as for masters.
Hood: a blue hood of CNAA shape [a1], lined and bound 1″ red.
Hat: a black cloth square cap.

MASTERS
Gown: a black stuff gown of the Scottish MA pattern [m12].
Hood: a blue hood of the Cambridge full shape [f1], lined and bound 1″ with the degree colour. The neckband is reversed to show the lining colour:
MBA: white.

MCA: pink.
MLitt: a green hood, lined blue, bound 1″ gold.
MSc (Management): yellow.
MSc (Computing; Pure Science): green.
MSc (Civil Engineering; Construction; Engineering): silver.
MSc (Health and Social Science): yellow.

Hat: a black cloth square cap.

MASTERS OF PHILOSOPHY

Gown: a black stuff gown of the Scottish MA pattern [m12], with 2½″ gold facings.

Hood: a green hood of the Cambridge shape [f1], lined and bound 1″ gold. The neckband is reversed to show gold.

Hat: a black cloth square cap.

DOCTORS OF PHILOSOPHY and TAUGHT AND PROFESSIONAL DOCTORS

Undress gown: *none specified*

Dress robe: a maroon robe of the St Andrews doctors' pattern [d3]. The facings and the 2½″ cuffs are covered with gold silk.

Hood: a maroon hood of the Cambridge shape [f1]. The neckband is reversed to show the lining colour:
PhD: lined and bound 1″gold.
DBA: lined white, bound 2″ gold.

Hat: in full dress, a black cloth bonnet with gold cords and tassels.

HIGHER DOCTORS

Undress gown: *none specified*

Dress robe: a blue robe of the St Andrews doctors' pattern [d3]. The facings and the 2½″ cuffs are covered with gold silk.

Hood: a blue hood of the Cambridge shape [f1], lined and bound 1″ gold. The neckband is reversed to show gold.

Hat: in full dress, a blue cloth bonnet with gold cords and tassels.

ABERYSTWYTH UNIVERSITY
1872/2009

Aberystwyth was founded as the University College of Wales (UCW) in 1872, and was one of the three original constituent colleges of the federal University of Wales. It changed its name to The University of Wales Aberystwyth (UWA) in 1995, and with the granting of degree-awarding powers in 2007, to Aberystwyth University (by which name it had long been informally known). On gaining full independence in 2007, it initially awarded degrees of the University of Wales, but since 2009 has awarded its own degrees.

The robes make no reference to the University of Wales robes. The main colours are red and green, which are the college colours. The green is a grass green, and the red is a shade of crimson. Unusually, the PhD is given a red robe, while the higher doctors have a maroon one – a reversal of the usual practice.

UNDERGRADUATES
none specified

UNDERGRADUATE CERTIFICATES AND DIPLOMAS
none specified

FOUNDATION DEGREES
Gown: as for bachelors.

Hood: a black hood of the CNAA shape [a1], lined black, and bound on all edges with a red and green twisted cord.

Hat: a black cloth square cap.

BACHELORS
Gown: a black gown of the London BA pattern [b4], but with red and green twisted cords and red buttons on the sleeves.

Hood: a black hood of the CNAA shape [a1], lined and the cape bound ½″ green, and the cowl bordered inside 2″ red.

Hat: a black cloth square cap.

POSTGRADUATE CERTIFICATES AND DIPLOMAS
none specified

FIRST-DEGREE MASTERS
not awarded

MASTERS including MASTERS OF PHILOSOPHY
Gown: a black gown of the basic pattern [m10]. The armhole is bound ½″ inside and out red, and there is a green cord and button on the yoke.

Hood:

MPhil: a green hood of the London shape [f3], unlined, and the cowl bordered inside 3″ red.

All others: a black hood of the London shape [f3], lined green, and the cowl bordered inside 3″ red.

Hat: a black cloth square cap.

DOCTORS OF PHILOSOPHY and TAUGHT AND PROFESSIONAL DOCTORS

Undress gown: *none specified*

Dress robe: a red robe of the Cambridge pattern [d1], with facings and sleeve linings of green. There is a red cord and button on each sleeve.

Hood: a red hood of the London shape [f3], lined and the cape bound ½″ green.

Hat: in full dress, a black cloth bonnet with red cords and tassels.

HIGHER DOCTORS

Undress gown: *none specified*

Dress robe: a maroon robe of the Cambridge pattern [d1], with facings and sleeve linings of red. There is a green cord and button on each sleeve.

Hood: a maroon hood of the London shape [f3], lined and the cape bound ½″ green.

Hat: in full dress, a black velvet bonnet with green cords and tassels.

ANGLIA RUSKIN UNIVERSITY
1993

The Cambridge School of Art was opened by John Ruskin in 1858, and changed its name to Cambridge College of Arts and Technology in 1960. It initially prepared its students for London degrees and later for those awarded by the CNAA. In 1985 it merged with the Essex Institute of Higher Education to form Anglia Higher Education College, which gained Polytechnic status in 1991 (as Anglia Polytechnic), and became Anglia Polytechnic University (APU) in 1992. In 2005 it changed its name again, to Anglia Ruskin University.

All hoods and dress robes feature gold brocade: this is 'Cloister' pattern, and the gold is very dark, approaching orange in some cases.

UNDERGRADUATES
none specified

UNDERGRADUATE CERTIFICATES AND DIPLOMAS
Gown: as for bachelors.
Hood: a dark blue hood of the CNAA shape [a1], lined gold brocade, tipped mid-blue silk.
Hat: a blue cloth square cap.

FOUNDATION DEGREES
Gown: as for bachelors.
Hood: a dark blue hood of the CNAA shape [a1], lined gold brocade, tipped mid-blue silk.
Hat: a blue cloth square cap.

BACHELORS
Gown: a dark blue stuff gown of the basic pattern [b1].
Hood: a dark blue stuff hood of the Cambridge shape [f1], bordered inside the cowl 4″ gold brocade, and bound 1″ mid-blue on the cowl edge.
Hat: a blue cloth square cap.

POSTGRADUATE CERTIFICATES AND DIPLOMAS
none specified

FIRST-DEGREE MASTERS
not awarded

MASTERS including MASTERS OF PHILOSOPHY
Gown: a dark blue stuff gown of the basic pattern [m10].

Hood: a dark blue hood of the Cambridge shape [f1], fully lined gold brocade, and bound on the cowl edge 2″ mid-blue.

Hat: a black cloth square cap.

DOCTORS OF PHILOSOPHY and TAUGHT AND PROFESSIONAL DOCTORS

Undress gown: *none specified*

Dress robe: a dark blue robe of the Cambridge pattern [d1], the facings covered and the sleeves lined gold brocade.

Hood: a dark blue hood of the Cambridge shape [f1], lined and bound ¼″ gold brocade.

Hat: in full dress, a blue cloth bonnet with gold cords and tassels.

HIGHER DOCTORS

Undress gown: *none specified*

Dress robe: as for PhD, but with blue cords and buttons on the sleeves also.

Hood: as for PhD, but the binding is 1½″ wide.

Hat: in full dress, a blue velvet bonnet with gold cords and tassels.

THE ARCHITECTURAL ASSOCIATION SCHOOL OF ARCHITECTURE
1847

The School was founded in 1847, and formally established in 1890. It offers both undergraduate programmes, which lead to the AADip (the equivalent of a first degree), and postgraduate programmes, which include specialized courses in landscape urbanism, housing and urbanism, energy and the environment, histories and theories, building conservation, garden conservation, and environmental access, and lead to an MA, MSc, or MArch. It also offers an MPhil and a PhD. The masters' and PhD degrees are validated by the Open University.

The Association uses only one hood for all its awards, the difference in status being denoted by the gowns.

AADip and GRADUATE DIPLOMA

Gown: a black stuff gown of the basic bachelors' pattern [b1].

Hood: a black stuff hood of the Edinburgh simple shape [s4], bordered inside the cowl with two 1″ orange bands separated by 2″ black.

Hat: a black cloth square cap.

MASTERS including MASTERS OF PHILOSOPHY

Gown: a black stuff gown of the London MA pattern [m5], with 1″ orange on the outer edge of the facings.

Hood: as for AADip.

Hat: a black cloth square cap.

DOCTORS OF PHILOSOPHY

Undress gown: *none specified*

Dress robe: as for masters, but the facings wholly covered with orange.

Hood: as for AADip.

Hat: in full dress, a black cloth bonnet with orange cords and tassels.

UNIVERSITY OF THE ARTS, LONDON
2004

This university was formed from five colleges of art: Camberwell College of Arts (1898), Central St Martin's (1854), Chelsea College of Art and Design (1895), the London College of Communication (1894), and the London College of Fashion (1906). They were united as the London Institute in 1988, which gained degree-awarding powers in 1993. It initially decided not to apply for university status, as the individual colleges were well-known in their own right. However, university status was granted in 2004. Wimbledon College (formerly School) of Art (1890) joined in 2006.

The colours used are red, purple, and magenta, which, in combination with black, produce some striking robes.

UNDERGRADUATES
none specified

UNDERGRADUATE CERTIFICATES AND DIPLOMAS
Gown: a black stuff gown of the basic pattern [b1].
Hood: a black silk hood of the Cambridge shape, the cowl bordered inside 2″ magenta silk. The neckband is black, lined and bound ¼″ magenta.
Hat: a black cloth square cap.

FOUNDATION DEGREES
Gown: a black stuff gown of the basic pattern [b1].
Hood: of the Cambridge shape [f1], in black silk, bordered inside the cowl 1″ purple velvet, and 1″ red velvet set 1″ away. The neckband is black, lined and bound ¼″ magenta.
Hat: a black cloth square cap.

BACHELORS
Gown: a black stuff gown of the basic pattern [b1].
Hood: a black silk hood of the Cambridge shape [f1], bordered inside the cowl 4″ magenta silk, with 1″ purple velvet set ¼″ in. The neckband is black, lined and bound ¼″ magenta.
Hat: a black cloth square cap.

POSTGRADUATE CERTIFICATES AND DIPLOMAS
Gown: a black stuff gown of the basic pattern [b1].
Hood: a black silk hood of the Cambridge shape [f1], lined purple silk, with 1″ red velvet set ¼″ in. The neckband is black, lined and bound ¼″ purple.
Hat: a black cloth square cap.

MASTERS including MASTERS OF PHILOSOPHY

Gown: a black stuff gown of the basic pattern [m10]. For MPhil, the facings have 1″ purple ribbon on the outer edge.

Hood: a black silk hood of the Cambridge shape, lined and bound 1″ purple silk, with 1¼″ red velvet set flush. The neckband is black, lined and bound ¼″ purple.

Hat: a black cloth square cap. For honorary masters, it has a purple button and tassel.

DOCTORS OF PHILOSOPHY and TAUGHT AND PROFESSIONAL DOCTORS

Undress gown: *none specified*

Dress robe: a purple silk robe of the Cambridge pattern [d1], with facings and sleeve linings of magenta silk.

Hood: a purple silk hood of the Cambridge shape [f1], lined magenta silk.

Hat: in full dress, a purple velvet bonnet with magenta cords and tassels.

HIGHER DOCTORS

Undress gown: *none specified*

Dress robe: a magenta silk robe of the Cambridge pattern [d1], with facings and sleeve linings of purple (velvet on the facings, satin in the sleeves). The sleeves have a purple cord and button.

Hood: a magenta silk hood of the Cambridge shape [f1], lined purple silk.

Hat: in full dress, a purple velvet bonnet with magenta cords and tassels.

UNIVERSITY OF ASTON
1966

Established in 1895 as the Birmingham Municipal Technical School, it became a College of Advanced Technology. In common with the other CATs, Aston achieved university status in 1966.

All hoods and the doctors' robes are trimmed with 'Aston silk'. This is blood crimson, with the university's armorial shield woven in at 5″ intervals. All hoods are made in the Aston simple shape, which is the same as the Surrey simple shape [s10], but the cowl edge is permanently turned out for 3″; the 3″ border on the bachelors' and the PhD hood is placed on this turnout. The PhD is unique among doctors in having a part-lined hood. The shape of the gown, with its coat-style sleeves, is apparently based on the white laboratory coat.

UNDERGRADUATES
none specified

UNDERGRADUATE CERTIFICATES AND DIPLOMAS
Gown: as for bachelors.

Hood: a black stuff hood of Aston shape [s10], the neckband only faced with black silk, showing one shield on each side.

Hat: a black cloth square cap.

FOUNDATION DEGREES
Gown: as for bachelors.

Hood: a black stuff hood of the Aston shape [s10], the neckband only faced with Aston silk, showing one shield on each side.

Hat: a black cloth square cap.

BACHELORS and FIRST-DEGREE MASTERS
Gown: a black stuff gown of Aston pattern [d7]. This has narrow sleeves, just wider than a coat sleeve. The facings are carried round the neck as a collar, into which the body of the gown is gathered in wide pleats.

Hood: a black stuff hood of the Aston shape [s10], bordered for 3″ Aston silk; four shields show on each side. This pattern is carried on to the front of the neckband, which is plain red.

Hat: a black cloth square cap.

POSTGRADUATE CERTIFICATES AND DIPLOMAS
Gown: as for bachelors.

Hood: a black stuff hood of Aston shape [s10], lined plain crimson, the neckband only faced with Aston silk, showing one shield on each side.

Hat: a black cloth square cap.

MASTERS including MASTERS OF PHILOSOPHY

Gown: as for bachelors.

Hood: a hood of the Aston shape [s10], lined Aston silk.

MPhil: the shell of the hood is blue.

All others: the shell of the hood is black.

Hat: a black cloth square cap.

DOCTORS OF PHILOSOPHY and TAUGHT AND PROFESSIONAL DOCTORS

Undress gown: as for bachelors.

Dress robe: the bachelors' gown, but in claret cloth.

Hood: a claret cloth hood of the Aston shape [s10], bordered for 3″ Aston silk.

Hats: in undress, a black cloth square cap; in full dress a black cloth bonnet with red cords and tassels.

HIGHER DOCTORS

Undress gown: as for PhD.

Dress robe: the bachelors' gown, but in red cloth, with the addition of 3″ facings covered with Aston silk, and 5″ cuffs covered with gold silk.

Hood: a gold cloth hood of the Aston shape [s10], lined Aston silk.

Hats: in undress, a black cloth square cap; in full dress, a black velvet bonnet with gold cords and tassels.

NOTES

1. Originally the PhD wore the black gown, with red facings, and the higher doctors wore the red gown now used by PhD.

BANGOR UNIVERSITY
1884

Bangor was founded as the University College of North Wales (UCNW) in 1884, and was one of the three original constituent colleges of the federal University of Wales. It changed its name to University of Wales, Bangor (UWB) in 1995, and with the granting of degree-awarding powers in 2007, to Bangor University (by which name it had often been informally known). The first Bangor degrees to be awarded were four honorary doctorates in 2009; earned Bangor degrees have been awarded since 2010.

Red and gold are the heraldic colours; the college colours are green and yellow.

UNDERGRADUATES
none specified

UNDERGRADUATE CERTIFICATES AND DIPLOMAS
Gown: as for bachelors.

Hood: a black hood of the CNAA shape [a1], fully lined black, and bordered inside the cowl ½″ red and ½″ gold (the red is nearer the edge).

Hat: a black cloth square cap.

FOUNDATION DEGREES
Gown: as for bachelors.

Hood: a black hood of the Cambridge shape [f1], fully lined black, and bordered inside the cowl 1″ red and 1″ gold (the red is nearer the edge).

Hat: a black cloth square cap.

BACHELORS
Gown: a black gown of the Wales bachelors' pattern [b6].

Hood: a black hood of the Cambridge shape [f1], lined black, and the cowl bordered inside 5″ gold, with 1″ red on the edge.

Hat: a black cloth square cap.

POSTGRADUATE CERTIFICATES AND DIPLOMAS
Gown: as for masters.

Hood:

PGCE: a black hood of the Cambridge shape [f1], lined black, and the cowl bordered inside 5″ red, with 1″ gold on the edge.

PG Diploma: as for PGCE, but with a second 1″ band of gold set ½″ away from the first.

Hat: a black cloth square cap.

FIRST-DEGREE MASTERS

Gown: as for bachelors.

Hood: as for bachelors, but with a second 1″ band of red set ½″ away from the first.

Hat: a black cloth square cap.

MASTERS including MASTERS OF PHILOSOPHY

Gown: a black gown of the Wales masters' pattern [m4].

Hood:

MPhil: a black hood of the Cambridge shape [f1], lined red; bound on all edges 1″ gold.

All others: a black hood of the Cambridge shape [f1], lined and the cape bound ¾″ red; the cowl bordered inside 1″ gold.

Hat: a black cloth square cap.

DOCTORS OF PHILOSOPHY and TAUGHT AND PROFESSIONAL DOCTORS

Undress gown: *none specified*

Dress robe: a maroon robe of the Cambridge pattern [d1]. The facings are covered with red, with 1″ gold on the outer edge; the sleeves are lined red with a gold cord and button. There is a gold cord and button on the yoke.

Hood: a maroon hood of the Cambridge shape [f1], lined red, and bound on all edges 1″ gold.

Hat: in full dress, a black cloth bonnet with gold and red cord and tassels.

HIGHER DOCTORS

Undress gown: *none specified*

Dress robe: a scarlet cloth robe of the Cambridge pattern [d1], the sleeves lined and the facings covered with red silk. There is 1″ gold on the outer edge of each facing, and a gold cord and button holding each sleeve.

Hood: a scarlet cloth hood of the Cambridge shape [f1, lined red silk, and bound 1″ inside and out gold.

Hat: in full dress, a black velvet bonnet with gold and red cord and tassels.

UNIVERSITY OF BATH
1966

The University of Bath can trace its roots to the Bristol Trade School, established in 1856. In 1885, the school became part of the Society of Merchant Venturers, and was renamed the Merchant Venturers' Technical College. The Bath School of Pharmacy was founded in 1907, and became part of the Technical College in 1929. In 1949, the college came under the control of the Bristol Education Authority and was renamed the Bristol College of Technology; the name was subsequently changed again in 1960 to the Bristol College of Science and Technology when it became one of ten Colleges of Advanced Technology: they were all granted university status in 1966.

The robes for Bath were designed by George Shaw, and incorporate old-gold grosgrain as a base colour to recall the colour of Bath stone. The scheme is simple, and has adapted well to the addition of new degrees. It is not clear why the Science hoods do not have a faculty colour: when asked about this, Dr Shaw said he could not remember. The DMus robes are an interesting revival of the ancient use of cream brocade for this degree.

UNDERGRADUATES

Gown: a black stuff gown of the Oxford scholar's pattern [u2], but with the forearm seam left open for the lower 6″, with a black button at the top of the slit.

Hat: a black cloth square cap.

UNDERGRADUATE CERTIFICATES AND DIPLOMAS

none specified

FOUNDATION DEGREES

Gown: as for bachelors.

Hood: an old-gold grosgrain hood of the Leeds simple shape [s7], lined old-gold grosgrain.

Hat: a black cloth square cap.

BACHELORS

Gown: a black stuff gown of the basic pattern, but with the forearm seam left open for the lower 6″, with a black button at the top of the slit [b7].

Hood: an old-gold grosgrain hood of the Leeds simple shape [s7], lined olive green taffeta. There is a 1″ ribbon of the degree colour laid on the turnout, set 1″ in:

BA: pale yellow.
BArch: light crimson.
[BEd: orange.]
BEng: no ribbon.
BMus: cream damask.
BPharm: no ribbon.

BSc: no ribbon.

Hat: a black cloth square cap.

POSTGRADUATE CERTIFICATES AND DIPLOMAS

none specified

FIRST-DEGREE MASTERS
(MBiochem, MBiol, MChem, MMath, MPhys; and MArch, MEng, and MPharm since 2001)

Gown: as for other masters.

Hood: an old-gold grosgrain hood of the Leeds simple shape [s7], lined light blue taffeta. There is a 1″ ribbon of olive green laid on the turnout, set 1″ in.

Hat: a black cloth square cap.

MASTERS including MASTERS OF PHILOSOPHY (but not ChM)

Gown: a black stuff gown of Bath masters' pattern [m16]. This is the basic pattern, but there is an inverted-T armhole, with a black button at the top of the vertical slit, and the front corner of the sleeve is cut at 45 degrees [m16].

Hood: an old-gold grosgrain hood of the Leeds simple shape [s7], lined light blue taffeta. There is a 1″ ribbon of degree colour laid on the turnout, set 1″ in.

MA: pale yellow.

MArch: light crimson (*until 2001; since then it is a first-degree master*).

MBA: dark blue.

MEd: orange.

MEng: purple (*until 2001; since then it is a first-degree master*).

MPharm: no ribbon (*until 2001; since then it is a first-degree master*).

MPhil: red.

MRes: gold.

MSc: no ribbon.

Hat: a black cloth square cap.

MASTERS OF SURGERY (ChM)

Undress gown: as for PhD.

Dress robe: as for PhD, with the facings and upper edge of the cuffs bound 1″ pale blue.

Hood: an old-gold grosgrain hood of the Leeds simple shape [s7], lined crimson taffeta. There is a 1″ ribbon of pale blue laid on the turnout, set 1″ in.

Hats: in undress, a black cloth square cap; in full dress, a black cloth bonnet with silver cords and tassels.

DOCTORS OF PHILOSOPHY and
TAUGHT AND PROFESSIONAL DOCTORS

Undress gown: as for masters, with Cambridge lace round the armhole.

Dress robe: a crimson cloth robe of the Oxford pattern [d2], with facings and 9″ cuffs of old-gold. The outer edge of the facing and the upper edge of the cuff are edged 1″ ribbon of the degree colour:
DBA: dark blue (from 2008, olive green).
EdD: olive green.
EngD: olive green.
DHealth: olive green.
MD: pink (was dark crimson).
PhD: no ribbon.

Hood: an old-gold grosgrain hood of the Leeds simple shape [s7], lined crimson taffeta. There is a 1″ ribbon of the degree colour (as above) laid on the turnout, set 1″ in.

Hats: in undress, a black cloth square cap; in full dress, a black cloth bonnet with silver cords and tassels.

HIGHER DOCTORS

Undress gown: as for PhD.

Dress robe: a scarlet cloth robe of the Oxford pattern [d2], with facings and 9″ cuffs of old-gold. The outer edge of he facing and the upper edge of the cuff are edged 1″ ribbon of the degree colour:
DLitt: yellow.
LL.D: white.
DSc: no ribbon.
DMus: a cream silk damask robe, with facings and cuffs of old-gold.

Hood: an old-gold grosgrain hood of the Leeds simple shape [s7], lined scarlet taffeta. There is a 1″ ribbon of the degree colour (as above) laid on the turnout, set 1″ in.
DMus: old-gold lined cream silk damask.

Hats: in undress, a black cloth square cap; in full dress, a black cloth bonnet with gold cords and tassels.

NOTES

1. Holders of the honorary degrees of DArts and DEng wear the DLitt and DSc robes respectively.

BATH SPA UNIVERSITY
2006

The Bath Academy of Art was founded in 1898. The present institution was formed in 1975 as Bath College of Higher Education by the merger of the Bath College of Education and Newton Park College of Education. In 1992, the college was granted taught degree-awarding powers and in 1999 adopted the name Bath Spa University College. In 2005, it was granted university status, and became Bath Spa University. Research degree-awarding powers were granted in 2008 (until then, the MPhil and PhD were awarded by the University of the West of England).

The hoods are azure blue and silver, these being the principal colours of the university's coat of arms.

UNDERGRADUATES
none specified

UNDERGRADUATE CERTIFICATES AND DIPLOMAS
none specified

FOUNDATION DEGREES
Gown: as for bachelors.
Hood: an azure blue hood of the Edinburgh shape [s4], lined silver-grey satin, bordered inside the cowl 1″ azure blue.
Hat: a dark blue cloth square cap.

BACHELORS
Gown: a dark blue stuff gown of the basic pattern [b1].
Hood: an azure blue hood of the Edinburgh shape [s4], lined silver-grey satin, bordered inside the cowl 2″ azure blue.
Hat: a dark blue cloth square cap.

POSTGRADUATE CERTIFICATES AND DIPLOMAS
Gown: as for bachelors.
Hood: as for bachelors, but the cowl edge is further bound ½″ white.
Hat: a dark blue cloth square cap.

MASTERS
Gown: a dark blue stuff gown of the basic pattern [m10].
Hood: an azure blue hood of the Cambridge shape [f1], lined and the cape bound 1″ silver-grey satin.
Hat: a dark blue cloth square cap.

MASTERS OF PHILOSOPHY

Gown: a dark blue stuff gown of basic pattern [m10], with silver-grey facings.

Hood: an azure blue hood of the Cambridge full shape [f1], lined and the cape bound 1″ silver grey, with a 1" band of azure blue inside the cowl set 1″ in.

Hat: a dark blue cloth square cap.

DOCTORS OF PHILOSOPHY

Undress gown: *none specified*

Dress robe: an azure blue robe of Cambridge pattern [d1], the facings covered and the sleeves lined with silver grey. The sleeves are held with blue cords and buttons.

Hood: as for MPhil.

Hat: a blue cloth bonnet with silver cords and tassels.

UNIVERSITY OF BEDFORDSHIRE
2006

The University of Luton (1995; *q.v.*) merged with the Bedford campus of de Montfort University (*q.v.*) in 2006 to form the University of Bedfordshire. New robes were designed.

UNDERGRADUATES
none specified

UNDERGRADUATE CERTIFICATES AND DIPLOMAS
Gown: a black stuff gown of the basic pattern [b1].
Scarf: A waist length red scarf, bound 1″ royal blue on the inside edge, and 1″ white on the outside edge.

FOUNDATION DEGREES
Gown: a black stuff gown of the basic pattern [b1].
Hood: a red hood of the CNAA shape [a1], lined white, the cowl bordered inside ½″ royal blue.
Hat: a black cloth square cap.

BACHELORS
Gown: a black stuff gown of the basic pattern [b1].
Hood: a red hood of the CNAA shape [a1], lined white, the cape bound 1″ inside and out royal blue.
Hat: a black cloth square cap.

POSTGRADUATE CERTIFICATES AND DIPLOMAS
Gown: a black stuff gown of basic masters' pattern. [m10]
Scarf: a waist length red scarf, bound 1″ royal blue on the inside edge, and 1″ white on the outside edge.
Hat: a black cloth square cap.

FIRST-DEGREE MASTERS
not awarded

MASTERS including MASTERS OF PHILOSOPHY
Gown: a black stuff gown of the basic pattern [m10].
Hood:
MPhil: a red hood of the Cambridge shape [f1], lined white, bordered inside the cowl for 1″, and the cape bound 1″ inside and out, royal blue.
All others: a red hood of the Cambridge shape [f1], lined white, the cowl bordered inside 2″royal blue.

Hat: a black cloth square cap.

DOCTORS OF PHILOSOPHY and TAUGHT AND PROFESSIONAL DOCTORS

Undress gown: *none specified*

Dress robe: a red robe of the Oxford pattern [d2], with facings and 10″ cuffs of white. There is 1″ royal blue along the outer edge of the facings, and at the base of the cuff.

Hood:

PhD: as for MPhil.

Professional doctorates: a red hood of the Cambridge shape [f1], lined white, the cowl bordered 1″ royal blue set 1″ in, and the cape bound 1″ inside and out royal blue.

Hat: in full dress, a black cloth bonnet with blue cords and tassels.

HIGHER DOCTORS

Undress gown: *none specified*

Dress robe: a red robe of the Oxford pattern [d2], with facings and 10″ cuffs of white. There is 2″ royal blue along the outer edge of the facings, and at the base of the cuff.

Hood: a red hood of the Cambridge shape [f1], lined white, and the cowl bordered inside 2″ and the cape bound 1″ with royal blue.

Hat: in full dress, a black velvet bonnet with blue cords and tassels.

QUEEN'S UNIVERSITY, BELFAST
1909

This was one of the three Queen's Colleges established in 1884. In 1909, it became a university in its own right, while the other two (Cork and Galway), together with the Catholic University in Dublin, formed the National University of Ireland. For further history, see the Royal University of Ireland entry.

The original robes of QUB were simply transferred from the Royal University of Ireland (*q.v.*), and bound with light blue watered silk as a mark of difference. In the case of bachelors and masters, the shape was altered to the simple shape, to conform with the BA.

Faculty colours

Arts and Letters: dark blue.
Agriculture: dark primrose.
Dental Surgery: dove grey.
Divinity: white (BD, BTh, MTh); black (DD).
Education: mauve.
Engineering: eau-de-nil green.
Health Science: dark grey.
Laws: pink.
Library Studies: mid-blue.
Medicine, Surgery, and Obstetrics: scarlet.
Medical Science: purple.
Science: light green.
Science (Applied Science and Technology): dark green.
Science (Economics, Accounting, Management, IT): light rose pink.
Science (Food): dark primrose.
Science (Social): dark rose pink.

UNDERGRADUATES
none specified

UNDERGRADUATE CERTIFICATES AND DIPLOMAS
Gown: as for bachelors.
Hood:
DipNursSt: a black hood of the Irish simple shape [s3], lined black, and bound on all edges 1″ light blue.
Hat: a black cloth square cap.

FOUNDATION DEGREES
Gown: as for bachelors.

Hood: a black hood of the Irish simple shape [s3], lined gold, bound on all edges 1″ light blue.
Hat: a black cloth square cap.

BACHELORS

Gown: a black stuff gown with bell sleeves, which are gathered as the London BA [b4] (*see Note 1*).
Hood: a black hood of the Irish simple shape [s3], lined faculty colour, bound on all edges 1″ light blue. Exceptions:
BA: lined white fur, bound light blue.
BA(GenSt): dark blue, lined white fur, bound light blue.
BLegSc: lined russet brown.
BMus: a dark blue hood, lined white, bound light blue.
BSW: dark rose.
BTh: lined white (same hood as BD).
Hat: a black cloth square cap.

POSTGRADUATE CERTIFICATES AND DIPLOMAS

none specified

FIRST-DEGREE MASTERS

Gown: as for bachelors.
Hood: a hood of the Irish simple shape [s3]:
MEng: black, lined eau-de-nil, the cowl bordered inside 2″ red silk, and bound light blue.
MSci: red, lined light green, the cowl bordered inside 2″ red silk, and bound light blue.
Hat: a black cloth square cap.

MASTERS including MASTERS OF PHILOSOPHY

Gown: a black stuff gown of Dublin MA pattern [m3].
Hood: a red silk hood of the Irish simple shape [s3], lined the faculty colour, bound on all edges 1″ light blue. Exceptions:
MA: black, lined dark blue, bound light blue.
MA(Ed): red, lined dark blue, bound light blue.
MAO: lined purple, bound light blue (same as MMedSc).
MArch: white, lined dark green, bound light blue.
MBA: lined gold, bound light blue.
MDiv: lined white, bound light blue (same as MTh).
MSc(Nur): lined dark grey, bound light blue (same as MHealthSc)
MSc(Mid): as MSc(Nur), but the cowl also bordered 2″ purple.
MSW: lined dark rose, bound light blue (same as MSocSc).
Hat: a black cloth square cap.

ALL DOCTORS

Undress gown: as for masters.

Dress robe: a scarlet robe of the Oxford pattern [d2], with facings and sleeves as below. There is 1″ light blue along the outer edge of the facings.
DClinPsy: red.
DD: black (facings only).
DLitt: white.
LL.D: pink.
MD: scarlet.
DMedSc: purple.
DMus: dark blue.
PhD: violet.
DSc: light green.
DSc(Agr): dark primrose.
DSc(Econ): light rose.
DSc(Ed): mauve.
DSc(Eng): dark green.
DSocSc: dark rose.
DUniv: light blue, with no binding.

Hood: a scarlet hood of the Irish full shape [f2], lined the same colour as faces the robe, and bound on all edges 1″ light blue.

Hats: in undress, a black cloth square cap; in full dress, a black velvet bonnet with gold cords and tassels.

NOTES

1. The bachelors' gown appears to be in abeyance, and the basic gown [b1] is supplied.
2. Superseded hoods:
   MAO: black, lined purple, bound light blue.
   BComSc: black, lined old-gold, bound light blue (until 1949).
   MComSc: old-gold, lined white, bound light blue (until 1949).
   MScEcon: dark rose, lined white, bound light blue (1949 until the early 1970s).
3. Hoods transferred from the RUI are:
   BA; MA; MB; MD; DLitt; LL.D; MusD: BEng; MAO.

UNIVERSITY OF BIRMINGHAM
1900

The earliest beginnings of the university can be traced back to the Birmingham Medical School, founded in 1828. In 1843 the medical school changed its name to Queen's College. In 1875, Sir Josiah Mason, a Birmingham industrialist and philanthropist, founded Mason Science College. In 1882, the Departments of Chemistry, Botany, and Physiology were transferred from Queen's to Mason Science College, followed by the Departments of Physics and Comparative Anatomy. The transfer of the Medical School to Mason Science College gave considerable impetus to the growing importance of that college. It was incorporated as Mason University College in January 1898, and was granted a Royal Charter in 1900. The Charter also included provision for a Faculty of Commerce, as was appropriate for a university founded by industrialists and based in a city with enormous business wealth. The faculty, the first of its kind in Britain, was founded in 1901. Queen's College still remains as a theological college, part of the Queen's Foundation.

Faculty colours

The scheme, when first drawn up, relied on faculty colours, with a three-inch border in the bachelors' hoods, and full linings in the master's and doctors' hoods, doubtless based on the London scheme. However, as will be seen, the increasing number of degrees and the insistence on degree-specific hoods has meant the addition of bindings to create new hoods. Some of the bindings are of incongruous colours: *e.g.*, the MSci wears the BSc hood with a Music binding; the BEng&Com wears the BEng hood with a Divinity binding. The foundation degree hood is an anomaly, and does not fit the scheme, either in shape or material.

All the faculty silks are of watered silk. This may have been an attempt to find some distinguishing feature, similar to the choice of shot silks at Wales. They are listed here, but owing to the very complicated nature of the bindings, all hoods have been listed individually.

Arts and Letters: electric blue (this is very pale).
Commerce: terra-cotta.
Dentistry: garnet red.
Divinity: cobalt blue.
Education: primrose yellow.
Engineering: purple.
Laws: bronze green (this is effectively olive green).
Medicine: cardinal red (this is effectively dark scarlet).
Music: tangerine.
Nursing: rose red.
Philosophy (post-1997): bottle green (or 'forest' green).
Science: silver-grey.

UNDERGRADUATES

Gown: a black stuff gown of the Oxford scholar's pattern [u2], but with the whole forearm seam left open.

Hat: a black cloth square cap.

UNDERGRADUATE CERTIFICATES AND DIPLOMAS

none specified

FOUNDATION DEGREES

Gown: a black stuff gown of the basic pattern [b1].

Hood: a dark blue hood of the CNAA shape [a1], part-lined gold, and the cape edged outside for ½″ mid-blue.

Hat: a black cloth square cap.

BACHELORS

Gown: a black stuff gown of the Cambridge BA pattern [b2].

Hood: a black stuff hood of the London shape [f3], bordered inside the cowl edge as follows; where no separate binding colour is specified, the border is brought out to form a ¼″ binding.

BA: electric blue.

BCom: terra-cotta.

BD: cobalt blue (originally fully lined).

BDS: garnet red.

BEd: primrose yellow.

BEdStud: primrose yellow.

BEng: purple.

BEng,BCom: purple, bound ½″ terra-cotta [double degree].

BEng&Com: purple, bound ½″ cobalt blue.

BLitt: electric blue, bound ½″ white.

LL.B: bronze green.

MB,ChB: cardinal red.

BMedSci: cardinal red, bound ½″ grey.

BMus: tangerine.

BNurs: rose red.

BPhil: bottle green.

BPhil(Ed): primrose yellow, bound ½″ white.

BPhysio: rose red, bound ½″ white.

BSc: silver-grey.

BSc,BCom: silver-grey, bound ½″ terra-cotta; the neckband is grey lined and bound terra-cotta [double degree].

BSocSc: terra-cotta, bound ½″ grey; the neckband is terra-cotta, lined and bound grey.

BTh: electric blue, bound ½″ cobalt blue.

Hat: a black cloth square cap.

POSTGRADUATE CERTIFICATES AND DIPLOMAS

none specified

FIRST-DEGREE MASTERS

Gown: as for bachelors.

Hood: a black stuff hood of the London shape [f3], bordered inside as follows; where no separate binding colour is specified, the border is brought out to form a ¼″ binding:

MChem: grey, bound ½″ tangerine.
MEng: purple, bound ½″ white.
MEng&Man: white.
MMath: grey, bound ½″ tangerine.
MNatSci: grey, bound ½″ bronze green.
MPhys: grey, bound ½″ tangerine.
MSci: grey, bound ½″ tangerine.

Hat: a black cloth square cap.

MASTERS including MASTERS OF PHILOSOPHY

Gown: a black stuff gown of the Cambridge MA pattern [m2], with an inverted-T armhole.

Hood: a black stuff hood of the London shape [f3], fully lined as follows; where no separate binding colour is specified, the lining is brought out on all edges for ¼″; separate bindings are applied to cape and cowl:

MA: electric blue.
MAppPsy: grey, bound ½″ cobalt blue.
MBA: terra-cotta, bound 1″ white on the cowl only.
MCDH: grey (originally lined garnet, then garnet bound white).
ChM: cardinal red.
ClinPsyM: grey, bound ½″ white.
MCom: terra-cotta.
MDS: garnet red.
MDentSc: grey (originally garnet bordered silver-grey).
MEd: primrose yellow.
MHS: rose red, bound ½″ royal blue.
MIS: terra-cotta, bound ½″ cobalt blue.
MJur: bronze green, bound ½″ grey.
MLitt: electric blue, bound ½″ garnet red.
LL.M: bronze green.
MMedSci: cardinal red, bound ½″ grey.
MMus: tangerine.
MPhil: bottle green [since 1997; *see Note 1*].
MPH: cardinal red, bound ½″ cobalt blue.

MPM: terra-cotta, bound ½″ lime green.
MRes: bottle green, bound ½″ white.
MSc: silver-grey [in all Faculties and Schools].
[MSc(Eng): purple.]

Hat: a black cloth square cap.

TAUGHT AND PROFESSIONAL DOCTORS (ApEd&ChildPsyD, DBA, EdD, EdPsyD, EngD, HScD, HScD(Clin), SocScD, ThD)

Undress gown: as for masters.

Dress robe: a crimson cloth robe of the Cambridge pattern [d1], the facings covered and the sleeves lined bottle green, and with 1″ primrose along the outer edge of the facings.

Hood: a crimson cloth hood of the London shape [f3], lined primrose yellow.

Hats: in undress, a black cloth square cap; in full dress, a black velvet bonnet with gold cords and tassels.

DOCTORS OF PHILOSOPHY *(see Note 1)*

Undress gown: as for masters.

Dress robe: a crimson cloth robe of the Cambridge pattern [d1], the facings covered and the sleeves lined bottle green.

Hood: a crimson cloth hood of the London shape [f3], in crimson cloth, lined bottle green.

Hats: in undress, a black cloth square cap; in full dress, a black velvet bonnet with gold cords and tassels.

HIGHER DOCTORS

Undress gown: as for masters, but with a row of lace along the outer edge of each facing.

Dress robe: a scarlet cloth robe of the Cambridge pattern [d1], the facings covered and the sleeves lined as follows:
DD: cobalt blue.
DEng: purple.
LL.D: bronze green.
DLitt: electric blue.
MD: cardinal red.
DSc: silver-grey.
DSocSci: terra-cotta, edged silver-grey.
DUniv: bright royal blue.

Hood: a scarlet cloth hood of the London shape [f3], lined as the robe. The DSocSci hood is lined terra-cotta, and bound silver-grey.

Hats: in undress, a black cloth square cap; in full dress, a black velvet bonnet with gold cords and tassels.

MPhil in Plant Breeding and Crop Improvement
–Joint degree with the University of Reading.

Gown: a black stuff gown of Cambridge MA pattern [m2].

Hood: a dark blue silk hood of the Cambridge full shape [f1], lined and bound silver-grey watered silk.

Hat: a black cloth square cap.

NOTES

1. Before 1997, the robe and hood for PhD were lined with the silk of the faculty in which the degree was taken. The hoods for the MPhil were as follows:
   Arts: black, lined electric blue, bound white.
   Commerce and Social Studies: black, lined terra-cotta, bound crimson.
   Education: black, lined primrose, bound white.
   Engineering: black, lined purple, bound crimson.
   Medicine and Dentistry: black, lined cardinal, bound green.
   Science: black, lined silver-grey, bound crimson.
2. Women who graduated before 1985 may wear the Oxford ladies' cap.
3. Licentiates in Dental Surgery (LDS) wore a black gown of [b4] pattern, with dark red cord along the facings and round the yoke, the sleeves looped with a dark red cord and a black button.

BIRMINGHAM CITY UNIVERSITY
1993

Although Birmingham had a Polytechnic between 1843 and 1853, that from which BCU was formed was created in 1971 from five different colleges, with more colleges being added in the mid-1970s. It was run by Birmingham City Council. In 1992 it became the University of Central England in Birmingham. Two more colleges were absorbed in 1995: Birmingham and Solihull College of Nursing and Midwifery, and the West Midlands School of Radiography. In June 2007, the University was renamed Birmingham City University.

The scheme of robes used is simple, and grade-specific. Its diagnostic feature is the cream brocade linings of the hoods.

UNDERGRADUATES
none specified

UNDERGRADUATE CERTIFICATES and DIPLOMAS, and FOUNDATION DEGREES
Gown: as for bachelors.
Hood: a dark blue silk hood of the CNAA shape [a1], lined cream brocade [bordered ¼″ gold].
Hat: a dark blue cloth square cap.

BACHELORS
Gown: a dark blue stuff gown of the basic pattern [b1].
Hood: a dark blue silk hood of the Cambridge shape [f1], the cowl edge bordered inside the cowl with cream brocade, 8″ at the end of the cowl, tapering to 4″ at the neck, and bound ½″ gold silk.
Hat: a dark blue cloth square cap.

POSTGRADUATE CERTIFICATES AND DIPLOMAS
Gown: as for bachelors.
Hood: a dark blue silk hood of the Cambridge shape [f1], lined cream brocade, bound gold silk on all edges:
PGCerts: half an inch.
PGDips: one inch.
Hat: a dark blue cloth square cap.

MASTERS including MASTERS OF PHILOSOPHY
Gown: a dark blue stuff gown of the basic pattern [m10], with cream brocade facings.
Hood: a dark blue silk hood of Cambridge shape [f1], lined and bound as follows:
MA, MBA, MSc: lined cream brocade, and bound 1½″ gold silk on all edges.

MPhil: lined gold silk, and bound 1½″ cream brocade on all edges.

Hat: a dark blue cloth square cap.

DOCTORS OF PHILOSOPHY and TAUGHT AND PROFESSIONAL DOCTORS

Undress gown: *not specified.*

Dress robe: a scarlet robe of the Cambridge pattern [d1], the facings covered and sleeves lined cream brocade, and with 1″ gold silk along the outer edge of the facings.

Hood: a scarlet cloth hood of the Cambridge shape [f1], lined and bound 1″ cream brocade.

Hat: in full dress, a black cloth bonnet with scarlet cords and tassels.

HIGHER DOCTORS and DOCTOR OF THE UNIVERSITY

Undress gown: *not specified.*

Dress robe: a gold cloth robe of the Cambridge pattern [d1], the facings covered and the sleeves lined cream brocade. The sleeves have a gold cord and button.

Hood: a gold cloth hood of the Cambridge shape [f1], lined and bound 1″ cream brocade.

Hat: in full dress, a black velvet bonnet with gold cords and tassels.

THE BIRMINGHAM CONSERVATOIRE

Founded in 1859, and known as the Birmingham School of Music, it became part of the Polytechnic in 1971. It awarded its own diplomas (ABSM, LBSM, FBSM), which had their own robes (for which see Groves and Kersey, *Academical Dress of Music Colleges*). In 1993, it adopted the title Birmingham Conservatoire, and became a faculty of UCE. As such, although it still awards its own diplomas, they have been renamed and use BCU robes:

ADipBC, LDipBC: as for undergraduate certificates and diplomas.

Fellow by examination:

Gown: a dark blue cloth gown of the Cambridge doctors' pattern [d1], the sleeve lined gold, and with 2' gold on the outer edge of the facings.

Hood: a dark blue hood of the Cambridge shape [f1], lined and bound 1″ gold.

BISHOP GROSSETESTE UNIVERSITY COLLEGE, LINCOLN
1862/2008

Established in 1862 as Lincoln Training College, the college changed its name to Bishop Grosseteste College, to commemorate Robert Grosseteste, the scholarly thirteenth-century Bishop of Lincoln. The College gained degree-awarding powers in 2006; before that, all degree were validated by the University of Leicester, which is why the Leicester shape hood is used, and the three-colour cord which was used by Leicester to mark out the validated degrees (see the Leicester entry) has also been retained.

UNDERGRADUATES
none specified

UNDERGRADUATE CERTIFICATES AND DIPLOMAS
Gown: a black stuff gown of the basic bachelors' pattern [b1].
Hood: a blue hood of the Leicester simple shape [s6], piped on the edge of the turn-out and neckband with a twisted cord of blue, green, and gold.
Hat: a black cloth square cap.

FOUNDATION DEGREES
Gown: a black stuff gown of the basic bachelors' pattern [b1].
Hood: a blue hood of the Leicester simple shape [s6], the turn-out part covered with red, and piped on the edge of the turn-out and neckband with a twisted cord of blue, green, and gold.
Hat: a black cloth square cap.

BACHELORS
Gown: a black stuff gown of the basic bachelors' pattern [b1].
Hood: a blue hood of the Leicester simple shape [s6], lined red, and piped on the edge of the turn-out and neckband with a twisted cord of blue, green, and gold.
Hat: a black cloth square cap.

POSTGRADUATE CERTIFICATES AND DIPLOMAS
Gown: a black stuff gown of the basic masters' pattern [m10].
Hood:
Graduate Teacher Programme: same as undergraduate certificates.
PGCE, ProfGradCerEd: a blue hood of the Cambridge shape [f1], lined red, and piped on the cowl with a twisted cord of blue, green, and gold.
Hat: a black cloth square cap.

MASTERS including MASTERS OF PHILOSOPHY

Gown: a black stuff gown of the basic pattern [m10].

Hood: a blue hood of the Cambridge shape [f1], lined red, the cowl bordered inside with ½″ buttercup yellow, set 1″ in, and piped on the cowl with a twisted cord of blue, green, and gold.

Hat: a black cloth square cap.

DOCTOR OF THE UNIVERSITY (DUniv)

Undress gown: *none specified*

Dress robe: a red robe of the Cambridge pattern [d1], the facings and sleeve linings of blue. There is 1″ buttercup yellow along the outer edge of the facings, and a yellow cord and button on each sleeve.

Hood: a red hood of the Cambridge shape [f1], lined blue, and the cowl bordered inside with 3″ green shot blue silk (same as Wales Arts), and piped on the cowl with a twisted cord of blue, green, and gold; the cape is bound with 1″ yellow.

Hat: in full dress, a black velvet bonnet with cords and tassels of blue, green, and gold.

UNIVERSITY OF BOLTON
2004

Bolton Institute of Higher Education was formed in 1982 by the merger of the Bolton Institute of Technology and Bolton College of Education (Technical). Bolton Institute was granted the right to award taught degrees in 1990, with the powers to award research degrees in 1994. In April 2004, the Institute was granted university status.

The robes are based round three colours, using the grade-hood system.

UNDERGRADUATES
none specified

UNDERGRADUATE CERTIFICATES AND DIPLOMAS
Gown: as for bachelors.
Hood: a cardinal red silk hood of the Leeds simple shape [s7], lined yellow silk.
Hat: a black cloth square cap.

BACHELORS
Gown: a black stuff gown of the basic pattern [b1].
Hood: a cardinal red silk hood of the Leeds simple shape [s7], lined yellow silk, with one 1″ band of dark green on the turn-out, set 1″ in.
Hat: a black cloth square cap.

POSTGRADUATE CERTIFICATES AND DIPLOMAS
Gown: as for bachelors.
Hood: a cardinal red silk hood of the Leeds simple shape [s7], lined yellow silk, with two 1″ bands of dark green on the turn-out, set 1″ apart.
Hat: a black cloth square cap.

MASTERS including MASTERS OF PHILOSOPHY
Gown: a black stuff gown of the basic pattern [m10].
Hood: a cardinal red silk hood of the Cambridge shape [f1], lined yellow silk, and the cowl bordered inside 1″ dark green.
For honorary masters and MUniv, the cape is also bound green.
Hat: a black cloth square cap.

DOCTORS OF PHILOSOPHY and TAUGHT AND PROFESSIONAL DOCTORS
Undress gown: as for masters.
Dress robe: a cardinal red robe of the basic masters' pattern [m10]. The facings are covered in yellow, with 1″ green on the outer edges.

Hood: a cardinal red hood of the Cambridge shape [f1], lined and the cape bound yellow silk, and bordered inside the cowl with 1″ dark green.

Hats: in undress, a black cloth square cap; in full dress, a black cloth bonnet with green cords and tassels.

HIGHER DOCTORS

Undress gown: *none specified*

Dress robe: a cardinal red cloth robe of the Cambridge pattern [d1], with facings and sleeve linings of yellow silk. The sleeves are looped with a dark green cord and button, and the facings have 1″ dark green on the outer edge.

Hood: a cardinal red cloth hood of the Cambridge full shape [f1], lined yellow, and bound on all edges 1″ green silk.

For honorary doctors and the DUniv, the robes are the same as for honorary masters.

Hat: in full dress, a black velvet bonnet with green cords and tassels.

UNIVERSITY OF BOURNEMOUTH
1993

The University of Bournemouth was founded in 1913 as Bournemouth Municipal College, becoming Bournemouth College of Technology during the 1970s. In 1976 it changed its name to Dorset Institute of Higher Education, and in 1990 it became Bournemouth Polytechnic. Full university status was granted in 1992. It has two campuses: Talbot Campus in Poole, and Lansdowne Campus, just outside Bournemouth town centre.

The robes are a simple grade-specific scheme.

UNDERGRADUATES
none specified

UNDERGRADUATE CERTIFICATES AND DIPLOMAS
Gown: as for bachelors.
Hood: a mid-blue hood of the CNAA shape [a1], lined black, tipped white.
Hat: a black cloth square cap.

FOUNDATION DEGREES
none specified

BACHELORS
Gown: a black stuff gown of the basic pattern [b1].
Hood: a mid-blue hood of the Cambridge shape [f1], lined 8″ gold, the cowl edge bound 1″ white.
Hat: a black cloth square cap.

POSTGRADUATE CERTIFICATES AND DIPLOMAS
Gown: as for bachelors.
Hood: as for masters.
Hat: a black cloth square cap.

FIRST-DEGREE MASTERS
none specified

MASTERS including MASTERS OF PHILOSOPHY
Gown: a black stuff gown of the basic pattern [m10].
Hood: a mid-blue hood of the Cambridge shape [f1], lined gold, the cowl edge bound 2″ white.
Hat: a black cloth square cap.

DOCTORS OF PHILOSOPHY and TAUGHT AND PROFESSIONAL DOCTORS

Undress gown: *none specified*

Dress robe: a mid-blue robe of the Cambridge pattern [d1], the facings covered and the sleeves lined gold.

Hood: a mid-blue hood of the Cambridge shape [f1], lined gold, bound on all edges 1″ white.

Hat: in full dress, a black velvet bonnet with gold cords and tassels.

HIGHER DOCTORS

Undress gown: *none specified*

Dress robe: as for PhD, but the sleeves bound white.

Hood: as for PhD, but bound 2″ white.

Hat: in full dress, a black velvet bonnet with gold cords and tassels.

BPP COLLEGE OF PROFESSIONAL STUDIES
2008

BPP College, which is owned by BPP Holdings plc, is composed of the Law School and the Business School and is situated in city-centre locations in Leeds, London, and Manchester. Each School has close links with the relevant business professions. In 2008 it gained the right to award taught degrees in both Schools.

The hoods are based on the Leeds model, using three shades of blue, and also the Leeds simple shape.

UNDERGRADUATES
none specified

GRADUATE DIPLOMAS
Gown: a black stuff gown of the basic pattern [b1].
Hood: a dark blue hood of the Leeds simple shape [s7], lined mid-blue, with 1″ light blue on the turn-out, set 1″ in.
Hat: a black cloth square cap.

BACHELORS
Gown: a black stuff gown of the basic pattern [b1].
Hood: a light blue hood of the Leeds simple shape [s7], lined mid-blue, with 1″ dark red on the turn-out, set 1″ in.
Hat: a black cloth square cap.

POSTGRADUATE DIPLOMAS
Gown: a black stuff gown of the basic pattern [b1].
Hood: a light blue hood of the Leeds simple shape [s7], lined dark blue, with 1″ mid-blue on the turn-out, set 1″ in.
Hat: a black cloth square cap.

MASTERS
Gown: a black stuff gown of the basic pattern [m10].
Hood: a dark blue hood of the Leeds simple shape [s7], lined dark red, bound on all edges light blue.
Hat: a black cloth square cap.

UNIVERSITY OF BRADFORD
1963

The University of Bradford has its origins in the Bradford School of Weaving, Design, and Building, dating from 1860, which in 1882 became the Bradford Technical College. In 1957, the Bradford Institute of Technology was formed to take on the provision of higher education courses. It became a College of Advanced Technology, and in 1966, like the other CATs, it became a university. It has three campuses: the main campus located on Richmond Road, the School of Health on Trinity Road, and the School of Management at Emm Lane.

The diagnostic feature of the hoods and doctors' robe is the use of saffron silk. It is unclear why the higher doctors have faculty borders, but the lower degrees do not.

UNDERGRADUATES
none specified

UNDERGRADUATE CERTIFICATES AND DIPLOMAS
Gown: a black gown of the basic pattern [b1], with a black cord and button on the yoke.

Hood: a black hood of the Edinburgh shape [s4], the cowl bordered inside ½″ saffron.

Hat: a black cloth square cap.

FOUNDATION DEGREES
Gown: as for bachelors.

Hood: a black hood of the CNAA shape [a1], bordered inside the cowl and outside the cape ½″ saffron.

Hat: a black cloth square cap.

BACHELORS and FIRST-DEGREE MASTERS
Gown: a black stuff gown of the Cambridge MA pattern [m2], with a black cord and button on the yoke.

Hood: a black stuff hood of the Cambridge shape [f1], bordered inside the cowl 4″ saffron silk.

Hat: a black cloth square cap.

POSTGRADUATE CERTIFICATES AND DIPLOMAS
Gown: as for bachelors.

Hood: as for undergraduate certificates.

Hat: a black cloth square cap.

MASTERS including MASTERS OF PHILOSOPHY

Gown: a black stuff gown of the Cambridge MA pattern [m2], with a black cord and button on the yoke.

Hood: a black stuff hood of the Cambridge shape [f1], lined saffron silk.

Hat: a black cloth square cap.

ALL DOCTORS

Undress gown: as for masters.

Dress robe: a scarlet cloth robe of the Cambridge pattern [d1], with facings and sleeve linings of saffron silk.

Hood: a scarlet hood of the Cambridge shape [f1], lined as follows:

PhD: lined saffron.
EdD: lined saffron, the cowl bordered 3″ maroon.
DEng: lined saffron, the cowl bordered 3″ mid-green.
LL.D: lined saffron, the cowl bordered 3″ dark navy blue.
DLitt: lined saffron, the cowl bordered 3″ white.
DSc: lined saffron, the cowl bordered 3″ mid-blue.
DTech: lined saffron, the cowl bordered 3″ violet.
DUniv: lined saffron, the cowl bordered 3″ silver-grey.

Hats: in undress, a black cloth square cap; in full dress, a black velvet bonnet.

NOTES

1. The University now 'does not permit' the wearing of the black cloth square cap during graduation ceremonies, but it still forms part of the robes.

UNIVERSITY OF BRIGHTON
1993

The University was formed from Brighton Polytechnic in 1992. The Polytechnic was established in 1968 by a merger of Brighton College of Technology and Brighton College of Art, and was further expanded by mergers in 1976 with Brighton College of Education and in 1979 with the East Sussex College of Higher Education at Eastbourne. It was awarded full university status in 1992.

All hoods and robes are trimmed with a special damask, woven with the double elm-leaf symbol of the university.

UNDERGRADUATES
none specified

UNDERGRADUATE CERTIFICATES AND DIPLOMAS
Gown: as for bachelors.
Hood: a black hood of the CNAA shape [a1], fully lined light blue leaf damask.
Hat: a black cloth square cap.

FOUNDATION DEGREES
Gown: as for bachelors.
Hood: a black hood of the CNAA shape [a1], fully lined light blue leaf damask, and the cowl edge bordered 1″ reflex blue damask.
Hat: a black cloth square cap.

BACHELORS
Gown: a black stuff gown of the basic pattern [b1].
Hood: a black silk hood of the London shape [f3], fully lined reflex blue leaf damask.
Hat: a black cloth square cap.

POSTGRADUATE CERTIFICATES AND DIPLOMAS
Gown: as for bachelors.
Hood: a black silk hood of the London shape [f3], fully lined reflex blue leaf damask, the cowl bordered inside with 1″ light blue leaf damask.
Hat: a black cloth square cap.

FIRST-DEGREE MASTERS
Gown: as for bachelors.
Hood: a black silk hood of the London shape [f3], fully lined reflex blue leaf damask, bordered inside the cowl 1″ pale purple damask.
Hat: a black cloth square cap.

MASTERS

Gown: a black stuff gown of the basic pattern [m10].
Hood: a black silk hood of the London shape [f3], fully lined pale purple leaf damask.
Hat: a black cloth square cap.

MASTERS OF PHILOSOPHY

Gown: a black stuff gown of the basic pattern, with 1″ purple ribbon on outer edge of the facings.
Hood: a black silk hood of the London shape [f3], fully lined pale purple leaf damask, bordered inside the cowl 1″ reflex blue damask.
Hat: a black cloth square cap.

DOCTORS OF PHILOSOPHY and TAUGHT AND PROFESSIONAL DOCTORS

Undress gown: *none specified*
Dress robe: a claret cloth robe of the Oxford pattern [d2], with facings and 5″ cuffs of reflex blue leaf damask.
Hood: a claret cloth hood of the London shape [f3], fully lined reflex blue damask.
Hat: in full dress, a black cloth bonnet with reflex blue cords and tassels.

HIGHER DOCTORS

Undress gown: *none specified*
Dress robe: a scarlet cloth robe of the Oxford pattern [d2], with facings and 5″ cuffs of reflex blue leaf damask.
Hood: a scarlet cloth hood of the London shape [f3], fully lined reflex blue damask.
Hat: in full dress, a black velvet bonnet with reflex blue cords and tassels.

JOINT MASTER'S DEGREE WITH THE UNIVERSITY OF SUSSEX.

Gown: as for Sussex masters.
Hood: a black alpaca hood of the Sussex shape [s8], lined dove grey silk, bordered gold and red silk.
Hat: a black cloth square cap.

BRIGHTON-SUSSEX MEDICAL SCHOOL

— *see following entry*

BRIGHTON AND SUSSEX MEDICAL SCHOOL 2003

BSMS is one of four new medical schools created as part of a strategy of increasing the number of qualified doctors from the UK working in the NHS. The first intake of students began their five-year medical degree programmes in September 2003.

Degrees are awarded jointly by the Universities of Sussex and Brighton. The bachelor's hoods follow the revised Sussex model, except that there are two school colours instead of one. Robes for the higher degrees have yet to be designed.

BACHELOR OF MEDICINE AND BACHELOR OF SURGERY

Gown: a black stuff gown of the basic pattern [b1].

Hood: a black hood of Sussex shape [s8], the cowl bordered 6″ pale blue silk, and edged 1″ eau-de-nil green silk.

Hat: a black cloth square cap.

BACHELOR OF SCIENCE IN MEDICAL SCIENCE

Gown: a black stuff gown of the basic pattern [b1].

Hood: a black hood of Sussex shape [s8], the cowl bordered 6″ eau-de-nil green silk, and edged 1″ pale blue silk.

Hat: a black cloth square cap.

POSTGRADUATE DIPLOMAS

Gown: a black stuff gown of the basic pattern [b1].

Hood: a black hood of London shape [f3], lined eau-de-nil green, the cowl bordered 1″ pale blue inside.

Hat: black cloth square cap.

MASTERS

Gown: a black stuff gown of the basic pattern [m10].

Hood: a black hood of London shape [f3], lined pale blue, the cowl bordered 1″ eau-de-nil green inside.

Hat: a black cloth square cap.

DOCTORS OF PHILOSOPHY

Undress gown: *none specified*

Dress robe: a claret robe of Oxford pattern [d2], with facings and cuffs of dark blue. The facings are bordered 1″ eau-de-nil green and 1″ pale blue on the outer edge.

Hood: a claret hood of London shape [f3], lined dark blue, the cowl bordered 1″ pale blue and 1″ eau-de-nil green inside.

DOCTORS OF MEDICINE (MD)

Undress gown: *none specified*

Dress robe: a claret cloth robe of the Oxford pattern [d2], with facings and 6″ cuffs of dark blue. The facings are bordered on the outer edge with 1″ pale blue and 1″ eau-de-nil green.

Hood: of the London shape [f3], in claret, lined with dark blue, and the cowl bordered inside 1″ pale blue and 1″ eau-de-nil green.

HIGHER DOCTORS

Undress gown: *none specified*

Dress robe: a scarlet robe of Oxford pattern [d2], with yellow facings and cuffs. The facings are bordered 1″ eau-de-nil green and 1″ pale blue on the outer edge.

Hood: a scarlet hood of London shape [f3], lined yellow, the cowl bordered 1″ pale blue and 1″ eau-de-nil green inside.

UNIVERSITY OF BRISTOL
1909

The earliest antecedent of the University was the engineering department of the Merchant Venturers' Technical College (founded as a school as early as 1595), which became the Engineering faculty. University College, Bristol was founded in 1876, and prepared its students for London degrees. The University College was the first such institution in the country to admit women on the same basis as men. However, women were forbidden to take examinations in medicine until 1906. The University received its Royal Charter in 1909, assisted by the financial support of the Wills and Fry families, who had made their fortunes in tobacco plantations and chocolate, respectively. It is thus one of the original 'red brick' universities.

The robes are the first to introduce a 'grade-specific' scheme – *i.e.*, one hood for bachelors, one for masters, *etc.* (It is not clear why the LL.B, MB, and BMus have special hoods). In this case the hoods all have shells of the same colour ('university red'), and are differentiated by the colour of the linings. The combination of the university red hood with the scarlet doctoral gown is not a happy one.

UNDERGRADUATES

Gown: a black stuff gown of the Oxford scholar's pattern [u2].
Hat: a black cloth square cap.

UNDERGRADUATE CERTIFICATES AND DIPLOMAS

none specified

FOUNDATION DEGREES

t.b.a.

BACHELORS

Gown: a black stuff gown of the Cambridge BA pattern [b2]. For MB, it may be of silk.

Hood: a dull red silk or stuff hood, of the Cambridge shape [f1], lined as follows:

MB: fully lined with silk of a lighter shade of red, and bound on all edges ¾″ white silk.

LL.B: fully lined with silk of a lighter shade of red, and bound on all edges ¾″ violet silk.

BMus: fully lined and bound on all edges ¼″ lavender silk (*degree not awarded since the 1960s*).

All other bachelors: lined 'so far as the visible parts are concerned' with silk of a lighter shade of the same red. The intention appears to be that the hood is lined to a depth of ten inches or more, so it appears fully lined (*see Note*), but over the years this has shrunk to a border of three or four inches inside the cowl.

Hat: a black cloth square cap.

POSTGRADUATE CERTIFICATES AND DIPLOMAS

none specified

MASTERS, including MASTERS OF PHILOSOPHY and FIRST-DEGREE MASTERS

Gown: a black stuff or silk gown of the Bristol pattern [m9]. The sleeves have rounded corners, and a concavity in the base.

Hood: a dull red silk hood of the Cambridge shape [f1], lined but not bound white silk.

Hat: a black cloth square cap.

DOCTORS OF PHILOSOPHY and TAUGHT AND PROFESSIONAL DOCTORS (since 2004 this includes DOCTORS OF MEDICINE)

Undress gown: as for masters.

Dress robe: a scarlet cloth robe of the Oxford pattern [d2], the facings and sleeves covered in violet silk.

Hood: a dull red silk hood of the Cambridge shape [f1], lined but not bound violet silk.

Hats: in undress, a black cloth square cap; in full dress, a black velvet square cap.

HIGHER DOCTORS

Undress gown: as for masters, but with a triangle of embroidery towards the top of the sleeve.

Dress robe: a scarlet cloth robe of the Oxford pattern [d2], the facings only covered with salmon pink watered silk.

Hood: a dull red silk hood of the Cambridge shape [f1], lined but not bound salmon pink watered silk.

Hats: in undress, a black cloth square cap; in full dress, a black velvet bonnet with gold cords and tassels.

NOTES

1. *Athena, a Year-Book of the Learned World* for 1920 indicates that the bachelors' hood was fully lined red. The reduction to 'so far as the visible parts are concerned' may well be a later economy measure. It lists the MB, which at that time seems not to have had the white binding, but not the LL.B and BMus, the other exceptions. It also lists the PhD as sharing the higher doctors' hood.

BRUNEL UNIVERSITY
1966

Acton Technical College was founded in 1929. In 1957 the college was divided into Acton Technical College, which continued to cater for further education, and Brunel College of Technology at Uxbridge was dedicated to higher education. In 1961 it was awarded the status of College of Advanced Technology, and in 1962 it was officially named Brunel College of Advanced Technology; it was the tenth College of Advanced Technology in the country, and the last to be awarded this title. In 1966, in common with many other CATs, Brunel was transformed into a technological university.

The academic dress features 'Brunel blue' velvet, which is a dark azure blue. The PhD robes were changed in response to graduate pressure, as the dark brown robes were not popular. It is unfortunate that their robes no longer have the diagnostic Brunel velvet.

UNDERGRADUATES
none specified

NON-DEGREE AWARDS
until 1998:

Gown: a black stuff gown of the basic bachelors' pattern [b1].

Epitoge: a black silk epitoge bound ½″ Brunel blue velvet on all edges.

Hat: a black cloth square cap.

from 1999:

Gown: a black undergraduate style gown trimmed with Brunel blue velvet ribbon 1″ wide on front facings and yoke.

Hat: a black cloth square cap.

BACHELORS
Gown: a black stuff gown of the basic pattern [b1].

Hood: a black stuff hood of Edinburgh simple shape [s4], fully lined white, and the cowl bordered inside 1½″ Brunel blue velvet.

Hat: a black cloth square cap.

POSTGRADUATE CERTIFICATES AND DIPLOMAS
none specified

ALL MASTERS including MASTERS of PHILOSOPHY
Gown: a black stuff gown of the basic pattern, [m10].

Hood: a Brunel blue hood of the Cambridge shape[f1], lined silver, and the cowl bordered inside 2½″ Brunel blue velvet.

Hat: a black cloth square cap.

MASTERS OF THE UNIVERSITY (MUniv)

Robe: a black robe of the Oxford pattern [d2], with 5″ facings and 5″ cuffs in Brunel blue velvet.

Hood: a black hood in the Cambridge shape [f1], lined silver and the cowl bordered inside 3½″ Brunel blue velvet.

Hat: a black cloth square cap.

DOCTORS OF PHILOSOPHY and PROFESSIONAL DOCTORS

until June 1996

Undress gown: as for masters.

Dress robe: a mushroom (dark brown) cloth robe of the Oxford pattern [d2], with 4″ facings and 4″ cuffs of Brunel blue velvet.

Hood: a mushroom cloth hood in the Cambridge shape [f1], lined and the cape bound scarlet silk, the cowl bordered inside 3½″ with Brunel blue velvet.

Hats: in undress, a black cloth square cap; in full dress, a black cloth bonnet with scarlet cords and tassels.

from July 1996

Undress gown: as for masters.

Dress robe: a mid-blue (not Brunel blue) panama robe of the Cambridge pattern [d1]. The facings are covered with gold silk, edged 1″ scarlet ribbon. The sleeves are lined mid-blue panama. There is a scarlet cord and button on each sleeve and on the yoke.

Hood: a mid-blue panama hood of the Cambridge shape [f1], lined and bound 1″ on the cape with gold silk. The cowl is bordered inside with 1″ scarlet ribbon.

Hats: in undress, a black cloth square cap; in full dress, a black cloth bonnet with scarlet cords and tassels.

HIGHER DOCTORS

Undress gown: as for masters.

Dress robe: a scarlet robe of the Oxford pattern [d2], with 6″ facings and 7″ cuffs in Brunel blue velvet.

Hood: a scarlet hood of the Cambridge shape [f1], lined and bound gold, and the cowl bordered inside with 4½″ Brunel blue velvet.

Hats: in undress, a black cloth square cap; in full dress, a black velvet bonnet with gold cords and tassels.

UNIVERSITY OF BUCKINGHAM
1983

Founded in 1973, as University College Buckingham, this is the UK's sole private university. Some of Buckingham's founding academics migrated from the University of Oxford, disillusioned or wary of aspects of the late 1960s ethos. It was initially incorporated (as University College, Buckingham) in 1973, and received a Royal Charter in 1983. The University offers traditional degrees over a shorter time-span: students at Buckingham study for eight terms over two years, rather than nine terms over three; there is a fourth term during what is the Long Vacation elsewhere. The main campus is in Buckingham, with another in Milton Keynes.

Until it was chartered in 1983, its courses led to licences – originally designated LArts, LSc, *etc.*, and later LUCB. The robes for these are noted at the end; they formed the basis for the full scheme.

Faculty colours

Arts and Letters: pink.
Business Administration: light blue.
Economic Science (Business): lemon.
Laws: scarlet.
Science (Computing Science, IT, Psychology): maroon.

UNDERGRADUATES
none specified

UNDERGRADUATE CERTIFICATES AND DIPLOMAS
none specified

BACHELORS
Gown: a black stuff gown of the London BA pattern [b4].
Hood: a blue stuff hood of Edinburgh shape [s4], lined white silk, and with a 1″ ribbon of faculty colour set 1″ in on all edges.
Hat: a black cloth square cap.

POSTGRADUATE CERTIFICATES AND DIPLOMAS
Gown: a black gown of the London BA pattern [b4].
Hood:
PGCE: a blue stuff hood of Edinburgh shape [s4], lined white silk.
PGDip: a blue silk hood of the Cambridge shape [f1], lined white silk.
Hat: a black cloth square cap.

MASTERS

Gown: a black stuff gown of the Oxford MA pattern [m1].

Hood: a blue silk hood of the Cambridge shape [f1], lined as follows:

MPhil: lined blue silk, with a 2″ white ribbon set 1″ in on the cowl edge.

MBA: lined blue silk, with a 2″ light blue ribbon set 1″ in on the cowl edge.

All others: lined white silk, with a 2″ ribbon of the faculty colour set 1″ in on the cowl edge.

Hat: a black cloth square cap.

DOCTORS OF PHILOSOPHY

Undress gown: a black stuff gown of the Oxford MA pattern [m1].

Dress robe: a maroon cloth robe of the Oxford pattern, with facings and 4″ cuffs of blue silk. The facings continue round onto the yoke.

Hood: a maroon cloth hood of the Cambridge shape [f1], lined blue silk.

Hat: a black cloth bonnet with blue cords and tassels.

DOCTORS OF MEDICINE

Undress gown: a black stuff gown of the Oxford MA pattern [m1].

Dress robe: a dark blue cloth robe of the Oxford pattern, with facings and 4″ cuffs of dark red silk. The facings continue round onto the yoke.

Hood: a dark blue cloth hood of the Cambridge shape [f1], lined as follows:

MD (taught): lined dark red silk.

MD (research): as for the taught MD, but the cowl is bordered inside 1½″ cream, set ½″ in.

Hats: in undress, a black cloth square cap; in full dress, a black cloth bonnet with blue cords and tassels.

HIGHER DOCTORS

Undress gown: a black stuff gown of the Oxford MA pattern [m1].

Dress robe: a scarlet cloth robe of the Oxford pattern, with facings and 4″ cuffs of blue silk. The facings continue round onto the yoke.

Hood: a scarlet cloth hood of the Cambridge shape [f1], lined blue silk, with a 2″ ribbon of the faculty colour set 1″ in on the cowl edge.

DUniv: a gold ribbon.

Hats: in undress, a black cloth square cap; in full dress, a black velvet bonnet with old-gold cords and tassels.

Former Licences (LUCB, LArts, LSc, LL.L)

Gown: a black stuff gown of the London BA pattern [b4].

Hood: a blue stuff hood of the Edinburgh shape [s4], lined white silk.

Hat: a black cloth square cap.

BUCKINGHAMSHIRE NEW UNIVERSITY
2007

In 1893, a Science and Art School was established in High Wycombe, which immediately started to play an important role in providing evening classes to the residents of the town and the surrounding region. The High Wycombe College of Art and Technology merged in 1975 with the Newland Park College of Education in Chalfont St Giles to form Buckinghamshire College of Higher Education. In 1999 it became Buckinghamshire Chilterns University College, and in 2007 its application for university status was successful.

UNDERGRADUATES
none specified

UNDERGRADUATE CERTIFICATES AND DIPLOMAS
Gown: as for bachelors.
Hood: a burgundy hood of the CNAA shape [a1], lined grey.
Hat: a black cloth square cap.

BACHELORS
Gown: a black stuff gown of the basic pattern [b1].
Hood: a cardinal red hood of the Edinburgh shape [s4], lined silver-grey, the cowl edge bordered inside 2″ cardinal red velvet, and piped grey cord.
Hat: a black cloth square cap.

POSTGRADUATE CERTIFICATES AND DIPLOMAS
Gown: as for bachelors.
Hood: a silver-grey hood of the Cambridge shape [f1], lined black, the cowl edge bordered inside 2″ cardinal red velvet.
Hat: a black cloth square cap.

MASTERS including MASTERS OF PHILOSOPHY
Gown: a black stuff gown of the basic pattern [m10].
Hood: a cardinal red panama hood of the Cambridge shape [f1], lined silver-grey, the cowl edge bordered inside 3″ cardinal red velvet, and piped old-gold cord.
Hat: a black cloth square cap.

DOCTORS OF PHILOSOPHY and TAUGHT AND PROFESSIONAL DOCTORS
Undress gown: *none specified*
Dress robe: a cardinal red robe of the Oxford pattern [d2], with facings and 4″ cuffs of burgundy velvet.

Hood: a cardinal red hood of the Cambridge shape [f1], lined old-gold, the cowl edge bordered inside 3″ burgundy velvet, and piped black cord.

Hat: in full dress, a burgundy cloth bonnet with either black or gold brim and cords and tassels in the opposite colour.

HIGHER DOCTORS

Undress gown: *none specified*

Dress robe: a cardinal red cloth robe of the Oxford pattern [d2], with facings and 4″ cuffs of cardinal red velvet.

Hood: as PhD, but bordered cardinal red velvet

Hat: in full dress, a cardinal red cloth bonnet with black cloth brim and gold cords and tassels.

UNIVERSITY OF CAMBRIDGE
1209

The University of Cambridge has its origins in a migration of students from Oxford in 1209, following a dispute with the townsfolk there; other migrations went to Stamford and to Northampton but these nascent universities were fairly quickly closed down. Teaching had happened at Cambridge as early as 1201. It was recognized as a *universitas* in 1233, and as a *studium generale* in 1290. Like Oxford, it is a collegiate university, and comprises thirty-one colleges, of which the oldest surviving is Peterhouse (St Peter's College), founded 1284.

As at Oxford, the academic robes descend from those in use in the Middle Ages, but they followed a different path of evolution from Oxford's, and thus the two systems were very different by the end of the seventeenth century. Unlike Oxford, the dress of undergraduates is a matter of College, and not University, regulation. The system was revised in the 1930s, unfortunately ignoring several historic features. It is adapting to the addition of new degrees fairly well, although the new bachelors' degrees which rank below BA (BEd, BTh) and the professional doctorates (VetMD, EngD) have caused problems. The system is distinctive in that each degree had not only its own hood but also its own gown, so that the degree of the wearer is identifiable even if not wearing a hood, although this is breaking down, as some degrees now share the same gown.

The neckbands of all hoods are made of, and lined with, the same material as the shell. Several hoods rely on differences in material to tell them apart: notably the MLitt (black cloth lined scarlet silk) and PhD (black silk lined scarlet cloth), and the MSc (black cloth shell) and MSci (black silk shell). All graduate gowns and dress robes include 'strings' – two long pieces of ribbon sewn inside the facings. These are black for black gowns, and scarlet for the dress robes, but black for DD and dark cherry for MusD. In the case of holders of the status of BA or MA, the strings are omitted.

UNDERGRADUATES

Gown: The basic gown is a smaller version of the BA gown: a black stuff gown of the Cambridge pattern [u1].

The following use the basic gown, without modification:

Churchill, King's, Peterhouse, Queens', Robinson.

The following use the basic gown, modified as follows:

Christ's: with box pleats on the facings from shoulder to waist, and a pleated strip round the sleeve slit.

Corpus Christi: the facings covered with black velvet.

Emmanuel: with box pleats on the facings from shoulder to waist.

Fitzwilliam: with a black velvet strip either side of the sleeve slit.

Magdalene: the sleeve below the slit is gathered and held by a black cord and button.

St Catharine's: the facings are machined in vertical rows.

Selwyn: the facings are covered with mid-blue stuff.

Sidney Sussex: the sleeve-slit is surrounded by rows of small chevrons.

Trinity Hall: the sleeve below the slit is left open and held across by two buttons and a cord.

The following use the basic gown, but without the sleeve-slit, and further modified as noted:

Clare: three black velvet chevrons on each sleeve.

Downing: the sleeve is gathered into six broad pleats, and held by three black cords and buttons.

Jesus: the sleeve is gathered into six broad pleats, with a black velvet strip from the top of the pleats to the top of the forearm seam.

St John's: four horizontal black velvet bars on each sleeve.

Pembroke: the sleeve is gathered and held by a black cord and button (similar to [b4]).

Clare Hall, Darwin, Hughes Hall, Lucy Cavendish, St Edmund's, Wolfson: the sleeve gathered and held by a blue cord and button. (similar to [b4]).

Trinity: the gown is dark blue, and the facings are black; there is a 2″ edging of black inside each sleeve.

Other colleges:

Newnham, Murray-Edwards (formerly New Hall), Homerton: the basic gown, without the slit, but the lower four inches of the seam left open.

Girton: as Newnham, *etc.*, but the lower twelve inches are left open.

Gonville and Caius: a dark blue gown, with the whole forearm seam left open. The facings and yoke are covered in black velvet, and there is a black velvet strip either side of the open seam.

Hat: a black cloth square cap.

UNDERGRADUATE CERTIFICATES AND DIPLOMAS

none specified

FOUNDATION DEGREES

not awarded

BACHELORS

Gown:

BA: a black stuff gown of the Cambridge BA pattern [b2].

BTh: as BA, but with a black cord and button on the yoke.

BD: as MA, but in black silk, and with a black cord and button on the yoke.

The following degrees use a black stuff gown of the Cambridge MB pattern [b3], with cords and buttons added to the sleeves:

MB: one black twisted cord, with a black button at the top.

VetMB: as MB, but with a second button at the base of the cord.

LL.B: two black twisted cords, with a black button at the top of each.

BChir: three black twisted cords, with a black button at the top of each.

BEd: four black twisted cords, with a black button at the top of each.

MusB: as MB, but with two further buttons at the base of the turned-back triangle.

Hood: a hood of the Cambridge full shape [f1]:

BA: black stuff, half-lined and the cape bound 1″ white fur.

BChir: 'mid-cherry' (magenta) silk, half-lined white fur, but the cape not bound.

BD: black silk, lined black silk.

BEd: black stuff, lined royal blue silk, the cowl bordered inside 4″ and the cape bound 1″ white fur.

LL.B: 'light cherry' (pink) silk, half-lined and the cape bound 1″ white fur.

MB: 'mid-cherry' (magenta) silk, half-lined and the cape bound 1″ white fur.

MusB: 'dark cherry' (maroon) satin, half-lined and the cape bound 1″ white fur.

BTh: black stuff lined black silk, the cape bound 1″ white fur.

VetMB: as MB, but the cape is bound 2″ fur.

Hat: a black cloth square cap.

POSTGRADUATE CERTIFICATES AND DIPLOMAS

none specified

MASTERS including FIRST-DEGREE MASTERS (MEng, MSci)

Gown: all wear a black stuff gown of the Cambridge MA pattern [m2]. Black cords and buttons are placed above the arm slit as follows:

MA: none.

MASt: same as MEng.

MBA: four buttons arranged in a square, joined by twisted cords.

MChir: three single 5″ cords placed horizontally, ½″ apart.

MEd: five buttons placed in a quincunx, and joined with twisted cords to form a saltire.

MEng: one button, in the centre of a 5″ circle of black twisted cord.

MFin: four buttons, arranged in a lozenge, joined by twisted cords.

MLitt: three buttons placed vertically, 2½″ apart, joined by twisted cords.

LL.M: two single 5″ cords, placed horizontally, ½″ apart.

MMath: same as MEng.

MMus: three buttons placed to form a triangle, point upwards, joined by twisted cords.

MPhil: two buttons placed vertically, 2½″ apart, joined by a twisted cord.

MRes: two buttons placed vertically, joined by two black cords.

MSc: three buttons placed horizontally, 2½″ apart, joined by twisted cords.

MSci: same as MEng.

MSt: five buttons placed to form a cross, joined by twisted cords.

Hood: a black hood of the of the Cambridge full shape [f1] (black cloth for MASt, MBA, MEng, MFin, MLitt, MMath, MPhil, MRes, and MSc, black silk otherwise), fully lined, but not bound, as follows:

MA: white silk.

MASt: gold silk.

MBA: grass green silk.

MChir: mid-cherry silk.
MEd: light blue silk.
MEng: bronze silk.
MFin: light green silk.
MLitt: scarlet silk.
LL.M: light cherry silk.
MMath: slate blue silk.
MMus: dark cherry satin.
MPhil: royal blue silk.
MRes: dark plum red (Sarum red) silk.
MSc: pink shot light blue silk.
MSci: pink shot light blue silk.
MSt: yellow silk.

Hat: a black cloth square cap.

DOCTORS OF PHILOSOPHY and PROFESSIONAL DOCTORS

Undress gown:

PhD, VetMD, EngD: the MA gown, with 4″ of doctors lace set horizontally 3″ above the armhole.

EdD: also has four buttons in a horizontal row over the lace, joined by black cord.

Dress robe:

PhD, VetMD, EngD: the MA gown in black silk, with scarlet cloth facings, *or* the undress gown with scarlet cloth facings.

EdD: the undress gown, with scarlet cloth facings.

Hood: a black silk hood of the Cambridge full shape [f1], lined as follows:

PhD: lined scarlet cloth.
EdD: lined light blue silk, the cowl bordered inside with 4″ scarlet cloth.
EngD: lined bronze silk, the cowl bordered inside with 4″ scarlet cloth.
VetMD: lined scarlet cloth, the cowl bordered inside 4″ mid-cherry silk.

Hats: in undress, a black cloth square cap; in full dress, a black velvet bonnet with gold cords and tassels.

HIGHER DOCTORS

Undress gown:

DD: a black silk gown with pudding sleeves [d8], which are folded under and ruched round the elbow. There is a black cord and button on the yoke. More usually, the MA gown in black silk with a black cord and button on the yoke is worn. Both gowns are worn with a black silk scarf.

LittD: the MA gown, with a vertical row of doctor's lace from the arm slit to the sleeve head.

LL.D: the flap-collar gown. [d4].

MD: as LL.D, but with doctors' lace round the armhole, continuing to the sleeve-head; across the base of the sleeve, along the facings, and round the collar.

MusD: as MD, but with a second row of lace along the base of the collar.

ScD: the MA gown, with a horizontal row of doctor's lace along the upper edge of the arm slit.

Dress robe:

DD: a scarlet cloth robe of the Cambridge pattern [d1], with facings and sleeve linings of turquoise shot rose silk. The sleeve is held back by a black cord and button, and there is another black cord and button on the yoke.

MusD: a cream brocade robe of the Cambridge MusD pattern [d3], with facings and cuffs of dark cherry satin. The sleeve is held back by a dark cherry cord and button.

Others: a scarlet cloth robe of the Cambridge pattern [d1], with facings and sleeve linings of silk as follows. The sleeve is held back by a scarlet cord and button.

LittD: scarlet silk.

LL.D: light cherry silk.

MD: mid-cherry silk.

ScD: pink shot light blue silk.

Hood:

MusD: a cream brocade hood of the Cambridge shape [f1], lined dark cherry satin.

Others: a scarlet cloth hood of the Cambridge shape [f1], lined as the dress robe.

Hats: in undress, a black cloth square cap; in full dress, a black velvet bonnet with gold cords and tassels, except DD, who wears a Bishop Andrewes cap [h4].

NOTES

1. During the 1939–45 war, an alternative BA hood was licensed for economic reasons, with the white fur replaced by white cloth, thus:

   a black stuff hood of the Cambridge shape [f1], the cowl bordered inside 8″ white cloth, and the cape bound 1″ white cloth.

   Permission to wear this hood has never been withdrawn, and it is still listed in the Regulations. It is unclear whether this modification was also permitted for other bachelors. It seems not to have been in use at Oxford, Dublin, Durham, Lampeter, or Belfast, all of which have fur-lined BA hoods.
2. From 1889 until the 1934 revision, the doctors (DD, LL.D, MD, MusD, PhD) wore the same robes and hoods as they do now. All masters wore the MA gown and hood. The BD and BA wore the same robes as now; the MB a hood of black lined crimson; the LL.B the BA hood, though it had used the MA one at times; and the MusB the BA hood.
3. Holders of the status of Student in Civil Law (SCL) – those reading for the LL.B without first taking the BA – wore the BA robes. This status was abolished during the latter half of the 19th century, possibly during the reforms of 1858.
4. DDs wear a black silk scarf with both dress robe and undress gown.

CANTERBURY CHRIST CHURCH UNIVERSITY
2005

Christ Church College was founded in 1962 by the Church of England as a teacher training college. In the early 1970s, the first degree programme, the BEd, awarded by the University of Kent, was established. In 1977 the College began to offer joint honours degrees in other subjects. In the late 1980s the College was substantially enlarged by the addition of Health Studies. In 1995, the College was awarded taught degree awarding powers, and it changed its name to Canterbury Christ Church University College. It became a full university in 2005. It also has campuses at Broadstairs, Tunbridge Wells, and Medway. In September 2007 the University opened a campus in Folkestone (known as University Centre Folkestone) in collaboration with the University of Greenwich. In 2010 it gained Research Degree Awarding Powers.

UNDERGRADUATES
none specified

UNDERGRADUATE CERTIFICATES AND DIPLOMAS
Gown: a dark blue gown of the basic bachelors' pattern [b1].
Hood: none.
Hat: a dark blue cloth square cap.

FOUNDATION DEGREES
none specified

BACHELORS
Gown: a black stuff gown of the basic pattern, [b1].
Hood: a cardinal red hood of the CNAA shape [a1], lined purple.
Hat: a black cloth square cap.

POSTGRADUATE CERTIFICATES AND DIPLOMAS
none specified

FIRST-DEGREE MASTERS
not awarded

MASTERS including MASTERS OF PHILOSOPHY
Gown: a black stuff gown of the basic pattern [m10].
Hood:
MPhil: a purple hood of the Oxford full shape [f5], lined red; the cowl bound 1″ white.
All others: a purple hood of the Burgon shape [s2], lined cardinal red.
Hat: a black cloth square cap.

DOCTORS OF PHILOSOPHY and
TAUGHT AND PROFESSIONAL DOCTORS

Undress gown: *none specified*

Dress robe: a purple robe of the Oxford pattern [d2], the facings and sleeves covered with cardinal red. There is 1″ white along the outer edge of the facings, and on the sleeves where the purple and red meet.

Hood: a purple hood of the Oxford full shape [f5], lined and bound as follows:
PhD: lined cardinal red, bound on all edges 1″ white.
DClinPsy: lined cardinal red, the cowl edge bound 1″ white.

Hat: in full dress, a purple cloth bonnet with white cords and tassels.

CARDIFF UNIVERSITY
2004

Cardiff was founded in 1884 as the University College of South Wales and Monmouthshire, and became one of the three original constituent colleges of the University of Wales in 1893. In 1988 it merged with the neighbouring University of Wales Institute of Science and Technology (UWIST) to form the University of Wales College of Cardiff. In 2004 UWCC merged with another neighbour, the Welsh National College of Medicine, and became independent of the federal University of Wales, with its own degree-awarding powers with the name Cardiff University, which it had been using informally since the mid-1990s. Although all other degrees will be Cardiff degrees, those in medicine and dentistry will continue to be awarded by the University of Wales until the General Medical and General Dental Councils recognize the MB,BCh(Cardiff) and BDS(Cardiff)as 'registrable qualifications'.

All hoods are of the Oxford simple shape, in 'Cardiff red' – this is a tomato red – and lined according to the grade of degree.

UNDERGRADUATES
none specified

UNDERGRADUATE CERTIFICATES AND DIPLOMAS
none specified

BACHELORS
Gown: a black gown of the London BA pattern [b4].
Hood: a Cardiff red hood of the Oxford simple shape [s1], lined white taffeta.
Hat: a black cloth square cap.

FIRST-DEGREE MASTERS and MB,BCh and BDS
Gown: a black gown of the London BA pattern [b4].
Hood: a Cardiff red hood of the Oxford simple shape [s1], lined white taffeta, bordered inside the cowl with 3″ royal blue.
Hat: a black cloth square cap.

POSTGRADUATE CERTIFICATES
Gown: a black gown of the London BA pattern [b4].
Hood: a Cardiff red hood of the Oxford simple shape [s1], lined beige taffeta.
Hat: a black cloth square cap.

POSTGRADUATE DIPLOMAS
Gown: a black gown of the London BA pattern [b4].
Hood: a Cardiff red hood of the Oxford simple shape [s1], lined powder blue taffeta.

Hat: a black cloth square cap.

MASTERS (taught course)

Gown: a black gown of the basic pattern [m10].

Hood: a Cardiff red hood of the Oxford simple shape [s1], lined royal blue taffeta.

Hat: a black cloth square cap.

MASTERS OF PHILOSOPHY

Gown: a black gown of the basic pattern [m10].

Hood: a Cardiff red hood of the Oxford simple shape [s1], lined lilac taffeta.

Hat: a black cloth square cap.

DOCTORS OF PHILOSOPHY and TAUGHT AND PROFESSIONAL DOCTORS

Undress gown: *none specified*

Dress robe: a Cardiff red robe of the Cambridge doctors' pattern [d1]; the facings are covered and the sleeves lined forest green taffeta; the facings are bound on the outer edge with 1″ silver grey, and the sleeves are held with a silver-grey cord and button.

Hood: a Cardiff red hood of the Oxford simple shape [s1], lined forest green taffeta, bordered inside the cowl with 3″ silver-grey.

Hat: in full dress, a black velvet bonnet with black and silver silk cords and tassels.

HIGHER DOCTORS

Undress gown: *none specified*

Dress robe: a Cardiff red robe of the Cambridge doctors' pattern [d1]; the facings are covered and the sleeves lined pale gold taffeta; the facings are bound on the outer edge with 1″ silver-grey, and the sleeves are held with a silver-grey cord and button.

Hood: a Cardiff red hood of the Oxford simple shape [s1], lined pale gold taffeta, bordered inside the cowl with 3″ silver-grey.

Hat: in full dress, a black velvet bonnet with black and silver silk cords and tassels.

UNIVERSITY OF CENTRAL ENGLAND

— *see Birmingham City University*

UNIVERSITY OF CENTRAL LANCASHIRE, PRESTON
1993

The University of Central Lancashire ('UCLan') is based in Preston. It was founded in 1828, as 'The Institution for the Diffusion of Useful Knowledge'. It changed its name to Harris Technical College in 1899, and in 1932 to Harris Art College. In 1952 it became simply Harris College, and in 1973 it was designated Preston Polytechnic. The name was again changed, to Lancashire Polytechnic, in 1984, and it became the University of Central Lancashire in 1993.

In 2004, UCLan took over the former Northumbria University campus in Carlisle. This campus, along with the university's Newton Rigg campus near Penrith, has been part of the University of Cumbria (*q.v.*) since 2007.

All hoods are trimmed with the University's special damasked red silk.

UNDERGRADUATES
none specified

UNDERGRADUATE CERTIFICATES AND DIPLOMAS
Gown: as for bachelors.
Hood: a grey hood of the Oxford simple shape [s1], the cowl bordered inside 2″ university red silk.
Hat: a black cloth square cap.

FOUNDATION DEGREES
Gown: a black stuff gown of the basic bachelors' pattern [b1].
Hood: a grey hood of the CNAA shape [a1], lined black, tipped university red silk.
Hat: a black cloth square cap.

BACHELORS
Gown: a black stuff gown of the basic pattern [b1].
Hood: a grey hood of the CNAA shape [a1], lined university red silk.
Hat: a black cloth square cap.

POSTGRADUATE CERTIFICATES AND DIPLOMAS
Gown: a black stuff gown of the basic bachelors' pattern [b1].
Hood: a grey hood of the CNAA shape [a1, lined and the cowl bordered inside 2″ university red silk and 1″ black.
Hat: a black cloth square cap.

FIRST-DEGREE MASTERS
not awarded

MASTERS including MASTERS OF PHILOSOPHY
Gown: a black stuff gown of the basic pattern [m10].
Hood: a black silk hood of the Cambridge shape [f1], lined and bound 2½″ university red silk, the cape edged outside with 1″ silver grey set next to the red binding.
Hat: a black cloth square cap.

MASTERS honoris causa
Gown: a grey stuff gown of the basic pattern [m10], with facings of university red silk.
Hood: a grey hood of the CNAA shape [a1], lined university red silk.
Hat: a black cloth square cap.

DOCTORS OF PHILOSOPHY and TAUGHT AND PROFESSIONAL DOCTORS
Undress gown: as for masters.
Dress robe: a grey cloth robe of the Cambridge pattern [d1], with facings and sleeve linings of university red silk.
Hood: a grey cloth hood of the Cambridge shape [f1], lined university red silk.
Hats: in undress, a black cloth square cap; in full dress, a grey cloth bonnet with red cords and tassels.

HIGHER DOCTORS
Undress gown: as for PhD.
Dress robe: as for PhD, but with a grey cord and button on each sleeve.
Hood: a grey cloth hood of the Cambridge shape [f1], lined and bound 2″ university red silk.
Hats: in undress, a black cloth square cap; in full dress, a grey cloth bonnet with gold cords and tassels.

NOTES
1. Holders of undergraduate awards formerly used the following hoods:
   HND, HNC: a grey hood of the CNAA shape [a1], part-lined university red silk.
   All others: as HND, but with 1″ black between the red silk and grey body.

UNIVERSITY OF CHESTER
1839/2005

The University of Chester was founded in 1839 as Chester Diocesan Training College – the UK's first purpose-built teacher-training college. In 1910, Chester College began its association with the University of Liverpool, becoming a formally affiliated college of the University in 1930. Women were first admitted in 1962, and the College's name was changed to Chester College of Education in 1963. In 1974, the number of courses was expanded to include BA and BSc degrees. To reflect its wider remit, the College was renamed again, as Chester College of Higher Education. By 1995, Chester had earned the right to call itself University College Chester. In 1999 the government changed the requirements for university colleges to include only those that had their own degree-awarding powers, so the college had to revert to the title Chester College of Higher Education, though the more descriptive 'Chester, a College of the University of Liverpool' was frequently used in publicity material. It was granted taught degree-awarding powers in 2003, allowing it to be known as University College Chester once again. In 2005, University College Chester was finally awarded full university status and became the University of Chester. This was followed by the right to award research degrees in 2007.

All hoods are lined white with a red stripe, which reflects the basis of the armorial bearings, a red cross on a silver field.

Faculty colours.

Arts: bright red
Business Administration (MBA only): light blue.
Education: dark green
Laws: gold
Ministry: magenta
Science: mid-blue
Theology: purple

UNDERGRADUATES
none specified

UNDERGRADUATE CERTIFICATES AND DIPLOMAS

Gown: a black stuff gown of the basic bachelors' pattern [b1], with a black cord and button on the yoke.

Hood: a black hood of Edinburgh shape [s4], lined as follows:

Certificates: the cowl bordered 3″ white, with 1″ red laid in the centre.

Diplomas: the cowl bordered 5″ white, with 1″ red set 1″ in from the edge.

Hat: a black cloth square cap.

FOUNDATION DEGREES

Gown: a black stuff gown of the basic bachelors' pattern [b1], with a black cord and button on the yoke.

Hood: a black hood of the Leeds shape [s7], lined white, with 1″ red set in the middle of the turn-out.

Hat: a black cloth square cap.

BACHELORS

Gown: a black stuff gown of the basic bachelors' pattern [b1], with a black cord and button on the yoke.

Hood: a hood of the Leeds shape [s7] in faculty colour, lined white, with 1″ red set in the middle of the turn-out.

Hat: a black cloth square cap.

POSTGRADUATE CERTIFICATES AND DIPLOMAS

Gown: a black stuff gown of the basic masters' pattern [m10], with a black cord and button on the yoke.

Hood: as for undergraduate diplomas.

Hat: a black cloth square cap.

FIRST-DEGREE MASTERS

not awarded

MASTERS including MASTERS OF PHILOSOPHY

Gown: a black stuff gown of the basic pattern [m10], with a black cord and button on the yoke.

Hood: a hood of the Cambridge shape [f1] in faculty colour, lined white, with 1″ red inside the cowl set 1″ in.

MPhil: the body of the hood is black.

MLitt (honorary only): as for honorary doctors.

Hat: a black cloth square cap.

DOCTORS OF PHILOSOPHY and TAUGHT AND PROFESSIONAL DOCTORS

Undress gown: *none specified*

Dress robe: a maroon robe of the Cambridge pattern [d1], the facings and sleeve-linings of white; there is 1″ red set in the centre of the facings.

Hood: a maroon hood of the Cambridge shape [f1], lined as follows:

PhD: lined white, with 1″ red inside the cowl set 1″ in.

Professional Doctorates: lined and the cape bound 1″ white, with 1″ red inside the cowl set 1″ in.

Hat: in full dress, a black cloth bonnet with maroon cords and tassels.

HONORARY DOCTORS

Undress gown: *none specified*

Dress robe: a scarlet robe of the Cambridge pattern [d1], with the facings and sleeve-linings of white; there is 1″ red set in the centre of the facings.

Hood: a gold hood of the Cambridge shape [f1], lined white, with 1″ red inside the cowl set 1″ in.

Hat: in full dress, a black cloth bonnet with gold cords and tassels.

UNIVERSITY OF CHICHESTER
1839/2005

The university dates back to 1839, when a college for training schoolmasters was established at what is now the Chichester campus, known as Bishop Otter College. In 1873, the campus became a training institute for women teachers, men being re-admitted to the College in the 1950s. The second campus, at Bognor Regis, was opened as an emergency teacher-training institute in 1946. Because of the proximity of Chichester and Bognor Regis, the two colleges merged in 1977 to form the West Sussex Institute of Higher Education, with degrees being awarded by CNAA, and later by the University of Southampton. Between 1995 and 1999, it was known as Chichester Institute of Higher Education. It gained degree-awarding powers in 1999, becoming known as University College Chichester, and became recognized as a full university in October 2005.

All hoods feature the colours 'champagne' and 'lido blue'. Champagne is a dark yellow; lido blue is similar to royal blue.

UNDERGRADUATES
none specified

FOUNDATION DEGREES
Gown: a black stuff gown of the basic bachelors' pattern [b1].
Hood: a champagne hood of the Edinburgh shape [s4], lined champagne, and the cowl edge bordered inside ½″ lido blue.
Hat: a black cloth square cap.

UNDERGRADUATE CERTIFICATES AND DIPLOMAS
Gown: a black stuff gown of the basic bachelors' pattern [b1].
Hood: a champagne hood of the Edinburgh shape [s4], lined champagne, and the cowl edge bordered inside 3″ lido blue.
Hat: a black cloth square cap.

BACHELORS
Gown: a black stuff gown of the London BA pattern [b4], with twisted cords of champagne and lido blue, and a blue button.
Hood: a champagne hood of the Edinburgh shape [s4], lined lido blue.
Hat: a black cloth square cap.

POSTGRADUATE CERTIFICATES AND DIPLOMAS
Gown: as for bachelors.
Hood: a champagne hood of the Edinburgh shape [s4], lined lido blue, and the cowl edge bordered inside 3″ champagne.
Hat: a black cloth square cap.

MASTERS

Gown: a black stuff gown of the Oxford MA pattern [m1], with a twisted cord of champagne and lido blue, and a gold button, on the yoke.

Hood: a lido blue hood of the Edinburgh shape [s4], fully lined champagne.

If awarded *honoris causa*, the cowl is also bordered ½″ gold lace.

Hat: a black cloth square cap.

Although robes have been designed for them, research degrees (MPhil, PhD) are currently awarded by the University of Southampton.

MASTERS OF PHILOSOPHY

Gown: as for other masters.

Hood: a lido blue hood of the Cambridge shape [f1], lined and bound ⅜″ champagne.

Hat: a black cloth square cap.

DOCTORS OF PHILOSOPHY and TAUGHT AND PROFESSIONAL DOCTORS

Undress gown: *none specified*

Dress robe: a royal blue cloth robe of the Oxford pattern [d2], with facings and cuffs of champagne.

Hood: a champagne hood of the Cambridge shape [f1], lined and bound 2″ lido blue.

Hat: in full dress, a blue cloth bonnet with champagne and lido blue cords and tassels.

HIGHER DOCTORS

Undress gown: *none specified*

Dress robe: same as for PhD.

Hood: a royal blue panama robe of the Cambridge shape [f1], lined and bound 2″ champagne.

If awarded *honoris causa*, the cowl is also bordered ¾″ gold lace.

Hat: in full dress, a blue cloth bonnet with champagne and lido blue cords and tassels.

CITY UNIVERSITY
1963

City University traces its origin to the Northampton Institute, established in 1894, and named after the Marquess of Northampton, who donated the land on which the Institute was built, between Northampton Square and St John Street in Islington. The Institute was designated a College of Advanced Technology in 1957, and received its Royal Charter in 1966, becoming The City University.

The scheme of academic dress is very simple, being based round two colours: maroon and gold. As noted below, the hoods originally had coloured neckbands indicating the area of study; this may have been based on the practice at Imperial College.

UNDERGRADUATES
none specified

UNDERGRADUATE CERTIFICATES AND DIPLOMAS
Gown: as for bachelors.
Hood:
Grad Cert and Grad Dip: as for bachelors.
Others: none.
Hat: a black cloth square cap.

FOUNDATION DEGREES
Gown: as for bachelors.
Hood: none.
Hat: a black cloth square cap.

BACHELORS
Gown: a black stuff gown of the Cambridge BA pattern [b2].
Hood: a maroon silk hood of the Oxford simple shape [s1], fully lined gold silk. The neckband is gold.
Hat: a black cloth square cap.

POSTGRADUATE CERTIFICATES AND DIPLOMAS
Gown: as for bachelors.
Hood: a maroon silk hood of the Cambridge shape [f1], unlined. The neckband is gold.
Hat: a black cloth square cap.

FIRST-DEGREE MASTERS and MASTERS by TAUGHT COURSE
Gown: a black stuff gown of the Cambridge MA pattern [m2], with inverted-T armholes.

Hood: a maroon silk hood of the Cambridge shape[f1], lined and bound on all edges ½″ gold silk. The neckband is gold.

Hat: a black cloth square cap.

MASTERS by RESEARCH

Gown: a black stuff gown of the Cambridge MA pattern [m2], with inverted-T armholes.

Hood: a maroon silk hood of the Cambridge shape[f1], in maroon silk, lined and bound on the cape ½″ gold silk; the cowl is bordered inside 1″ maroon silk. The neckband is gold.

Hat: a black cloth square cap.

DOCTORS OF PHILOSOPHY and TAUGHT AND PROFESSIONAL DOCTORS

Undress gown: as for masters.

Dress robe: a maroon cloth robe of the Cambridge MA pattern [m2], with 2″ gold silk on the facings, and ½″ gold silk round the inverted-T armholes.

Hood: a maroon silk hood of the Cambridge shape [f1], the lining divided vertically when worn, maroon on the left side and gold on the right. The neckband is gold.

Hats: in undress, a black cloth square cap; in full dress, a black cloth bonnet with maroon cords and tassels.

HIGHER DOCTORS

Undress gown: as for PhD.

Dress robe: as for PhD, but the facings are 5″ wide, and the sleeve below the armhole is also covered in gold silk.

Hood: as for PhD, but the shell of the hood is of scarlet cloth.

Hats: in undress, a black cloth square cap; in full dress, a black velvet bonnet with maroon cords and tassels.

NOTES

1. Since 2007, all neckbands have been gold. Until then the discipline (not the title) of the degree awarded was shown by the colour of the neckband:
   Engineering: blue
   Laws: scarlet.
   Nursing: white.
   Performing Arts: gold.
   Science: grey
   Social Science: olive green.
   DD *honoris causa*: purple.

THE COLLEGE OF LAW, HOLBORN, LONDON.
1962

The College of Law was created by the Law Society by combining its own School of Law with the tutorial firm Gibson and Weldon. Student numbers grew to around 4,500 a year by the mid-1990s. A few years later, the College severed its links with the Law Society. In 2006 the College was granted limited degree-awarding powers by the Privy Council. It may award the taught degrees of Bachelor and Master of Laws, and the *honoris causa* Doctorate of Laws. It has campuses in Birmingham, Chester, Guildford, London (Bloomsbury and Moorgate), Manchester, and York.

BACHELORS OF LAWS

Gown: a black stuff gown of the basic pattern [b1].

Hood: a red hood of the Surrey simple shape [s10], lined dark blue, the cowl bordered inside 1″ silver grey.

Hat: a black cloth square cap.

MASTERS OF LAWS

Gown: a black stuff gown of the basic pattern [m10].

Hood: a red hood of the Cambridge shape [f1], lined dark blue, the cowl bordered inside 2″ silver grey.

Hat: a black cloth square cap.

DOCTORS OF LAWS

Undress gown: *none specified*

Dress robe: a red robe of the Cambridge pattern [d1], with facings and sleeve linings of dark blue. There is 1″ silver-grey on the outer edge of the facings, and the sleeves are held by silver-grey cord and buttons.

Hood: a red hood of the Cambridge shape [f1], lined dark blue, the cowl bordered inside, and the cape bordered outside, 1″ silver grey.

Hat: in full dress, a black velvet bonnet with dark blue cords and tassels.

COUNCIL FOR NATIONAL ACADEMIC AWARDS (CNAA)
1963-1992

The Council was set up to validate courses run by the polytechnics and various other institutions of higher education, and to award the degrees those courses led to: it did this in over 140 such institutions, and was thus the largest degree-awarding body in the UK. With the transformation of the polytechnics into universities in 1992, the CNAA was closed down, although obviously its robes will be seen for some years yet. The bachelors' and masters' hoods are now used by the Open University for its validated degrees since the OUVS took over the responsibility for awarding degrees in institutions without degree-awarding powers.

The robes are notable for being the first institution to use the Aberdeen-style hood since Aberdeen invented it in the 1870s, although it has its own, rather more generously cut, version. It has, probably as a result of its use at many institutions, been a very popular choice of shape in the post-1992 universities.

UNDERGRADUATES
none ever specified

UNDERGRADUATE CERTIFICATES AND DIPLOMAS
Gown: as for bachelors. No hood.

BACHELORS
Gown: a black stuff gown of the basic pattern [b1].
Hood: a gold panama hood of the CNAA shape [a1], lined turquoise silk.
Hat: a black cloth square cap.

GRADUATE and POSTGRADUATE CERTIFICATES AND DIPLOMAS
Gown: as for bachelors. No hood.

FIRST-DEGREE MASTERS
Gown: as for bachelors.
Hood: a gold panama hood of the CNAA shape [a1], lined turquoise silk, and the cowl edge bordered inside 1″ white silk.
Hat: a black cloth square cap.

MASTERS including MASTERS OF PHILOSOPHY
Gown: a black stuff gown of the basic pattern [m10].
Hood: a gold panama hood of the CNAA shape [a1], lined white silk.
Hat: a black cloth square cap.

DOCTORS OF PHILOSOPHY and TAUGHT AND PROFESSIONAL DOCTORS

Undress gown: as for masters.

Dress robe: a black robe of the same pattern as the masters' gown, with the facings and yoke covered with maroon silk.

Hood: a gold panama hood of the CNAA shape [a1], lined maroon silk.

Hats: in undress, a black cloth square cap; in full dress, a black cloth bonnet with maroon cords and tassels.

HIGHER DOCTORS

Undress gown: as for PhD.

Dress robe: a gold panama robe of the same pattern as the masters' gown, with the facings covered in cream St Aidan pattern brocade.

Hood: a gold panama hood of the CNAA shape [a1], lined and bound with cream St Aidan pattern brocade.

Hats: in undress, a black cloth square cap; in full dress, a black cloth bonnet with gold cords and tassels.

UNIVERSITY OF COVENTRY
1993

The University can trace its roots as far back as Coventry College of Design, founded in 1843. In 1970 Coventry College of Art amalgamated with Lanchester College of Technology and Rugby College of Engineering Technology. The resulting institution was called Lanchester Polytechnic, after the Midlands automotive industry pioneer, Dr Frederick Lanchester. In 1987 the name was changed to Coventry Polytechnic, and in 1992 it became the University of Coventry.

The blue and the gold hood linings are damasked with the University's phoenix emblem.

UNDERGRADUATES
none specified

UNDERGRADUATE CERTIFICATES AND DIPLOMAS
Gown: as for bachelors.
Hood: a black silk hood of the CNAA shape [a1, lined blue damask and tipped gold damask.
Hat: a black cloth square cap.

FOUNDATION DEGREES
none specified

BACHELORS
Gown: a black stuff gown of the basic pattern [b1].
Hood: a gold silk hood of the Cambridge shape [f1], the cowl bordered inside 4″ blue damask.
Hat: a black cloth square cap.

MASTERS including FIRST-DEGREE MASTERS, MASTERS OF PHILOSOPHY, and POSTGRADUATE CERTIFICATES AND DIPLOMAS
Gown: a black stuff gown of the basic pattern [m10].
MPhil: the facings are gold damask.
All others: the facings are blue damask.
Hood: a gold silk hood of the Cambridge shape, lined blue damask.
Hat: a black cloth square cap.

DOCTORS OF PHILOSOPHY
Undress gown: as for masters.
Dress robe: a royal blue panama robe of the Cambridge pattern [d1], with facings and sleeve linings of gold damask.
Hood: a blue panama hood of the Cambridge shape [f1], lined gold damask.

Hats: in undress, a black cloth square cap; in full dress, a blue cloth bonnet with gold cords and tassels.

HIGHER DOCTORS

Undress gown: as for PhD.

Dress robe: as for PhD, but with a blue cord and button on each sleeve, and on the yoke.

Hood: a blue panama hood of the Cambridge shape [f1], lined and bound 1½″ gold damask.

Hats: in undress, a black cloth square cap; in full dress, a black cloth bonnet with gold cords and tassels.

DOCTOR OF CLINICAL PSYCHOLOGY (DClinPsy) – joint degree with the University of Warwick.

Undress gown: *none specified*

Dress robe: a black robe of the Cambridge doctor's shape [d1], with 3″ silk facings (1½″ scarlet on the inner edge and 1½″ royal blue on the outer edge); the sleeves are lined royal blue silk and bordered inside with 2″ scarlet silk, and gathered at the elbows with dark blue cord and buttons.

Hood: a scarlet hood of the CNAA shape [a1], lined royal blue.

Hat: in full dress, a black bonnet with scarlet and blue cords and tassels.

CRANFIELD UNIVERSITY
1969/1993

The University can trace its history back to 1946, when the College of Aeronautics opened on the former Royal Air Force base of RAF Cranfield. It incorporated the former National College of Agricultural Engineering established at Silsoe during the 1950s. In 1969 it was chartered as Cranfield Institute of Technology, with its own postgraduate degree-awarding powers. An academic partnership with the Royal Military College of Science at Shrivenham, whose roots can be traced back to 1772, was formed in 1984, when bachelors' degrees were introduced. In 1993 a further Royal Charter changed the institution's name to Cranfield University. By 2008, the Silsoe campus was closed, and courses taught there transferred to Cranfield.

The robes are very simple, and the original scheme did not have them for bachelors. It is not clear why the division between the two areas was made. 'Neyron' rose is a rich pink shade.

UNDERGRADUATES
none specified

CERTIFICATE of MEMBERSHIP OF CRANFIELD UNIVERSITY (CMCU)
Gown: a black gown of the basic pattern [b1].
Hood: none.
Hat: a black cloth square cap.

BACHELORS
Gown: a black gown of the basic pattern [b1].
Hood: an old-gold corded silk hood of the Oxford simple shape [s1], lined as follows:
Agriculture, food production, and rural land use: spectrum green silk.
Military science, technology, and management: scarlet silk.
Hat: a black cloth square cap.

FELLOWSHIP IN MANUFACTURING MANAGEMENT (FMM)
Gown: as for masters.
Hood: an old-gold corded silk of the Oxford simple shape [s1], the cowl bordered inside 4″ royal blue silk, and 1″ gold. [s1]
Hat: a black cloth square cap.

FIRST-DEGREE MASTERS
not awarded

MASTERS, including MASTERS OF PHILOSOPHY

Gown: a black gown of the basic pattern [m10], with inverted-T armhole, and an old-gold cord and button on the yoke.

Hood: an old-gold corded silk hood of the Oxford simple shape [s1], lined royal blue silk.

Hat: a black cloth square cap.

DOCTORS OF PHILOSOPHY and TAUGHT AND PROFESSIONAL DOCTORS

Undress gown: as for masters.

Dress robe: the master's gown, with facings of neyron rose cloth.

Hood: a gold hood of the Oxford simple shape [s1], lined neyron rose cloth.

Hats: in undress, a black cloth square cap; in full dress, a black velvet bonnet with gold cords and tassels.

HIGHER DOCTORS

Undress gown: as for masters.

Dress robe: a neyron rose cloth robe of the Cambridge pattern [d1], with facings and sleeve linings of royal blue.

Hood: a neyron rose cloth hood of the Cambridge shape [f1], lined royal blue silk.

Hats: in undress, a black cloth square cap; in full dress, a black velvet bonnet with gold cords and tassels.

UNIVERSITY FOR THE CREATIVE ARTS
2008

In August 2005 the University College for the Creative Arts at Canterbury, Epsom, Farnham, Maidstone and Rochester was established through the merger of the Surrey University Institute of Art and Design and the Kent Institute of Art and Design. It became the University for the Creative Arts in 2008.

UNDERGRADUATES
none specified

FOUNDATION DEGREES
Gown: a black stuff gown of the basic pattern [b1].
Hood: a black hood of the Edinburgh shape [s4], the cowl bordered inside 3″ red and 1″ grey.
Hat: a black cloth square cap.

BACHELORS
Gown: a black stuff gown of the basic pattern [b1].
Hood: a black hood of the Edinburgh shape [s4], lined red, bordered inside the cowl for 3″ with grey.
Hat: a black cloth square cap.

PROFESSIONAL GRADUATE CERTIFICATE IN EDUCATION
Gown: a black stuff gown of the basic pattern [b1].
Hood: a black hood of the Edinburgh shape [s4] lined red, bordered inside the cowl with 3″ grey and 1½″red.
Hat: a black cloth square cap.

POSTGRADUATE CERTIFICATES and DIPLOMAS
Gown: a black stuff gown of the basic masters' pattern [m10].
Hood: a black hood of the Edinburgh shape [s4], lined grey, bordered inside the cowl 3″ red.
Hat: a black cloth square cap.

MASTERS
Gown: a black stuff gown of the basic pattern [m10].
Hood: a red hood of the Edinburgh shape [s4], lined grey, bordered inside the cowl with 3″ black and ¼″ red.
Hat: A black cloth square cap.

HONORARY MASTERS

Gown: a black stuff gown of the basic pattern [m10], with 2½″ red facings.
Hood: as for other masters.
Hat: a black velvet bonnet with red cords and tassels.

UNIVERSITY OF CUMBRIA
2007

This university was formed in 2007 by an amalgamation of St Martin's College, Cumbria, Cumbria Institute of the Arts, and the Cumbrian campuses of the University of Central Lancashire. It has five campuses, at Carlisle, Newton Rigg, Penrith, Ambleside, and Lancaster, as well as a teacher-education centre in London. The hood colours were designed to reflect the natural colours of the region.

UNDERGRADUATES
none specified

'INTERMEDIATE AWARDS' (DipHE, FdA, FdSc, FdTech)
Gown: a black stuff gown of the basic pattern [b1].
Hood: a silver-grey hood of the Burgon shape [s2], lined bright green, and the cowl bordered inside with 1″ black.
Hat: a black cloth square cap.

BACHELORS
Gown: a black stuff gown of the basic pattern [b1].
Hood: a silver-grey hood of the Burgon shape [s2], lined bright green, and the cowl bordered inside with two black ribbons, ½″ wide, set ½″ apart.
Hat: a black cloth square cap.

POSTGRADUATE CERTIFICATES and DIPLOMAS
Gown: a black stuff gown of the basic masters' pattern [m10].
Hood: a silver-grey hood of the Cambridge shape [f1], lined as follows:
Certificates: lined green, the cowl bordered inside with 1″ black.
Diplomas: lined bright green, the cowl bordered inside with two black ribbons, ½″ wide, set ½″ apart.
Hat: a black cloth square cap.

FIRST-DEGREE MASTERS
not awarded

MASTERS
Gown: a black stuff gown of the basic pattern [m10].
Hood: a silver-grey hood of the Cambridge shape [f1], lined and the cape bound 1″ bright green, and the cowl bordered inside with 1″ black.
Hat: a black cloth square cap.

MASTERS OF PHILOSOPHY, DOCTORS OF PHILOSOPHY, TAUGHT AND PROFESSIONAL DOCTORS, and HIGHER DOCTORS

not yet awarded

DE MONTFORT UNIVERSITY, LEICESTER
1992

Leicester Polytechnic was created in 1969 through the amalgamation of Leicester College of Technology and Leicester College of Art. The polytechnic was established as a corporation in 1989, and was granted university status in 1992, since when it has absorbed several other colleges. In 2001 the Lincolnshire campuses merged with the University of Lincolnshire and Humberside (creating the University of Lincoln) and in 2003 de Montfort withdrew from Milton Keynes. The Faculty of Education and Contemporary Studies at the Bedford campus was recently merged with the University of Luton to create the University of Bedfordshire. De Montfort now has two campuses: Leicester City Campus, and Charles Frears. The name commemorates Simon de Montfort, Earl of Leicester, who is widely credited with establishing the first parliament in 1265.

The robes were designed in-house at Northams. All hoods and doctors' robes include the colour 'university red', which is a very pale brick red, almost crushed-strawberry pink. Its inspiration was the wall in the Council Chamber where the decision was made. An anomaly is that the professional doctorates are granted the same robes as the higher doctors, and not the PhD robes. This is probably the result of the original regulations specifying the PhD as an exception to the other doctors, and then the DBA, *etc.*, being added later, and the regulations not being updated.

Degree colours

Arts: mid blue.
Business Administration: lilac.
Chemistry: pale green.
Design: purple.
Education: brown.
Engineering: grey.
Laws: light blue.
Medical Science: pale green.
Pharmacy: dark green.
Philosophy: white.
Science: bright green.

UNDERGRADUATES

none specified

UNDERGRADUATE CERTIFICATES and DIPLOMAS ('LICENTIATES') and PGCE

Gown: as for bachelors.

Scarf: a gold silk scarf, lined and edged for 1″ university red silk. It reaches to the waist in front, and the ends are mitred, and finished with a red and gold tassel. There is a similar tassel hanging from the lower edge at the centre. The university emblem is embroidered on each end.

Hat: a black cloth square cap.

FOUNDATION DEGREES (all faculties)

Gown: as for bachelors.

Hood: a black hood of the CNAA shape [a1], lined university red, the cowl bound 1″ gold.

Hat: a black cloth square cap.

BACHELORS

Gown: a black gown of basic pattern [b1].

Hood: a gold silk hood of the CNAA shape [a1], lined university red, and the cowl bordered inside 1″ with the degree colour.

Hat: a black cloth square cap.

POSTGRADUATE CERTIFICATES AND DIPLOMAS and GradDipArch

Gown: as for bachelors.

Hood: a gold silk hood of the CNAA shape [a1], lined university red.

Hat: a black cloth square cap.

FIRST-DEGREE MASTERS

Gown: as for bachelors.

Hood: a gold hood of the Cambridge shape [f1], lined university red, and the cowl bordered 1″ with the degree colour.

Hat: a black cloth square cap.

MASTERS including MASTERS OF PHILOSOPHY

Gown: a black gown of the basic pattern [m10], with an inverted-T armhole.

Hood: a gold hood of the Cambridge shape [f1], lined university red, and the cowl bordered 1″ with the degree colour.

Hat: a black cloth square cap.

PROFESSIONAL DOCTORS (DBA, DFin, AdminD)

Undress gown: as for masters.

Dress robe: the higher doctors' robe.

Hood: a gold hood of the Cambridge shape [f1], lined and the cape bound for 1½″ university red, and the cowl bordered 1½″ with the degree colour.

AdminD: *t.b.a.*

DFin: *t.b.a.*

DBA: lilac.

Hats: in undress, a black cloth square cap; in full dress, a black cloth bonnet, with red and gold cords and tassels.

DOCTORS OF PHILOSOPHY

Undress gown: as for masters.

Dress robe: the masters' gown, with facings of gold, the outer edge bordered 1″ university red. The yoke is covered with gold silk, and has a red cord and button.

Hood: a gold hood of the Cambridge shape [f1], lined and the cape bound for 1½″ university red, and the cowl bordered 1½″ white.

Hats: in undress, a black cloth square cap; in full dress, a black cloth bonnet, with red and gold cords and tassels.

HIGHER DOCTORS

Undress gown: as for masters.

Dress robe: a gold silk robe of [m10] pattern, with inverted -T armhole. The facings and yoke are covered with university red silk, and there is a gold cord and button on the yoke.

Hood: a gold hood of the Cambridge shape [f1], lined and the cape bound for 1½″ university red, and the cowl bordered 1½″ with the degree colour.

Hats: in undress, a black cloth square cap; in full dress, a black velvet bonnet, with red and gold cords and tassels.

NOTES

1. A 're-graduation hood' is used. This is the same as a bachelor's hood, but bordered in yellow. It is used for alumni of the University's predecessor institutions, who are awarded a BSc *honoris causa.*

UNIVERSITY OF DERBY
1993

At least two dozen bodies have contributed to the university's formation. The first was founded in 1851 as the Derby Diocesan Institution for the Training of Schoolmistresses, which flourished for 120 years before merging in 1977 with another college to form what was then known as the Derby Lonsdale College of Higher Education. In 1853 the Derby School of Art was established, which in 1870 became the Derby Central School of Art and the Derby Central School of Science. In 1885, the two schools were reunited as the Derby School of Art and Technical Institution. Less than a decade later, in 1892, three more mergers took place and the institution became the Derby Municipal Technical College. Further mergers and amalgamations took place over the following years, until the Derbyshire College of Higher Education came into being. In 1992, it became a university: at that time, the only college of higher education in the country to be upgraded directly to university status.

The academic dress is simple, and grade-specific. The neckbands of all hoods are faced with the main lining colour.

UNDERGRADUATES
none specified

UNDERGRADUATE CERTIFICATES AND DIPLOMAS
Gown: as for bachelors.
Hood: a black hood of the CNAA shape [a1], part-lined pale blue, and bordered scarlet.
Hat: a black cloth square cap.

ADVANCED DIPLOMAS
Gown: as for bachelors.
Hood: a black hood of the Burgon shape [s2], the cowl bordered inside 2″ light blue, and bound 1″ scarlet.
Hat: a black cloth square cap.

FOUNDATION DEGREES
Gown: as for bachelors.
Hood: a black hood of the Cambridge shape [f1], the cowl bordered inside 2″ scarlet, and bound 1″ light blue.
Hat: a black cloth square cap.

BACHELORS
Gown: a black stuff gown of basic pattern [b1].
Hood: a black hood of the Cambridge shape [f1], the cowl bordered inside 4″ scarlet, and bound 1½″ pale blue.

Hat: a black cloth square cap.

POSTGRADUATE CERTIFICATES AND DIPLOMAS

Gown: as for bachelors.

Hood: a dark blue hood of the Cambridge shape [f1], the cowl bordered inside 4″ scarlet and bound 1½″ pale blue.

Hat: a black cloth square cap.

FIRST-DEGREE MASTERS

not awarded

MASTERS including MASTERS OF PHILOSOPHY

Gown: a black stuff gown of basic pattern [m10]. For MPhil, it has scarlet facings.

Hood: a black hood of the Cambridge shape [f1], lined and bound on the cape for ¼″ scarlet, and bound on the cowl 2½″ pale blue.

Hat: a black cloth square cap.

TAUGHT AND PROFESSIONAL DOCTORS

Undress gown: *none specified*

Dress robe: a pale blue robe of the Cambridge pattern [d1], with facings and sleeve linings of maroon. The facings have 1″ dark blue on the outer edge, piped scarlet.

Hood: a pale blue hood of the Cambridge shape [f1], lined maroon, the cowl bordered inside 1″ dark blue, piped scarlet.

Hat: in undress, a black cloth square cap; in full dress, a black cloth bonnet with maroon cords and tassels.

If awarded *honoris causa*, the bonnet is of black velvet with navy cords and tassels.

DOCTORS OF PHILOSOPHY

Undress gown: *none specified*

Dress robe: a maroon robe of the Cambridge pattern [d1], with facings and sleeve linings of pale blue. The facings have 1″ dark blue on the outer edge, piped scarlet.

Hood: a maroon hood of the Cambridge shape [f1], lined pale blue, the cowl bordered inside 1″ dark blue, piped scarlet.

Hat: in full dress, a black cloth bonnet with maroon cords and tassels.

DOCTORS OF THE UNIVERSITY

Undress gown: *none specified*

Dress robe: a scarlet robe of the Cambridge pattern [d1], with facings and sleeve linings of dark blue. The facings are piped pale blue, and there is a pale blue cord and button on each sleeve.

Hood: a scarlet hood of the Cambridge shape [f1], lined dark blue, the cowl piped light blue.

Hat: in full dress, a black velvet bonnet with scarlet cords and tassels.

UNIVERSITY OF DUBLIN
1592

The University of Dublin was founded in 1592, when Queen Elizabeth I issued a charter for Trinity College, Dublin as 'the mother of a university', making it Ireland's oldest university. Unlike the universities of Oxford and of Cambridge, after which the University of Dublin was modelled, and both of which comprise several constituent colleges, there is just one Dublin college: Trinity College. Thus the designations 'Trinity College Dublin' and 'University of Dublin' are usually synonymous for practical purposes. However, in a remarkable High Court case of 1898, the Provost, Fellows, and Scholars of Trinity College were the claimants and the Chancellor, Doctors, and Masters of the University of Dublin were among the defendants, and the court held that Trinity College and the University of Dublin 'are one body'.

Although Shaw said 'there is a simple system of gowns and hoods' in use here, it is in fact one of the most complicated. Given a bachelor's hood, it is almost impossible to predict what the corresponding master's hood will be. Some (*e.g.* AgrB) change their black shell for a white one; others (*e.g.* BDentSc) change their lining colour instead; others add or remove a coloured binding; still others use a combination of two or more of these methods. There is a rudimentary system of faculty colours, but it is not consistent: gold is associated with Commerce, but appears in the lining of the BDentTech hood; the DEd hood is basically a Music hood. There can also be confusion between yellow (MPhil, PhD) and gold (business and commerce). Some degrees, especially the BSc, have further letters in brackets – as BSc(Surv), BSc(Pharm). These all wear the same hood as the BSc, unless otherwise noted. Previous editions have stated that doctors wear a bonnet; this is not so, and if a hat is desired, they wear the standard black square.

UNDERGRADUATES

Gown:

Scholars: as for bachelors.

All others: a black stuff gown of the same pattern as Oxford commoners, but of knee-length [u8]. The 'streamers', which are wider and reach only to the elbow, are decorated with three rows of small black tassels. There are also three rows of tassels under each armhole.

Hat: a black cloth square cap. Scholars wear a velvet one, which they continue to do after graduation.

UNDERGRADUATE CERTIFICATES AND DIPLOMAS

Gown: as for undergraduates.

Epitoge: a blue epitoge.

Hat: a black cloth square cap.

BACHELORS

Gown: a black stuff gown of basic BA pattern, but with smaller sleeves [b10].

Hood: hoods of the Dublin full shape [f2]. All hoods are bound with the lining colour for 1″, unless a separate colour is specified for the binding.

AgrB: black, lined and bound brown.
Agr(Forest)B: black, lined brown, bound 1″ green.
BA: black, half lined and bound fur; the neckband is black bound white silk.
BAI: black, lined and bound green.
[BAI(Elect); BAI(Mech): black, lined green, bound 1″ orange.]
BAO: black, lined and bound olive green.
BAS: *same as MusB.*
BArchSc: dark green, half-lined and bound fur.
BBS: black, lined and bound gold.
BCh: black, lined white bound 1″ dark blue.
BCom: *same as BBS.*
BD: black, lined and bound black.
BDentSc: myrtle green, lined black watered, bound 1″ crimson.
BDentTech: myrtle green, lined gold, bound 1″ crimson.
BEd: dark blue, lined and bound dark blue.
[BLitt: black, lined dark blue, bound 1″ white.]
BMusEd, BMusPerf: light blue, lined and bound rose.
BMS: *same as BSc.*
BNS: *same as BSc.*
BTS: *same as MusB.*
BSc: myrtle green, lined and bound black.
BSc(Bus & Inf Tech): green, lined and bound gold.
BSc(Ing): black, lined white bound 1″ green.
BSS: black, lined gold bound 1″ white.
BStSu: black, lined and bound yellow.
BTh: black, lined and bound 1″ black, the cowl bordered inside 1″ purple set 1″ in.
BTS: light blue, half-lined and bound fur.
BVS: *same as BSc.*
LL.B: black, lined and bound white.
MB: black, lined and bound 1″ crimson.
[MusB: light blue, half-lined and bound fur.]
MVB: black, lined maroon, bound 1″ olive green.
ScBTech: green, lined black, bound 1″ orange.

Hat: a black cloth square cap.

POSTGRADUATE CERTIFICATES AND DIPLOMAS

Gown: as for undergraduates.
Epitoge: a blue and black epitoge.
Hat: a black cloth square cap.

MASTERS including MASTERS OF PHILOSOPHY

Gown: a black stuff gown of the Dublin MA pattern [m3].

Hood: hoods of the Dublin full shape [f2].

AgrM: white, lined and bound brown.
Agr(Forest)M: white, lined brown, bound 1″ green.
LL.M: black, lined white, bound 1″ pink.
MA: black, lined and bound dark blue.
MAI: white, lined and bound dark green.
MAO: black, lined and bound purple.
MBA: *same as MComm.*
MCh: crimson, lined white, bound 1″ dark blue .
MComm: white, lined and bound gold.
MDentSc, MDentCh: myrtle green, lined pale blue, bound 1″ crimson.
MEd: white, lined dark blue, bound 1″ white.
MLitt: white, lined and bound dark blue.
MPhil: white, lined and bound yellow.
MSc: white, lined and bound myrtle green.
MSc(Econ), MSc(Mgmt): gold lined and bound white.
MSt: *same as MPhil.*
MSW: black,, lined gold, bound 1″ dark blue.
MTh: purple, lined purple, the cowl bordered inside 1″ black set 1″ in.
MVM: white, lined and bound maroon.

Hat: a black cloth square cap.

ALL DOCTORS

Undress gown: as for masters.

Dress robe: except where noted below, a scarlet robe of the Oxford pattern [d2], with facings and sleeves covered as follows:

DD: black velvet.
LL.D: pink.
MD: crimson.
LittD: dark blue.
ScD: myrtle green.
PhD: yellow.
MusD: robe of cream brocade, facings and sleeves of rose.
DClinPsy: robe of red, facings and sleeves of light green.
DEd: robe of light blue, facings and sleeves of rose.
DChDent: robe of scarlet, facings and sleeves of pale blue.

Hood: hoods of the Dublin full shape [f2], coloured, lined and bound as follows:

DD: scarlet, lined and bound black velvet.
LL.D: scarlet, lined and bound pink.
MD: scarlet, lined and bound crimson.
LittD: scarlet, lined and bound dark blue.
ScD: scarlet, lined and bound myrtle green.

PhD: scarlet, lined and bound yellow.
MusD: cream brocade, lined and bound rose.
DClinPsy: red, lined and bound light green.
DEd: light blue, lined rose, bound 1″ dark blue.
DChDent: scarlet, lined pale blue, bound myrtle green.

Hat: a black cloth square cap.

NOTES

1. The following hoods are given in various sources:

The 1911 *Encylopædia Britannica*:
DD: scarlet, lined black.
BD: black, unlined.
LL.D: scarlet lined pink.
LL.B: black, bordered white.
MD: scarlet, lined scarlet.
MB: black, lined fur.
MA: black, lined blue.
BA: black, lined fur.
MusD: crimson, lined white.
MusB: blue, lined fur.
LittD: scarlet, lined white.
ScD: scarlet, lined blue.
(Surgery and Engineering degrees not listed)

The 1903 *Boys' Own Paper* chart:
DD: scarlet, lined black.
BD: black, lined black.
LL.D: scarlet, lined pink.
LL.B: black, lined white.
MD: scarlet, lined pink.
MB: black, lined crimson bound fur.
MCh: crimson, lined white, bound blue.
BCh: crimson, lined black, bound blue.
MA: black, lined blue.
BA: black, lined fur.
MusD: white figured silk, lined crimson satin.
MusB: blue, lined fur.
BAI: black, lined green.
MAI: white, lined green.
ScD: black, lined myrtle green.
LittD: scarlet, lined blue.

The 1888 *Girls' Own Paper* article:
DD: scarlet, lined black.
BD: black, lined 'glossy' black.
LL.D: scarlet, lined pink.
LL.B: black, lined white.
MD: scarlet, lined crimson.
MB: black, lined crimson.
MS: crimson, lined white 'edged' blue.
BS: crimson, lined black 'edged' blue.
MA: black, lined dark blue.
BA: *not listed.*
MusD: white figured silk, lined crimson.
MusB: blue, edged fur.
BE: green, lined black (*i.e.*, BEng).
ME: green, lined white (*i.e.*, MEng).
(Degrees in Letters and in Science not listed)

Wood's *Ecclesiastical and Academical Colours*, 1875:
DD: scarlet, lined black.
BD: black, lined black.
LL.D: scarlet, lined pink.
LL.B: black, lined white.
MD: scarlet, lined crimson.
MB: black, lined crimson.
MS: crimson, lined white bound blue.
BS: crimson, lined black bound blue.
MA: black, lined dark blue.
BA: black, 'trimmed' fur.
MusD: crimson, lined white.
MusB: blue, 'trimmed' fur.
BEng: green, lined black.
MEng: green, lined white.
(Degrees in Letters and in Science not listed)

DUBLIN CITY UNIVERSITY
1989

Dublin City University (DCU) is situated between Glasnevin, Ballymun, and Whitehall on the Northside of Dublin. Created as the National Institute for Higher Education, Dublin, in 1975, on an ad-hoc basis, it enrolled its first students in 1980. It was intended at this stage that the institution become the unified structure under which the colleges of what later became Dublin Institute of Technology would unite, but by 1978 it became apparent that this would not be the case and instead an independent institution developed with a distinct identity and mission. The early focus of the institution was, in particular, on science and technology, although it has also had, and has, a large business school. It has recently developed a presence also in the performing arts and in the humanities. It was elevated by statute to university status (along with the University of Limerick) in 1989.

The robes rely on faculty colours, and gold braid as the diagnostic feature.

Faculty colours

Business Studies: drab.
Communications and Human Studies: white.
Computing and Maths: grey.
Distance Education: russet brown.
Education: light blue.
Engineering: orange.
Science: jade green.

UNDERGRADUATES

none specified

UNDERGRADUATE CERTIFICATES AND DIPLOMAS

Gown: as for bachelors.
Epitoge: an epitoge of the faculty colour, with two bars of dark blue, 1″ wide, with a narrow gold edging.
Hat: a black cloth square cap.

BACHELORS

Gown: a black stuff gown of basic pattern [b1].
Hood: a blue hood of the CNAA shape [a1], lined and bound on the cowl 1½″ faculty colour, and the cape bound ⅜″ gold braid.
Hat: a black cloth square cap.

POSTGRADUATE CERTIFICATES AND DIPLOMAS

Gown: as for bachelors.

Epitoge: an epitoge of faculty colour, with bars of dark blue, 1″ wide, with narrow gold edging:
Certificates: three bars
Diplomas: four bars.

Hat: a black cloth square cap.

MASTERS including MASTERS OF PHILOSOPHY

Gown: a black stuff gown of the Oxford MA pattern [m1].

Hood: of the CNAA shape [a1], in dark blue, lined and bound on the cowl 2½″ faculty colour, and the cape bound ⅜″ gold braid.

Hat: a black cloth square cap.

DOCTORS OF PHILOSOPHY and TAUGHT AND PROFESSIONAL DOCTORS

Undress gown: *none specified*

Dress robe: of the Oxford pattern [d2], in red, with facings and sleeves of dark blue. The facings are edged ⅜″ gold braid.

Hood: of the CNAA shape [a1], in dark blue, lined and bound on the cowl edge 4″ gold, and the cape bound ⅜″ gold braid.

Hat: in full dress, a black cloth bonnet with gold cords and tassels.

HIGHER DOCTORS

Undress gown: *none specified*

Dress robe: of the Oxford pattern [d2], in red, with facings and sleeves of dark blue. The facings are edged ⅜″ gold braid, and there is ⅜″ gold braid set on the sleeves 4″ from the cuff edge.

Hood: of the CNAA shape [a1], in dark blue, lined and bound on the cowl edge 4″ red, and the cape bound ⅜″ gold braid.

Hat: in full dress, a black cloth bonnet with gold cords and tassels.

DUBLIN INSTITUTE OF TECHNOLOGY
1998

The Dublin Institute of Technology was established as an autonomous institution under the DIT Act in 1992, but its origins go back to 1887 and the establishment of technical education in Ireland. It was formed by merging six colleges of higher education formerly under the City of Dublin Vocational Educational Committee. These were:

College of Technology, Kevin Street - founded in 1887
College of Music, Chatham Row - founded in 1890
College of Commerce, Rathmines - founded 1901
College of Marketing and Design, Mountjoy Square - founded in 1905
College of Technology, Bolton Streeet - founded in 1911
College of Catering, Cathal Brugha Street - founded in 1941

From 1975 until 1998, when it gained its own degree-awarding powers, the Institute awarded University of Dublin degrees. However, Dublin degrees appear to have been awarded until well after 2000. In the second edition, Shaw gave a part specification, and noted that DIT was revising its scheme of dress. The revised version follows.

Faculty colours

Applied Arts: white.
Built Environment: silver grey.
Business: drab.
Engineering: orange.
Science: gold.
Tourism and Food: magenta.

UNDERGRADUATES
none specified

UNDERGRADUATE CERTIFICATES AND DIPLOMAS

Gown: as for bachelors.
Epitoge: an epitoge of the faculty colour with 1″ stripes of blue at each end:
Certificates: two stripes.
Diplomas: three stripes.
Hat: a black cloth square cap.

FOUNDATION DEGREES
not awarded

BACHELORS

Gown: a black stuff gown of basic pattern [b1].
Hood: a hood in the faculty colour of the CNAA shape [a1], lined blue.
Hat: a black cloth square cap.

POSTGRADUATE CERTIFICATES AND DIPLOMAS

Gown: as for bachelors.

Hood: an epitoge of the faculty colour, with four 1″ stripes of blue at each end.

Hat: a black cloth square cap.

FIRST-DEGREE MASTERS

not awarded

MASTERS including MASTERS OF PHILOSOPHY

Gown: a black stuff gown of the basic pattern [m10].

Hood: a blue hood of the Dublin full shape [f2], lined and bound in the faculty colour.

MPhil: lined and bound in the faculty colour, with 1″ maroon set 1″ in inside the cowl and the neckband faced maroon.

Hat: a black cloth square cap.

ALL DOCTORS

Undress gown: *none specified*

Dress robe: a maroon robe of the Oxford pattern [d2], with facings of violet brocade, with 1″ gold on the outer edges. For honorary doctors, the gold edging is metallic oak-leaf braid; for PhD is it is gold silk. The sleeves are bordered 1″ inside with violet brocade.

Hood: a red hood of the Irish full shape [f2], lined and bound 1″ violet brocade.

Hat: in full dress, a black velvet bonnet with gold cords and tassels.

UNIVERSITY OF DUNDEE
1967

The University of Dundee is the successor of a number of academic institutions related to the University of St Andrews, dating back to 1881: University College, the Medical School, the Dental School and Dundee School of Economics, which (in 1953) became Queen's College, Dundee. Queen's College received its own Royal Charter in 1967 and became the University of Dundee.

The system follows that of several other universities, using a black hood lined with the faculty colour for masters, with a fur border for bachelors. Doctors wear a robe and hood of Stewart blue, the use of which reflects fact that the Virgin Mary is the patron of the City of Dundee. Although there is a faculty colour scheme, the number of exceptions makes it easier to list the degrees individually. Unlike Newcastle, which was part of Durham and formed its new scheme round the robes for the Durham degrees it awarded, the robes for the St Andrews degrees awarded at Dundee were not transferred to the new university, but an entirely new scheme was drawn up.

UNDERGRADUATES

Gown: a scarlet stuff gown, with split sleeves. The yoke, facings, and flap collar are covered with serge or flannel of Stewart blue.

Hat: a black cloth square cap.

UNDERGRADUATE CERTIFICATES AND DIPLOMAS

Gown: as for graduates.

Hood: a black hood of the Dundee shape [a6], lined Stewart blue and tipped black.

Hat: a black cloth square cap.

BACHELORS

Gown: a black stuff gown of Scottish master's pattern [m12].

Hood: a black silk hood of the Dundee shape [a6], in black silk, lined with the degree colour, and the cowl bound fur.

BA: tartan green.
BAcc: forget-me-not blue.
[BAdmin: forget-me-not blue.]
BArch: heliotrope.
BDS: ruby.
BDes: reseda green.
BEd: tuscan yellow.
BEng: powder blue.
BFin: forget-me-not blue.
LL.B: old gold.
MB,ChB: cherry.

BMedSc: clover.
BMid: clover.
BN: clover.
[BPhil: eggshell blue.]
BSc: buttercup.
BSc(Arch): gault grey.
[BSc(Eng): powder blue.]
BSc (environmental science): gault grey.

Hat: a black cloth square cap.

POSTGRADUATE CERTIFICATES AND DIPLOMAS

As for undergraduate certificates and diplomas.

FIRST-DEGREE MASTERS

Gown: as for bachelors.

Hood: a black silk hood of the Dundee shape [a6], lined as follows:
MA: tartan green.
MEng; MRes: powder blue.
MRes (law and accountancy): forget-me-not blue, the cowl bound fur.
MSci (science and engineering): buttercup.

Hat: a black cloth square cap.

MASTERS including MASTERS OF PHILOSOPHY

Gown: as for bachelors.

Hood: a black silk hood of the Dundee shape, [a6], lined with the degree colour.
MAcc: forget-me-not blue.
MBA: stone white.
[ChM: imperial purple.]
MChOrth: clover.
MDS, MDSc: ruby.
MDes: verdigris.
MEd: tuscan yellow.
MFA: verdigris.
LL.M: old gold.
MMEd: tuscan yellow.
MMedSc: clover.
MPhil: eggshell blue.
MPH: begonia (a shade of coral).
MRes: powder blue.
MSc: buttercup.
MSc (enviromental): gault grey.
MSc (medicine): clover.
MSSc: clover.
MSW: jade green.

Hat: a black cloth square cap.

DOCTORS OF PHILOSOPHY

Undress gown: as for masters.
Dress robe: as for masters, with facings of Stewart blue.
Hood: a Stewart blue silk hood of the Dundee shape [a6] lined eggshell blue.
Hats: in undress, a black cloth square cap; in full dress, a black cloth square cap, with an eggshell blue tassel.

HIGHER DOCTORS

Undress gown: as for masters.
Dress robe: a Stewart blue silk robe of the Oxford pattern [d2], with facings and sleeve cuffs of the same colour as the lining of the hood.
Hood: a Stewart blue silk hood of the Dundee shape [a6], lined with the degree colour:
DDS: ruby.
LL.D: old gold.
DLitt: smalt blue.
MD: cherry.
DSc: buttercup.
DScEng: powder blue.
DSc (environmental): gault grey.
Hats: in undress, a black cloth square cap; in full dress, a black velvet bonnet with degree-colour cords and tassels.

NOTES

1. Until 1991, the PhD had no dress robe, but wore the black undress gown.

UNIVERSITY OF DURHAM
1832

The University of Durham was founded by the Dean and Chapter of Durham in 1832, and gained the right to award degrees in 1837. It currently consists of sixteen colleges. In 1851, the College of Medicine in Newcastle became a college of Durham, and in 1871 was joined by the Durham College of Science, later named Armstrong College, Newcastle. In 1963, they became independent as the University of Newcastle-upon-Tyne, and the robes for the degrees in Laws, Medicine, Surgery, Dentistry, and Architecture, which had only ever been awarded through the Newcastle Division, were transferred to Newcastle's scheme. The BHy, which was awarded at Newcastle, was defunct by 1952, and is thus included here, as it was technically a Durham degree. The DHy is listed here and also under Newcastle, as it was awarded there after the split.

The scheme of academic dress is based heavily on Oxford, but with the use of 'palatinate purple' as a distinguishing mark. This colour is in fact a mauve colour, but which can vary from almost silver-grey to lilac, depending on the dye used. It is of interest as being the first scheme to be designed, and not to have evolved, as the Oxford, Cambridge, and Dublin schemes did. The scheme is a restricted-colour one, using black, white, mauve, and scarlet, together with fur, and the addition of old gold. It is starting to break down as more new degree-specific hoods are required.

UNDERGRADUATES

Gown: a black stuff gown with bell sleeves, modified as follows; it is worn mid-calf length:

Arts and Commerce: the sleeve is left open for the lower part of the forearm seam [u4].

Science: as Arts, but with a 1″ wide black velvet strip from the top of the slit to the shoulder.

Scholars: the sleeve is not slit or decorated [u2].

Theology: a black stuff gown with long pointed sleeves [b8].

Two of the colleges have their own gowns:

St Chad's: as for the Arts gown, but there is a green cord and button on each sleeve, to join the slit.

St Hild and St Bede: the same as the Oxford commoners' gown [u5]. This gown has never had official sanction.

Hat: a black cloth square cap.

UNDERGRADUATE CERTIFICATES AND DIPLOMAS

none specified (but see end of section)

FOUNDATION DEGREES

not awarded

BACHELORS

Gown:

BD: the MA gown.

[BHy: a black gown with a flap collar [d4], and with flaps over the armholes. There are four vertical rows of black braid from the shoulder to the base of the flap, and two concentric squares of black Durham bachelors' braid at the foot of each sleeve.]

BMus: the Oxford BMus gown [d4] with Oxford gimp.

All others: a black stuff gown with open sleeves, with the forearm seam left open for the lower ten inches, and held together at the hem by a black cord and button [b6].

Hood:

BA: a black stuff hood of full shape [f6], half-lined and bound fur.

[BAEcon and BCom: a black hood of Durham BSc full shape [f7], lined cerise silk, and the cape bound fur.]

[BArch: a black hood of full shape [f7], the cowl bordered 4″ sky blue, and the cape bound fur.]

[BCL: a palatinate purple silk hood of full shape [f7], unlined, and bound 1″ fur on all edges. *now used for MJur*]

BChem: a black stuff hood of full shape [f7], lined palatinate purple silk, the cowl bound fur, and the cape bound 1″ palatinate purple.

BD: a black silk hood of the Durham doctors' shape [f4], lined black silk.

BEd: a black stuff hood of full shape [f7], the cowl bordered inside 3″ palatinate purple silk, and the cape bound fur.

BEng: a black silk hood of full shape [f7], lined scarlet silk, the cowl bordered inside 3″ palatinate purple silk, and the cape bound fur.

[BHy: a black silk hood of full shape [f7], the cowl bound fur and bordered inside 3″ palatinate purple silk and 1″ scarlet silk, the cape not bound.]

[BLitt: an old gold satin hood of full shape [f7], unlined, and the cape bound fur.]

LL.B: a palatinate purple silk hood of full shape [f7], lined maroon silk, and the cape bound fur. *(see Note 1)*

[BMus: a palatinate purple silk hood of Oxford simple shape [s1], unlined, and the cowl edge bound with 1″ white silk brocade.]

BPhil: a black stuff hood of full shape [f7], the cowl bordered inside 4″ white silk, and the cape bound fur.

BPhys: as BChem, but the cape is bound dark purple instead of palatinate.

BSc: a palatinate purple silk hood of full shape [f7], bound on all edges with fur, and with 1″ scarlet cloth laid next the fur.

Hat: a black cloth square cap.

POSTGRADUATE CERTIFICATES AND DIPLOMAS

Gown: as BA.

Hood: a black stuff hood of Oxford simple shape [s1], lined as follows:

PGCE: lined black, the cowl bordered inside ½″ palatinate purple silk [s1].

PGDip: as PGCE, but with a second ½″ band of palatinate purple silk set 1″ away from the first.

Hat: a black cloth square cap.

FIRST-DEGREE MASTERS

Gown: as BA.

Hood: a black silk hood of Oxford simple shape [s1], lined and bound as follows:

MBus: *hood not yet decided*

MChem: lined palatinate purple silk, the cowl bound white fur, and bound 1″ palatinate purple silk on the opposite edge.

MEng: lined scarlet silk, the cowl bound ½″ palatinate purple silk.

MMath: lined cerise silk, and the cowl bound 1″ fur.

MMktg: *hood not yet decided*

MPhys: lined palatinate purple silk, the cowl bound white fur, and bound 1″ dark purple silk on the opposite edge.

MSci: lined palatinate purple silk, bound fur on the cowl, and bound 1″ scarlet silk on the opposite edge.

Hat: a black cloth square cap.

MASTERS

Gown:

MMus: a flap-collar gown [d4], with black Oxford gimp along the facings, round the collar and armholes, and a row from below the armhole to the foot of the sleeve in the centre of the sleeve.

All others: the Oxford MA gown [m1], but with a black cord and button on the yoke.

Hood:

MA: a black silk hood of Oxford simple shape [s1], lined and bound ¼″ palatinate purple silk.

[MAEcon and MCom: a black silk hood of Oxford simple shape [s1], lined and bound ¼″ cerise silk.]

MBA: a black silk hood of full shape [f7], lined palatinate purple silk, the cowl bordered inside 2½″ white silk, and bound ½″ scarlet silk on all edges.

MEd: a black silk hood of full shape [f7], lined white silk, and bound 1″ palatinate purple silk on all edges.

MEng(until 1996): a black silk hood of full shape [f7], lined palatinate purple silk, the cowl bordered inside 3½″ scarlet silk.

MEng: (since 1996): a black silk hood of Oxford simple shape [s1], lined scarlet, and bordered palatinate purple.

MJur: a palatinate purple silk hood of full shape [f7], unlined, and bound 1″ fur on all edges (*the former BCL hood*).

MLitt: a black silk hood of full shape [f7], lined old gold satin.

LL.M: a black silk hood of full shape [f7], lined palatinate purple silk, and bound ½″ white silk on all edges. *See Note 1.*

MMus: a black silk hood of full shape [f7], lined white silk brocade, and bound 1″ palatinate purple silk on all edges.

MPhil: a black silk hood of full shape [f7], lined scarlet silk, and bound ½″ palatinate purple silk on all edges.

MProfS: *not yet decided*

MRes: a palatinate purple silk hood of full shape [f7], lined and bound on all edges ¼″ white silk.

MSc: a black silk hood of full shape [f7], lined palatinate purple silk, and bound ½″ scarlet silk on all edges.

MSW: a palatinate purple silk hood of Oxford simple shape [s1], lined palatinate purple, and the cowl bound ½″ dark purple silk.

MTheol: a black silk hood of full shape [f7], lined black silk, and bound 1″ palatinate purple silk on all edges.

MTP: *not yet decided*

Hat: a black cloth square cap.

DOCTORS

Undress Gown:

DD: as for MA, with the addition of a black silk scarf.

PhD: as for MA, the cord and button on the yoke are palatinate purple.

DMus: the BMus gown, but with a 13″ slit in the back of the skirt.

[DHy: a black stuff gown with a flap collar [d4]; the corners of the collar are cut across at 45 degrees. There is Durham doctors' pattern braid along the facings, round the collar, round the armholes up to the sleeve head, and across the base of the sleeves.]

All others: as for MA.

Dress robe: a scarlet cloth robe of Oxford pattern [d2]. The sleeves and facings are covered as follows:

DBA: white silk, the facings bound 1″ palatinate purple silk and 1″ palatinate purple silk on the sleeves at the top of the white silk.

DCL: white silk.

EdD: faced with scarlet silk, bound on the inside edge with palatinate purple silk one inch wide. From the bottom edge, the sleeves are faced 4″ palatinate purple silk and 4″ white silk.

DD: palatinate purple silk.

[DHy: the lower one-third palatinate purple silk, the upper two-thirds scarlet silk, with 1″ white silk between.]

DLitt: old gold satin.

MD: palatinate purple cloth. *see Note 1*

DMin: faced with scarlet silk, edged with one inch palatinate purple silk. From bottom edge, the sleeves are faced with 8″ palatinate purple silk, edged with 1″ black silk.

PhD: scarlet silk, the facings bound 1″ palatinate purple, and 1″ palatinate purple silk on the sleeves at the top of the scarlet silk.

DSc: scarlet silk.
DMus: a white brocade robe with palatinate purple sleeves and facings.

Hood: all doctors' hoods are full shape [f4], coloured and lined as follows:
DBA: scarlet cloth lined white silk, bound 1″ palatinate purple silk on all edges.
DCL: scarlet cloth lined white silk.
EdD: scarlet cloth lined white silk, the cowl bordered 3″ palatinate purple silk.
DD: scarlet cloth lined palatinate purple silk.
[DHy: scarlet cloth lined scarlet silk, the cowl bordered 3″ palatinate purple silk and 1″ white silk.]
DLitt: scarlet cloth lined old gold satin.
MD: [to be decided] *see Note 1*
DMin: scarlet cloth lined palatinate purple silk, bound 1″ black silk on all edges.
DMus: white silk brocade lined palatinate purple silk.
PhD: scarlet cloth lined scarlet silk, bound on all edges 1″ palatinate purple silk.
DSc: palatinate purple cloth lined scarlet silk.

Hat: in undress, a black cloth square cap; in full dress, a black velvet John Knox cap with a black tuft.

FORMER UNDERGRADUATE DIPLOMAS

Licence in Theology (LTh; 1840-1946)

Gown: a black stuff gown of London BA pattern [b4], but with the sleeves gathered with a black 1″ velvet ribbon and black velvet button.

Hood: a black stuff hood, the cowl bordered inside 4″ and the cape bound 1″ black velvet. The cowl is also bound ¼″ palatinate purple silk. The shape is as the BA hood [f6], but with the liripipe cut off.

Associate in Theology (ATh; first awarded 1901; date of withdrawal unknown)

Gown: a black gown of the Oxford BA pattern [b8].

Hood: a black stuff hood of the same shape as the LTh, and bound on all edges ¼″ palatinate purple silk [so far as can be ascertained].

Associate in Science (ASc; first awarded 1879; date of withdrawal unknown)

Gown: as LTh.

Hood: a black stuff hood of the same shape as the LTh, the cowl bordered inside 4″ black velvet and bound ¼″ palatinate purple silk [so far as can be ascertained].

Licence in Sanitary Science (LSSc; from 1887; date of withdrawal unknown)

Gown: the BHy gown.

Hood: a black stuff hood of the same shape as the LTh. The cowl was bordered inside 1″ scarlet silk, and 2″ black velvet, and bound ¼″ palatinate purple silk [so far as can be ascertained].

There were also diplomas of Associate in Physical Science (APhysSc, first awarded 1874); Licentiate in Medicine (LM, first awarded 1856); Licentiate in Surgery (LS, first awarded 1872); and Diploma in Public Health (DPH, first awarded 1894). These appear not to have had any distinctive robes. Apart from the LTh, it is not clear when any of the other diplomas ceased to be awarded.

NOTES

1. The degrees of LL.B, LL.M, and MD listed here have been introduced since the split with Newcastle, which keeps the original robes for these degrees.
2. The LTh could be gained at a number of Anglican theological colleges, without residence in Durham. These included Queen's College, Birmingham; St John's College, Highbury (London College of Divinity); St Boniface College, Warminster.
3. DDs wear a black silk scarf with both dress robe and undress gown.

UNIVERSITY OF EAST ANGLIA, NORWICH
1963

The University of East Anglia (UEA) was one of the nine new foundations of the early 1960s, although discussions about founding a university in Norwich go back to the nineteenth century. It was originally organized on an interdisciplinary School system, rather than the traditional departmental one, although this has weakened in recent years.

The robes were designed by Cecil Beaton, and were designed to look well together at Congregation, but are not very suitable for everyday wear. Beaton was attempting to be innovative, but in fact appears to have taken his inspiration from seventeenth-century prints of Oxford academic dress. The use of dark blue gowns may have been influenced by the undergraduate gown of Gonville and Caius College in Cambridge, which is the Norfolk college. The colour of the facing of the hoods is determined by the degree title, not by the subject, School, or Faculty.

Degree colours

Arts and Letters: coral pink (FdA, BA, MA, LittD).
Business Administration: magenta (MBA) (same as Laws).
Chemistry: spectrum green (was yellow-gold 2005-2009) (MChem).
Civil Law: mauve (DCL).
Clinical Education: purple (MClinEd).
Clinical Psychology: pale blue (ClinPsyD).
Computer Science: spectrum green (MCmpSc).
Education: sky blue (BEd, MEd, EdD).
PGCE: beryl blue.
[BPhil(teaching): petrol blue.]
Engineering: saffron (BEng, MEng).
Laws: magenta (LL.B, LL.M, LL.D).
Mathematics: spectrum green (MMath).
Medicine: light grey (MB,BS, MS, MD).
Music: pale ('Beaton') pink. (MMus, MusD).
Natural Sciences: spectrum green (MNatSc).
Pharmacy: yellow-gold (MPharm).
Philosophy: scarlet (MPhil, PhD, [BPhil]).
[Physics: spectrum green (MPhys).]
Research: maroon (MRes).
Science: spectrum green (FdSc, BSc, MSc, ScD).
Social Work: pastel green (MSW, DSW).
All diplomas, etc: white.

UNDERGRADUATES

Gown: a dark blue sleeveless cape, of knee-length, with slits for the arms [u7]. The front opening is edged black.

Hat: a black skull-cap with upstanding brim.

UNDERGRADUATE-LEVEL CERTIFICATES AND DIPLOMAS

Gown: the BA gown.

Hood: a dark blue hood of the UEA shape [a4], the cowl bordered outside 2″ white.

Hat: a black cloth square cap.

FOUNDATION DEGREES

Gown: the BA gown.

Hood: a dark blue hood of UEA shape [a4], the cowl bordered outside 2″ of the degree colour.

Hat: a black cloth square cap.

BACHELORS

Gown: a dark blue gown of basic pattern [b1]. The yoke is semicircular, and the gown is gathered into it in flat pleats.

Hood: a dark blue hood of UEA shape [a4], the cowl bordered outside 6″ of the degree colour.

Hat: a black cloth square cap.

POSTGRADUATE CERTIFICATES AND DIPLOMAS

Gown: the MA gown.

Hood: a dark blue hood of UEA shape [a4], lined as follows:

PGCE: the cowl bordered outside 6″ beryl blue taffeta.

All others: the cowl bordered outside 6″ white taffeta.

Hat: a black cloth square cap.

FIRST-DEGREE MASTERS (MChem, MCompSc, MEng, MMath, MNatSc, MPharm, [MPhys])

Gown: the MA gown.

Hood: a dark blue hood of UEA shape [a4], the cowl bordered outside 6″ of the degree colour.

Hat: a black cloth square cap.

MASTERS (including MPhil)

Gown: a dark blue gown of the Cambridge MA pattern [m2], but with the same style of yoke as the bachelors.

Hood: a dark blue hood of UEA shape [a4], covered outside with taffeta of the degree colour, arranged in four folds.

Hat: a black cloth square cap.

DOCTORS OF PHILOSOPHY and TAUGHT AND PROFESSIONAL DOCTORS (ClinPsyD, EdD, MD, DSW)

Undress gown: *none specified*

Dress robe: the MA gown, with scarlet facings.

Hood: a dark blue hood of UEA shape [a4], covered outside with taffeta of the degree colour, arranged in four folds.

Hat: in full dress, a black velvet bonnet, with gold cords and tassels.

HIGHER DOCTORS

Undress gown: *none specified*

Dress robe: a dark blue robe, with loose-fitting coat-style sleeves. The sleeves and facings are of the degree colour.

Hood: a dark blue hood of Dublin shape [f2], lined and bound for 1″ with the degree colour.

Hat: in full dress, a black velvet bonnet, with gold cords and tassels.

NOTES

1. The higher doctors' hoods were originally made in the UEA shape, with the outside 'draped' with degree colour. They had no neckband, but were attached to the shoulders of the robe. It is not clear when (or why) the change to the Dublin shape was made: the published regulations still do not notice this change.
2. The original PhD hood likewise had no neckband, and was attached to the robe facings; the change was made in 1978.
3. The original masters' hat was replaced by the square cap by 1979; the bachelors' hat was replaced by the square in 1979.
4. The MSW used the MA hood from its inception in the mid-1980s until 2005.
5. The BPhil was a one-year postgraduate degree in the School of Social Sciences; only two were ever awarded, and it has long been defunct.
6. The BPhil(Tchg) was awarded from the mid-1980s to 1992.
7. Postgraduate diplomas and certificates other than PGCE were originally allowed merely the BA gown, without hood or hat. In 2005, they were allowed to wear the same robes as the PGCE, but since 2008, have had their own hood, bordered white.
8. Undergraduate diplomas and certificates were originally allowed merely the undergraduate gown, without hood or hat. In 2008, they were allowed to wear the BA gown, with their own hood, bordered white.
9. The Regulations list the rather oddly titled EdMPhil, which is awarded to EdD candidates who fail to reach the required standard. It has never been awarded, and it is unclear what robes would be used.

UNIVERSITY OF EAST LONDON
1992

The University of East London can trace its roots to the foundation in 1898 of the West Ham Technical Institute. In 1970 the North East London Polytechnic was formed from a merger of higher education colleges, including the West Ham Technical Institute in Stratford, and South East Essex Technical College in Barking. In 1989 the Polytechnic, became the Polytechnic of East London, and was granted university status in 1992. The original Victorian buildings, including University House, the former municipal library, and the Passmore Edwards Museum, now form the heart of the Stratford campus. A second campus was formally opened on the waterfront of the Royal Albert Dock by the new Mayor of London on his very first day in office in 2000. It was London's first new university campus for over half a century.

All hoods except the undergraduate certificate hood are lined with silk of chilli red, damasked with the University's emblem.

UNDERGRADUATES
none specified

UNDERGRADUATE CERTIFICATES AND DIPLOMAS
Gown: as for bachelors.
Hood: a dark blue hood of the CNAA shape [a1], lined plain chilli red silk.
Hat: a black cloth square cap.

FOUNDATION DEGREES
not awarded

BACHELORS
Gown: a dark blue stuff gown of basic pattern [b1].
Hood: a dark blue hood of the Cambridge shape [f1], the cowl bordered inside 4″ chilli red damask.
Hat: a dark blue cloth square cap.

POSTGRADUATE CERTIFICATES AND DIPLOMAS
Gown: as for bachelors.
Hood: a dark blue hood of the CNAA shape [a1], lined and bound chilli red.
Hat: a dark blue cloth square cap.

FIRST-DEGREE MASTERS
not awarded

MASTERS including MASTERS OF PHILOSOPHY

Gown: a dark blue stuff gown of basic pattern [m10].

Hood: a dark blue hood of the Cambridge shape [f1], lined and bound ¼″ chilli red damask.

Hat: a black cloth square cap.

DOCTORS OF PHILOSOPHY and TAUGHT AND PROFESSIONAL DOCTORS

Undress gown: *none specified*

Dress robe: a royal blue panama robe of the Cambridge pattern [d1], with facings and sleeve linings of chilli red damask.

Hood: a dark blue hood of the Cambridge shape [f1], lined and bound 1″ chilli red damask.

Hat: in full dress, a royal blue bonnet with chilli red cords and tassels.

HIGHER DOCTORS

Undress gown: *none specified*

Dress robe: as for PhD, but the facings have 1″ silver lace on the outer edges. There is a silver cord and button on each sleeve.

Hood: as for PhD, but the cowl is bordered inside 1″ silver lace.

Hat: in full dress, a dark blue bonnet chilli red cords and tassels.

EDGE HILL UNIVERSITY
2006

Edge Hill College was opened in 1885 and named after the district of Liverpool in which it was sited. It was the first non-denominational teacher training college for women in England. By 1892, Edge Hill was one of only two colleges in England combining teacher training and undergraduate academic programmes; it became a mixed college in 1959. The institution has since expanded rapidly; with further developments at Ormskirk and absorbing the former Sefton School of Health Studies. In 2005, Edge Hill was granted taught degree awarding powers, and in 2006 became Edge Hill University. Research degree awarding powers were granted in 2008; until then research degrees were awarded by the University of Lancaster.

UNDERGRADUATES
none specified

UNDERGRADUATE CERTIFICATES and DIPLOMAS; FOUNDATION DEGREES
Gown: a black stuff gown of the London BA pattern [b4].
Hood: a black hood of the CNAA shape [a1], lined grass green.
Hat: a black cloth square cap.

BACHELORS
Gown: a black stuff gown of London BA pattern [b4].
Hood: a black hood of the CNAA shape [a1], lined grass green, and the cowl bordered inside 1″ lilac.
Hat: a black cloth square cap.

POSTGRADUATE CERTIFICATES AND DIPLOMAS
Gown: a black stuff gown of London BA pattern [b4].
Hood: a black hood of the Cambridge shape [f1], lined lilac, and the cowl bordered inside 1″ grass green.
Hat: a black cloth square cap.

FIRST-DEGREE MASTERS
not awarded

MASTERS including MASTERS of PHILOSOPHY
Gown: a black stuff gown of basic pattern [m10].
MPhil: a black stuff gown of basic pattern [m10] with green facings.
Hood: a black hood of the Cambridge shape [f1], lined lilac, and the cowl bordered inside 1″ grass green. The cape is bordered outside 1″ pale gold. For honorary masters, the hood linings are of 'Lancashire Rose' pattern damask.

Hat: a black cloth square cap.

DOCTORS of PHILOSOPHY

Undress gown: *not specified.*

Dress robe: a purple panama robe of Oxford pattern [d2], with facings and 5″ cuffs of green.

Hood: a purple panama hood of Cambridge shape [f1], lined green, and the cowl bordered inside 1″ gold.

Hat: in full dress, a black cloth bonnet with purple cords and tassels.

HIGHER DOCTORS

Undress gown: *not specified*

Dress robe: a green panama robe of Oxford pattern [d2], with facings and 5″ cuffs of purple 'Lancashire Rose' pattern damask.

Hood: a green panama hood of Cambridge shape [f1], lined purple 'Lancashire Rose' pattern damask, and the cowl bordered inside 1″ gold.

Hat: in full dress, a black velvet bonnet with purple cords and tassels.

UNIVERSITY OF EDINBURGH
1582

The University's foundation is attributed to Bishop Robert Reid of St Magnus Cathedral, Kirkwall, who left the funds on his death in 1558 that ultimately provided the University's endowment. The University was formally established by a Royal Charter granted by James VI in 1582, becoming the fourth university in Scotland at a time when its more populous neighbour England had only two. In 2002, the University was re-organised from its nine faculties into three 'Colleges', and now comprises the Colleges of Humanities and Social Sciences (HSS), of Science and Engineering (CSE), and of Medicine and Veterinary Medicine (MVM). Within these Colleges are twenty-one Schools, which are of roughly equal sizes.

Although there is a logical system of faculty colours, there are so many hoods with variations that a full list has been given.

The Edinburgh College of Art degrees are validated by the University, but it has it own robes. These are listed separately, at the end of this entry.

UNDERGRADUATES

Gown: a scarlet stuff gown of the London pattern [u3].
Hat: a black cloth square cap.

UNDERGRADUATE CERTIFICATES AND DIPLOMAS

Gown: a black stuff gown of the Scottish MA pattern [m12].
Hood: a blue hood of the Edinburgh shape [s4], lined red, and bordered white.
Hat: a black cloth square cap.

BACHELORS

Gown: a black stuff gown of the Scottish MA pattern [m12].
Hood: a hood of the Edinburgh shape [s4], in black silk (except BMus), lined with the degree colour, and bound on the cowl with fur. Where a border is specified, it is inside the cowl, next to the fur binding.

BA: lined white.
BA(Div): lined white, bordered 1″ purple set 3″ in from the fur.
BA(RelSt): lined white, bordered 3″ purple.
BCom: lined pale primrose.
BD: lined purple.
[BDS: lined crimson, bordered 3″ ivory.]
BEd: lined pale blue.
BEng: lined green, bordered 3″ red.
LL.B: lined mid-blue.
MB,ChB: lined crimson.
BMedSc: lined crimson, bordered 3″ green.

BMus: a scarlet silk hood, lined white, and bound fur.
BNurs: lined white, bordered blue.
BSc: lined green.
BSc(SocSci): lined deep turquoise.
BSc(SocWk): lined mauve.
BSc(Vet): lined green.
BSc(Nurs): lined deep turquoise, bordered 2″ white.
BTech: divided lining, half green and half blue.
BVM&S: lined maroon, bordered 3″ golden yellow.

Hat: a black cloth square cap.

POSTGRADUATE CERTIFICATES AND DIPLOMAS

Gown: as for bachelors.

Hood: a hood of the Edinburgh simple shape, coloured and lined as follows:
PGDE, PGCI: a green hood, lined blue.
All others: a blue hood, lined white, bound red.

Hat: a black cloth square cap.

MASTERS including MASTERS OF PHILOSOPHY and FIRST DEGREE MASTERS

Gown: as for bachelors.

Hood: a hood of the Edinburgh shape [s4], in black silk (except ChM and MMus), lined with the degree colour. Where a border is specified, it is inside the cowl.
MA: lined white.
MA(Div): lined white, bordered 1″ purple set 3″ in from the edge.
MA(RelSt): lined white, bordered 3″ purple.
MArch: lined orange-brown.
MBA: lined pale primrose.
ChM: a black velvet hood, lined gold.
MChem: lined green, bordered 3″ white.
MChemPhys: lined green, bordered 3″ white.
MChinSt: lined white, bordered 3″ yellow.
MClinDent: lined white, bordered 3″ red.
MCouns: lined deep turquoise, bordered 3″ mauve.
MEarthSci: lined green, bordered 3″ white.
MEd: lined pale blue.
MEng: lined green, bordered 3″ red.
MInf: lined green, bordered 3″ white.
LL.M: lined mid-blue.
MLA: lined white, bordered 3″ green, with 1″ brown in the middle of the green.
MLitt: lined royal blue shot maize, bordered 3″ ivory.
MMus: a scarlet silk hood, lined white.
MPhil: lined silver, bordered 3″ royal blue shot brown.
MPhys: lined green, bordered 3″ white.

MSc: lined white, bordered 3″ green.
MSc(Soc): lined deep turquoise, bordered 3″ white.
MSW: lined mauve.
MTeach: lined white, bordered blue.
MTh: lined purple.
MVetSc: lined maroon, bordered 3″ green.

Hat: a black cloth square cap.

DOCTORS OF PHILOSOPHY and TAUGHT AND PROFESSIONAL DOCTORS

Undress gown: as for bachelors.

Dress robe: the undress gown, faced red.

Hood: a black hood of the Edinburgh shape [s4], lined as follows:
PhD: blue shot brown, bordered 3″ red.
DClinPsychol: silver grey bordered 3″ deep turquoise.
EdD: pale blue, bordered 3″ red.
DPsychol: grey.

Hat: in undress, a black cloth square cap; in full dress a black velvet John Knox cap.

HIGHER DOCTORS

Undress gown: as for bachelors.

Dress robe: a robe of the Cambridge pattern [d1], but with shorter sleeves. The robe is of scarlet cloth, with facings, sleeve linings, and yoke of scarlet silk. The yoke is edged with a scarlet cord, and there are four scarlet buttons along its lower edge.

Hood: a hood of the Edinburgh shape [s4], except DD, LL.D, MD, and DDS. The hoods for these degrees are the same shape, but also have an appended cape, converting it into a full shape [f8]. The cape is the same colour as the lining, with a black backing. The hoods are of black cloth (except DMus), lined as follows:
DDS: crimson, bordered 3″ ivory [f8].
DD: purple [f8].
LL.D: mid-blue [f8].
DLitt: royal blue shot maize [s4].
MD: crimson [f8].
DMus: scarlet cloth, lined rich white silk [s4].
DSc: green [s4].
DSc(SocSc): deep turquoise [s4].
DVM&S: maroon, bordered 3″ golden yellow [s4].
Dr.h.c: 'oatmeal' – a yellowish shade [s4].

Hat: in undress, a black cloth square cap; in full dress a black velvet John Knox cap.

NOTES

1. The obsolete degree of BL had a black hood of the Edinburgh shape [s4], bordered 3″ mid-blue, bound fur.

2. The green used for science and related degrees is an olive green. Prior to 1874, the science colour was lemon yellow.
3. Until 1991, the PhD had no dress robe, but used the black gown only, and the hood did not have the red border.
4. The 1911 *Encylopædia Britannica* entry, and *Athena: A Year-Book of the Learned World* (1920) give a DPhil, with a black hood, lined white silk shot with 'Vesuvius', which is a shade between tan and orange. The DPhil was replaced by the PhD.
5. Originally the doctors' robes had facings and sleeve linings of faculty colour; it is not known when the change to scarlet was made.
6. Holders of the obsolete diploma of LTh wore the black gown, and an epitoge of black, edged with ½″ purple silk. It was gathered on the shoulder into a purple button.

EDINBURGH COLLEGE OF ART

The hoods for all awards have the lining split horizontally, the line of division forming a chevron, point upwards. In all cases the lower portion when worn is purple.

FIRST DEGREES (BA, BArch, MA)

Gown: as bachelors.

Hood: a black hood of the Edinburgh shape [s4], lined blue and purple, the cowl bordered inside 1″ gold set 1″ in.

POSTGRADUATE DIPLOMA

Gown: as bachelors.

Hood: a black hood of the Edinburgh shape [s4], lined blue and purple, the cowl bordered inside 1″ red set 1″ in.

MASTERS (MFA, MArch, MDes, MSc, MLA, MPhil)

Gown: as bachelors.

Hood: a black hood of the Edinburgh shape [s4], lined red and purple, the cowl bordered inside 2″ gold set 1″ in.

DOCTOR OF PHILOSOPHY (PhD)

Undress gown: *none specified*

Dress robe: a blue robe of the Cambridge pattern [d1], with gold facings and sleeve linings.

Hood: a blue hood of the Edinburgh shape [s4], lined gold and purple, the cowl bordered inside 3″ blue set 1″ in.

EDINBURGH NAPIER UNIVERSITY
1992

The Napier Technical College was established in 1964, taking its name from John Napier, the inventor of logarithms, who was born on the site of the University's Merchiston campus. In 1974, Napier merged with the Edinburgh College of Commerce to form Napier College of Commerce and Technology, which was renamed Napier Polytechnic in 1986. It gained full university status as Napier University in June 1992. In January 2009, it changed its name to Edinburgh Napier University, and adopted a new scheme of academic dress. The former scheme is given below the current one. It is not clear if pre-2009 graduates may wear the new robes, or must wear the old ones.

UNDERGRADUATES
none specified

UNDERGRADUATE CERTIFICATES AND DIPLOMAS
Gown: as for bachelors.
Hood: a black hood of the Edinburgh shape [s4], the cowl bound 1″ Napier red (a shade of maroon).

BACHELORS
Gown: a black gown of the basic pattern [b1], with a black cord and button on the yoke.
Hood: a black hood of the Edinburgh shape [s4], lined Napier red.

POSTGRADUATE CERTIFICATES AND DIPLOMAS
Gown: as for masters.
Hood: a black hood of the Edinburgh shape [s4], lined blue, the cowl edge bordered inside 1″ Napier red.

MASTERS including MASTERS OF PHILOSOPHY
Gown: a black gown of Scottish MA pattern [m12].
Hood: a black hood of the Edinburgh simple shape [s4], lined as follows:
MPhil: lined Napier red, the cowl edge bordered inside 3″ blue, with 1″ green between the red and the blue.
All others: lined blue, the cowl edge bordered inside 3″ Napier red.

DOCTORS OF PHILOSOPHY and TAUGHT AND PROFESSIONAL DOCTORS
Undress gown: *none specified*
Dress robe: a red robe of the same pattern as the bachelors' gown, with 3″ facings of blue.
Hood: same as MPhil.

HIGHER DOCTORS

Undress gown: *none specified*

Dress robe: a blue cloth robe of the Cambridge pattern [d1], with facings and sleeve linings of Napier red. There is 1″ silver lace along the outer edge of each facing, and a silver cord and button on each sleeve.

Hood: a blue hood of the Cambridge shape [f1], lined and bound 1″ Napier red.

Robes used 1992–2008

The original system used the gowns to differentiate between the levels of degree, and a single set of hoods, one per faculty, regardless of the level of degree (except for non-degree awards). Buttons on the gowns were used to hold the hoods, which were provided with buttonholes, in place. Hats were not specified, nor were robes for the higher doctors.

The hoods were as follows. All were made in the London shape [f3], in black cloth, lined and bound on all edges with 1½″ of silk of the faculty colour.

Arts and Social Sciences: Alice blue (BA, MA, MPhil, PhD, DLitt).
Business Studies: rust (MBA).
Design: Wedgwood blue (BDes).
Engineering and Computing Science: yellow (BEng, MPhil, PhD).
Health and Life Sciences: forest green (BSc).
Laws: eggplant purple (LL.M).
Midwifery: forest green (BMid).
Music: Post Office red (BMus).
Nursing: forest green (BN).
Science: imperial purple (BSc, MSc, MPhil, PhD, DSc).

Undergraduate and postgraduate diploma and certificate holders, except HNC and HND, used the same hoods, but the binding was only ½″, the lining colour decided by the faculty in which the diploma was taken.

UNDERGRADUATES

none specified

UNDERGRADUATE CERTIFICATES AND DIPLOMAS

Gown: as for bachelors.

Hood:

HNC, HND: a black hood of CNAA shape [a1], lined crimson, and bordered inside the cowl edge 3″ white silk.

All others: the relevant faculty diploma hood.

BACHELORS

Gown: a black gown of basic pattern [b1]. The facings were piped on the outer edge and across the top with Napier tartan. There was a black and blue cord and a black button on the yoke, and a button covered with Napier tartan on each facing, 2½″ from the top.

Hood: the relevant faculty hood.

POSTGRADUATE CERTIFICATES AND DIPLOMAS

Gown: as for masters.

Hood: the relevant faculty diploma hood.

MASTERS including MASTERS OF PHILOSOPHY

Gown: a black stuff gown of basic pattern [m10], as follows:

MPhil: The 4″ facings were covered in silk of Napier red, and piped across the top and on the outer edge with Napier tartan. There was a black, white, and blue cord and black button on the yoke. There were buttons covered with Napier tartan on the facings, 2½″ below the top.

All others: The facings were covered in striped silk of black, blue, and white, and piped on the outer edge and across the top with yellow cord. There was a black, white, and blue cord and black button on the yoke, and a button covered with Napier tartan on each facing, 2½″ from the top.

Hood: the relevant faculty hood.

DOCTORS OF PHILOSOPHY and TAUGHT AND PROFESSIONAL DOCTORS

Undress gown: *none specified*

Dress robe: as for MPhil.

Hood: the relevant faculty hood.

HIGHER DOCTORS

none specified

UNIVERSITY OF ESSEX
1965

In July 1959, Essex County Council accepted a proposal that a university be established in the county, and a formal application was made to the University Grants Committee. Initially intended to be in Chelmsford, the eventual site chosen was at Wivenhoe, just outside Colchester.

Red was chosen as the university colour, and it features in all the hoods and robes. Referred to as 'university red' it is a shade of pillar-box red.

UNDERGRADUATES
none specified

UNDERGRADUATE CERTIFICATES AND DIPLOMAS
Gown: as for bachelors,
Hood: a black hood of the Edinburgh shape [s4], bordered inside 1″ bright red.
Hat: a black cloth square cap.

FOUNDATION DEGREES
Gown: as for bachelors.
Hood: a black hood of the Oxford simple shape [s1], the cowl bordered 2″ inside bright red.
Hat: a black cloth square cap.

BACHELORS
Gown: a black gown of basic pattern [b1].
Hood: a black hood of the Oxford simple shape [s1], lined, but not bound, bright red.
Hat: a black cloth square cap.

POSTGRADUATE CERTIFICATES AND DIPLOMAS
Gown: as for masters.
Hood: a black hood of the Cambridge shape [f1], the cowl edge bordered 1″ white and 1″ bright red.
Hat: a black cloth square cap.

FIRST-DEGREE MASTERS
not awarded

MASTERS including MASTERS OF PHILOSOPHY
Gown: a black gown of the Oxford MA pattern [m1].
Hood: a black silk hood of the Cambridge shape [f1], lined bright red, and the cowl bordered inside as follows:

MA, MSc, MEnvSt, [MBA]: 1″ white silk.
LL.M: 1″ white silk and 1″ black silk.
MPhil: 3″ white silk.

Hat: a black cloth square cap.

DOCTORS OF PHILOSOPHY and TAUGHT AND PROFESSIONAL DOCTORS

Undress gown: *none specified*

Dress robe: a black cloth robe of the Oxford pattern [d2], the sleeves (but not facings) are of maroon cloth.

Hood: a red hood of the Oxford full shape [f5], lined as follows:
PhD: lined maroon silk.
All others: lined maroon silk, bordered inside the cowl 1″ black silk.

Hat: in full dress, a black cloth bonnet with maroon cords and tassels.

HIGHER DOCTORS

Undress gown: *none specified*

Dress robe: a red robe of the Oxford pattern [d2], with facings and 8″ cuffs of black silk. Facings and cuffs are edged 1″ white silk, but 2″ for honorary doctors.

Hood: a red silk hood of the Cambridge shape [f1], lined and bound white silk. There is a black ribbon inside the cowl edge, set ½″ in, 1″ wide, but 2″ wide for honorary doctors.

Hat: in full dress, a black velvet bonnet with red cords and tassels.

NOTES

1. The neckbands of bachelors' hoods were originally black lined red. They were changed in 1993, so that they are now black, with a narrower piece of red silk sewn on the front, giving the effect of a red band bound black.

UNIVERSITY OF EXETER
1955

University education in Exeter began in 1922 with the conversion of the previous Royal Albert Memorial College into the University College of the South-West of England. With further growth in the 1920s and 1930s, it was granted increasing autonomy, but full independence was delayed by the Second World War. The university college received its Royal Charter and became the University of Exeter in December 1955.

The original scheme had the hoods and robes trimmed with silk in a faculty colour, most of which were fairly similar shades of blue. In 1986 they were abolished and replaced with one shade of blue for all. The hoods are stated to be of cloth (*i.e.,* wool-based) but now are usually made in other materials, notably the doctors' hoods, which, if made of, and lined with, cloth would be very heavy.

The faculty colours were:

Arts: kingfisher blue.
Arts(Social Sciences): dark blue.
Divinity (DD only): kingfisher blue.
Education: ultramarine blue.
Engineering: salvia blue.
Laws: purple.
Music: kingfisher blue.
Science: turquoise.

UNDERGRADUATES

Gown: a black stuff gown of the Cambridge basic pattern [u1]. Scholars wore the same gown, but with dark green facings and yoke. It is not known when it was introduced, nor if it is still current.

Hat: none.

UNDERGRADUATE CERTIFICATES AND DIPLOMAS

none specified

FOUNDATION DEGREES

not awarded

BACHELORS

Gown: a black stuff gown of the Cambridge BA pattern [b2].

Hood: a dove grey cloth hood of the Cambridge shape [f1], bound on all edges 2″ spectrum blue silk.

BPhil: further bound white cord on the outer edge.

Hat: a black cloth square cap.

POSTGRADUATE CERTIFICATES AND DIPLOMAS

none specified

FIRST-DEGREE MASTERS

Gown: as for masters.

Hood: a dove grey cloth hood of the Cambridge shape [f1], bound on all edges 2″ spectrum blue silk, and further bound gold cord on the outer edge.

Hat: a black cloth square cap.

MASTERS including MASTERS OF PHILOSOPHY

Gown: a black stuff gown of the Cambridge MA pattern [m2].

Hood: a dove grey cloth hood of the Cambridge shape [f1], lined spectrum blue silk.

Hat: a black cloth square cap.

DOCTORS OF PHILOSOPHY and TAUGHT AND PROFESSIONAL DOCTORS

Undress gown: as for masters, but with Cambridge lace round the armhole.

Dress robe: the masters' gown, with facings of spectrum blue silk.

Hood: a dove grey cloth hood of the Cambridge shape [f1], lined scarlet cloth.

Hat: in undress, a black cloth square cap; in full dress, a black cloth bonnet with spectrum blue cords and tassels.

HIGHER DOCTORS

Undress gown: as for masters, but with Cambridge lace round the armhole and the yoke.

Dress robe: a scarlet cloth robe of the Cambridge pattern [d1], with facings and sleeve linings of spectrum blue.

Hood: a scarlet cloth hood of the Cambridge shape [f1], lined dove grey cloth, and bound on all edges spectrum blue silk.

Hat: in undress, a black cloth square cap; in full dress, a black cloth bonnet with spectrum blue cords and tassels.

THE FACULTY OF THEOLOGY OF THE PRESBYTERIAN CHURCH OF IRELAND
1881

The Faculty was granted a Royal Charter in 1881, and has the right to award the degrees of BD (examined) and DD (*honoris causa* only). It does this through Union College, Belfast, which is a constituent college of Queen's University, Belfast; most students take the QUB BD or BTh, and so the BD is rarely awarded.

Gown: none has ever been specified. A black gown of a common pattern is worn.
Hood: originally of Edinburgh simple shape [s4] or (rarely) Belfast simple shape [s3], but now usually Dublin full shape [f2]:
BD: a black hood, lined purple, bound fur.
DD: a black hood, lined (and bound) purple.

UNIVERSITY COLLEGE, FALMOUTH
2005

University College Falmouth was founded in 1902 as the Falmouth School of Art. It became Falmouth College of Arts; when it received degree-awarding powers in March 2005 it took the title University College. In April 2008 it merged with Dartington College of Arts, adding a range of performance courses. The college is located on three different campuses across Cornwall and Devon; it is the first higher education institution in Cornwall to be able to award degrees under its own name.

The shade 'Cornish gold' is featured in all the hoods and some gowns. It is a rich yellow-gold.

UNDERGRADUATES
none specified

UNDERGRADUATE CERTIFICATES AND DIPLOMAS
none specified

FOUNDATION DEGREES
not awarded

BACHELORS
Gown: a black stuff gown of basic pattern [b1].
Hood: a black hood of the CNAA shape [a1], lined white, the cowl bordered inside ½″ Cornish gold.
Hat: a black cloth square cap.

POSTGRADUATE CERTIFICATES AND DIPLOMAS
Gown: a black stuff gown of basic pattern [b1].
Hood: a black hood of the CNAA shape [a1], lined white, the cowl bordered inside 1″ Cornish gold.
Hat: a black cloth square cap.

MASTERS including MASTERS OF PHILOSOPHY
Gown: a black stuff gown of basic pattern [m10], with an inverted-T armhole, and faced 2″ Cornish gold.
Hood: a black hood of the CNAA shape [a1], lined white, the cowl bordered inside 2″ Cornish gold.
Hat: a black cloth square cap.

DOCTORS OF PHILOSOPHY and TAUGHT AND PROFESSIONAL DOCTORS

not yet awarded

HIGHER DOCTORS

not yet awarded

UNIVERSITY OF GLAMORGAN
1992

The University of Glamorgan was founded in 1913 as a School of Mines based in Trefforest to serve the large coal mining industry in the South Wales valleys. It later became Glamorgan Polytechnic, then the Polytechnic of Wales, before finally becoming the University of Glamorgan in 1992. In 2004 it merged with Merthyr Tydfil College, and it entered a 'strategic alliance' with the Royal Welsh College of Music and Drama in 2006, which now awards Glamorgan degrees. A new campus in Cardiff city centre, the Atrium, was opened in 2005. The University thus has four campuses: Trefforest, Glyntaff, Merthyr Tydfil, and the Atrium. It has also a number of specialised partner colleges throughout South Wales, such as Barry College for aeronautical engineering.

All hoods and the doctoral robes are bordered or lined university silk: gold with the 'G' logo embroidered into it in blue and light gold.

UNDERGRADUATES
none specified

HND and HNC
Gown: as for bachelors.
Hood: a blue hood of the Cambridge shape [f1], bordered inside plain gold silk.
Hat: a black cloth square cap.

BACHELORS, FOUNDATION DEGREES and FIRST-DEGREE MASTERS
Gown: a black gown of basic pattern [b1].
Hood: a blue hood of the Cambridge shape [f1], bordered inside 4″ university gold silk.
Hat: a black cloth square cap.

POSTGRADUATE CERTIFICATES AND DIPLOMAS
Gown: as for masters.
Hood: the bachelors' hood.
Hat: a black cloth square cap.

MASTERS (including MPhil)
Gown: a black gown of basic pattern [m10].
Hood: a blue hood of the Cambridge shape[f1], fully lined university gold silk.
Hat: a black cloth square cap.

DOCTORS OF PHILOSOPHY and TAUGHT AND PROFESSIONAL DOCTORS
Undress gown: *none specified*

Dress robe: a dark blue robe of the basic masters' pattern [m10], with an inverted-T armhole, the facings and the sleeves below the armholes covered with university gold silk.

Hood: a blue hood of the Cambridge full shape [f1], lined and bound 1″ university gold silk.

Hat: in full dress, a black cloth bonnet with gold cords and tassels.

HIGHER DOCTORS

Undress gown: *none specified*

Dress robe: a gold robe of the basic masters' pattern [m10], with an inverted-T armhole, the facings and the sleeves below the armholes covered with blue.

Hood: a blue hood of the Cambridge full shape [f1], lined and bound 2″ university gold silk.

Hat: in full dress, a black velvet bonnet with gold cords and tassels.

NOTES

1. Holders of sub-degree awards until 2002 wore a hood of CNAA shape [a1], in green, lined white, and tipped red. This was the old Polytechnic hood.

UNIVERSITY OF GLASGOW
1451

The University of Glasgow was founded in 1451 by a papal bull of Pope Nicholas V, as a result of King James II's wish that Scotland should have two Universities to equal England's Oxford and Cambridge. It is the second oldest university in Scotland, the oldest being the University of St Andrews, founded in 1410. The Universities of St Andrews, Glasgow, and Aberdeen are ecclesiastical foundations, while Edinburgh was a secular foundation.

The system of academic dress is simple: bachelors and masters have a black hood with faculty colour lining, the bachelors being marked by a scarlet cord binding. Doctors have a scarlet hood and robe with faculty colour lining, except for the PhD, which has a black hood and robe. The new 'practitioner doctorates' have PhD-style robes, and in 2001 the MD and DDS were 'down-graded' from scarlet robes to black ones, and they wear the hoods formerly used by the now-obsolete ChM and MDS. As several degrees share hoods, and some have an extra border, it has been simplest to list every hood.

UNDERGRADUATES

Gown: a scarlet stuff gown with bell sleeves. The faculty may be indicated by a narrow band of silk on each facing at breast-level of the same colour as the lining of the hood of the lowest degree in the faculty.

Hat: a black cloth square cap.

UNDERGRADUATE CERTIFICATES AND DIPLOMAS

none specified

BACHELORS

Gown: a black stuff gown of the Oxford BA pattern [b8].

Hood: a black stuff hood of the Glasgow shape [f9], lined and bound ¼″ silk as follows, and bound on the cape and lower edge of the neckband with a narrow scarlet cord:

BA: purple.
BAcc: slate grey.
BAH: terra-cotta, bordered inside the cowl 3″ gold.
BCLD(SocSci): sky blue.
[BCommEdCommDev: sky blue.]
BDS: emerald green.
BD: light cherry (pink).
BEd: bluebell.
BEng: plum.
BES: gold.
BFLS: slate grey, bordered inside the cowl 3″ Venetian red.

BIBA: orange, bordered inside the cowl 3″ purple.
LL.B: Venetian red.
[BL: bordered 3″ Venetian red.]
BMedSci: scarlet, bordered inside the cowl 3″ emerald green.
MB,ChB: scarlet.
BMus: azure blue.
BN: cornflower blue.
BSc: gold.
BTechEd: plum, bordered inside the cowl 3″ bluebell.
BTechS: plum, bordered inside the cowl 3″ bluebell.
BTh: light cherry (pink), bordered inside the cowl 3″ bluebell.
BVMS: terra-cotta.

Hat: a black cloth square cap.

POSTGRADUATE CERTIFICATES AND DIPLOMAS

none specified

MASTERS including MASTERS OF PHILOSOPHY and FIRST DEGREE MASTERS (MA, MEng, MSci)

Gown: a black stuff gown of Scottish MA pattern [m12].

Hood: a black silk or stuff hood of the Glasgow shape [f9], lined and bound for ¼″ silk as follows:
MA: purple (also MA(SocSci).
MAcc: slate grey.
[MAppSc: gold.]
MBA: orange.
[ChM: scarlet.]
MCC: sky blue .
[MDS: emerald.]
MEd: bluebell.
MEng: plum.
MFA (Creative Writing): purple, bound on all edges 1″ beige.
MFin: slate grey, bordered inside the cowl 3″ Venetian red.
LL.M: Venetian red.
MLitt: purple, bound on all edges 1″ white (before 2009: lined white).
MML: Venetian red, bound on all edges 1″ white.
MMLE: Venetian red, bound on all edges 1″ white.
MM: cornflower blue, bound on all edges 1″ white.
MMus: azure blue.
MN: cornflower blue.
MPhil: crimson (before 2009: lined white.)
MPC: gold.
MPH: gold.
MRes: gold.

MSci: gold, bound with scarlet cord, as bachelors.
MSc: gold.
MSc(Adult & ContEd): gold.
[MSc(DentSc): gold]
MSW: sky blue.
MTh: light cherry (pink).
[MUA: orange.]
MVS: terra-cotta.
MVPH: terra-cotta, bound on all edges 1″ gold.
International Master's Degree in Russian, Central and East European Studies: white, bordered inside the cowl 3″ purple silk. (*This degree appears to have no abbreviation.*)

Hat: a black cloth square cap.

DOCTORS OF PHILOSOPHY and TAUGHT AND PROFESSIONAL DOCTORS

Undress gown: a black silk or stuff gown, with bell sleeves [d2], and a flap collar.

Dress robe: as the undress robe, but the facings and collar (but not the sleeves) are covered with silk to match the hood lining.

Hood: a black silk hood of the Glasgow shape [f9], lined and bound ¼″ silk as follows:
PhD: crimson.
MD: scarlet.
DDS and DCD: emerald green.
DBA: orange.
DClinPsy: gold.
EdD: bluebell.
EngD: plum.

Hat: a black cloth square cap.

HIGHER DOCTORS

Undress gown: as PhD.

Dress robe: a scarlet cloth robe of the Cambridge pattern [d1], with facings and sleeve-linings to match the hood lining. There is a cord and button on the yoke.

Hood: a scarlet cloth hood of the Glasgow shape [f9], lined and bound ¼″ silk as follows:
DD: white.
[DDSc: emerald green, bordered inside the cowl 3″ gold.]
DEng: plum.
LL.D: Venetian red.
DLitt: purple.
DMus: azure blue.
DSc: gold (also for DSc in Dentistry, in Engineering, and in Medicine).
DVMS: terra-cotta.

DVS, DVM: terra-cotta.

DUniv: black, bordered 1″ gold.

Hat: in undress, a black square cap; in full dress, a black velvet John Knox cap.

SCOTTISH AGRICULTURAL COLLEGE

Gown: a black stuff gown of the Oxford BA pattern [b8].

Hood: a black stuff hood of the Glasgow shape [f9]:

BTechnol: lining split vertically when worn, sedge green on the right and bugloss blue on the left.

Hat: a black cloth square cap.

GLASGOW SCHOOL OF ART

BACHELORS

Gown: a black stuff gown of the Oxford BA pattern [b8].

Hood: a black stuff hood of the Glasgow shape [f9], lined and bound ¼″ silk as follows, and bound on the cape and lower edge of the neckband with a narrow scarlet cord:

BA in Design or in Fine Art: lining split vertically when worn, malachite green on the right and white on the left.

BArch: lime-flower green.

BDes: lining split vertically when worn, smalt blue on the right and saffron on the left.

Hat: a black cloth square cap.

MASTERS

Gown: a black stuff gown of Scottish MA pattern [m12].

Hood: a black silk or stuff hood of the Glasgow shape [f9], lined as follows:

MArch: lime-flower green.

MDes: lining split vertically when worn, malachite green on the right and swiss white on the left.

MEDes: lining split vertically when worn, smalt blue on the right and saffron on the left (European Design).

MFA: lining split vertically when worn, malachite green on the right and swiss white on the left.

Hat: a black cloth square cap.

NOTES

1. Until 1936, bachelors' hoods were bound on the cape 1″ scarlet cloth, when it was changed to scarlet cord.

2. Bachelors who are also Masters of Arts may wear hoods with black silk shells, and wear the MA gown with their bachelor's hood.
3. If awarded before 2001, the MD and DDS had robes and hoods of scarlet, with linings and facings of scarlet (MD) or emerald (DDS).

4. A number of the faculty silks are tied to flower colours:
   Purple: bell heather, *erica cinerea.*
   Gold: whin blossom, *ulex europæus.*
   Bluebell: bluebell of Scotland, *campanula rotundiflora.*
   Orange: slender St John's wort, *hypericum pulchrum.*
   Lime-flower: lime flower, *tilia europæa.*
   Sedge green: bottle sedge, *carex rostrata.*
   Bugloss: viper's bugloss, *echium vulgare.*

5. Obsolete hoods and robes:
   DLitt: robe and hood lined violet silk (until 1936).
   DPhil: replaced by PhD in 1936, had a scarlet robe and hood, lined with the MA silk.
   BD: as MA, but bordered inside the cowl 3″ black velvet.
   Under the original nineteenth-century scheme, doctors wore hoods of black velvet lined with faculty colour silk.
   LTh: a black gown as for bachelors, and a black epitoge edged with Divinity pink.

GLASGOW CALEDONIAN UNIVERSITY
1993

Glasgow Caledonian University was formed in 1993 by the merger of The Queen's College, Glasgow and Glasgow Polytechnic. The Queen's College traces its origins to 1875 when the Glasgow School of Cookery was established. In 1908, the Glasgow School of Cookery merged with the West End School of Cookery (1878) to form the Glasgow and West of Scotland College of Domestic Science. The Glasgow College of Technology (later known as Glasgow Polytechnic) was formed in 1971 by the merger of two separate colleges: the College of Science and Technology and the College of Commerce. The Queen's College and Glasgow Polytechnic merged in 1992 and the combined institution was granted University status in 1993.

A completely new set of robes was brought into use in July 2010. The former set, used from 1993, is at the end of the entry. As with the previous scheme, hats are specifically stated not to be part of the academic dress.

Faculty colours

Arts: Post Office red.
Business Administration: deep magenta.
Engineering: imperial purple.
Nursing: buttercup yellow.
Science: malachite green.
Laws: light grey.

UNDERGRADUATES

none specified

UNDERGRADUATE CERTIFICATES AND DIPLOMAS

Gown: as for bachelors.

Hood: a black hood of the Edinburgh shape [s4], fully lined black, the cowl bordered inside 1″ mid-blue.

BACHELORS

Gown: a black stuff gown of the basic pattern [b1].

Hood: a black hood of Edinburgh shape [s4], lined mid-blue, the cowl bordered inside 3″ faculty colour.

POSTGRADUATE CERTIFICATES AND DIPLOMAS

Gown: as for masters.

Hood: a black hood of the Edinburgh shape [s4], fully lined black, the cowl bordered inside 3″ mid-blue.

MASTERS including MASTERS OF PHILOSOPHY

Gown: a black gown of the Scottish MA pattern [m12]. For MPhil there are mid-blue facings.

Hood:

MPhil: a mid-blue hood, fully lined university mid-blue of the Edinburgh shape [s4], the cowl bordered 1″ champagne gold.

All others: a black hood of the Edinburgh shape [s4], lined mid-blue, the cowl bordered inside 3″ faculty colour, and 1″ champagne gold.

DOCTORS OF PHILOSOPHY and TAUGHT AND PROFESSIONAL DOCTORS

Undress gown: *none specified*

Dress robe: a mid-blue gown of the Scottish MA pattern [m12], with champagne gold facings.

Hood: a mid-blue hood of the Cambridge shape [f1], lined and bound as follows:

PhD: bound champagne gold.

Professional doctors: lined and bound Post Office red.

HIGHER DOCTORS

t.b.a.

Robes used 1993–2010

The hoods were a variant of the Edinburgh simple shape, with very wide neckbands (about 6″), which reversed. Hats were specifically stated not to be part of the academic dress.

UNDERGRADUATES

none specified

UNDERGRADUATE CERTIFICATES AND DIPLOMAS

Gown: a black stuff gown of the Oxford BA pattern [b8].

Hood: a black hood of the Caledonian shape [s11], lined as follows:

Certificates: lined light blue satin.

Diplomas: lined light blue satin, the cowl edge bordered ½″ white satin.

BACHELORS

Gown: a black stuff gown of the Oxford BA pattern [b8].

Hood: a black hood of the Caledonian shape [s11], lined light blue satin, the cowl edge bordered 1″ white satin.

POSTGRADUATE CERTIFICATES AND DIPLOMAS

Gown: a black gown of the Scottish masters' pattern [m12].

Hood: a black hood of the Caledonian shape [s11], lined light blue satin, the cowl edge bordered ½″ gold satin.

MASTERS including MASTERS OF PHILOSOPHY

Gown: a black gown of the Scottish masters' pattern [m12]. For the MPhil, there are light blue satin facings.

Hood: a black hood of the Caledonian shape [s11], lined light blue satin, the cowl edge bordered 1″ gold satin.

DOCTORS OF PHILOSOPHY and TAUGHT AND PROFESSIONAL DOCTORS

Undress gown: *none specified*

Dress robe: a light blue panama gown of the Scottish masters' pattern [m12], with an inverted-T armhole. The outer edge of the facings is bound 1″ gold satin. Each facing also has six gold bars, 1″ wide, piped on the top edge with red, three at breast level, and three about 12″ from the base. Within each group, the bars are set 1″ apart, and slope down from the outer to the inner edge of the facings; if they met, they would form inverted chevrons.

Hood: a light blue hood of the Caledonian shape [s11], lined light blue satin, the cowl edge bordered 1″ gold, and piped red. On the cowl seam, there are three gold buttons.

UNIVERSITY OF GLOUCESTERSHIRE
2001

The university succeeds a large number of merged and name-changed institutions of further and higher education. Its history began with the Mechanics Institute founded in 1834. From 1992, Cheltenham and Gloucester College of Higher Education (CGCHE) was permitted to award taught degrees. It was awarded university status in 2001 as the University of Gloucestershire. It has five campuses, three in Cheltenham, one in Gloucester, and one in London for PGCEs.

UNDERGRADUATES
none specified

UNDERGRADUATE CERTIFICATES AND DIPLOMAS
Gown: as for bachelors.
Hood: a mid-blue hood of the Leeds simple shape [s7], lined mid-blue.
Hat: a black cloth square cap.

FOUNDATION DEGREES
Gown: as for bachelors.
Hood: a mid-blue hood of the Leeds simple shape [s7], lined mid-blue, with 1″ white on the turn-out.
Hat: a black cloth square cap.

BACHELORS
Gown: a black stuff gown of basic pattern [b1].
Hood: a mid-blue hood of the Leeds simple shape [s7], lined cardinal red, the cowl bordered 1″ white in the turn-out, set 1″ in.
Hat: a black cloth square cap.

POSTGRADUATE CERTIFICATES AND DIPLOMAS
Gown: as for bachelors.
Hood: a cardinal red hood of the Leeds simple shape [s7], lined mid-blue.
Hat: a black cloth square cap.

MASTERS including MASTERS OF PHILOSOPHY
Gown: a black stuff gown of basic pattern [m10].
Hood: a cardinal read hood of the Leeds simple shape [s7], lined mid-blue, the cowl bordered 1″ white on the turn-out, set 1″ in.
Hat: a black cloth square cap.

DOCTORS OF PHILOSOPHY and TAUGHT AND PROFESSIONAL DOCTORS

Undress gown: *none specified*

Dress robe: a cardinal red robe of the Oxford pattern [d2], with facings and sleeves covered with mid-blue. There is 1″ white on the outer edge of the facings and at the top of the blue on the sleeves.

Hood: a cardinal red hood of the Cambridge shape [f1], lined mid-blue, bound on all edges 1″ white inside and out.

Hat: in full dress, a cardinal red cloth bonnet with blue cords and tassels.

HIGHER DOCTORS

Undress gown: *none specified*

Dress robe: a mid-blue robe of the Oxford pattern [d2], with facings and sleeves covered with cardinal red. There is 1″ silver oak-leaf lace on the outer edge of the facings and at the top of the blue on the sleeves.

Hood: a mid-blue hood of the Cambridge shape [f1], lined cardinal red, bound on all edges ½″ inside and out with silver oak-leaf lace.

Hat: in full dress, a black cloth bonnet with gold cords and tassels.

GLYNDŴR UNIVERSITY
2008

Founded as Wrexham School of Science and Arts in 1887, it offered courses for London external students from 1924. In 1927 it changed its name to the Denbighshire Technical Institute (Denbighshire Technical College in 1939) and following mergers with a number of other colleges, it became the North-East Wales Institute (NEWI) in 1975, awarding degrees of the University of Wales from 1993, becoming a full member in 2004. In 2008 it gained university status, again changing its name. It is named after Owain Glyndŵr.

At present it is still awarding degrees of the University of Wales, and robes have thus not been designed.

UNIVERSITY OF GREENWICH
1993

The history of the University dates back to 1890, when Woolwich Polytechnic was founded. In 1970, it merged with various other higher education institutions to form Thames Polytechnic. In the following years, Dartford College (1976), Avery Hill College (1985), Garnett College (1987) and parts of Goldsmiths College and the City of London College (1988) were incorporated, extending the range of subjects taught considerably. In 1992, Thames Polytechnic was granted university status as the University of Greenwich.

The robes feature silk damask ('Cloister' pattern) in two colours; blue, which is a shade of azure, and gold, which is very rich and approaches orange. The doctors' robe are made of St Aidan damask. They also use a scarlet silk, with the University's armorial bearings woven into it in colour.

UNDERGRADUATES
none specified

UNDERGRADUATE CERTIFICATES AND DIPLOMAS
Gown: as for bachelors.

Hood: a black silk hood of the Oxford simple shape [s1], lined blue damask, and the cowl bordered inside 2″ plain scarlet silk; neckband blue damask.

Hat: a black cloth square cap.

FOUNDATION DEGREES
Gown: as for bachelors.

Hood: a black silk hood of the Cambridge shape [f1], lined blue damask, and the cowl bordered inside 2″ scarlet woven silk; neckband blue damask.

Hat: a black cloth square cap.

BACHELORS
Gown: a black stuff gown of basic pattern [b1].

Hood: a black silk hood of the Cambridge shape [f1], lined and bound on the cape for 1″ blue damask, and the cowl bordered inside 3″ scarlet woven silk; neckband scarlet woven silk.

Hat: a black cloth square cap.

POSTGRADUATE CERTIFICATES AND DIPLOMAS
Gown: a black stuff gown of basic pattern [b1].

Hood: a black silk hood of the Cambridge shape [f1], lined and bound on the cape for 1″ gold damask, and the cowl bordered inside 3″ scarlet woven silk; neckband scarlet woven silk.

Hat: a black cloth square cap.

MASTERS including MASTERS OF PHILOSOPHY

Gown: a black stuff gown of basic pattern [m10]. For MPhil, the facings are of scarlet woven silk.

Hood: a blue damask hood of the Cambridge shape [f1], lined and bound 1″ on all edges scarlet woven silk.

Hat: a black cloth square cap.

DOCTORS OF PHILOSOPHY and TAUGHT AND PROFESSIONAL DOCTORS

Undress gown: *none specified*

Dress robe: a gold damask robe of the Cambridge pattern [d1], with sleeve linings of scarlet woven silk; the facings are gold, with 2″ scarlet woven silk on the outer edges. There is a blue cord and button on each sleeve, and on the yoke.

Hood: a gold damask hood of the Cambridge shape [f1], lined scarlet woven silk, and the cowl bordered inside 1″ blue damask.

Hat: in full dress, a gold damask bonnet with blue cords and tassels.

HIGHER DOCTORS

Undress gown: *none specified*

Dress robe: a gold damask robe of the Cambridge pattern [d1], with yoke and sleeve linings of blue damask; the facings are gold, with 2″ scarlet woven silk on the outer edges. There is a gold cord and button on each sleeve, and on the yoke.

Hood: a gold damask hood of the Cambridge shape [f1], lined scarlet woven silk, bound on all edges 1″ blue damask inside and out.

Hat: in full dress, a gold damask bonnet with blue cords and tassels.

LONDON GUILDHALL UNIVERSITY
1992–2002

In 1848 the Metropolitan Evening Classes for Young Men in Crosby Hall, Bishopsgate, London, with student fees at one shilling per session, were established in response to a call by Charles Blomfield, the Bishop of London. Subjects on the original curriculum included Greek, Latin, Hebrew, English, History, Mathematics, Drawing and Natural Philosophy. This fledgling college came under royal patronage following the visit of Prince Albert to the classes in 1851. In 1861 the classes were reconstituted and named the City of London College. Over the next twenty years, the College was one of the pioneers in the introduction of commercial and technical subjects. In 1891 the College joined the Birkbeck Institute and the Northampton Institute (*see* City University) to form the notional City Polytechnic. However this attempted federation did not function in practice, as each institution continued to operate more or less independently. The City Polytechnic concept was dissolved in 1906, and the City of London College came under the supervision of London County Council. In 1970 the College merged with Sir John Cass College to form the City of London Polytechnic. From 1992, it was called London Guildhall University. In 2002 the university merged with the University of North London and the new institution became London Metropolitan University. London Guildhall University was so named in order to show its links with the City of London and the City's many guilds and livery companies. It had no connexion with the Guildhall School of Music and Drama (based at the Barbican Centre).

The Guildhall hoods featured two silks, black and scarlet, damasked with the University's logo.

UNDERGRADUATES
none specified

UNDERGRADUATE CERTIFICATES AND DIPLOMAS
Gown: as for bachelors.
Hood: a black silk hood of the Burgon shape [s2], lined black damask, the cowl bordered inside 1″ silver.
Hat: a black cloth square cap.

FOUNDATION DEGREES
never awarded.

BACHELORS
Gown: a black stuff gown of basic pattern [b1].
Hood: a plain black silk hood of the Burgon shape [s2], lined scarlet damask.
Hat: a black cloth square cap.

POSTGRADUATE CERTIFICATES AND DIPLOMAS

Gown: as for bachelors.

Hood: as for masters.

Hat: a black cloth square cap.

FIRST-DEGREE MASTERS

never awarded.

MASTERS except Masters of Philosophy

Gown: a black stuff gown of the Oxford MA pattern [m1].

Hood: a plain black silk hood of the Burgon shape [s2], lined scarlet damask, the cowl bordered inside 1″ silver.

Hat: a black cloth square cap.

MASTERS OF PHILOSOPHY

Gown: a black stuff gown of the Oxford MA pattern [m1], with facings of scarlet damask.

Hood: a scarlet damask hood of the Burgon shape [s2], lined black damask.

Hat: a black cloth square cap.

DOCTORS OF PHILOSOPHY

Undress gown: as for masters.

Dress robe: a black cloth robe of the Oxford pattern [d2], with facings and sleeve cuffs of scarlet damask.

Hood: a scarlet damask hood of the Burgon shape [s2], lined black damask, the cowl bordered inside 1″ silver.

Hat: in undress, a black cloth square cap; in full dress, a black cloth bonnet with scarlet cords and tassels.

HIGHER DOCTORS

Undress gown: as for PhD.

Dress robe: a scarlet cloth robe of the Oxford pattern [d2], with facings and sleeve cuffs of black damask.

Hood: a scarlet cloth hood of the Oxford full shape [f5], lined black damask, the cowl bordered inside 1″ silver.

Hat: in undress, a black cloth square cap; in full dress, a black cloth bonnet with gold cords and tassels.

HARPER ADAMS UNIVERSITY COLLEGE
near Newport, Shropshire
1901

The College opened its doors to six students in April 1901, and offered certificate courses, very much of a practical nature. A College Diploma of a more scientific nature was also on offer, but the National Diploma in Agriculture had less appeal, being considered by many as far too theoretical. Although the College sought to educate the sons of the smaller and tenant farmer groups, students tended to come from the wealthier farming and professional backgrounds. Women were admitted in 1916.

Higher education courses were started in 1981, and in 1996 Harper Adams was awarded its own degree-awarding powers for its taught courses. Research was also a growth area and it was increasingly undertaken by postgraduate students. The first award of a PhD to a student at Harper Adams was in 1989. Until 2007, the research degrees were awarded by the Open University.

UNDERGRADUATES
none specified

UNDERGRADUATE CERTIFICATES AND DIPLOMAS
Gown: a black stuff gown of the London BA pattern [b4].

Hood: a dark blue silk hood of the CNAA shape [a1], lined gold, and tipped light blue.

Hat: a black cloth square cap.

FOUNDATION DEGREES
Gown: a black stuff gown of basic pattern [b1].

Hood: a dark blue silk hood of the CNAA shape [a1], lined light blue, and tipped gold.

Hat: a black cloth square cap.

BACHELORS
Gown: a black stuff gown of the London BA pattern [b4].

Hood: a dark blue silk hood of the CNAA shape [a1], lined gold, the cowl edge bordered 1″ light blue.

Hat: a black cloth square cap.

POSTGRADUATE CERTIFICATES AND DIPLOMAS
Gown: a black stuff gown of basic masters' pattern [m10], with 1″ gold on the outer edge of each facing.

Hood: a dark blue silk hood of the CNAA shape [a1], lined light blue, the cowl edge bordered 1″ gold.

Hat: a black cloth square cap.

FIRST-DEGREE MASTERS

Gown: a black stuff gown of the London BA pattern [b4].
Hood: a dark blue hood of the Cambridge shape [f1, lined gold. the cowl bordered 1″ light blue.
Hat: a black cloth square cap.

MASTERS (including Masters of Philosophy)

Gown: a dark blue stuff gown of the basic pattern [m10].
Hood: a gold cloth hood of the Cambridge shape [f1], lined light blue silk.
Hat: a black cloth square cap.

DOCTORS OF PHILOSOPHY

Undress gown: *none specified*
Dress robe: a dark blue panama robe of the Cambridge pattern [d1], with facings and sleeve linings of gold silk.; there is a gold cord and button on each sleeve.
Hood: a light blue panama hood of the Cambridge shape [f1], lined gold silk.
Hat: in full dress, a dark blue panama bonnet with gold cords and tassels.

HONORARY DOCTORS

Undress gown: *none specified*
Dress robe: a gold panama robe of the Cambridge pattern [d1], with facings and sleeve linings of dark blue silk.; there is a dark blue cord and button on each sleeve.
Hood: a dark blue panama hood of the Cambridge shape [f1], lined gold silk.
Hat: in full dress, a gold panama bonnet with dark blue cords and tassels.

NOTES

1. The foundation degrees initially wore the same robes as the undergraduate certificates and diplomas.

HERIOT–WATT UNIVERSITY, EDINBURGH
1966

Heriot–Watt University can trace its origins to 1827, when the 'School of Arts of Edinburgh for the Education of Mechanics in Such Branches of Physical Science as are of Practical Application in their Several Trades' was established. By 1966, when the University received its Royal Charter, it had a respected reputation in the fields of science and engineering.

The bachelors' and masters' hoods were heavily revised in 2007. Previously there had been a faculty colour system, with bachelors wearing a black hood lined faculty colour, bordered gold, and masters a black hood lined faculty colour. See the end of the entry for these.

UNDERGRADUATES
none specified

UNDERGRADUATE CERTIFICATES AND DIPLOMAS
Gown: as for bachelors.
Hood: the hood of any degree that may be held.
Hat: a black cloth square cap.

BACHELORS and GRADUATE CERTIFICATES AND DIPLOMAS
Gown: a black stuff gown of the Scottish MA pattern [m12].
Hood: a black hood of the Cambridge shape [f1], lined blue.
Hat: a black cloth square cap.

POSTGRADUATE CERTIFICATES AND DIPLOMAS
Gown: as for bachelors.
Hood: a black hood of the Cambridge shape [f1], lined blue, the cowl bordered inside 1″ gold.
Hat: a black cloth square cap.

MASTERS including MASTERS OF PHILOSOPHY
Gown: as for bachelors.
Hood: a hood of the Cambridge shape [f1], as follows:
Taught Masters: black, lined blue, cowl and cape edged gold.
MPhil: black, lined magenta.
MLitt: black, lined purple (Edinburgh Business School; Management and Languages).
MLitt: pillar box red, lined silver grey (School of Textiles and Design).
Hat: a black cloth square cap.

ALL DOCTORS

Undress gown: as for bachelors.

Dress robe: a robe of Oxford pattern [d2], but with the front of the sleeve gathered with a cord and button as on [b4]. The whole robe, including the cords and buttons, is made in the same colour as the shell of the hood; there are no sleeve linings.

Hood: a hood of the Cambridge shape [f1], as follows:

PhD, EngD: magenta, lined white.

DSc (Science): light blue, lined white (Engineering and Physical Sciences; Physical Sciences only, Mathematics and Computer Sciences; Life Sciences).

DSc (Engineering): dark blue, lined white (Engineering only; Institute of Petroleum Engineering; Built Environment).

DSc (Textiles and Design): pillar box red, lined white (School of Textiles and Design).

DEng: dark blue, lined white.

DLitt: purple, lined white (Edinburgh Business School; Management and Languages).

DLitt: pillar box red, lined white (School of Textiles and Design).

DUniv: gold, lined white.

Hat: a black cloth square cap.

Former scheme (pre-2007)

Faculty colours

Economic and Social Studies: purple.
Education: green.
Environmental Studies: red.
Engineering Sciences: dark blue.
Fine Art and Design: burgundy moiré.
Physical sciences: light blue.
Textiles: silver grey.
Philosophy: magenta.
Non-faculty BSc: black.
DUniv: gold.

The hoods for bachelors' and masters' degrees were black, fully lined with the faculty colour. Bachelors' degrees were distinguished by a 1″ gold border inside the cowl, except as follows:

BA (Faculty of Environmental Studies): facing laid 2″ inside the cowl.

BArch (Faculty of Environmental Studies): facing laid 1″ inside the cowl.

Doctors' hoods were of the faculty colour fully lined white silk. The degrees of DLitt and DSc were awarded in several faculties; a DSc and a DLitt awarded in Engineering Sciences would both have worn the same hood: dark blue lined white.

The gowns and robes were as they are now.

UNIVERSITY OF HERTFORDSHIRE
1992

In 1951, the chairman of the de Havilland company, Alan Samuel Butler, gave land in Hatfield to Hertfordshire County Council for educational use in perpetuity. The Council decided to use this to build and operate Hatfield Technical College, which trained aerospace engineers for Hatfield's then-dominant aerospace industry. In 1967, it became Hatfield Polytechnic. With the passage of the Further and Higher Education Act in 1992, it gained university status.

The scheme of dress is grade-specific, and based round the university colours of grey, white, and purple. All hoods are grey, and the grade is denoted by the lining colour. The bachelors' gown reflects the fact that the College originally taught for London degrees, and the masters' gown and the hood shape mark the CNAA link.

UNDERGRADUATES

Gown: as for bachelors.

Hat: a black cloth square cap.

UNDERGRADUATE CERTIFICATES AND DIPLOMAS

Gown: as for bachelors.

Hood:

Certificates: no hood.

Diplomas: a grey cloth hood of the CNAA shape [a1], lined grey silk.

Higher Diplomas: a grey cloth hood of the CNAA shape [a1], lined grey silk, the cowl bordered inside 1″ white watered silk.

Hat: a black cloth square cap.

FOUNDATION DEGREES

Gown: as for bachelors.

Hood: a grey cloth hood of the CNAA shape [a1], lined grey silk, the cowl bordered inside 1″ white watered silk.

Hat: a black cloth square cap.

BACHELORS

Gown: a black stuff gown of London BA pattern [b4].

Hood: a grey cloth hood of the CNAA shape [a1], lined white watered silk.

Hat: a black cloth square cap.

POSTGRADUATE CERTIFICATES AND DIPLOMAS

Gown: as for bachelors.

Hood:

Certificates: no hood.

Diplomas: a grey cloth hood of the CNAA shape [a1], lined grey silk, the cowl bordered inside 1″ purple watered silk.

Hat: a black cloth square cap.

FIRST-DEGREE MASTERS

Gown: as for bachelors.

Hood: a grey cloth hood of the CNAA shape [a1], lined white watered silk, the cowl bordered inside 1″ purple watered silk.

Hat: a black cloth square cap.

MASTERS including MASTERS OF PHILOSOPHY

Gown: a black stuff gown of basic pattern [m10].

Hood: a grey cloth hood of the CNAA shape [a1], lined as follows:

MPhil: lined purple watered silk, the cowl bordered inside 1″ red watered silk.

All others: lined purple watered silk.

Hat: a black cloth square cap.

DOCTORS OF PHILOSOPHY and PROFESSIONAL DOCTORS

Undress gown: as for masters.

Dress robe: a dark red cloth robe of the Oxford pattern [d2], the facings and 5″ cuffs of purple watered silk.

Hood: a grey cloth hood of the CNAA shape [a1], lined dark red watered silk, the cowl bordered inside 1″ purple watered silk.

Hat: in undress, a black cloth square cap; in full dress, a black cloth bonnet with grey cords and tassels.

HIGHER DOCTORS

Undress gown: as for the PhD.

Dress robe: a purple cloth robe of the Oxford pattern [d2], the facings and 5″ cuffs covered with white St Aidan damask.

Hood: a grey cloth hood of the CNAA shape [a1], lined purple watered silk, the cowl bordered inside 2″ white St Aidan damask.

Hat: in undress, a black cloth square cap; in full dress, a black velvet bonnet with grey cords and tassels.

NOTES

1. Until 2005, the higher doctors' hood was grey, lined white St Aidan damask.

HIGHER EDUCATION AND TRAINING AWARDS COUNCIL (IRELAND)
2001

HETAC (the Higher Education and Training Awards Council) was established on 11 June 2001, under the Qualifications (Education and Training) Act 1999. It is the successor to the National Council for Educational Awards (NCEA, established 1972) and is the qualifications awarding body for third-level education and training institutions outside the university sector. The providers of courses which lead to HETAC awards are called 'recognised institutions', and they are recognised under the Qualifications (Education and Training) Act, 1999 (Section 24). Some of these institutions may have 'delegation of authority' which allows them to make HETAC awards in their own name. This is currently limited to the Institutes of Technology and is often limited to certain award levels at institutions.

The bachelors' degree are awarded with or without honours, but there is no difference in the robes. There is no MPhil, but the four master's degrees (MA, MSc, MBus, MEng) can be awarded for research.

The NCEA robes are listed at the end of this article.

Faculty colours

Arts: pale blue.
Business: cream.
Engineering: orange.
Music: salmon pink.
Science: yellow-gold.

UNDERGRADUATES

none specified

CERTIFICATES, HIGHER CERTIFICATES and HIGHER DIPLOMAS

Gown: as for bachelors.

Epitoges:

For the following, an epitoge in the faculty colour, with horizontal dark blue bands, 1″ wide, set 1½″ apart:
Higher Certificate: three bands at each end.
Higher Diploma: four bands at each end.

For the following a dark blue epitoge, edged all round:
Special Purpose Awards: ½″ emerald green.
Supplemental Awards: ½″ cerise.
Minor Awards: ½″ silver grey.

Hat: a black cloth square cap.

BACHELORS

Gown: a black stuff gown of the London BA pattern [b4].

Hood: a dark blue hood of the Irish simple shape [s3], lined and bound faculty colour.

Hat: a black cloth square cap.

POSTGRADUATE CERTIFICATES AND DIPLOMAS

Gown: as for bachelors.

Epitoge: an epitoge in the faculty colour, with horizontal dark blue bands, 1″ wide, set 1½″ apart, four on the broad portion, and five on the narrow.

Hat: a black cloth square cap.

MASTERS

Gown: a black stuff gown of the Oxford MA pattern [m1].

Hood: a dark blue hood of the Irish full shape [f2], lined and bound faculty colour.

Hat: a black cloth square cap.

DOCTORS OF PHILOSOPHY

Undress gown: *none specified*

Dress robe: a dark blue robe with narrow bell sleeves [d3], and a flap collar. The facings and collar are covered with old gold silk, and the bottom 4″ of the sleeves are bound old gold.

Hood: *none.*

Hat: in full dress, a dark blue velvet bonnet, with gold cords and tassels.

HIGHER DOCTORS

Undress gown: *none specified*

Dress robe: a dark blue robe with narrow bell sleeves [d3], and a flap collar. The facings and collar are covered with scarlet silk, and the bottom 4″ of the sleeves are bound scarlet.

Hood: *none.*

Hat: in full dress, a dark blue velvet bonnet, with scarlet cords and tassels.

NOTES

1. The published regulations state that the masters' hoods are of faculty colour lined and bound blue, but pictures seen indicate they are made as specified above.
2. The published regulations refer to hoods for doctors, but there is no specification.

NCEA robes (1972–2001)

The NCEA robes were as follows:

Faculty colours

Arts: blue.

Business: cream.
Design: brown.
Engineering: orange.
Science: gold
Technology: grey.

The red used for the hood shells was a deep scarlet.

CERTIFICATES and DIPLOMAS

Gown: a black stuff gown of basic pattern [b1].

Epitoge: an epitoge in the faculty colour with horizontal red bands, 1″ wide, set 1½″ apart:

1-year certificate: one band.
2-year certificate: two bands.
Diploma: three bands.
Diploma in Hotel Management: three bands of fur.

Hat: a black cloth square cap.

BACHELORS

Gown: a black stuff gown of basic pattern [b1].

Hood: a red hood of the Irish simple shape [s3], lined and bound ¼″ faculty colour.

Hat: a black cloth square cap.

GRADUATE DIPLOMAS

Gown: a black stuff gown of basic pattern [b1].

Epitoge: an epitoge in the faculty colour with four horizontal red bands, 1″ wide, set 1½″ apart:

Hat: a black cloth square cap.

MASTERS

Gown: a black stuff gown of the Oxford MA pattern [m1].

Hood: a red hood of the Irish full shape [f2], lined faculty colour.

Hat: a black cloth square cap.

DOCTORS OF PHILOSOPHY

Undress gown: *none specified*

Dress robe: a dark green robe of the Oxford MA pattern [m1], the facings covered with gold.

Hood: a red hood of the Irish full shape [f2], lined gold.

Hat: in full dress, a black cloth bonnet, with red cords and tassels.

HIGHER DOCTORS

Undress gown: *none specified*

Dress robe: a dark green robe, of the Oxford pattern [d2], the facings covered with black edged gold.

Hood: a red hood of the Irish full shape [f2], lined and bound ½″ faculty colour.
Hat: a black velvet bonnet, with faculty colour cords and tassels.

UNIVERSITY OF THE HIGHLANDS AND ISLANDS
2011

The University was previously known as the 'UHI Millennium Institute' (Institiùd OGE nam Mìle Bliadhna), which goes back to 1992, when the UHI Project was set up. It is a federation of 13 colleges and research institutions in the Highlands and Islands of Scotland delivering higher education. Its Executive Office is in Inverness. In April 2001 the Scottish Parliament awarded UHI Higher Education Institute status, and it now provides university-level courses. UHI degrees were validated by the Open University Validation Service (OUVS), the University of Strathclyde, and the University of Aberdeen until 2008, when the UHI was awarded taught degree awarding powers. University status was granted in February 2011.

UNDERGRADUATES
none specified

UNDERGRADUATE CERTIFICATES AND DIPLOMAS
none specified

BACHELORS
Gown: a black stuff gown of basic pattern [b1].

Hood: a black hood of the Edinburgh shape [s4], lined purple, the cowl bordered inside 1″ grey set ½″ in.

Hat: a black cloth square cap.

POSTGRADUATE CERTIFICATES AND DIPLOMAS
none specified

MASTERS
Gown: a black stuff gown of the Scottish masters' pattern [m12].

Hood: a grey hood of the Edinburgh shape [s4], lined purple.

Hat: a black cloth square cap.

UNIVERSITY OF HUDDERSFIELD
1992

The University traces its roots back to a Science and Mechanic Institute founded in 1825. In 1958 it became a College of Technology, and was redesignated Huddersfield Polytechnic in 1970. It became a university in 1992.

The robes are based around the original Polytechnic hood, which was peacock blue lined turquoise. The lining was changed to navy blue, and faculty colours introduced.

Faculty colours

Arts: white.
Architecture: emerald.
Business Administration: orange.
Design: purple.
Education : grey
Engineering: red.
Laws: lilac.
Philosophy: maroon.
Science: yellow.

UNDERGRADUATES

none specified

UNDERGRADUATE CERTIFICATES AND DIPLOMAS

Gown: as for bachelors.
Hood: a cyan hood of the CNAA shape [a1], bordered 4″ navy.
Hat: a black cloth square cap.

FOUNDATION DEGREES

Gown: as for bachelors.
Hood: a cyan hood of the CNAA shape [a1], lined cyan, tipped navy [a1].
Hat: a black cloth square cap.

BACHELORS

Gown: a black gown of the basic bachelors' gown [b1].
Hood: a cyan hood of the CNAA shape [a1], lined navy, the cowl bordered inside 1″ faculty colour.
Hat: a black cloth square cap.

POSTGRADUATE CERTIFICATES AND DIPLOMAS

Gown: as for bachelors.
Hood: a cyan hood of the CNAA shape [a1], lined navy.

Hat: a black cloth square cap.

FIRST-DEGREE MASTERS

Gown: as for bachelors.

Hood: a cyan hood of the CNAA shape [a1], lined navy; the cape has a 1″ band of navy set 1″ in.

Hat: a black cloth square cap.

MASTERS, including MASTERS OF PHILOSOPHY

Gown: a black gown of the basic shape [m10], with an inverted-T armhole.

Hood: a cyan hood of the CNAA shape [a1], lined navy, the cowl bordered inside 2″ faculty colour. MPhil is bordered 3″.

Hat: a black cloth square cap.

DOCTORS OF PHILOSOPHY and TAUGHT AND PROFESSIONAL DOCTORS

Undress gown: *none specified*

Dress robe: a cardinal red gown in the same shape as the masters' gown. The facings and yoke are covered in cyan, and there is a red cord and button on the yoke.

Hood: a cyan hood of the CNAA shape [a1], lined as follows:

PhD: lined navy, the cowl bordered inside 3″ maroon (same as MPhil).

EdD: as PhD, but with 1″ grey between the maroon and navy.

Hat: in full dress, a black bonnet, with cyan cords and tassels.

HIGHER DOCTORS

Undress gown: *none specified*

Dress robe: as for the PhD.

Hood: a cyan hood of the CNAA shape [a1], lined navy, the cowl bordered inside 3″ old gold.

Hat: in full dress, a red bonnet, with cyan cords and tassels.

UNIVERSITY OF HULL
1954

Founded as University College Hull in 1927, it was granted a charter in 1954. The robes were designed by Charles Franklyn, and include his various signatures: the London BA gown, the Burgon and London shape hoods, and the use of a shade of light blue.

As originally designed, the faculty was indicated by coloured cords on the sleeves and yoke of the bachelors' gowns, and on the yoke of masters', doctors' undress and dress robes. These were abolished in 1989, and replaced by black ones for black gowns, and claret or scarlet ones for the doctors' dress robes.

Faculty colours

Arts: silver.
Economic Science: grey.
Education: white.
Laws: blue.
Music: cream.
Science: rich gold.
Theology: scarlet.

There was no MMus degree originally, and the robes now used by it were used by the BMus from 1954 until 1962. The BMus now uses the same robes as all other bachelors.

UNDERGRADUATES

Gown: a black gown of the London undergraduate pattern [u3].
Hat: a black cloth square cap.

UNDERGRADUATE CERTIFICATES AND DIPLOMAS

Gown: as for bachelors.
Hood: a black hood of the CNAA shape [a1], bordered as follows:
Certificates: bordered 1″ turquoise silk.
Diplomas: bordered 3″ turquoise silk.
Hat: a black cloth square cap.

FOUNDATION DEGREES

Gown: as for bachelors.
Hood: as for undergraduate diplomas.
Hat: a black cloth square cap.

BACHELORS

Gown: a black gown of the London BA pattern [b4].
Hood: a black silk hood of the Burgon shape [s2], lined but not bound with turquoise silk.
Hat: a black cloth square cap.

BACHELORS OF DIVINITY, of PHILOSOPHY, and of ARTS IN EDUCATION

(these degrees are currently in abeyance; BD last awarded 1978; BPhil 1995; BA(Ed) 1989)

Gown: the masters' gown.

Hood: a black cloth hood of the Oxford full shape [f5], lined but not bound with turquoise silk.

Hat: a black cloth square cap.

POSTGRADUATE CERTIFICATES AND DIPLOMAS

Gown: as for masters.

Hood: the certificate or diploma hood as appropriate (*see* Undergraduate Certificates and Diplomas)

PGCE: a black hood of the CNAA shape [a1], lined turquoise silk.

Hat: a black cloth square cap.

FIRST-DEGREE MASTERS

Gown: as for bachelors.

Hood: as for masters.

Hat: a black cloth square cap.

MASTERS OF MUSIC

Gown: a black silk gown of the [d4] pattern, with black gimp decoration on the skirt and sleeves, as for the Oxford BMus.

Hood: a cream silk brocade hood of the Burgon shape [s2], lined but not bound with turquoise silk.

Hat: a black cloth square cap.

MASTERS OF THEOLOGY

Gown: a black gown of the Oxford MA pattern [m1].

Hood: a black cloth hood of the Oxford full shape [f5], lined but not bound with turquoise silk.

Hat: a black cloth square cap.

ALL OTHER MASTERS including MASTERS OF PHILOSOPHY

Gown: a black gown of the Oxford MA pattern [m1].

Hood: a black silk hood of the London shape [f3], lined and the cape bound ⅜″ turquoise silk.

Hat: a black cloth square cap.

DOCTORS OF PHILOSOPHY and TAUGHT AND PROFESSIONAL DOCTORS

Undress gown: as for masters.

Dress robe: a claret cloth robe of the Oxford pattern [d2], the facings and sleeves covered with turquoise silk.

Hood: a claret cloth hood of the Oxford full shape [f5], lined but not bound with turquoise silk.

Hat: in undress, a black cloth square cap; in full dress, a black cloth bonnet with claret cords and tassels.

DOCTORS OF MUSIC

Undress gown: as for the MMus.

Dress robe: a cream silk brocade robe of the Oxford pattern [d2], the facings and sleeves covered with turquoise silk.

Hood: a cream silk brocade hood of the Oxford full shape [f5], lined but not bound with turquoise silk.

Hat: in undress, a black cloth square cap; in full dress, a black cloth bonnet with cream cords and tassels.

HIGHER DOCTORS

Undress gown: as for masters.

Dress robe: a scarlet cloth robe of the Oxford pattern [d2], the facings and sleeves covered with turquoise silk.

Hood: a scarlet cloth hood of the Oxford full shape [f5], lined but not bound with turquoise silk.

Hat: in undress, a black cloth square cap; in full dress, a black velvet bonnet with scarlet cords and tassels.

DD: in undress, a black cloth square cap; in full dress, a black velvet soft square cap ('Cranmer cap') lined scarlet silk.

HULL–YORK MEDICAL SCHOOL
2003

The founding of a new medical school as part of the University of Hull was considered in the Report of the Royal Commission on Medical Education 1965–68 (Todd Report), published 1968, but it did not materialize. HYMS was opened as a part of the government's initiative to train more medical doctors.

The robes draw on the schemes of both universities, most notably in the alternating use of the gowns. The gowns used for bachelors and masters depend on where the ceremony is held; it alternates year by year between Hull and York. It is unclear whether this restricts a graduate to the use of the gown in which they graduated.

UNDERGRADUATES
none specified

UNDERGRADUATE CERTIFICATES AND DIPLOMAS
none specified

BACHELORS
Gown:
if at York: a grey stuff gown of basic pattern [b1].
if at Hull: a black stuff gown of London BA pattern [b4].
Hood: a black hood of the Burgon shape [s2]:
BMedSci: lined turquoise, the cowl bordered inside 2″ dark blue.
BSc(MedSc): lined dark blue, bordered inside 2″ turquoise.
MB,BS: lined dark blue, bordered inside 1″ turquoise and 1″ orange, set 1″ apart.
Hats: a grey or black cloth square cap, to match the gown.

POSTGRADUATE CERTIFICATES AND DIPLOMAS
none specified

ALL MASTERS including MASTERS OF PHILOSOPHY
Gown:
if at Hull: a black stuff gown of Oxford pattern [m1] with a black cord and button on the yoke.
if at York: a grey gown of basic pattern [m10] with an inverted-T armhole.
Hood:
MSc: a black hood of the Cambridge shape [f1], fully lined orange and bordered inside the cowl 1″ turquoise ribbon. The cape is bordered outside 1″ dark blue. The neckband is black, bound 1″ turquoise on top edge and 1″ dark blue on bottom edge.

MPhil: a maroon panama hood of the Cambridge shape [f1], fully lined and the cape bound 25mm dark blue; bordered inside the cowl 1″ turquoise ribbon. The neckband is maroon, bound 1″ turquoise on top edge and 1″ dark blue on bottom edge.

Hats: a grey or black cloth square cap, to match the gown.

DOCTORS OF MEDICINE (taught degree)

Gown: a dark blue gown of the Oxford doctors' pattern [d2], with 4″ facings to show 3″ of turquoise with 1″ of orange on the outer edge; the sleeves are faced for 10″ with turquoise with 1″ orange at the top.

Hood: a dark blue hood of the Cambridge shape [f1], fully lined and cape edge bound 1″ turquoise. The cowl edge is bordered inside 1″ orange ribbon. The dark blue neckband is 3″ wide, bound 1″ orange on top edge and 1″ turquoise on bottom edge.

Hat: a dark blue cloth bonnet with turquoise cord and tassels.

DOCTORS OF PHILOSOPHY (research degree)

Undress gown: *none specified*

Dress robe: a maroon panama robe of the Oxford pattern [d2], with 4″ facings to show 3″ dark blue with 1″ of orange on the outer edge. The sleeves are faced for 10″ with dark blue with 1″ orange at the top.

Hood: a maroon panama hood of the Cambridge shape [f1], fully lined and the cape bound 25mm dark blue. The cowl is bordered inside 1″ turquoise ribbon. The maaroon neckband is bound 1″ turquoise on top edge and 1″ dark blue on bottom edge.

Hat: in full dress, a maroon cloth bonnet with turquoise cord and tassels.

UNIVERSITY OF HUMBERSIDE

— *see University of Lincoln*

IMPERIAL COLLEGE, LONDON
1907/2007

The Imperial College of Science, Technology, and Medicine has a long history, and was brought into being in 1907 by combining three other institutions: the Royal College of Science, the Royal School of Mines, and the City and Guilds Institute, which remained as 'constituent institutions' of Imperial. It then became part of the University of London. The Imperial College School of Medicine was added as a fourth institution in 1997, and Wye College, near Ashford in Kent, was subsumed in 2000. Degree-awarding powers were granted in 2003, and it became independent of the University of London in 2007.

In addition to the London degree, graduates were awarded an Associateship of one of the three colleges, as appropriate (ARCS, ARSM, ACGI). These diplomas had their own robes (see end of article), and these were more often worn at college-based graduations than the London robes. There was also a postgraduate research-based Diploma of Imperial College (DIC), which also had its own robes. As will be seen, the new robes have been developed from the old diploma robes.

UNDERGRADUATES
none specified

UNDERGRADUATE CERTIFICATES AND DIPLOMAS
none specified

FOUNDATION DEGREES
not awarded

BACHELORS
Gown: a black stuff gown of the basic pattern [b1].
Hood: a black hood of Cambridge shape [f1], the cowl bordered 6″ white watered silk inside, with 1″ purple velvet set ½″ in. The neckband is coloured as follows:
BSc (science): saffron.
BEng and BSc in Engineering: silver grey.
MB,BS: scarlet.
Hat: a black cloth square cap.

POSTGRADUATE CERTIFICATES AND DIPLOMAS
Gown: a black stuff gown of the basic masters' pattern [m10].
Hood: a black hood of Cambridge shape [f1], lined white watered silk, with 1″ purple velvet set ½″ in. The neckband is black.
Hat: a black cloth square cap.

FIRST DEGREE MASTERS

Gown: a black stuff gown of the basic bachelors' pattern [b1].

Hood: the relevant bachelors' hood is worn:

MSci (science): as BSc.
MSci (engineering): as BEng.
MEng: as BEng.

MASTERS including MASTERS OF PHILOSOPHY

Gown: a black stuff gown of the basic pattern [m10].

Hood: a black hood of Cambridge shape [f1], lined as follows:

MPhil: lined purple watered silk, the cowl bordered inside with 1″ white velvet set ½″ in. The neckband is black.

All others: lined and bound on the cape for ½″ white watered silk; the cowl is bordered inside 1″ purple velvet set ½″ in. The neckband is coloured as follows, the colour depending on the faculty, and not the degree title:

MBA: pink.
MEd (medicine): scarlet.
MPH: scarlet.
MRes (business): pink.
MRes (engineering): silver grey.
MRes (humanities): purple, bound white watered silk.
MRes (medicine): scarlet.
MRes: (science): saffron.
MSc (engineering): silver grey.
MSc (humanities): purple, bound white watered silk.
MSc (medicine): scarlet.
MSc (science): saffron.

Hat: a black cloth square cap.

DOCTORS OF PHILOSOPHY and TAUGHT AND PROFESSIONAL DOCTORS

Undress gown: *none specified*

Dress robe: a purple cloth robe of Cambridge pattern [d1]. The facings are covered with white watered silk, with 1″ purple velvet set ½″ from the outer edge. The sleeves are lined purple watered silk, with white cords and buttons.

Hood: a purple cloth hood of Cambridge shape [f1], lined white watered silk, with 1″ purple velvet set ½″ in. The neckband is purple.

Hat: in full dress, a black velvet bonnet with purple cords and tassels.

HIGHER DOCTORS

Undress gown: *none specified*

Dress robe: a purple cloth robe of Cambridge pattern [d1]. The facings are covered with white watered silk, with 1″ purple velvet set ½″ from the outer edge. The sleeves are lined white watered silk, with purple cords and buttons.

Hood: a purple cloth hood of Cambridge shape [f1], lined and bound white watered silk, with 1″ purple velvet set ½″ in. The neckband is purple.

Hat: in full dress, a black cloth bonnet with gold cords and tassels.

ASSOCIATES and DIPLOMATES

Gown: a black stuff gown of the basic pattern [b1], save that the sleeve is left open for the entire length of the forearm.

Hood: a black hood of Oxford simple shape [s1], bordered inside the cowl 6″ white watered silk, with 1″ purple velvet set on it, 1″ from the edge. The neckbands are coloured as follows:

DIC: black lined and bound white watered.

ARCS: white lined and bound white watered.

ARSM: gold lined and bound white watered.

ACGI: red lined and bound white watered.

Honorary Associates of the College wore the same gown and hood, but the shell of the hood was maroon.

Honorary Fellows wore the same gown in scarlet, and a similar hood, with scarlet shell, and fully lined white watered silk.

INSTITUTE OF EDUCATION, LONDON
1902/2008

The Institute was founded in 1902 as a teacher-training body as the London Day Training Centre, under the joint auspices of the University of London and the LCC. In 1932 it changed its name to the Institute of Education. It was awarded a Royal Charter in 1987, and became a School of the University of London. It gained degree-awarding powers in 2008.

UNDERGRADUATES
none specified

UNDERGRADUATE CERTIFICATES AND DIPLOMAS, AND FOUNDATION DEGREES
Gown: as for bachelors.
Hood: a black hood of Cambridge shape [f1], the cowl bordered inside with 2″ dark blue silk, with ½″ yellow laid in the middle. The neckband is blue.
Hat: a black cloth square cap.

BACHELORS
Gown: a black stuff gown of London BA pattern [b4]
Hood: a black hood of Cambridge shape [f1], the cowl bordered inside with 5″ dark blue silk, the cowl edge bound ½″ yellow. The neckband is blue.
Hat: a black cloth square cap.

POSTGRADUATE CERTIFICATES (including PGCE), DIPLOMAS, AND ADVANCED DIPLOMAS
Gown: a black stuff gown of London BA pattern [b4].
Hood: a black hood of Cambridge shape [f1], the cowl bordered inside with 5″ dark blue silk, the cowl edge bound 1½″ yellow. The neckband is blue.
Hat: a black cloth square cap.

FIRST DEGREE MASTERS
not awarded

MASTERS including MASTERS OF PHILOSOPHY
Gown: a black stuff gown of London MA pattern [m5].
Hood: a black hood of Cambridge shape [f1], lined as follows:
MPhil: lined dark blue, bound 1″ yellow on all edges. The neckband is blue.
All others: lined dark blue, the cowl bound 2″ yellow. The neckband is blue.
Hat: a black cloth square cap.

DOCTORS OF EDUCATION

Undress gown: *none specified*

Dress robe: a dark blue robe of Cambridge pattern [d1], the sleeves lined and the facings covered with black. There is ½″ yellow on the outer edge of the facings, and the sleeves are held by a yellow cord and button.

Hood: a dark blue hood of Cambridge shape [f1], lined black, the cowl bordered inside 1″ yellow. The neckband is blue.

Hat: in full dress, a black cloth bonnet with yellow cords and tassels.

DOCTORS OF PHILOSOPHY

Undress gown: *none specified*

Dress robe: a dark blue robe of Cambridge pattern [d1], the sleeves lined and the facings covered with black. There is 1″ yellow on the outer edge of the facings, and the sleeves are held by a yellow cord and button.

Hood: a dark blue hood of Cambridge shape [f1], lined black, and bound on all edges with 1″ yellow. The neckband is blue.

Hat: in full dress, a black cloth bonnet with yellow cords and tassels.

HIGHER DOCTORS

Undress gown: *none specified*

Dress robe: a dark blue robe of Cambridge pattern [d1], the sleeves lined yellow, and the facings covered with black. The sleeves are held by a black cord and button.

Hood: a dark blue hood of Cambridge full shape [f1], lined yellow. The neckband is yellow.

Hat: in full dress, a black velvet bonnet with yellow cords and tassels.

JOHN MOORES UNIVERSITY, LIVERPOOL
1992

Originally founded as a small mechanics institution, the Liverpool Mechanics' School of Arts, in 1825, the institution grew over the centuries by amalgamating with different colleges, eventually becoming Liverpool Polytechnic. It became a university in 1992 under the new title of 'Liverpool John Moores University'. The University took its name from Sir John Moores, the founder of the Littlewoods empire, which has been synonymous with Liverpool since it began in 1923.

All hoods use the University's embossed silk – grey, dark blue, or scarlet – which has the armorial shield as the motif.

UNDERGRADUATES
none specified

UNDERGRADUATE CERTIFICATES AND DIPLOMAS
Gown: as for bachelors.
Hood: a dark blue hood of the CNAA shape [a1], lined with grey embossed silk.
Hat: a black cloth square cap.

FOUNDATION DEGREES
Gown: as for bachelors.
Hood: a dark blue hood of the CNAA shape [a1], fully lined with grey embossed silk, the cowl bordered inside with 2″ dark blue ribbon, set 1″ in.
Hat: a dark blue cloth square cap.

BACHELORS and FIRST-DEGREE MASTERS
Gown: a dark blue stuff gown of basic pattern [b1].
Hood: a dark blue hood of Cambridge shape [f1], the cowl bordered inside with 4″ grey embossed silk.
Hat: a dark blue cloth square cap.

POSTGRADUATE CERTIFICATES AND DIPLOMAS
Gown: as for bachelors.
Hood: a dark blue hood of Cambridge shape [f1], part-lined with blue embossed silk.
Hat: a dark blue cloth square cap.

MASTERS including MASTERS OF PHILOSOPHY
Gown: a dark blue stuff gown of basic pattern [m10]. For MPhil, the gown has 2″ wide facings of grey embossed silk.
Hood: a dark blue hood of Cambridge shape [f1], lined with grey embossed silk.

Hat: a dark blue cloth square cap.

DOCTORS OF PHILOSOPHY and TAUGHT AND PROFESSIONAL DOCTORS

Undress gown: as for masters

Dress robe: a scarlet cloth robe of Cambridge pattern [d1], with facings and sleeve linings of dark blue embossed silk.

Hood: a scarlet hood of Cambridge shape [f1], lined with dark blue embossed silk.

Hat: in undress, a dark blue cloth square cap; in full dress, a dark blue velvet bonnet with scarlet cords and tassels.

HIGHER DOCTORS

Undress gown: as PhD.

Dress robe: a dark blue robe of Cambridge pattern [d1], with the sleeves lined and facings covered with scarlet embossed silk.

Hood: a dark blue hood of Cambridge shape [f1], lined with scarlet embossed silk.

Hat: in undress, a dark blue cloth square cap; in full dress, a scarlet velvet bonnet with dark blue cords and tassels.

UNIVERSITY OF KEELE
1949/1962

Founded as the University College of North Staffordshire in 1949, Keele had from the start the right to award its own BA under the ægis of Oxford, Birmingham, and Manchester, resembling in this St David's College, Lampeter. Graduates wishing to read for higher degrees were able to do so at Keele, but the degrees were awarded by other universities – principally Birmingham, but also Manchester, Southampton, and Sheffield. Full university status was granted in 1962.

The BA hood dates from 1949, the others from 1962. The hoods are based on the university's heraldic colours of gold and red, although it is unclear why the higher degrees have a red rather than a gold lining. The use of purple rather than scarlet for the higher doctors was much commented on at the time, but in fact goes back to a mediæval precedent – although it is probable that they did not know of this.

UNDERGRADUATES

Gown: a black gown of the London undergraduate pattern [u3], but with the forearm seam left open.
Hat: a black cloth square cap.

UNDERGRADUATE CERTIFICATES AND DIPLOMAS

none specified

BACHELORS

Gown: a black gown of basic pattern [b1].
Hood: a black hood of Cambridge shape [f1], the cowl bordered with six inches of gold silk, and piped on the cowl edge with a red cord.
Hat: a black cloth square cap.

POSTGRADUATE CERTIFICATES AND DIPLOMAS

Gown: as for bachelors.
Hood: a black hood of Edinburgh shape [s4], the cowl bordered inside 2″ gold silk, and piped with a red cord.
Hat: a black cloth square cap.

FIRST-DEGREE MASTERS

Gown: as for bachelors.
Hood: as for masters.
Hat: a black cloth square cap.

MASTERS including MASTERS OF PHILOSOPHY

Gown: a black gown of Oxford MA pattern [m1], with a black gimp frog at the top of each sleeve.

Hood: a black hood of Cambridge shape [f1], fully lined with red silk, and piped on all edges with gold cord.

Hat: a black cloth square cap.

DOCTORS OF PHILOSOPHY, of EDUCATION, and of MEDICINE

Undress gown: as for masters.

Dress robe: the masters' gown, with facings of gold silk.

Hood: a gold silk hood of Cambridge shape [f1], fully lined with red silk.

Hat: in undress, a black cloth square cap; in full dress a black velvet bonnet with red (PhD) or yellow (MD, EdD) cords and tassels.

HIGHER DOCTORS

Undress gown: as for masters.

Dress robe: a purple cloth robe of Cambridge pattern [d1], the sleeves lined with purple silk of a lighter shade and held with a gold cords and buttons. The facings are edged with gold cord.

Hood: a purple cloth hood of Cambridge shape [f1], fully lined with red silk, and piped on the cowl edge with a gold cord.

Hat: in undress, a black cloth square cap; in full dress, a black velvet bonnet with gold cords and tassels.

NOTES

1. The obsolete BEd had a hood bordered with silver silk instead of gold. There have been listings that show the BSc as bordered red and piped gold, but this is incorrect, and was never the case.

UNIVERSITY OF KENT
1965

A university in Canterbury was first considered in 1947, when an anticipated growth in student numbers led several localities to seek the creation of new universities. The university's original name, chosen in 1962, was the University of Kent at Canterbury, reflecting the fact that the campus straddled the boundary between the county borough of Canterbury and Kent County Council. The idea of calling the new institution the University of Canterbury was opposed by the University of Canterbury in New Zealand. Its charter was granted in 1965. During the 1990s and 2000s the University expanded beyond its original campus. It now has campuses in Medway, Tonbridge, and Brussels, and has recently dropped the 'at Canterbury' from its title.

The robes are unexceptionable, except for the 'hoods', which are of a nature peculiar to this university, being a flap or cape held together in front by cords and buttons. These 'hoods' have no cowl at all. Previous statements that they were designed by Hardy Amies are now known to be incorrect, although it is not known who was responsible for them. The Arts colour is officially listed as green, but it is very hard to tell from yellow.

UNDERGRADUATES
none specified

UNDERGRADUATE CERTIFICATES AND DIPLOMAS
Gown: as for bachelors.
Hood:
Certificate: a dark blue hood of CNAA shape [a1].
Diploma: a red hood of CNAA shape [a1].
Hat: a black cloth square cap.

FOUNDATION DEGREES
Gown: as for bachelors.
Hood: a bronze cloth hood of Kent shape [a3], with a central V-shaped panel of velvet:
FdA: yellow-green.
FdSc: purple.
if from a validated institution: 'Canterbury' (light) blue silk.
Hat: a black cloth square cap.

BACHELORS
Gown: a black stuff gown of basic pattern [b1].
Hood: a silver cloth hood of Kent shape [a3], with a central V-shaped panel of velvet:
BA (humanities): yellow-green.

BA(maths), BSc: purple.
BA(Soc), LL.B [BSocSc]: grey.
BA, BSc, BEng (info tech): royal blue.
[BEd: red silk.]
BA, BSc from accredited colleges: 'Canterbury' (light) blue silk.

Hat: a black cloth square cap.

POSTGRADUATE CERTIFICATES AND DIPLOMAS

Gown: as for bachelors.
Hood: a red hood of CNAA shape [a1], lined dark blue.
Hat: a black cloth square cap.

FIRST-DEGREE MASTERS

Gown: as for bachelors.
Hood: as for the relevant bachelor.
Hat: a black cloth square cap.

MASTERS

Gown: a black stuff gown of basic pattern [m10].
Hood: a gold cloth hood of Kent shape [a3], with a central V-shaped panel of velvet:
MA, MPhil (Humanitites): yellow-green.
MSc, MA(Maths), MBioTech, MPhil: purple.
MASoc, LL.M, MBA, MEBA, MBS, MSc(Soc), MPhil: grey.
MA, MSc, MPhil (IT): royal blue.
MA, MPhil from accredited colleges: 'Canterbury' (light) blue silk.

Hat: a black cloth square cap.

MASTERS OF PHILOSOPHY

Gown: as for other masters.
Hood: a gold cloth hood of Kent shape [a3], with a central V-shaped panel of velvet of the colour of the discipline in which the degree was taken, or 'Canterbury' (light) blue silk if taken through an accredited college. The cords and buttons are wine-colour.

DOCTORS OF PHILOSOPHY and TAUGHT AND PROFESSIONAL DOCTORS

Undress gown: as for masters.
Dress robe: the masters' gown, but with facings of scarlet velvet.
Hood: a red cloth hood of Kent shape [a3], with a central V-shaped panel of velvet of the colour of the discipline in which the degree was taken, or 'Canterbury' (light) blue silk if taken through an accredited college.
Hat: in undress, a black cloth square cap; in full dress, a black cloth bonnet with maroon cords and tassels.

HIGHER DOCTORS

Undress gown: as for masters.

Dress robe: a scarlet cloth robe of Oxford pattern [d2]. The facings are of scarlet velvet, and there are two 5″ bands of scarlet velvet on the sleeves, set 5″ apart. For DCL, the velvet is purple.

Hood: a scarlet cloth hood of the Kent shape [a3], with a central V-shaped panel of velvet:

DCL: black, outlined with gold cord.

DLitt, DD, DMus: yellow-green.

DSc: purple.

DLitt(Soc), LL.D, [DSocSc]: grey.

Hat: in undress, a black cloth square cap; in full dress, a black velvet bonnet with maroon cords and tassels, but gold for DCL.

KING'S COLLEGE, LONDON
1829/2007

King's College was founded in 1829 as an Anglican response to the establishment in 1826 of the militantly secular 'London University' – later University College, London (*q.v.*). In 1836 the two colleges became the founding colleges of the federal University of London. The college absorbed a number of other colleges over the years, notably Queen Elizabeth College, and Chelsea College. It was granted degree-awarding powers in 2003, but did not start to exercise them until 2007. The College has always awarded an Associateship (AKC), and still does. The robes for this are discussed in Note 1.

The robes for King's were designed by Vivienne Westwood. Hats are specifically stated not to be part of the scheme. The gowns have a gold metal button on each shoulder, embossed with the College's lion emblem, to which the hood is buttoned; there are no neckbands (see Note 2), but the hood binding continues over the shoulders to form loose facings to the gowns, hanging to about knee-level. They are about 4″ wide. The colour of the binding depends on the School in which the degree was taken, not its title. Thus a BSc in physics is bound coral, while a BSc in sociology is bound gold.

Faculty colours

Biomedical and Health Sciences: orange.
Dental Institute: fuchsia.
Humanities: green.
Institute of Psychiatry: deep red.
Law: silver.
Medicine: purple.
Nursing and Midwifery: lilac.
Physical Science and Engineering: coral.
Social Science and Public Policy: gold.

UNDERGRADUATES
none specified

UNDERGRADUATE CERTIFICATES AND DIPLOMAS
none specified

FOUNDATION DEGREES
not awarded

BACHELORS

Gown: a black stuff gown of KCL pattern [m19]. This is a master's pattern gown, with the sleeve open from the shoulder to 8″ above the boot, which is cut square (as [m10]). It has broad flat pleats at the back and a flap collar, as on the [d4] gown.

Hood: a black hood of KCL simple shape [s12], which is a large cowl, lined with black taffeta, and the cowl edge bound 4″ inside and out with school colour.

POSTGRADUATE CERTIFICATES AND DIPLOMAS

none specified

MASTERS including MASTERS OF PHILOSOPHY and FIRST-DEGREE MASTERS

Gown: a black stuff gown of KCL pattern [m19]; the sleeve openings are bound with 4″ inside and out with school colour. For MPhil the bindings are of the same blue as used for the PhD.

Hood: a black hood of the KCL full shape [f12], lined with black taffeta, bound on all edges 4″ inside and out with school colour. For MPhil the bindings are of the same blue as used for the PhD.

TAUGHT AND PROFESSIONAL DOCTORS

Undress gown: *none specified*

Gown: a blue gown of KCL pattern [m19], the sleeve openings bound 4″ inside and out with dark red.

Hood: a blue hood of the same shape as masters [f12], lined blue taffeta, and bound dark red 4″ inside and out on all edges.

DOCTORS OF PHILOSOPHY and of MEDICINE

Undress gown: *none specified*

Dress robe: a dark red robe of KCL pattern [m19], the sleeve openings bound 4″ inside and out with blue.

Hood: a dark red hood of the same shape as masters [f12], lined dark red taffeta, and bound blue 4″ inside and out on all edges.

HIGHER DOCTORS

Undress gown: *none specified*

Dress robe: a scarlet cloth robe of KCL pattern [m19], the sleeves bound gold 4″ inside and out.

Hood: a scarlet hood of the same shape as masters [f12], lined scarlet, bound gold 4″ inside and out on all edges.

NOTES

1. The College has always awarded the diploma of Associate, designated AKC, for which there were no robes. Since 2008, holders of the AKC wear, in addition to

their gown and hood, an epitoge on the left shoulder, embroidered with the College's lion emblem.

2. The Theological Associateship, (originally designated ThA,KCL, but latterly AKC) was offered as an ordination training award from 1846 to 1972. This had the following robes:
   Gown: a black gown of basic pattern [m10]. Occasionally it was made with ½″ black velvet round the armholes; the facings were sometimes covered with black velvet.
   Hood:
   1846-1862: none.
   1862-1882: a black stuff hood of Oxford simple shape[s1], lined and bound mauve silk.
   1882-1909: a black stuff hood of Oxford simple shape[s1], bordered inside 1″ and outside ¼″ mauve silk.
   1909-1972: a black stuff hood of Cambridge shape [f1], bound on all edges 1″ mauve silk.
   Hat: a black cloth square cap, the skull bound black velvet.
   These robes became obsolete when the theological AKC was withdrawn in 1972.

3. In 2009, following representation from clergy, an alternative version of the hood, with neckband, has been approved, for use in church over a surplice. This version cannot be hired, and may not be worn at degree ceremonies.

UNIVERSITY OF KINGSTON
1992

The university's roots go back to the Kingston Technical Institute, which opened in 1899. It became Kingston Polytechnic in 1970, and was granted university status in 1992.

There are only two hoods used by this University: one for all earned awards, and one for awards made *honoris causa*. The difference in degree is marked by the styles of the gown, which have Continental origins.

The 'university blue' is a bright turquoise colour.

UNDERGRADUATES
none specified

UNDERGRADUATE CERTIFICATES AND DIPLOMAS
Gown: a black gown, with loose sleeves, less full than the [d2] robe, and black facings which continue round the neck to form a collar.
Hood: a grey panama hood of Cambridge shape [f1], fully lined, but not bound, with university blue.
Hat: a black cloth square cap.

FOUNDATION DEGREES
Gown: a black gown, with loose sleeves, less full than the [d2] robe, and black facings which continue round the neck to form a collar. There is 1″ blue set on the sleeves, 8″ from the bottom.
Hood: a grey panama hood of Cambridge shape [f1], fully lined, but not bound, with university blue.
Hat: a black cloth square cap.

BACHELORS
Gown: a black gown, with loose sleeves, less full than the [d2] robe, and 2½″ university blue facings which continue round the neck to form a collar.
Hood: a grey panama hood of Cambridge shape [f1], fully lined, but not bound, with university blue.
Hat: a black cloth square cap.

POSTGRADUATE CERTIFICATES AND DIPLOMAS
Gown: a black gown, with loose sleeves, less full than the [d2] robe, and 4″ university blue facings which continue round the neck to form a collar.
Hood: a grey panama hood of Cambridge shape [f1], fully lined, but not bound, with university blue.

Hat: a black cloth square cap.

FIRST-DEGREE MASTERS

Gown: a black gown, with loose sleeves, less full than the [d2] robe, and black facings which continue round the neck to form a collar. There is 3″ university blue set on the sleeves, 8″from the bottom.

Hood: a grey panama hood of Cambridge shape [f1], fully lined, but not bound, with university blue.

Hat: a black cloth square cap.

MASTERS including MASTERS OF PHILOSOPHY

Gown: a black stuff gown with loose sleeves, less full than the [d2] robe, with black facings. These are 5½″ wide at the top, and 7½″ wide at the hem. The outer edge has four university blue pleats, 2″ increasing to 4″.

Hood: a grey panama hood of Cambridge shape [f1], fully lined, but not bound, with university blue.

Hat: a black cloth square cap.

DOCTORS OF PHILOSOPHY and TAUGHT AND PROFESSIONAL DOCTORS

Undress gown: *none specified*

Dress robe: a grey panama gown with loose sleeves, less full than the [d2] robe, with grey facings. These are 5½″ wide at the top, and 7½″ wide at the hem. The outer edge has four university blue pleats, 2″ increasing to 4″. The 8″ cuffs are university blue, and there is a 1″ band of blue set 1″ above them.

Hood: a grey panama hood of Cambridge shape [f1], fully lined, but not bound, with university blue.

Hat: in full dress, a grey panama bonnet with university blue cords and tassels.

HIGHER DOCTORS

Undress gown: *none specified*

Dress robe: a mid-blue panama gown with loose sleeves, less full than the [d2] robe, with university blue facings. These are 5½″ wide at the top, and 7 ½″ wide at the hem. The outer edge has four grey pleats, 2″ increasing to 4″. The 8″ cuffs are university blue.

Hood: a grey panama hood of Cambridge shape [f1], fully lined, but not bound, with university blue.

Hat: in full dress, a university blue panama bonnet with grey cords and tassels.

MASTERS *honoris causa*

Gown: a university blue stuff gown with loose sleeves, less full than the [d2] robe, with university blue facings. These are 5½″ wide at the top, and 7½″ wide at the hem. The outer edge has four black pleats, 2″ increasing to 4″. The cuffs are black.

Hood: a grey panama hood of Cambridge shape [f1], fully lined, but not bound, with university blue. There is 1″ university blue on the outside of the cape, set 1″ in.
Hat: a black cloth square cap

DOCTORS *honoris causa*
Gown: as for higher doctors.
Hood: as for masters *honoris causa.*
Hat: as for higher doctors.

LAMBETH DEGREES

Lambeth degrees are awarded by the Archbishop of Canterbury in his own right. They are designated 'Lambeth' from his London Palace, and that follows the degree designation: *e.g.*, MA(Lambeth). Occasionally the form 'Cantuar:' (for Canterbury) is encountered, but this appears to be incorrect.

The robes used are identical with those of Oxford or Cambridge: which set is used depends on the *alma mater* of the awarding archbishop. However, when George Carey (1991-2002) became the first archbishop without an Oxford or Cambridge degree, there was heated discussion as to whether the robes of his *alma mater,* London, were to be used, with the University of London being very much in favour. In the event, he continued to use the Oxford robes, which his predecessor, Robert Runcie, had used, and this use has continued under Rowan Williams. This could mean that the Oxford robes will become the default ones.

It would appear, however, that the custom of using the Oxford or Cambridge robes is the result of historical development. When the degrees were first awarded, the robes of the two universities were practically identical, having been totally identical originally. As the two universities developed significant differences in their schemes, the common original became lost, and thus the custom of using the variant of the archbishop's university came into being. Some commentators have held that a recipient of a Lambeth degree who is already a graduate should wear the robes of the corresponding degree in their own university, but it is unknown to what extent this happened – if ever it did – nor what would happen if the university concerned did not have the relevant faculty (*e.g.*, a BD being awarded to a graduate of Sheffield).

If the lost original were restored for use, it would have all doctors wearing scarlet robes and hoods, trimmed or lined with rose-pink silk, and MAs black silk hoods, probably with a rose-pink lining, as (arguably) would BDs.

In 1905, Randall Davidson instituted the Lambeth Diploma of **Scholar in Theology** (STh), initially for women, but later opened to men. Holders of the STh wear the following robes:

Gown: a black stuff gown of London BA pattern [b4], with blue cords and buttons on the sleeves.

Hood: a black hood of Cambridge shape [f1], the lining is split horizontally when worn, white over light blue. (Occasionally, a hood lined with light blue and the cowl bordered inside with 8″ white is used.)

In 1990, Robert Runcie instituted an examination by thesis for the MA; in 2007, Rowan Williams extended this provision by adding the PhD, and replacing the MA with the MPhil. The robes used for the examined degrees are the same as for all other Lambeth degrees.

SAINT DAVID'S COLLEGE, LAMPETER
1822

Founded in 1822, the College gained the right to award the BD in 1852, and the BA in 1865. The LD was introduced in 1884, and died out around 1940. The degrees (but not the diplomas) were placed in suspension when the College became a constituent institution of the University of Wales in 1971 as St David's University College. At that time, the Privy Council awarded it full degree-awarding powers, which would be revived should the College cease to be part of that University. The name was changed to the University of Wales Lampeter in 1996; in 2010 the college united with Trinity College Carmarthen to form 'The University of Wales: Trinity St David'. Late in 2010, it was announced that Swansea Metropolitan University was to merge with the new TSD.

The BD hood has been used since around the mid-1970s for the various Licences the College awards in its own right, such as the LTh; these are equivalent of the third year of an honours degree. The LicDD, a post-PhD award, was introduced in 2007, but withdrawn by 2011.

UNDERGRADUATES

Gown: a black gown of Oxford scholars' pattern [u1], but with the forearm sleeve left open. Scholars had a velvet strip 1″ wide (called 'tabs') from shoulder to waist on the facings of their gowns. The Senior Scholar had 2″ tabs on his gown.

Hat: a black cloth square cap.

BACHELOR OF ARTS (BA)

Gown: a black gown of Cambridge BA pattern [b2].

Hood: a black silk hood of Cambridge shape [f1], half lined and bound 'miniver' – white fur with black spots. (Unlike the Cambridge BA, the Lampeter hood usually has the cowl fur bound over the edge for about an inch.)

Hat: a black cloth square cap.

BACHELOR OF DIVINITY (BD)

Gown: a black gown of the Lampeter BD pattern [m7] – *i.e.,* with two crescent cuts on each sleeve.

Hood: a black silk hood of Cambridge shape [f1], lined violet silk, bound ½″ white silk on all edges.

Hat: a black cloth square cap.

LICENTIATE IN DIVINITY (LD)

Gown: as for undergraduates.

Hood: a black stuff hood of Cambridge shape [f1], lined black Italian cloth, bound ½″ white silk on all edges.

Hat: a black cloth square cap.

COLLEGE LICENCES since 1971 (LTh, etc)

Gown: the Wales BA gown [b6].

Hood: a black silk hood of Cambridge shape [f1], lined violet silk, bound ½″ white silk on all edges.

Hat: a black cloth square cap.

LICENTIATE IN DIVINITY (DOCTORAL) (LicDD)

Holders of this award wear the robe and hood of the PhD (or other doctorate) which they already hold. In addition, a scarlet cape of elbow length, trimmed with white fur on the lower edge, is worn over the gown and under the hood. The cape is open in front, and held by a single button at the neck. The hat is a scarlet bonnet with white cords and tassels.

NOTES

1. Initially, the BA and BD hoods could be made in either the Cambridge or the Oxford shape [s1] – and in the early days Oxford was the more usual shape. The Cambridge shape seems to have been fixed by about 1885.

2. The original pattern for the LD had a semi-circular cape, similar to the Durham BA [f6]. (The use of 'LicDiv' as the abbreviation for the LD, found in some older works on academic dress, was incorrect.)

UNIVERSITY OF LANCASTER
1966

The University was established by Royal Charter in 1964, as part of the expansion of higher education. The University is collegiate, with eight undergraduate colleges, and one postgraduate college.

The main University colour is a pale grey – 'Quaker' grey – which reflects the influence the Quakers had in the region. Although the various degrees are differentiated by colours, they are not used entirely systematically. For example, all Science degrees have gold, but dark blue goes from LL.B to MBA, while the LL.M has purple. Originally, all students received a BA, which is why the BA hood is the 'basic' hood; the BSc was introduced later. Likewise the MA was seen as the basic postgraduate degree, while the MSc and MLitt were the higher ones: this explains why the MA is bound on the cowl only.

UNDERGRADUATES

Gown: a grey stuff gown of London pattern [u3], with a red yoke. This is in abeyance.
Hat: a black cloth square cap.

UNDERGRADUATE CERTIFICATES AND DIPLOMAS

none specified

FOUNDATION DEGREES

Gown: as for bachelors.
Hood: a black hood of CNAA shape [a1], lined bright red, and tipped grey.
Hat: a black cloth square cap.

BACHELORS

Gown: a black stuff gown of basic pattern [b1].
Hood: a black silk hood of Burgon shape [s2], lined grey, and bordered ½″ bright red silk inside the cowl edge. There is a further ½″ band of silk set ½″ away:
BA: no extra band.
BBA: royal blue.
[BEd: white.]
BEng: orange.
LL.B: dark blue.
BMus: light blue.
BPhil: dark green.
BSc: gold.
Hat: a black cloth square cap.

POSTGRADUATE CERTIFICATES AND DIPLOMAS

Gown: as for bachelors.

Hood: a black hood of CNAA shape [a1], lined grey, and tipped bright red.

FIRST-DEGREE MASTERS

Gown: as for bachelors.

Hood: the same as the bachelor's hoods, except that the extra band is 2″ wide:

MEng: tangerine.

All others: yellow.

Hat: a black cloth square cap.

MASTERS including MASTERS OF PHILOSOPHY

Gown: a black stuff gown of Lancaster pattern [m11]. This the same as the Cambridge MA, but the base of the sleeve is cut back at 45 degrees. For MLitt, there are two vertical rows of black velvet on each sleeve, 1″ wide, and 1½″ long, set ½″ apart.

Hood: a black hood of Cambridge shape [f1], lined with bright red, and bound on all edges for 1½″ as follows:

MA: grey (bound on cowl only)

MBA: dark blue.

LL.M: purple.

MLitt: royal blue.

MMus: light blue (this is very pale)

MPhil: the lining is brought out on all edges for 1½″.

MRes: cowl bound yellow, and the cape bound gold.

MSc: gold.

Hat: a black cloth square cap.

DOCTORS OF PHILOSOPHY and TAUGHT AND PROFESSIONAL DOCTORS

Undress gown: as for masters, and with a single row of black Birmingham lace round each armhole and round the yoke.

Dress robe: a grey cloth robe of Cambridge pattern [d1], with facings and sleeve linings of bright red. There are grey cords and button on the sleeves and yoke.

Hood: a bright red cloth hood of Cambridge shape [f1], lined with silk of the same shade.

Hat: in undress, a black cloth square cap; in full dress a black cloth bonnet with red cords and tassels.

HIGHER DOCTORS

Undress gown: as PhD, but with two rows of black Birmingham lace round the armholes and on the yoke.

Dress robe: a bright red cloth hood of Cambridge pattern [d1], with facings and sleeves linings as follows:

LL.D: grey.
DLitt: blue.
DSc: gold.
DMus: cream brocade (until some point before 1986, red brocade)

Hood: a bright red cloth hood of Cambridge shape [f1], lined with the same silk as the dress robe.

Hat: in undress, a black cloth square cap; in full dress a black velvet bonnet with red cords and tassels.

NOTES

1. Originally, the MSc had the same gown as the MLitt.

UNIVERSITY OF LEEDS
1904

Founded in 1874 as Yorkshire College of Science, it changed its name to Yorkshire College in 1878. In 1884 it amalgamated with the Leeds Medical School, founded 1831. From 1887, it was one of the three colleges of the Victoria University. It was chartered as the University of Leeds on 25 April 1904.

The original scheme, which relied on three shades of green, with the addition of white for masters and scarlet for doctors, is now in grave danger of collapsing, owing to the increasing number of new degree titles that are being introduced. Although a white lining has always been the marker of a master's degree, there are two that have no white at all (MPH and MHSc), and one (MPsychoth) where it is reduced to the band on the lining. It would be easy to simplify it to a 'grade hood' system, with one hood for all bachelors (green lined green), one for masters (green lined white), *etc*, by following Exeter and reducing the several shades of green to one.

All hoods, except those for doctors and MPhil, are made in a special form of the simple shape. The cowl edge is permanently turned out for about 4″, and shows the lining colour. Where there is a 1″ band, it is placed on this turned-out portion, in many cases set 1″ away from its edge. Bachelors' hoods are generally made in one of more shades of green, while masters' hoods usually have a white lining, although there are exceptions to both, notably the MPhil, which has the only black hood in the scheme. The diploma hoods, introduced in 2004, all have maroon shells. Although this seems to introduce an extraneous colour, it is explained by the fact that the university colours are green, white, and maroon.

The black gowns are trimmed with black Leeds lace, which is illustrated on page 42. The published regulations on the website say that hats do not now form part of the scheme, and are not to be worn at ceremonies. However, they did once, and so are included here.

UNDERGRADUATES

Gown: a black stuff gown of Oxford scholars' pattern [u2].
[**Hat:** a black cloth square cap.]

UNDERGRADUATE CERTIFICATES AND DIPLOMAS

Gown: as for bachelors.
[Licentiate in Dental Surgery – LDS: a black stuff gown with elbow-length bell sleeves, the facings and yoke covered with middle green, and the sleeves bordered 2″ middle green outside and 2″ white inside.]
Hood: a maroon hood of Leeds simple shape [s7], lined as follows:
CertHE: lined light green.
DipHE: lined middle green.

Advanced Diplomas: lined middle green, with a 1″ band of light green.
Graduate Diplomas/Graduate Certificates: lined dark green.
[**Hat:** a black cloth square cap.]

FOUNDATION DEGREES

Gown: as for bachelors.
Hood: a maroon hood of Leeds simple shape [s7], lined middle green with a 1″ band of dark green.
[**Hat:** a black cloth square cap.]

BACHELORS

Gown: a black stuff gown of basic pattern [b1], with Leeds lace round the yoke and along the forearm seam.
Hood: a hood of Leeds simple shape [s7]:
BA: dark green lined dark green.
[BA (Collegiate): dark green lined dark green, with a 1″ band of middle green.]
[BBroadcasting: light green lined light green, with a 1″ band of middle green.]
[BCom: light green lined dark green.]
BChD: dark green lined middle green.
BDes: middle green lined light green.
[BD: dark green lined white, with a 1″ band of scarlet set 1″ in.]
[BEd: dark green with a 1″ band of light green.]
BEng: middle green lined dark green.
BHSc: middle green lined middle green, with a 1″ band of light green.
LL.B: light green lined light green.
MB,ChB: dark green lined light green.
BMus: dark green lined dark green, with a 1″ band of white watered silk set 1″ in.
BPerfArts: light green lined light green, with a 1″ band of dark green.
BSc: middle green lined middle green.
[BSc (Collegiate): middle green lined middle green, with a 1″ band of dark green. *now used for MChem, etc*]
[**Hat:** a black cloth square cap.]

FIRST-DEGREE MASTERS

Gown: as for bachelors
Hood: a middle-green hood of Leeds simple shape [s7], lined as follows:
MEng: lined dark green, with a 1″ band of middle green.
MChem, MGeog, MGeol, MGeophys, MMath, MPhys, MDes, MInformatics, MNatSci, MEnv, MGeosciences: lined middle green, with a 1″ band of dark green.
[**Hat:** a black cloth square cap.]

POSTGRADUATE CERTIFICATES AND DIPLOMAS

Gown: as for masters.

Hood: a maroon hood of Leeds simple shape [s7], lined as follows:
Postgraduate Certificates: lined light green, with a 1″ band of white silk.
Postgraduate Diplomas: lined middle green, with a 1″ band of white silk.

MASTERS including MASTERS OF PHILOSOPHY

Gown: a black stuff gown of the Lampeter BD pattern [m7]: it has a crescent cut on both sides of each sleeve, and has Leeds lace round the armholes and the yoke.

Hood: a hood of Leeds simple shape [s7], (except MPhil):
MA: dark green with white lining.
MBA: light green lined white, with a 1″ band of dark green set 1″ in.
MBS: *same as* MA.
[MCFS: *same as* MMedSc.]
[MCom: *same as* MBA.]
ChM: dark green with white lining, with a 1″ band of light green.
MChD: dark green lined white, with a 1″ band of middle green.
MDSc: dark green lined white, with a 1″ band of dark green set 1″ in.
MEd: dark green lined white, with a 1″ band of middle green set 1″ in.
MFA: *same as* MA.
MHSc: *same as* ChM.
LL.M: light green lined white.
MMedSc: *same as* ChM.
MMid: *same as* ChM.
MMus: dark green lined white, with a 1″ band of white watered silk set 1″ in.
MPH: dark green lined light green, with a 1″ band of dark green set 1″ in.
MPhil: a black stuff or silk hood of Cambridge shape [f1], lined with middle green and bound ½″ scarlet on all edges.
MPsychObs:[1] dark green lined light green, with a 1″ band of white silk set 1″ in.
MPsychother: *same as* MPsychObs.
MSc middle green lined white.
MSc(Eng): middle green lined white, with a 1″ band of dark green set 1″ in.
MRes: as for the equivalent taught master's degree in the appropriate faculty.

[**Hat:** a black cloth square cap].

DOCTORS OF PHILOSOPHY and TAUGHT AND PROFESSIONAL DOCTORS

Undress gown: as for masters.

Dress robe: a mid-green robe of Cambridge pattern [d1], the sleeves lined with the same colour. The facings are of mid-green cloth, with 2″ mid-green silk on the outer edge, and a narrow band of scarlet down the centre of each facing between the silk and the cloth.

Hood: a mid-green hood of Cambridge shape [f1], lined and bound as follows:
PhD: lined mid-green, bound ½″ scarlet on all edges.
DClinPsy: lined scarlet, bound ½″ dark green on all edges.

[1] Originally designated MPsObSt.

EdD: lined and bound ½″ white on all edges.

All others: lined white, bound ½″ scarlet on all edges.

[**Hat:** in undress, a black cloth square cap; in full dress, a black velvet bonnet with gold cords or tassels.]

HIGHER DOCTORS

Undress gown: as for masters.

Dress robe: a scarlet cloth robe of Cambridge pattern [d1], with facings and sleeve linings as follows. The facings are 5″ wide, and have the silk on the outer 2½″, the rest showing the scarlet cloth. In the case of those which have an 'edging', it is placed along the centre of the facing, between the silk and the scarlet, and also round the edge of the sleeve, on the inside.

DD: dark green sleeve linings, white facings.
DDS: dark green sleeve linings, mid-green facings.
DLitt: dark green.
DSc: mid-green.
MD: dark green, edged 1″ light green.
DSc(Eng): middle green, edged dark green. [*formerly DEng*]
LL.D: light green.
DMus: dark green, edged 1″ white watered silk.

Hood: a scarlet cloth hood of Cambridge shape [f1], lined as follows:

DD: dark green, bound 1″ white on all edges.
DDS: dark green, bound mid-green on all edges.
DLitt: dark green.
LL.D: light green.
DSc: mid-green.
DSc(Eng): mid-green, bound 1″ dark green on all edges. [*formerly DEng*]
MD: dark green, bound 1″ light green on all edges.
DMus: dark green, the cowl bordered inside 1″ white watered silk set 1″ in.

[**Hat:** in undress, a black cloth square cap; in full dress, a black velvet bonnet with gold cords and tassels.]

NOTES

1. Until 2006, holders of the various diplomas wore 'scarves'. These were about 6″ wide, reaching to the waist when worn, with pointed ends, and shaped at the neck. They were coloured as follows:
   CertHE: light green.
   DipHE: middle green.
   Graduate Certificates and Diplomas: dark green.
   Postgraduate Diplomas: light green, with 1″ white on all edges.

LEEDS METROPOLITAN UNIVERSITY
1992

Leeds Polytechnic was formed in 1970 from the amalgamation of four colleges. These were: Leeds College of Technology. (1824); Leeds College of Commerce (1845); part of Leeds College of Art (1846), the remaining part becoming Jacob Kramer College; Yorkshire College of Education and Home Economics, (1874). In 1976 James Graham College and the City Of Leeds and Carnegie College of Physical Education joined Leeds Polytechnic. In 1998 a merger with Harrogate College established the Harrogate campus. It was chartered as a university in 1992.

The robes were originally designed round the use of just two colours – gold and blue, with red added for doctors. However, in 2005 the masters' hoods were changed to purple and green, which appears to be an arbitrary choice, until it is understood that the university's logo is a stripe of purple, green, gold, blue, and red, against a black background. Thus all five of the colours are now included in the robes. The yellow is an ochre shade, the purple a deep mauve, the blue a rich peacock blue, and the green is malachite green.

UNDERGRADUATES
none specified

UNDERGRADUATE CERTIFICATES AND DIPLOMAS
Gown: as for bachelors.
Hood: a gold silk hood of CNAA shape [a1], bordered 3″ blue inside the cowl.
Hat: a black cloth square cap.

FOUNDATION DEGREES
Gown: as for bachelors.
Hood: a gold hood of CNAA shape [a1], lined with the same colour, tipped blue, bound ½″ blue on the cowl.
Hat: a black cloth square cap.

BACHELORS
Gown: a black stuff gown of basic pattern [b1].
Hood: a gold silk hood of CNAA shape [a1], lined and bound 1″ blue on all edges.
Hat: a black cloth square cap.

POSTGRADUATE CERTIFICATES AND DIPLOMAS
Gown: as for bachelors.
Hood: a purple hood of CNAA shape [a1], lined malachite green.
Hat: a black cloth square cap.

MASTERS including MASTERS OF PHILOSOPHY

Gown: a black stuff gown of basic pattern [m10].

Hood: a purple hood of the London shape [f3], lined as follows:

MPhil: lined malachite green, bound ⅜″ old gold on the cowl.

All others: lined malachite green.

Hat: a black cloth square cap.

DOCTORS OF PHILOSOPHY and TAUGHT AND PROFESSIONAL DOCTORS

Undress gown: *none specified*

Dress robe: a claret panama robe of Cambridge pattern [d1]. The facings are blue, and the sleeve-linings gold. There is a blue cord and button on the yoke.

Hood: a gold hood of London shape [f3], lined and bound 1″ blue.

Hat: in full dress, a black cloth bonnet with dark blue cords and tassels.

NOTES

1. Obsolete hoods:

   Foundation degrees (until 2005): a gold hood of CNAA shape [a1], lined and bound blue, the cowl bordered ½″ gold set 1″ in.

   Postgraduate diplomas: a gold silk hood of CNAA shape [a1], lined and bound 1″ blue. There is 1″ gold inside the cowl edge, set 1″ in.

   Masters (until 2005): a gold hood of CNAA shape [a1], lined and bound 2″ blue.

   MPhil: a gold hood of London shape [f3], lined and bound 1″ blue.

UNIVERSITY OF LEICESTER
1957

The University was founded as the Leicester, Leicestershire, and Rutland College in 1918. In 1927 it became University College, Leicester, and 1957 it was chartered as the University of Leicester.

The robes were the first to make any kind of break from traditional styles. Notably, the hood shapes are developments of the simple and Aberdeen shapes. Both have permanently turned-out cowls (on the simple shape, this may be an influence from Leeds), but where a binding is applied to a hood, it is not placed on the actual edge of the turned-out cowl, but on the folded edge. All hoods are made in bright cherry (save that the doctors' hoods are effectively inside out). The PhD wears a master's style hood, which explains why the MPhil (a later introduction) has to share the MA hood, although several other universities make the MPhil and PhD share a hood.

Faculty colours

Arts and Letters: silver-grey.
Business Administration: gold.
Education: tartan green.
Engineering: purple.
Laws: black.
Medicine: pale turquoise.
Music: cream brocade.
Philosophy: light cherry watered (PhD); silver-grey (MPhil).
Science: royal blue.

UNDERGRADUATES

Gown: a black stuff gown of Oxford scholars' pattern [u2].
Hat: a black cloth square cap.

UNDERGRADUATE CERTIFICATES AND DIPLOMAS

none specified

FOUNDATION DEGREES

Gown: as for bachelors.
Hood: a cherry red hood of Leicester simple shape [s6], with 2″ faculty silk on the turned-out portion.
Hat: a black cloth square cap.

BACHELORS

Gown: a black stuff gown of basic pattern [b1].
Hood: a cherry red hood of Leicester simple shape [s6], lined with faculty silk.

BMedSci: lined turquoise, and bound with royal blue.
BSocSc: *same as* BA.
BPhil(Ed) lined silver-grey, and bound with tartan green.

Hat: a black cloth square cap.

POSTGRADUATE CERTIFICATES AND DIPLOMAS

none specified

FIRST-DEGREE MASTERS

Gown: as for bachelors.

Hood: a cherry red hood of Leicester simple shape [s6], lined as follows, and with a white cord on the lower edge of the turned-out portion:
MChem, MGeol, MMath, MPhys: lined royal blue.
MEng: lined purple.

Hat: a black cloth square cap.

MASTERS including MASTERS OF PHILOSOPHY

Gown: a black stuff gown of basic shape, but with a small quarter-circle cut on both sides of the sleeve [m8], and an inverted-T armhole.

Hood: a cherry red hood of Leicester masters' shape [a2], lined with faculty silk.
MBA(Ed): lined gold and bound tartan green.
MPhil: *same as* MA.
MRes: lined mauve.

Hat: a black cloth square cap.

DOCTORS OF PHILOSOPHY and TAUGHT AND PROFESSIONAL DOCTORS

Undress gown: as for masters, but with black Birmingham lace along the facings and round the yoke.

Dress robe: same as the undress gown, but the lace is cherry red.

Hood: a cherry red hood of Leicester masters' shape [a2], lined as follows:
DClinPsy: royal blue.
EdD: tartan green.
PhD: cherry red watered silk.

Hat: a black cloth square cap.

HIGHER DOCTORS

Undress gown: as PhD, but with a flap collar, which is trimmed with lace.

Dress robe: a cherry red cloth robe of Oxford pattern [d2], the facings and lower 8″ of the sleeves with faculty colour. There is a cord and button of the faculty colour on the yoke.

Hood: a hood of the appropriate faculty colour, of the Leicester doctors' shape [a5], lined with cherry red.

Hat: in undress, a black cloth square cap; in full dress a black velvet modified biretta.

NOTES

1. For degrees validated by Leicester at other colleges, the hoods are bound with tri-colour cords, as follows:

   Newman College, Birmingham: blue, gold, and red.

   Bishop Grosseteste College, Lincoln: used a cord of green, blue, and gold, but gained its own degree-awarding powers in 2008; see its own entry.

UNIVERSITY OF LIMERICK
1989

The University of Limerick was established in 1972 as the National Institute for Higher Education, Limerick and became a university by statute in 1989 in accordance with the University of Limerick Act. The University was the first university established since the foundation of the Free State in 1922; Dublin City University was established later the same day.

The gold edging on the hoods is officially called 'corporate gold braid', but is in fact gold silk.

Faculty colours

Arts: white.
Business: drab.
Engineering: orange.
Laws: blue.
Medicine: red-white.
Science: gold.
Technology: silver-grey.

UNDERGRADUATES
none specified

UNDERGRADUATE CERTIFICATES AND DIPLOMAS
Gown: as for bachelors.
Epitoge: of the faculty colour, with three gold bands at each end, each 1½″ wide.
Hat: a black cloth square cap.

BACHELORS
Gown: a black stuff gown of basic pattern [b1].
Hood: a black hood of CNAA shape [a1], lined faculty colour, and bound 1″ yellow-gold on the cowl edge, inside and out.
Hat: a black cloth square cap.

POSTGRADUATE CERTIFICATES AND DIPLOMAS
Gown: as for bachelors.
Epitoge: of the faculty colour, with four gold bands at each end, each 1½″ wide.
Hat: a black cloth square cap.

FIRST-DEGREE MASTERS
not awarded

MASTERS including MASTERS OF PHILOSOPHY

Gown: a black stuff gown of Oxford MA pattern [m1].

Hood: a black hood of CNAA shape [a1], lined white, bordered 3″ faculty colour inside the cowl, and bound yellow-gold 1″ on the cowl edge, inside and out.
MA: the hood is bordered 3″ blue.

Hat: a black cloth square cap.

DOCTORS OF PHILOSOPHY and TAUGHT AND PROFESSIONAL DOCTORS

Undress gown: as for masters.

Dress robe: a scarlet robe of Oxford MA pattern [m1].

Hood: a black hood of Durham BSc shape [f7], lined maroon, and bound 1″ yellow-gold on the cowl edge, inside and out.

Hat: in undress, a black cloth square cap; in full dress, a black cloth bonnet with maroon cords and tassels.

HIGHER DOCTORS

Undress gown: as PhD.

Dress robe: a scarlet robe of Oxford pattern [d2], with facings and sleeves of the faculty colour. There is 1″ yellow-gold set in 1″ from the edge of the facings, and 1″ from the base of the sleeves.

Hood: a scarlet hood of Durham BSc shape [f7], lined white, and bound 1″ yellow-gold on the cowl edge, inside and out.

Hat: in undress, a black cloth square cap; in full dress, a black cloth bonnet with gold cords and tassels.

UNIVERSITY OF LINCOLN
1992

The university can trace its origins to the Hull School of Art, founded in 1861. It was joined by Endsleigh Training College in 1905, and the Central College of Commerce in 1911. With some other colleges, in 1976, they became the Hull College of Higher Education, later the Humberside College of Higher Education, and Humberside Polytechnic in 1990. This was chartered as Humberside University in 1992. In response to local demands, a university campus was opened in Lincoln in 1996, and attached to the university, which then became the University of Humberside and Lincoln. In 2001, the Hull campus was transferred to the University of Hull, and the name was again changed to University of Lincoln.

The robes are very traditional, and designed round the university's colours of blue and yellow.

UNDERGRADUATES
none specified

UNDERGRADUATE CERTIFICATES AND DIPLOMAS
Gown: as for bachelors.
Hood: a black hood of Wales simple shape [s6], the cowl bordered 4″ bright blue, and bound ½″ yellow. The neckband is not bound.
Hat: a black cloth square cap.

FOUNDATION DEGREES
Gown: as for bachelors.
Hood: a black hood of Wales simple shape [s5], the cowl bordered inside 2″ yellow and bound ½″ blue. The neckband is not bound.
Hat: a black cloth square cap.

BACHELORS (except BArch)
Gown: a black stuff gown of basic pattern [b1].
Hood: a black hood of the Wales simple shape [s6], lined bright blue, and the cowl bound ½″ yellow on all edges. The neckband is not bound.
Hat: a black cloth square cap.

POSTGRADUATE CERTIFICATES and DIPLOMAS, and BACHELORS OF ARCHITECTURE
Gown: as for bachelors.
Hood: a black hood of Wales simple shape [s6], the cowl lined bright blue, and bound 1″ yellow on all edges. The neckband is bound ½″ yellow.
Hat: a black cloth square cap.

MASTERS

Gown: a black stuff gown of basic pattern [m10].

Hood: a dark blue hood of Wales simple shape [s6], lined bright blue, and the cowl bound yellow, 2″ inside and ½″ outside. The neckband is bound ½″ yellow.

If the degree is awarded *honoris causa,* the hood is lined yellow and bordered blue.

Hat: a black cloth square cap.

MASTERS OF PHILOSOPHY

Gown: a black stuff gown of basic pattern [m10].

Hood: a claret cloth hood of Cambridge shape [f1], lined and bound bright blue on all edges.

Hat: a black cloth square cap.

DOCTORS OF PHILOSOPHY and TAUGHT AND PROFESSIONAL DOCTORS

Undress gown: *none specified*

Dress robe: a claret cloth robe of Cambridge pattern [d1], with facings and sleeve linings of bright blue. There is a claret cord and blue button on each sleeve, and on the yoke.

Hood: a claret cloth hood of Cambridge shape [f1], lined and bound as follows:

PhD: lined and bound bright blue on all edges.

EdD: lined and the cape bound with bright blue, the cowl bound ½″ yellow.

Hat: in full dress, a black cloth bonnet with blue cords and tassels.

HIGHER DOCTORS

Undress gown: *none specified*

Dress robe: a scarlet cloth robe of Cambridge pattern [d1], with facings and sleeve linings of bright blue. There is a scarlet cord and blue button on each sleeve, and on the yoke.

Hood: a scarlet cloth hood of Cambridge shape [f1], lined and bound bright blue on all edges.

Hat: in full dress, a black velvet bonnet with blue cords and tassels.

UNIVERSITY OF LIVERPOOL
1903

The University was established in 1881 as University College Liverpool, admitting its first students in 1882. In 1884, it became part of the federal Victoria University. Following a Royal Charter and Act of Parliament in 1903, it became an independent university called the University of Liverpool, with the right to confer its own degrees.

The scheme is logical at root, but has had to accommodate a large number of exceptions due to the growing number of degree titles. Although historically the bachelors have always worn fur bindings, it is noteworthy that recently-introduced bachelors degrees (*e.g.*, BClinSc, BNurs) have hoods without fur (possibly owing to growing dislike of fur – even artificial), thus appearing to be masters. This is compounded by the use of a single black gown for all graduates, which is also used by the undergraduates if needed. Thus a Liverpool undergraduate looks like a Cambridge MA.

The hoods have their lining silk brought out on all edges to form a binding ¼″ wide, unless there is a fur binding; fur bindings are placed on the cowl edge only.

Faculty colours

Although the university has series of faculty colours, as listed below, there are so many exceptions that the full range of hoods has been given.

Arts: apple-blossom pink.
Commerce: citron.
Dentistry: 'dark red' (actually a dull magenta).
Education: green.
Engineering: orange.
Laws: 'bronze' (a shot silk of red and green).
Medicine: lavender.
Science: slate blue.
Theology: ecclesiastical purple.
Veterinary Science: grey.

All hoods are made in the Edinburgh shape [s4]. Linings are turned out for ¼″ where there is no other binding.

UNDERGRADUATES

Gown: a black gown of Cambridge MA pattern [m2], with a black cord and button on the yoke.
Hat: none.

UNDERGRADUATE CERTIFICATES AND DIPLOMAS

none specified

[FOUNDATION DEGREES]

These were awarded only at University College Chester, and thus ceased when it became a university itself.

Gown: a black gown of Cambridge BA pattern [b2].
Hood: a black hood, lined black, bordered 2″ white ribbon inside the cowl.
Hat: a black cloth square cap.

BACHELORS

Gown: a black gown of Cambridge MA pattern [m2], with a black cord and button on the yoke.
Hood:

BA (all Faculties): black cloth, lined apple blossom silk and bound white fur.
BArch: black cloth, lined white silk, bordered inside on both edges with a narrow line of black velvet set 1″ in, and bound white fur.
[BClinSci: black cloth, lined lavender silk, the cowl bordered inside 3″ slate-blue silk set 1″ in.]
[BCom: black cloth, lined citron silk, bound white fur.]
BDes: black cloth, lined silver grey silk, bound white fur.
BDS: black cloth, lined dark red silk, bound white fur.
[BEd: black cloth, lined green silk, bound white fur.]
BEng black cloth, lined orange silk, bound white fur.
LLB: black cloth, lined bronze silk, bound white fur.
MB,ChB: black cloth, lined lavender silk, bound white fur.
[BMus: dark blue silk, lined mid-blue silk, bound white fur.]
BN: black cloth, lined white silk, the cowl bordered inside 3″ lavender silk set 1″ in.
BPhil: black cloth, lined yellow silk, bound white fur.
BSc (all Faculties from 2005, Faculty of Science only prior to 2005): black cloth, lined slate-blue silk, bound white fur.
[BSc (Faculty of Medicine until 2005): black cloth, lined lavender silk, the cowl bordered inside 3″ white silk, set 1″ in.]
[BSc (Faculty of Engineering until 2005): black cloth, lined orange silk, the cowl bordered inside 3″ white silk set 1″ in.]
[BSc (Faculty of Veterinary Science until 2001): black cloth, lined forest green silk.
[BSc (Faculty of Veterinary Science 2001 to 2004): black cloth, lined grey silk, the cowl bordered inside 3″ white silk, set 1″ in.]
[BSc (Faculty of Social and Environmental Studies until 2005): black cloth, lined apple-blossom silk, the cowl bordered inside 3″ of white silk set 1″ in.]
[BTh: black cloth, lined ecclesiastical purple silk, bound white fur.]
BVSc: black cloth, lined grey silk, bound white fur.

Hat: a black cloth square cap.

POSTGRADUATE CERTIFICATES AND DIPLOMAS

none specified

FIRST-DEGREE MASTERS

Gown: a black gown of Cambridge MA pattern [m2], with a black cord and button on the yoke.

Hood:

MPhys, MMath, MChem, MESc: black cloth, lined slate-blue silk, the cowl bordered inside 2″ white ribbon, set 1″ in.

MEng: black silk or cloth, lined orange silk, the cowl bordered inside 2″ white ribbon, set 1″ in.

MPlan: black cloth, lined apple-blossom silk, the cowl bordered inside 2″ white ribbon set 1″ in.

Hat: a black cloth square cap.

MASTERS

Gown: a black gown of Cambridge MA pattern [m2], with a black cord and button on the yoke.

Hood:

MA (1903-1978, and since 2001): black silk or cloth, lined apple-blossom silk.

MA (1978 to 2001): black cloth, lined yellow silk.

[MAnimSc: black silk or cloth, lined terracotta silk.]

[MArAd], MARM: black silk or cloth, lined yellow silk, the cowl bordered inside with a narrow line of black velvet set 1″ in.

MArch: black silk or cloth, lined white silk and bordered inside on both edges with a narrow line of black velvet set 1″ in.

MBA: black silk or cloth, lined gold silk, the cowl bordered inside with one broad line of white ribbon.

MCD: black silk or cloth, lined white silk, the cowl bordered inside with one broad line of black velvet.

ChM, MChOrth, [MChOtol], MClinPsychol, MCommH, [MObstGyn], [MPsychMed], MPH, [MRad], MTCH&CP, MTropMed: black silk or cloth, lined lavender silk.

[MCom: black silk or cloth, lined citron silk.]

MDes: black silk or cloth, lined silver grey silk taffeta.

MDS, MDentSci: black silk or cloth, lined dark red silk.

MEd: black silk or cloth, lined green silk.

[MEng: black silk lined orange silk.]

LLM: back silk or cloth, lined bronze silk.

MMus: black silk or cloth, lined royal blue silk.

MPA: black silk or cloth, lined white silk, the cowl bordered inside 1″ scarlet ribbon, set 1″in.

MPhil (since 2004): black silk, lined scarlet silk, the cowl bordered inside 1″ black velvet on all edges, set 1″ in.

MPhil (1978–2004): black silk, lined apple-blossom silk.

[MPsych: black silk or cloth, lined purple silk.]

MRes: black silk, lined white silk, the cowl bordered inside 1″ scarlet velvet on all edges, set 1″ in.

MSc (all Faculties from 2005): black silk or cloth, lined slate-blue silk.

MSc (Faculty of Medicine until 2005): black silk or cloth, lined lavender silk.

MSc (Faculty of Veterinary Science until 2005): black cloth, lined burgundy silk.

MSc (Faculty of Social and Environmental Studies until 2005): black cloth, lined apple-blossom silk, the cowl bordered inside with two narrow lines of black velvet.

MSc (Eng): black silk or cloth, lined orange silk.

[MTD: black silk or cloth, lined white silk, the cowl bordered inside with one broad line of orange velvet.]

[MTheol: black silk or cloth, lined ecclesiastical purple silk.]

MVSc: black silk or cloth, lined grey silk.

Hat: a black cloth square cap.

TAUGHT AND PROFESSIONAL DOCTORS

Undress gown: a black gown of Cambridge MA pattern [m2], with a black cord and button on the yoke.

Dress robe: a scarlet cloth robe of Cambridge doctors' pattern [d2], with facings and sleeve linings of scarlet silk, and 1″ black velvet on the outer edge of the facings.

Hood:

DClinPsychol: scarlet cloth, lined lavender silk, bordered 1″ black velvet set 1″ in.

DDentSc: scarlet cloth, lined dark red silk, the cowl bordered 1″ black velvet set 1″ in.

Hat: a black cloth square cap.

DOCTORS OF PHILOSOPHY

Undress gown: a black gown of Cambridge MA pattern [m2], with a black cord and button on the yoke.

Dress robe: a scarlet cloth robe of Cambridge doctors' pattern [d2], with facings and sleeve linings of black silk, bordered 1″ scarlet velvet on all edges, set 1″ in.

Hood: scarlet cloth, lined black silk, bordered 1″ scarlet velvet on all edges, set 1″ in.

Hat: a black cloth square cap.

HIGHER DOCTORS

Undress gown: a black gown of Cambridge MA pattern [m2], with a black cord and button on the yoke.

Dress robe: a scarlet cloth robe of Cambridge doctors' pattern [d2], with facings and sleeve linings of the faculty colour.

Hood: scarlet cloth, lined with the faculty colour:

DEng: orange.

LittD: apple-blossom.

LL.D: bronze.

MD: lavender.

DMus: dark blue.
DSc: slate blue.
DVSc: grey.

Hat: a soft black velvet square ('John Knox') cap.

NOTES

1. [LDS: a black gown, the facings edged ¼″ dark red silk.]
2. Originally, all graduates were entitled to wear detachable facings of faculty colour on their gowns. It is not known when this practice was introduced, nor when it ceased.
3. The MCD hood was originally lined white, with two narrow bands of peach velvet inside the cowl. This had changed to the current hood by 1954.
4. The MD is no longer considered a higher doctorate, but the robes were designed when it was, hence its inclusion in that section.
5. The BTh and MTh were awarded only through Chester College, and the BEd only through Chester and through Liverpool Hope. As they have both gained university status, it is assumed that these degrees and hoods are now obsolescent.
6. Women who graduated before 1998 may wear the Oxford soft cap.
7. The Laws silk is called 'bronze', and is red shot green. This is different from the bronze shot silk of Wales Science, which is yellow shot black.

LIVERPOOL HOPE UNIVERSITY
2005

Two of the University's founding institutions were teacher-training colleges: the Anglican St. Katharine's in Warrington (founded 1844) and the Roman Catholic Notre Dame in Liverpool city centre (founded 1856). A second Roman Catholic teacher-training college, Christ's College, opened in 1965. In 1980 the three Colleges joined in an ecumenical federation as Liverpool Institute of Higher Education (LIHE). In 1995 new instruments and articles of government established a single, unified, ecumenical College, and a new name, Liverpool Hope. By 1994, it had become a fully accredited institution of the University of Liverpool. Hope gained its own taught degree awarding powers in August 2002. The Privy Council approved the title Liverpool Hope University in July 2005, granting Hope full University status.

The robes are simple, being grade-specific. It is one of the few universities to make a difference in the hoods of bachelors, depending on whether the degree is Ordinary or with Honours.

UNDERGRADUATES
none specified

UNDERGRADUATE CERTIFICATES AND DIPLOMAS
none specified

FOUNDATION DEGREES
Gown: a blue stuff gown of basic bachelors' pattern [b1].
Hood: a red hood of Oxford simple shape [s1], lined gold.
Hat: a blue cloth square cap.

BACHELORS
Gown: a blue stuff gown of basic pattern [b1].
Hood: a red hood of Oxford simple shape [s1], lined and edged as follows:
Ordinary degrees: lined gold, the cowl bordered inside 1″ emerald green set 1″ in.
Honours degrees: lined gold, the cowl bordered inside with two 1″ bands of emerald green set 1″ apart.
Hat: a blue cloth square cap.

POSTGRADUATE CERTIFICATES AND DIPLOMAS (except PGCE)
Gown: a blue stuff gown of basic masters' pattern [m10].
Hood: a gold hood of Oxford simple shape [s1], lined red, the cowl bordered inside 1″ emerald green set 1″ in.
Hat: a blue cloth square cap.

POSTGRADUATE CERTIFICATE in EDUCATION (PGCE)

Gown: a blue stuff gown of basic bachelors' pattern [b1].

Hood: a gold hood of Oxford simple shape [s1], lined red.

Hat: a blue cloth square cap.

MASTERS

Gown: a blue stuff gown of basic masters' pattern [m10].

Hood: a gold hood of Oxford simple shape [s1], lined red, the cowl bordered inside with two 1″ bands of emerald green set 1″ apart.

Hat: a blue cloth square cap.

HONORARY DOCTORS

Dress robe: a dark blue robe of Oxford pattern [d2], with red facings and sleeve coverings. There is 1″ green along the outer edge of the facings, and at the top of the red on the sleeves.

Hood: a gold-yellow hood of Cambridge shape [f1], lined red, the cape bound 1″ green, and the cowl bound 1″ blue.

Hat: in full dress, a dark blue bonnet with red cords and tassels.

All other degrees are currently validated by the University of Liverpool.

UNIVERSITY OF LONDON
1836

The University of London was formed in 1836 from two pre-existing colleges, University College London (1826) and King's College (1829) (*qq.v.*). A number of other colleges joined the federation over the years, some of which merged during the 1980s, and a number of which have now broken away from the federal University and are awarding their own degrees, and thus have separate entries.

There has always been an external system at London, whereby anyone may present themselves for examination without having undertaken a course of instruction in one of the colleges. Several colleges outside London – such as Hull, Exeter, and Leicester – made use of this facility until they became universities themselves and could award their own degrees, or came under the ægis of the CNAA.

Until Convocation was abolished in 2003, membership conferred various differences in the academic dress: see Note 1. The scheme currently in use is the second one; the original is to be found at the end of this entry in an appendix. The original PhD robes had no extra binding; the faculty colour binding on the hood and robe was introduced as an option in 1930, and eventually became compulsory; the same for the MPhil hood. When it was decided in 1997 to stop indicating the faculty, instead of simply removing the faculty bindings and reverting to the original robes, it was decided to use a blue binding. Thus Philosophy now has two faculty colours.

Faculty colours

Arts: russet brown.
Business Administration: fawn.
[Commerce: deep orange.]
Dentistry: olive green corded silk.
Divinity: sarum red.
Education: eau-de-nil green.
Engineering: pale turquoise.
[Humanities: pale pink].
Laws: mid-blue.
Medicine and Surgery: violet.
Music: white watered silk.
Pharmacy: old gold.
Philosophy: claret (and royal blue).
Science: light gold (lemon shot white).
Veterinary Medicine: lilac.
All degrees introduced after 1994: silver grey (black shot white).

UNDERGRADUATES

Gown: a black gown with short pointed sleeves [u3].

Hat: a black cloth square cap.

UNDERGRADUATE CERTIFICATES AND DIPLOMAS

none specified

FOUNDATION DEGREES

Gown: as for BA.

Hood: a black hood of London shape [f3], the cowl bound 1″ faculty colour silk.

Hat: a black cloth square cap.

BACHELORS

Gown:

Faculties of Arts, Commerce, Divinity, Education, Engineering, Humanities, and Science: a black gown with open sleeves, gathered at the elbow with a black cord and button [b4]. For BD, there is a black cord and sarum red button on the yoke.

Faculty of Laws: a black flap-collar gown [d4], with a slit behind. (This is the solicitor's gown.)

Faculties of Medicine, Dentistry, Pharmacy, Veterinary Medicine, and Music: as for LL.B, but the base of the sleeve is hollowed out into a double ogee curve, and there is no slit.

Hood: a black hood of London shape [f3], lined white silk, bordered inside 3″ and bound ¼″ on the cowl edge with faculty colour.

BMus: as for other bachelors, but the hood is made of light blue silk.

BMedSci: as for other bachelors, but bordered with 3″ violet, with 1″ pale gold set in the centre.

Hat: a black cloth square cap.

POSTGRADUATE CERTIFICATES and DIPLOMAS, EXTRA-MURAL DIPLOMAS, and GRADUATE DIPLOMAS

Gown: as for BA.

Hood: a black hood of London shape [f3], the cowl bound with a triple cord of red, white, and blue.

Hat: a black cloth square cap.

FIRST-DEGREE MASTERS

Gown: as for BA.

Hood: a black hood of London shape [f3], fully lined and bound ¼″ on all edges with the faculty colour.

MSci: same as MSc (but see Note 6).

Hat: a black cloth square cap.

MASTERS

Gown:

Faculties of Arts, Commerce, Divinity, Education, Engineering, Humanities, and Science: a black gown of Cambridge MA pattern, but the with lower point also rounded off [m4]. For MTh, there is a black cord and sarum red button on the yoke.

Faculties of Laws, Medicine, Dentistry, Pharmacy, Veterinary Medicine, and Music: as for the relevant bachelors.

Hood: a black hood of London shape [f3], fully lined and bound ¼″ on all edges with the faculty colour.

MMus: as for other masters, but the hood is made of mid-blue silk.

Hat: a black cloth square cap.

MASTERS of PHILOSOPHY (MPhil) and of PHILOSOPHICAL STUDIES (MPhilStud)

Gown: as for the master in the faculty in which the degree is taken, but with a 1″ claret ribbon along each facing.

Hood: a black hood of London shape [f3], fully lined with claret silk and bound ¼″ royal blue silk on all edges.

Hat: a black cloth square cap.

TAUGHT AND PROFESSIONAL DOCTORS

Undress gown: as for masters in the same faculty.

Dress robe: a claret cloth robe of Cambridge pattern [d2], the sleeves lined and the facings covered with ruby silk (red shot white).

Hood: a claret cloth hood of London shape [f3], lined with ruby silk.

Hat: in undress, a black cloth square cap; in full dress, a black velvet bonnet with claret cords and tassels.

DOCTORS OF PHILOSOPHY

Undress gown: as for masters in the same faculty.

Dress robe: a claret cloth robe of Cambridge pattern [d2], the sleeves lined and the facings covered with claret silk; the facings are bound on the outer edge with 1″ royal blue.

Hood: a claret cloth hood of London shape [f3], fully lined with claret silk, and bound 1″ royal blue silk on all edges.

Hat: in undress, a black cloth square cap; in full dress, a black velvet bonnet with claret cords and tassels.

HIGHER DOCTORS

Undress gown: as for masters in the same faculty.

Dress robe: a scarlet cloth robe of Cambridge pattern [d2], the sleeves lined and the facings covered with faculty colour silk.

Hood: a scarlet cloth hood of London shape [f3], fully lined with faculty colour silk.

Hat: in undress, a black cloth square cap; in full dress, a black velvet bonnet with cords and tassels of faculty colour.

NOTES

1. Until the abolition of Convocation in 2003, only members might wear the white lining in the bachelors' hoods; non-members wore their hood with just the three-inch faculty border. Masters who were members of Convocation wore their hoods with a 1″ white binding on the cowl. (For MPhil, it was a 1″ facing inside the faculty binding.)
2. Until 1998, the full dress robes were allowed only to doctors who were members of Convocation; all others wore only the black gown with the hood.
3. Holders of the following degrees who were members of Convocation might wear their gowns made in coloured silk:
   BMus and MMus: light blue;
   MS: violet;
   MDS: olive green.
4. Originally the PhD robe and hood and the MPhil hood had no bindings; from 1930 to 1997 they were bound with faculty colour. Technically optional, it was rare to see them without.
5. Although the PhD and MPhil lining is specified as 'claret', the original PhD robes were lined with the same crimson-shot-orange silk as is used for the MA at Oxford.
6. The DMus robes were originally those now used by the MMus; the DMus gained its scarlet robes in 1910.
7. The original MSci hood was black, bordered inside with 3″ pale gold set 1″ in. If a member of Convocation, there was a 1″ white binding on the cowl edge.

ORIGINAL SCHEME (in use 1844–c.1862)

London originally had no academic robes. Their adoption seems to have been prompted by a clerical graduate who inquired what hood he was entitled to wear, and the following scheme was drawn up. It should be compared with the contemporary scheme drawn up for Durham, which relies heavily on 'Oxbridge' models. The details that follow are taken from Northam's workbook. The gown patterns were specified, but not the hood shapes, although it is reasonable to assume they were all of the London shape [f3]. It is interesting that the Laws and Medicine colours were carried over into the new scheme. Also worthy of note is the MA hood, which resembles the Durham MA and the first AKC (instituted 1862) hoods in colour. The use of coloured gowns was also transferred to the new scheme: the violet one going to the MS, and the blue one to the DMus (see note 5 above). The extensive use of velvet on gowns, hoods, and caps will be noted. The Senate Minutes make several references to the 'indistinctive' nature of the BA hood (it was frequently mistaken for a literate's hood), and it was suggested it should be lined with gold silk, and bordered with 3″ black velvet, and the MA hood altered to match, although this seems not to have happened. It is not clear what prompted the revision of 1862.

UNDERGRADUATES

Gown: a black gown, 'the sleeve buttoned and pleated' (*i.e.* as the current BA gown [b4]) with black velvet facings.

Hat: a black cloth square cap, bound black velvet, with a black silk tassel and black velvet button.

BACHELORS of ARTS

Gown: a black gown as for Cambridge BA, with black velvet facings.

Hood: a black hood of full shape, bordered 3″ black velvet.

Hat: a black cloth square cap, bound black velvet, with a black silk tassel and black velvet button.

MASTERS of ARTS

Gown: a black gown of Oxford MA pattern, with 'a crescent of black velvet over the armhole'; the facings, 4½″ at the top widening to 8″ at the base, of black velvet, 'divided in the middle' (*i.e.* the effect is of two velvet stripes).

Hood: a black hood, lined lavender silk, bordered inside with two 3″ bands of lavender velvet, set 1″ apart.

Hat: a black velvet square cap, with a black silk tassel and black velvet button.

BACHELORS of LAWS

Gown: the same gown as the MA, but made throughout in blue, the facings not divided.

Hood: a blue hood, bordered 3″ blue velvet.

Hat: a blue cloth square cap, bound blue velvet, with a blue silk tassel and blue velvet button.

DOCTORS of LAWS

Gown: the same gown as the MA, but made throughout in blue, the yoke covered in blue velvet.

Hood: a blue hood, lined blue silk, bordered inside with two 3″ bands of blue velvet, set 1″ apart.

Hat: a blue cloth square cap, 'bound black velvet and crimson', with a blue silk tassel and blue velvet button.

BACHELORS of MEDICINE

Gown: the same gown as the MA, but made throughout in violet.

Hood: a violet hood, bordered 3″ violet velvet.

Hat: a black cloth square cap, bound black velvet, with a black silk tassel and violet velvet button.

DOCTORS of MEDICINE

Gown: the same gown as the MA, but made throughout in violet, the yoke covered in violet velvet.

Hood: a violet hood, lined violet silk, bordered inside with two 3″ bands of violet velvet, set 1″ apart.

Hat: a violet cloth square cap, bound violet velvet, with a violet silk tassel and violet velvet button.

UNIVERSITY COLLEGE, LONDON
1828/2007

UCL, as it is always known, was founded in 1828 as 'London University', and with King's College was one of the first two colleges of the University of London. It gained degree-awarding powers in 2007, and the scheme below was drawn up at that time. It demonstrates its links with the University of London by using the London BA and MA gowns, and, interestingly, by using its higher doctors' robes unchanged. Blue and purple are the college colours.

UNDERGRADUATES
none specified

UNDERGRADUATE CERTIFICATES AND DIPLOMAS
none specified

FOUNDATION DEGREES
none specified

BACHELORS
Gown: a black stuff gown of London BA pattern [b4].
Hood: a black cloth hood of CNAA shape [a1], lined purple silk.
Hat: a black cloth square cap.

POSTGRADUATE CERTIFICATES AND DIPLOMAS
Gown: as for bachelors.
Hood: a black cloth hood of CNAA shape [a1], lined black silk, the cowl bordered inside 1″ blue silk.
Hat: a black cloth square cap.

FIRST-DEGREE MASTERS (MSci, MEng)
Gown: as for bachelors.
Hood: a black cloth hood of CNAA shape [a1], lined blue silk.
Hat: a black cloth square cap.

MASTERS
Gown: a black stuff gown of London MA pattern [m5].
Hood: a black cloth hood of CNAA shape [a1], lined silver-grey silk.
Hat: a black cloth square cap.

MASTERS OF PHILOSOPHY and of SURGERY

Gown: a black stuff gown of London MA pattern [m5]. The facings are covered with silk: purple for MPhil, blue for MS.

Hood: a black cloth hood of CNAA shape [a1], lined and bound as follows:

MPhil: lined silver-grey silk, bound purple silk.

MS: lined purple silk, bound blue silk on all edges.

Hat: a black cloth square cap.

SPECIALIST DOCTORS (DClinPsy, DEdPsy, EngD)

Undress gown: *none specified*

Dress robe: a silver-grey cloth robe of Cambridge pattern [d1], the facings covered with blue silk, and the sleeves lined silver grey silk, with a blue cord and button.

Hood: a silver-grey cloth hood of CNAA shape [a1], lined blue silk.

Hat: in full dress, a black velvet bonnet with silver-grey cords and tassels.

DOCTORS OF PHILOSOPHY and of MEDICINE

Undress gown: *none specified*

Dress robe: a silver-grey cloth robe of Cambridge pattern [d1], with facings and sleeve-linings as follows:

PhD: the facings covered with red silk, and the sleeves lined silver-grey silk, with a red cord and button.

MD: the facings covered with purple silk, and the sleeves lined silver-grey silk, with a purple cord and button.

Hood: a silver-grey cloth hood of CNAA shape [a1], lined as follows:

PhD: red silk.

MD: purple silk.

Hat: in full dress, a black velvet bonnet with silver-grey cords and tassels.

HIGHER DOCTORS

Holders of these degrees (DLit, LL.D, DSc, DSc(Econ), DSc(Eng), DSc(Med)) wear the same robes as prescribed for these degrees at the University of London.

NOTES

1. The hood formerly used for college awards was black, of CNAA shape [a1], lined blue and tipped purple.

LONDON BUSINESS SCHOOL
1964

The London Institute of Business Management was founded in 1964, later becoming the London Graduate School of Business Studies. In 1970 it moved into its current specially-designed building in Sussex Place. It was granted a Royal Charter in 1986, which formally acknowledged the change of name to the London Business School, a name it had been using for some time. This charter gave it the right to confer degrees, although it remains a graduate school of the University of London. It awards only postgraduate degrees.

All hoods are lined with a special dark blue 'embossed' silk, the pattern being a diapering of small squares.

MASTERS

Gown: a black stuff gown of basic pattern [m10], with an inverted-T armhole.

Hood: a black hood of CNAA shape [a1], lined with blue embossed silk, and bordered ½″ inside the cowl and outside the cape with the degree colour:
MBA: red.
MIF (Master in Finance): cobalt blue.
MManage: cream.
MSc: gold.

Hat: a black cloth square cap.

DOCTORS OF PHILOSOPHY

Undress gown: *none specified*

Dress robe: a maroon robe of Cambridge pattern [d1], with 1″ white on the outer edge of the facings, and a white cord and button on each sleeve.

Hood: a maroon hood of Cambridge shape [f1], lined and the cape bound ½″ with blue embossed silk. The cowl is bordered inside 1″ white.

HIGHER DOCTORS

Undress gown: *none specified*

Dress robe: a scarlet robe of Cambridge pattern [d1], with 1″ white on the outer edge of the facings, and a white cord and button on each sleeve.

Hood: a scarlet hood of Cambridge shape [f1], lined and the cape bound ½″ blue embossed silk. The cowl is bordered inside 1″ white.

LONDON METROPOLITAN UNIVERSITY
2002

LMU was formed by a merger of the University of North London and Guildhall University, *qq.v.* The robes of the new institution do not make any reference to the robes of either of its predecessors. The grey used is very pale, and the violet is a quite strong spectrum violet.

UNDERGRADUATES
none specified

UNDERGRADUATE CERTIFICATES AND DIPLOMAS
Gown: as for bachelors.
Hood: a grey cloth hood of the Oxford simple shape, lined as follows:
Foundation certificates, and FE awards: bordered 1″ violet inside the cowl.
Intermediate level awards: bordered 3″ violet inside the cowl.
Hat: a black cloth square cap.

FOUNDATION DEGREES
Gown: as for bachelors.
Hood: a grey cloth hood of Oxford simple shape [s1], fully lined violet.
Hat: a black cloth square cap.

BACHELORS
Gown: a black stuff gown of basic pattern [b1].
Hood: a violet hood of Oxford simple shape, fully lined grey.
Hat: a black cloth square cap.

POSTGRADUATE CERTIFICATES AND DIPLOMAS
Gown: as for masters.
Hood:
Professional development awards: a grey hood of Cambridge shape [f1], fully lined violet.
PGCert and PGDip: violet hood of Cambridge shape [f1], fully lined grey.
Hat: a black cloth square cap.

FIRST-DEGREE MASTERS
not awarded

MASTERS
Gown: a black stuff gown of basic pattern [m10].
Hood: a violet hood of Cambridge shape [f1], lined violet, bordered 2″ grey inside the cowl.

Hat: a black cloth square cap.

MASTERS OF PHILOSOPHY

Gown: a black stuff gown of basic pattern [m10], with facings of violet, with 1″ grey on the outer edge.

Hood: a grey hood of Cambridge shape [f1], lined and bound 1″ violet.

Hat: a black cloth square cap.

DOCTORS OF PHILOSOPHY and TAUGHT AND PROFESSIONAL DOCTORS

Undress gown: *none specified*

Dress robe: a grey cloth robe of Oxford pattern [d2], with facings and 8″ cuffs of violet.

Hood: a grey hood of Cambridge shape [f1], lined and bound 1″ violet.

Hat: in full dress, a violet bonnet with grey cords and tassels.

HIGHER DOCTORS

Undress gown: *none specified*

Dress robe: a violet cloth robe of Oxford pattern [d2], with facings and 8″ cuffs of grey.

Hood: a violet hood of Cambridge shape [f1], lined and bound 2″ grey.

Hat: in full dress, a black cloth bonnet with gold cords and tassels.

DEGREES *honoris causa*

Use the same robes as the higher doctors – including the MA(hc).

LONDON SCHOOL OF ECONOMICS
1895/2007

The London School of Economics and Political Science, usually referred to as The London School of Economics or LSE, was founded in 1895, and officially joined the federal University of London in 1900 as the Faculty of Economics, beginning to award its degrees from 1902. It remains a specialist single-faculty constituent college of the University. In 2007, along with several other London colleges, it was granted degree-awarding powers, and now awards its own degrees instead of London ones. The robes are based on the College's colours of violet, black, and gold.

UNDERGRADUATES
none specified

BACHELORS
Gown: a black stuff gown of basic pattern [b1].
Hood: a violet hood of Burgon shape [s2], the cowl bordered 4″ black watered silk, and bound ¾″ gold.
Hat: a black cloth square cap.

POSTGRADUATE CERTIFICATES AND DIPLOMAS
Gown: as for bachelors.
Hood: a violet hood of Burgon shape [s2], lined black watered silk, edged as follows:
Certificates: the cowl edge bound ½″ inside and out with gold.
Diplomas: the cowl edge bound 1″ inside and ½″ outside with gold.
Hat: a black cloth square cap.

MASTERS including MASTERS OF PHILOSOPHY
Gown: a black stuff gown of Oxford MA pattern [m1].
Hood: a violet hood of Cambridge shape [f1], lined with black watered silk, bound as follows:
MPhil: bound ½″ gold on all edges.
All others: bound ½″ gold on the cowl edge only.
Hat: a black cloth square cap.

DOCTORS OF PHILOSOPHY
Undress gown: as for masters.
Dress robe: a purple robe of Oxford pattern [d2], with facings and 8″ cuffs of black watered silk. There is 1½″ gold along the outer edge of the facings, and at the top of the cuffs.
Hood: a purple hood of Oxford full shape [f5], lined black watered silk, bound ½″ gold on the cape edge only.

Hat: in undress, a black cloth square cap; in full dress, a black cloth bonnet with purple cords and tassels.

HIGHER DOCTORS

Undress gown: as for masters

Dress robe: a purple robe of Oxford pattern [d2], with facings and 8″ cuffs of gold watered silk. There is 1½″ black along the outer edge of the facings, and at the top of the cuffs.

Hood: a purple hood of Oxford full shape [f5], lined gold watered silk, bound ½″ black on the cape edge only.

Hat: in undress, a black cloth square cap; in full dress, a black cloth bonnet with gold cords and tassels.

NOTES

1. There was a college hood, used for LSE's own awards. It was a black hood of London shape [f3], the cowl bound with a twisted cord of purple, gold, and black.

UNIVERSITY OF LOUGHBOROUGH
1966

The institution's roots date from 1909, when the then Loughborough Technical Institute was founded. The Institute was later renamed Loughborough College. In the early years, efforts were made to mimic the environment of an Oxbridge college, such as requiring students to wear gowns to lectures. In 1952 the College was divided into four separate institutions: Loughborough College of Technology, Loughborough College of Art, Loughborough College of Further Education and Loughborough Training College. In 1966, the Loughborough College of Advanced Technology, as it had then become, received University status.

The robes are based on the old College diploma hoods (see Note 2), and most hoods and robes feature purple, which is the university colour.

Degree colours

Arts and Letters: dark green.
Business Administration: peach.
Chemistry: pale green.
Computer Science: royal blue.
Education: green-grey.
Engineering: lilac.
Library Studies: red.
Mathematics: light blue.
Philosophy: maroon.
Physics: pink.
Science: grey.
Technology: yellow.
DUniv: white.

UNDERGRADUATES

Gown: a black stuff gown of Oxford scholars' pattern [u2].
Hat: a black cloth square cap.

UNDERGRADUATE CERTIFICATES AND DIPLOMAS

Gown: as for bachelors.
Hood: a purple stuff hood of Edinburgh simple shape [s4], unlined.
Hat: a black cloth square cap.

BACHELORS

Gown: a black stuff gown of London BA pattern [b4].
Hood: a purple stuff hood of Cambridge full shape [f1], lined, but not bound, with silk of degree colour.

Hat: a black cloth square cap.

POSTGRADUATE CERTIFICATES AND DIPLOMAS

Gown: as for masters.

Hood: a purple stuff hood of Edinburgh simple shape [s4], unlined.

Hat: a black cloth square cap.

FIRST-DEGREE MASTERS

Gown: as for bachelors.

Hood: a purple stuff hood of Cambridge full shape [f1], lined, but not bound, as follows:

MChem: pale green.
MCompSc: royal blue.
MEng: lilac.
MMath: pale blue.
MPhys: pink.

Hat: a black cloth square cap.

MASTERS

Gown: a black stuff gown of London MA pattern [m5].

Hood: a purple stuff hood of Cambridge shape [f1], lined and bound ½″ on all edges with silk of the degree colour.

Hat: a black cloth square cap.

MASTERS OF PHILOSOPHY

Gown: a black stuff gown of London MA pattern [m5].

Hood: a purple stuff hood of Cambridge shape [f1], lined white silk, bound 1″ maroon silk on all edges.

Hat: a black cloth square cap.

DOCTORS OF PHILOSOPHY and TAUGHT AND PROFESSIONAL DOCTORS

Undress gown: as for masters.

Dress robe: a purple stuff robe of the same pattern as the masters' gown [m5].

Hood: a hood of Cambridge shape [f1]:

PhD: purple stuff, lined and bound 1″ maroon.
EngD: lilac stuff, lined and bound 1″ purple.

Hat: in undress, a black cloth square cap; in full dress, a black cloth bonnet with maroon cords and tassels.

HIGHER DOCTORS

Undress gown: as PhD.

Dress robe: a scarlet cloth robe of Oxford pattern [d2]. The facings and bottom 4″ of the sleeves are covered with purple silk. There is a 1″ strip of silk of degree colour along the outer edge of each facing, and at the base of each sleeve.

Hood: a hood of degree colour silk, of Cambridge full shape [f1], lined and bound on all edges with 1″ scarlet silk.

Hat: in undress, a black cloth square cap; in full dress, a black cloth bonnet with cords and tassels of degree colour.

NOTES

1. The obsolete joint degrees of BSc,BEng and BTech,BEng, wore the BSc or BTech hood with a 1″ strip of purple silk on the lining, set 1½″ in.
2. Before it became a university, Loughborough College awarded a Diploma (DLC). Holders wore the London BA gown, with a purple stuff hood of Cambridge shape [f1], lined, but not bound, as follows:

   Athletics: green.
   Arts: originally red, then gold.
   Commerce: white.
   Education: crimson.
   Engineering: yellow.
   Physical Education: royal blue.
   Pure and Applied Science: grey.

These have become the bachelors' hoods.

UNIVERSITY OF LUTON
1993-2006

The University of Luton was founded as the Modern School in the 1890s. It became Luton College of Higher Education when it merged with Luton College of Technology and Putteridge Bury College of Education in the mid-1970s. It gained university status in 1993. It then merged with the Bedford campus of de Montfort University in 2006 to form the University of Bedfordshire (*q.v.*): new robes were designed, and so the Luton robes are now obsolescent.

UNDERGRADUATES
none specified

UNDERGRADUATE CERTIFICATES AND DIPLOMAS
Gown: as for bachelors.
Hood: a black hood of CNAA shape [a1], lined and bordered as follows:
One-year awards: lined blue, the cowl bordered inside 1½″ white.
Two-year awards: lined green, the cowl bordered inside 1½″ white.
Hat: a black cloth square cap.

FOUNDATION DEGREES
Gown: a black stuff gown of London BA pattern [b4].
Hood: a blue hood of CNAA shape [a1], lined green, the cowl bordered inside 1½″ white.
Hat: a black cloth square cap.

BACHELORS
Gown: a black stuff gown of London BA pattern [b4].
Hood: a blue hood of CNAA shape [a1], lined green.
Hat: a black cloth square cap.

POSTGRADUATE CERTIFICATES AND DIPLOMAS
Gown: a black stuff gown of London BA pattern [b4].
Hood: a green hood of Cambridge shape [f1], lined blue, bound white on all edges.
Hat: a black cloth square cap.

FIRST-DEGREE MASTERS
not awarded

MASTERS including MASTERS OF PHILOSOPHY

Gown: a black stuff gown of basic pattern [m10].

Hood:

MPhil: a blue hood of Cambridge shape [f1], lined white, bound green on all edges.

All others: a green hood of Cambridge shape [f1], lined white, bound blue on all edges.

Hat: a black cloth square cap.

DOCTORS OF PHILOSOPHY and TAUGHT AND PROFESSIONAL DOCTORS

Undress gown: *none specified*

Dress robe:

PhD: a blue robe of Cambridge pattern [d1], with white facings and sleeve linings.

Others: as PhD, but the facings have 1″ green on the outer edge.

Hood: a blue hood of Cambridge shape [f1], the cape lined and bound white, the cowl bound green.

Hat: in full dress, a blue velvet bonnet with white cords and tassels.

HIGHER DOCTORS

Undress gown: *none specified*

Dress robe: a blue cloth robe of Cambridge pattern [d1], with white facings and sleeve linings, and silver cords and buttons on sleeves and yoke.

Hood: a blue hood of Cambridge shape [f1], the cape lined and bound white, the cowl bound green.

Hat: in full dress, a blue velvet bonnet with silver cords and tassels.

UNIVERSITY OF MANCHESTER
2004

When UMIST and the Victoria University of Manchester (*qq.v.*) merged in 2003, they were both dissolved, and a new university was founded and chartered in the following year. Although the old Victoria University robes had been retained by Manchester in 1903, new robes have been designed for the fresh creation, which make reference to the old robes in neither patterns nor colours.

There is one black gown used, which is of traditional MA pattern but with a stylized 'M' cut out of the base of the sleeve [m18]. All hoods have a neckband which shows gold edged purple.

UNDERGRADUATES
none specified

UNDERGRADUATE CERTIFICATES AND DIPLOMAS
Gown: the university gown [m18].
Hood: a black stuff hood of CNAA shape [a1], lined black silk, the cowl edge bordered ½″ purple silk inside.

FOUNDATION DEGREES
not awarded

BACHELORS
Gown: the university gown [m18].
Hood: a black hood of Cambridge shape [f1], lined as follows:
MB (and other bachelors taking 5 or more years): fully lined purple, with a 1″ gold band set ½″ in, and a 1″ red band set ½″ away.
All others: bordered inside 4″ purple, with 1″ gold set ½″ in.
Hat: a black cloth square cap.

POSTGRADUATE CERTIFICATES AND DIPLOMAS
same as undergraduate certificates and diplomas

FIRST-DEGREE MASTERS
Gown: the university gown [m18].
Hood: a black hood of Cambridge shape [f1], fully lined purple, with a 1″ band of gold set ½″ in, and a second 1″ band set ½″ away.
Hat: a black cloth square cap.

MASTERS

Gown: the university gown [m18].

Hood: a black hood of Cambridge shape [f1], bound on all edges and fully lined purple.

Hat: a black cloth square cap.

MASTERS OF PHILOSOPHY

Gown: the university gown [m18]

Hood: a black hood of Cambridge shape [f1], fully lined purple, the cowl bordered inside 1½″ gold set flush with the edge, the cape bordered 1″ maroon on the outside.

Hat: a black cloth square cap.

DOCTORS OF PHILOSOPHY and TAUGHT AND PROFESSIONAL DOCTORS

Undress gown: *none specified*

Dress robe: a maroon cloth robe of Oxford pattern [d2], the facings and lower half of the sleeves covered with purple, with 1″ gold on the outer edge of the facings, and at the top and bottom of the purple on the sleeves.

Hood: a maroon cloth hood of Cambridge shape [f1], fully lined and bound purple.

Hat: in full dress, a black velvet bonnet with gold cords and tassels.

HIGHER DOCTORS

Undress gown: *none specified*

Dress robe: as for PhD, but the robe is made of scarlet cloth.

Hood: a scarlet cloth hood of Cambridge shape [f1], fully lined and bound purple, with 1″ gold set next to the purple binding on the outside of the cape.

Hat: in full dress, a black velvet bonnet with gold cords and tassels.

MANCHESTER METROPOLITAN UNIVERSITY
1992

In 1970, Manchester Polytechnic was formed from the Manchester College of Art and Design, the Manchester College of Commerce (founded 1889), and the John Dalton College of Technology. In 1977, the Polytechnic merged with the Didsbury College of Education and Hollings College, and in 1983 with the City of Manchester College of Higher Education. It became a University in 1992.

The University uses a red silk, with the full armorial achievement embroidered into it in colour. The blue is a deep sky blue.

UNDERGRADUATES
none specified

UNDERGRADUATE CERTIFICATES and DIPLOMAS, and FOUNDATION DEGREES
Gown: as for bachelors.
Hood: a blue silk hood of Oxford simple shape [s1], lined blue satin, bordered 3″ plain red silk inside the cowl.
Hat: a black cloth square cap.

BACHELORS and FIRST-DEGREE MASTERS
Gown: a black stuff gown of Cambridge BA pattern [b2].
Hood: a blue hood of Cambridge shape [f1], bordered 4″ red embroidered silk inside the cowl.
Hat: a black cloth square cap.

POSTGRADUATE CERTIFICATES AND DIPLOMAS
Gown: a black stuff gown of Cambridge BA pattern [b2].
Hood: a blue hood of Oxford simple shape [s1], bordered 2″ red embroidered silk inside the cowl.
Hat: a black cloth square cap.

MASTERS including MASTERS OF PHILOSOPHY
Gown: a black stuff gown of basic pattern m10].
Hood: a blue hood of Cambridge shape [f1], fully lined red embroidered silk.
Hat: a black cloth square cap.

DOCTORS OF PHILOSOPHY and TAUGHT AND PROFESSIONAL DOCTORS
Undress gown: *none specified*

Dress robe: a blue robe of Cambridge pattern [d1], with facings and sleeve linings of red embroidered silk.
Hood: a blue hood of Cambridge shape [f1], fully lined and bound 1″ red embroidered silk.
Hat: in full dress, a black cloth bonnet with mixed red and blue cords and tassels.

HIGHER DOCTORS

Undress gown: *none specified*
Dress robe: as PhD.
Hood: as PhD, but the lining is brought out for 2″.
Hat: in full dress, a black velvet bonnet with mixed red and blue cords and tassels.

UNIVERSITY OF MANCHESTER INSTITUTE OF SCIENCE AND TECHNOLOGY (UMIST)
1993-2003

The foundation of UMIST can be traced to 1824, when a group of Manchester businessmen and industrialists met to establish the Mechanics' Institute in Manchester, where artisans could learn basic science, particularly mechanics and chemistry. In 1883 the Institution was reorganised as a Technical School, using the schemes and examinations of the City and Guilds of London Institute, and was known as the Manchester Municipal School of Technology. In 1918, the institution changed its name again to Manchester Municipal College of Technology. During 1955 and 1956 the Manchester College of Science and Technology achieved independent university status under its own Royal Charter, and in 1966 the name finally changed to the University of Manchester Institute of Science and Technology. The Victoria University of Manchester retained close ties with it for the second half of the twentieth century, with UMIST students awarded a University of Manchester degree, until UMIST gained full autonomy in 1993. UMIST, together with the Victoria University of Manchester, ceased to exist on 1 October 2004, when they were combined in the new University of Manchester (*q.v.*).

The robes featured terra-cotta, which was the faculty colour of technology in the Victoria University. The doctors' hoods were made in an unusual pattern, with the base of the cape being cut to a point. The initial suggestion was that there should be a tassel hanging from it, but this did not happen.

UNDERGRADUATES
none specified

UNDERGRADUATE CERTIFICATES AND DIPLOMAS
none specified, but a bachelors' gown and cap were used at ceremonies

FOUNDATION DEGREES
not awarded

BACHELORS
Gown: a black stuff gown of Cambridge BA pattern [b2].
Hood: a navy blue silk hood of CNAA shape [a1], lined as follows:
BSc: oyster-white taffeta.
BEng: light blue taffeta.
Hat: a black cloth square cap.

POSTGRADUATE DIPLOMAS
Gown: as for masters.

Hood: a navy blue silk hood of CNAA shape [a1], lined gold taffeta, the cowl bordered inside 1″ terra-cotta taffeta.

Hat: a black cloth square cap.

FIRST-DEGREE MASTERS

Gown: as for masters.

Hood: a navy blue silk hood of CNAA shape [a1], lined as follows:

MEng: lined light blue taffeta, the cowl bordered 1″ terra-cotta taffeta inside.

all others: lined oyster-white taffeta, the cowl bordered 1″ terra-cotta taffeta inside.

Hat: a black cloth square cap.

MASTERS including MASTERS OF PHILOSOPHY

Gown: a black stuff gown of Manchester Victoria pattern [m6]. For MPhil it had 1″ terra-cotta along the outer edge of the facings.

Hood: a navy blue silk hood of the CNAA shape [a1], lined and bound as follows:

MSc: lined terra-cotta taffeta.

[MLitt: lined gold, bordered 1″ terra-cotta taffeta.]

MPhil: lined and bound 1″ terra-cotta taffeta.

Hat: a black cloth square cap.

MASTERS OF SCIENCE (*honoris causa*)

Dress robe: a black robe of Cambridge pattern [d2], the facings covered and the sleeves lined terra-cotta taffeta.

Hood: a black hood of the same shape as the PhD, lined terra-cotta taffeta.

Hat: a black cloth square cap.

DOCTORS OF PHILOSOPHY and TAUGHT AND PROFESSIONAL DOCTORS

Undress gown: *none specified*

Dress robe: a navy blue cloth robe of Manchester Victoria masters' pattern [m6], the facings and sleeves below the armhole covered with terra-cotta taffeta; the upper edge of the armhole is bound ½″ terra-cotta.

Hood: a navy blue cloth hood of full shape with short liripipe, and the base of the cape cut to form a point [f13], lined terra-cotta taffeta.

Hat: in full dress, a navy blue cloth bonnet with a navy silk ribbon.

HIGHER DOCTORS

Undress gown: *none specified*

Dress robe: a navy blue cloth robe of Cambridge pattern [d2], the facings covered and the sleeves lined as follows:

DLitt: gold taffeta, with a gold cord and button on each sleeve.

DSc: oyster-white taffeta, with an oyster-white cord and button on each sleeve.

DEng: light blue taffeta, with a light blue cord and button on each sleeve.

Hood: a navy blue hood of the same shape as PhD, lined as the robe.

Hat: in full dress, a navy blue bonnet with cords and tassels to match the hood lining.

ST PATRICK'S COLLEGE, MAYNOOTH
1795

Maynooth College was founded in 1795 as a seminary for the education of Roman Catholic priests, and by 1850 had become the largest seminary in the world. In addition to the courses in philosophy and theology required for the education of candidates for the priesthood, its curriculum included courses in the Humanities (Classics, English, Irish, and Modern Languages) and Natural Philosophy (including mathematics and experimental science). At the time of the celebration of the College's first centenary, permission was sought from Rome to confer canonical degrees in Philosophy, Theology, and Canon Law. This was achieved in 1896 with the grant of a Charter as a Pontifical University. Maynooth also became a 'recognised college' of the National University of Ireland, and this began to function in 1910, with faculties of Arts, Science, Philosophy, and Celtic Studies.

The student body of the College remained exclusively clerical until 1966, when lay students were admitted to the NUI courses of the College. In time, these courses became the predominant dimension of Maynooth's curriculum, and the teaching staff of the NUI became more numerous and varied in background. An Act of Dáil Éireann in 1997 restructured the National University of Ireland, and the 'recognised college' at Maynooth became the National University of Ireland, Maynooth (NUIM), independent of Saint Patrick's College. NUIM now has more than 6,500 students and in addition to its traditional faculties of Arts, Philosophy, Science, and Celtic Studies, it now includes courses in Finance, Computer Science, Software Engineering, and Electronic Engineering.

The College thus consists of two parts: NUI Maynooth, which awards NUI degrees and uses NUI robes, and St Patrick's College, which is a Pontifical University, and awards its own degrees. The robes for them, which are listed below, use epitoges instead of hoods. These are made of coloured velvet, backed with black stuff, and are divided along their length into the two colours as specified. The triangular portion is not pleated, and the roundel where the two parts join is not present.

DIPLOMAS

Gown: a black gown of basic pattern [b1].

Epitoges: an epitoge of the faculty colour with one band of ermine, one inch wide, placed at the base of each end.

Hat: a black cloth square cap.

BACHELORS

Gown: a black gown of basic pattern [b1].

Epitoges: an epitoge of the faculty colour with one band of ermine, three inches wide, placed at the base of each end:

BATh: purple and red (Bachelor of Arts and Theology).
BD: purple and green.
BTh: purple and gold.

Hat: a black cloth square cap.

HIGHER DIPLOMAS

Gown: a black gown of masters' pattern [m10].

Epitoges: these have two bands of ermine, one inch wide, placed at each end of the epitoge.

Hat: a black cloth square cap.

MASTERS AND LICENTIATES

Gown: a black gown of Oxford MA pattern [m1].

Epitoge: these have two bands of ermine, three inches wide, placed at each end of the epitoge:
MTh: purple and red.
MPS: *information not available.*
STL: purple and green.

Hat: a black cloth square cap.

DOCTORS

Gown: a black gown of Oxford pattern [d2] but with narrow bell sleeves. The facings and yoke are covered with black velvet.

Epitoges: these have three bands of ermine, three inches wide, placed at each end of the epitoge:
PhD: purple and red.
DD: purple and green.
DCanL: red and green.

Hat: a black velvet bonnet, with gold cords and tassels.

MEDWAY SCHOOL OF PHARMACY
(joint degrees of Greenwich and Kent)
2007

Medway School of Pharmacy was established as a collaboration between the Universities of Kent and Greenwich, in response to a shortage of qualified pharmacists in the south east of England. The School admitted its first students in September 2004, and its first graduates completed Foundation degrees in June 2007.

The robes use shells of bronze and silver for foundation degrees and bachelors, taken from the Kent system; the blue red and gold linings are taken from the Greenwich hoods.

UNDERGRADUATES
none specified

UNDERGRADUATE CERTIFICATES AND DIPLOMAS
not awarded

FOUNDATION DEGREES
Gown: a black stuff gown of basic bachelors' pattern [b1].

Hood: a bronze hood of Cambridge shape [f1], lined blue, the cowl bordered inside 2″ bright red.

Hat: a black cloth square cap.

BACHELORS
Gown: a black stuff gown of basic pattern [b1].

Hood: a silver hood of Cambridge shape [f1], lined blue, the cowl bordered inside 4″ bright red.

Hat: a black cloth square cap.

POSTGRADUATE CERTIFICATES AND DIPLOMAS
Gown: a black stuff gown of basic pattern [b1].

Hood: a dark blue hood of Cambridge shape [f1], lined gold, the cowl bordered inside 4″ bright red.

Hat: a black cloth square cap.

Higher degrees are not yet awarded.

UNIVERSITY OF MIDDLESEX
1992

The roots of Middlesex University go back to two educational institutions founded in the late 1880s: St Katherine's College, and the Hornsey School of Arts and Crafts. Middlesex Polytechnic was created in 1973, when Enfield College of Technology, Hendon College of Technology and Hornsey College of Art, were merged. The College of All Saints (St Katherine's College had united with Berridge House in 1964 to form All Saints) and Trent Park College joined the Polytechnic in 1978. The Polytechnic gained university status in 1992.

The robes follow a simple system, with the hoods lined with university colour (bright red) and bound with the faculty colour.

Faculty colours

Arts and Letters: white.
Business Administration: yellow.
Education: green.
Engineering: purple.
Laws: light blue.
Science: dark blue.

UNDERGRADUATES
none specified

UNDERGRADUATE CERTIFICATES AND DIPLOMAS
Gown: a black gown of basic pattern [b1].
Hood: none, except:
DipHE and AdvDip: a black hood of Cambridge shape [f1], the cowl bordered 3″ red.
Holders of the HND and HNC wear the BTEC hood.
Hat: a black cloth square cap.

FOUNDATION DEGREES
Gown: a black stuff gown of London BA pattern [b4].
Hood: a black hood of Cambridge shape, bordered 4″ red inside the cowl, bound 1″ faculty colour on the cowl edge.
Hat: a black cloth square cap.

BACHELORS
Gown: a black stuff gown of London BA pattern [b4]. For BPhil, there is 1″ red along the outer edge of the facings.

Hood: a black hood of Cambridge shape, bordered 4″ red inside the cowl, bound 1″ faculty colour on the cowl edge. There is no binding for BPhil.

Hat: a black cloth square cap.

POSTGRADUATE CERTIFICATES AND DIPLOMAS

Gown: as for masters.

Hood: as for the relevant bachelor – *e.g.*, PGCE wears the BEd hood.

Hat: a black cloth square cap.

FIRST-DEGREE MASTERS

Gown: as for bachelors.

Hood: a black hood of Cambridge shape [f1], lined red, bound 1″ purple on all edges.

Hat: a black cloth square cap.

MASTERS

Gown: a royal blue stuff gown of London MA pattern [m5].

Hood: a black hood of Cambridge shape [f1], lined red, bound 1″ faculty colour on all edges.

MProfStud: lined red, no binding.

MFA, MDes: as MA.

Hat: a black cloth square cap.

MASTERS OF PHILOSOPHY

Gown: a royal blue stuff gown of London MA pattern [m5], with red facings.

Hood: a royal blue hood of Cambridge shape [f1], lined red.

Hat: a black cloth square cap.

MASTER of the UNIVERSITY

Gown: as for other masters, but in grey.

Hood: a grey panama hood of Cambridge shape [f1], lined red.

Hat: a grey cloth square cap.

DOCTORS OF PHILOSOPHY and TAUGHT AND PROFESSIONAL DOCTORS

Undress gown: as for masters.

Dress robe: a scarlet robe of Cambridge pattern [d1], with red facings and sleeve linings.

Hood:

PhD: a grey panama hood of Cambridge shape [f1], lined and bound ¼″ red.

DProfStud, DPsy: a grey panama hood of Cambridge shape [f1], lined red.

Hat: in undress, a black cloth square cap; in full dress, a black cloth bonnet with red cords and tassels.

HIGHER DOCTORS

Undress gown: as PhD.

Dress robe: a grey panama robe of Cambridge pattern [d1], with red facings and sleeve-linings, and 1″ faculty colour along the outer edge of each facing.

Hood: a grey panama hood of Cambridge shape [f1], lined red, bound 1″ faculty colour.

Hat: in undress, a black cloth square cap; in full dress, a black cloth bonnet with gold cords and tassels.

If awarded *honoris causa*, neither the robe nor the hood have a faculty binding.

THE NATIONAL UNIVERSITY OF IRELAND
1909

The University consists of a number of Constituent Universities and Recognized Colleges. The Constituent Universities are: University College Dublin (UCD); University College Cork (UCC); NUI Galway (NUIG); and NUI Maynooth. The Recognized Colleges are: the Royal College of Surgeons in Ireland; St. Angela's College of Education, Sligo; the National College of Art and Design, Dublin; Shannon College of Hotel Management; the Institute of Public Administration; and Milltown Institute of Theology and Philosophy. For further history, see the Royal University of Ireland entry.

The initial simple faculty-based system had become so complicated with degree-specific hoods, that there were over sixty-six of them by 1999. In that year, the system was rationalized on a faculty basis, so that all degrees in the Faculty of Human and Social Sciences, for example, however they are designated, wear the faculty colour, fawn. The pre-1999 scheme is in the Appendix. A slight flaw is that white is the faculty colour for Arts, but is also used to line master's hoods, so that Arts has effectively two faculty colours. In common with several other universities, the MD is now re-classified as a PhD-level degree; the higher doctorate in medicine is designated DMed.

An announcement was made in January 2010 by the Minster for Education and Science that he intended to dissolve the NUI. UCD, UCC, NUIG and NUI Maynooth would become independent universities; it is not clear what would happen to the Recognized Colleges. At the time of writing, no further details are available.

Faculty colours

Arts: white (but the MA and the diploma hoods also have mid-blue).
Architecture: gold.
Agriculture: light green.
Celtic Studies: saffron.
Commerce: strawberry (this is a shade of purple, rather than pink).
Dentistry: silver grey.
Engineering: terra-cotta.
Food Science and Technology: orange.
Human and Social Sciences: fawn.
Laws: prune(this is a shade of violet).
Medicine (and related sciences): scarlet.
Music: coral.
Nursing and Midwifery: lilac.
Pharmacy: crimson.
Philosophy: maroon (MPhil and PhD).
Science: St Patrick's blue (very pale).
Veterinary Medicine: Celtic blue (mid-dark)

UNDERGRADUATES

None currently specified. (Formerly a black stuff gown of the Oxford scholar's shape [u2] and a black cloth square cap were prescribed.)

UNDERGRADUATE CERTIFICATES AND DIPLOMAS

Gown: a black gown, of Dublin undergraduate pattern [u8], but without the streamers.

Hood: a green hood, of Belfast simple shape [s3] without a liripipe, lined as follows:
Certificates: lined with the faculty colour.
Diplomas: lined white, bordered inside on all edges with the faculty colour.

Hat: black cloth square cap.

BACHELORS

Gown: a black stuff gown, of the basic pattern [b1].
LL.B: as for masters (see note 1).

Hood: a green hood, of Belfast simple shape [s3], lined with the faculty colour.
LL.B: a green hood, of Dublin full shape [f2], lined white, bordered prune.

Hat: a black cloth square cap.

POSTGRADUATE CERTIFICATES AND DIPLOMAS

Gown: as for bachelors.

Hood: a green hood, of Belfast simple shape [s3] without a liripipe, lined white, and bordered inside on all edges with the faculty colour.

Hat: black cloth square cap.

MASTERS (including MASTERS OF PHILOSOPHY)

Gown: a black stuff gown of Oxford MA pattern [m1].

Hood: a green hood of Dublin full shape [f2], lined white, and bound on all edges with the faculty colour, 3″ inside and 1″ outside.
MA: bound mid-blue.

Hat: black cloth square cap.

DOCTORS OF PHILOSOPHY and PROFESSIONAL DOCTORS

Undress gown: as for masters.

Dress robe: a scarlet robe of Oxford MA pattern [m1].

Hood: a green hood of Belfast full shape [f2], lined maroon, and bound 3″ inside and 1″ outside on all edges as follows:
PhD: faculty colour.
DPsychSc, DSocSc: fawn.
MD: scarlet.
DClinDent: silver-grey.
DBA: strawberry.

Hats: in undress, a black cloth square cap; in full dress, a black cloth bonnet with faculty colour cords and tassels.

HIGHER DOCTORS

Undress gown: as PhD.

Dress robe: a scarlet poplin robe of Oxford doctors' pattern [d2], with facings and cuffs of the faculty colour.

Hood: a green hood of Dublin full shape [f2], lined and bound 1″ with the faculty colour.

Hat: in undress, a black cloth square cap; in full dress, a black cloth bonnet with gold cords and tassels.

NOTES

1. The first degree in Laws is BCL, which wears a simple hood, green lined prune. The LL.B wears the same robes as the LL.M.
2. At one point, degrees awarded in two or more faculties were lined or bound black.
3. The *honoris causa* doctorates of Doctor of Arts and Doctor of Education wear the DLitt robes, with white trim.

FORMER HOODS

The 1999 revision affected only hoods; the gowns and dress robes remained the same. The pre-1999 hoods were as follows:

Bachelors: a green hood of Belfast simple shape [s3], lined as follows:

BA: lined white.
BA(Financial Studies): lined strawberry bordered 1½″ white.
BAgSc: lined light green.
BArch: lined old gold.
BBLS: lined strawberry bordered 1″ prune.
BBS: lined strawberry, bordered 1″ white (*same as BFS*).
BCL: lined prune.
BCS: lined white bordered 1″ strawberry.
BCom: lined strawberry.
BDS: lined grey, bordered 1″ scarlet.
BEd: lined white, bordered two 1″ bands of maroon set 1″ apart.
BEng: lined terra-cotta.
BFS: *same as BBS*.
BFST: lined orange.
BLittCelt: lined saffron.
LL.B: lined white, bordered 1″ bands of prune set 1″ apart (full shape).
MB: lined scarlet.
BMedSc: lined scarlet bordered 1″ St Patrick's blue and 1″ white.
BMus: lined coral.
MVB: lined Celtic blue.
BNurSt: lined white bordered 1″ scarlet.
BPA: lined strawberry, bordered two 1″ bands of white set 1″ apart.
BPharm: lined crimson.
BPhysio: lined scarlet bordered 1″ white.

BRadiog: lined St Patrick's blue bordered 1″ scarlet.
BSc: lined St Patrick's blue.
BSc(Arch): lined gold bordered 1″ St Patrick's blue.
BSc(Dairy): lined orange, bordered 1″ St Patrick's blue.
BSc(PH): lined lilac.
BScPharm: lined St Patrick's blue, bordered 1″ crimson.
BSocSc: lined white, bordered 1″ maroon.
BSW: lined white, bordered 1½″ maroon.
BTech: lined white bordered 1″ terra-cotta.

Masters: a green hood of Dublin full shape [f2], lined white and bordered as follows; the first colour is nearer the edge.
MA: 3″ mid-blue.
MAcc and MAccSt: 3″ strawberry with 1″ St Patrick's blue in the centre.
MAO: 3″ gold and 1″ scarlet.
MAgSc: 3″ light green.
MAnimSc: 1½″ Celtic blue and 1½″ St Patrick's blue.
MAppSc: two 1½″ bands of St Patrick's blue set 1½″ apart.
MArch: 3″ gold.
MArchSc: 1½″ gold and 1½″ St Patrick's blue.
MBA: 1″ maroon and 1″ strawberry set 1″ away.
MBS: 1½″ strawberry, and 3″ strawberry set 1½″ away.
MCh: 3″ scarlet.
MCom: 3″ strawberry.
MCoun: 3″ maroon with 1″ St Patrick's blue in the centre.
MDS: 1″ scarlet and 3″ grey.
MDevSt: 1″ light green, and 1″ strawberry set 1″ away.
MEd: 1½″ maroon and 1½″ St Patrick's blue set 1½″ away.
MED: two 1½″ bands of terra-cotta, set 3″ apart.
MEconSc: two 1½″ bands of strawberry, set 1½″ apart.
MEng: 3″ terra-cotta.
MEngSc: 1½″ terra-cotta and 1½″ St Patrick's blue.
MEqSt: 1″ light green and 1½″ St Patrick's blue.
MEqualSt: 1″ maroon, and 1″ prune set 1″ away.
MGC: 1″ St Patrick's blue, and 1″ maroon set 1″ away.
MIE: two 1½″ bands of terra-cotta, 1½″ apart.
MIT: 1″ terra-cotta, 1″ St Patrick's blue, and 1″ strawberry.
LL.M: 3″ prune.
MLArch: 1½″ light green and 1½″ gold.
MLIS: 1″ white, 1″ maroon, and 1″ St Patrick's blue.
MLittCelt: 3″ saffron.
MMgtSc: 2″ strawberry, and 1½″ strawberry set 3″ away.
MMedSc: 1½″ scarlet, 1½″ St Patrick's blue, 1½″ scarlet.
MMus: 3″ coral.
MPA: two 2″ bands of strawberry, set 2″ apart.

MPH: 3″ lilac.
MPhil: 3″ maroon.
MPsychSc: 1½″ St Patrick's blue and 1½″ maroon.
MRUP: 1½″ gold and 1½″ terra-cotta set 1½″ apart.
MRurDev: 2″ strawberry and 2″ maroon set 2″ away.
MSW: two 1″ bands of maroon set 1″ apart.
MSc: 3″ St Patrick's blue.
MScAg: 3″ light green, and 1″ St Patrick's blue.
MSc(Dairy): 1″ orange and 2″ St Patrick's blue.
MSc(VetMed): 1″ Celtic blue and 1″ St Patrick's blue, set 1″ away.
MSocSc: two 1½″ bands of maroon set 1½″ apart.
MUBC: 1″ gold and 1″ terra-cotta set 2″ away.
MVetM: 3″ Celtic blue.

Doctors: a green hood of Dublin full shape [f2], lined and bound as follows:
LL.D: prune.
MD: scarlet.
MusD: coral.
DLitt: white.
DLittCelt: saffron.
DSc: St Patrick's blue.
DScPH: lilac.
DVetM: Celtic blue.
DEconSc: white, with 3″ strawberry set 3″ in.
PhD: maroon, bordered 3″ with the faculty colour.

UNIVERSITY OF NEWCASTLE-upon-TYNE
1963

The University has its origins in the School of Medicine and Surgery which was established in Newcastle-upon-Tyne in 1834. In 1851, following a dispute amongst the teaching staff, the School was split into two rival institutions: the majority forming the Newcastle College of Medicine, with the others establishing themselves as the Newcastle-upon-Tyne College of Medicine and Practical Science. By 1852 the majority college was formally linked to the University of Durham and its teaching certificates were recognised by the University of London for graduation in medicine. The two colleges amalgamated in 1857 and renamed the University of Durham College of Medicine in 1870.

The College of Physical Science was founded in 1871, becoming the Durham College of Physical Science in 1883, and then renamed Armstrong College, after William George Armstrong, in 1904. Both institutions later became part of the University of Durham, whose 1908 Act formally recognised that the University consisted of two Divisions, Durham and Newcastle. By 1908, the Newcastle Division was teaching a full range of subjects in the Faculties of Medicine, Arts, and Science, which also included agriculture and engineering. Throughout the early 20th century, the medical and science colleges vastly outpaced the growth of their Durham counterparts and a Royal Commission in 1934 recommended the merger of the two colleges as King's College, Durham. Growth of the Newcastle Division of the federal Durham University led to tensions within the structure and in 1963 an Act of Parliament separated the two, creating the University of Newcastle-upon-Tyne.

The scheme of dress is not entirely satisfactory: the robes of the degrees which were only ever taught at Newcastle were retained (Medicine, Dentistry, and Laws) and new robes designed for the others. The university now uses basic faculty colours to which new hoods conform: old gold for Arts-based courses, royal blue for Science-based ones, and palatinate purple for medical ones. Hoods and robes marked * were originally part of the Durham scheme.

UNDERGRADUATES

Gown: a gown of black stuff, in the Oxford scholars pattern, but with the forearm seam left open.

Hat: black cloth square cap.

UNDERGRADUATE CERTIFICATES AND DIPLOMAS

Gown: as for bachelors.

Stoles: a royal blue stole, 9″ wide, with mitred ends, with coloured bands as follows:

Certificates: a single 1″ wide black band along the centre of the stole.

Diplomas: two 1″ wide black bands along the centre of the stole, set 1″ apart.

Hat: a black cloth square cap.

FOUNDATION DEGREES

Gown: as for bachelors.

Hood:

FdSc: a royal blue hood of Durham BSc shape [f7], bordered inside the cowl 1″ black set 1″ in.

Hat: a black cloth square cap.

BACHELORS

Gown:

BA, BArch, BSc, LL.B, BEng, BMedSc: black stuff, Durham BA pattern, [b5].

MB, BS, BDS, [BHy]: black gown with a flap collar [d4], but with flaps over the armholes. There are four vertical rows of black braid from the shoulder to the base of the flap, and two concentric squares of black braid at the foot of each sleeve. *See Note 2.*

Hood: a hood of the Durham BSc shape [f7], coloured and lined as follows:

BA: black stuff, the cowl bordered inside 3″ old gold silk, the cape bound with fur.

BArch: *same as* BA.

BDS: rose silk, lined ivory silk, the cape bound with fur.*

BEng: black stuff, the cowl bordered inside 3″ royal blue silk, and bound fur.

LL.B: maroon silk, lined palatinate purple, the cape bound with fur.

MB: scarlet silk, lined palatinate purple, the cape bound with fur.*

BMedSc: *same as* BSc.

BPhil: *same as* MA.

BS: rose silk, lined palatinate purple, the cape bound with fur.*

BSc: black stuff, the cowl bordered inside 3″ royal blue silk, the cape bound fur.

Hat: black cloth square cap.

POSTGRADUATE CERTIFICATES AND DIPLOMAS

Gown: as for bachelors.

Stoles: a royal blue stole, 9″ wide with mitred ends, and coloured bands as follows:

Certificates: a single 1″ wide scarlet band along the centre of the stole.

Diplomas: two 1″ wide scarlet bands along the centre of the stole, set 1″ apart.

Hat: black cloth square cap.

FIRST-DEGREE MASTERS (MChem, MComp, MEng, MMath, MPhys)

Gown: as for bachelors.

Hood: a black silk hood of Oxford simple shape [s1], lined royal blue silk, the cowl edge bound 1″ white silk

Hat: a black cloth square cap.

MASTERS including MASTERS OF PHILOSOPHY

Gown: a black stuff gown of the Oxford MA pattern [m1], with a black cord and button on the yoke.

Hood: a hood of Oxford simple shape [s1], coloured and lined as follows:

LL.M: maroon lined palatinate purple.*
MS: rose lined palatinate purple.*
[MDS: rose lined ivory.*]

The following hoods are of the Durham BSc shape [f7]:

MA: black lined old gold.
MLitt: black lined old gold, the cowl bordered inside 1″ scarlet.
MPhil (by research) black lined scarlet.
MRes: black lined royal blue, the cowl bordered inside 1″ scarlet.
MSc: black lined royal blue.
MSc(Integrated Graduate Development Scheme): black lined grey, the cowl bordered inside 3″ maroon.
MHPrac, MGPrac, MMPrac: black, lined and the cowl bound 1″ old gold.
The following use the MA hood:
MArch, MBA, MClinEd, MEd, MFA, MIntHsgSc, MLA, MMus, MPhil (by taught course), MTP.

Hat: a black cloth square cap.

DOCTORS OF PHILOSOPHY and TAUGHT AND PROFESSIONAL DOCTORS

Undress gown: as for masters, but with a scarlet cord and button on the yoke.

Dress robe: as for masters, but without the cord and button on the yoke. There are white silk facings, edged on the outer edge with:

PhD: 1″ scarlet.
DBA, EdD, DAppEdPsy, and DEdPsy: 1″ old gold.
EngD: 1″ royal blue.
DClinPsy: 1″ palatinate purple.

Hood: a scarlet cloth hood of Durham BSc shape [f7], lined and bound as follows:

PhD: lined scarlet.
DBA: lined gold, bound white on all edges.
DEdPsy: lined and bound gold on all edges.
DAppEdPsy: lined and bound gold on all edges, the cowl bordered inside 1″ white set 1″ in.
EdD: white, bound 1″ old gold on all edges.
EngD: lined royal blue, bound white on all edges.
DClinPsy: palatinate purple, bound 1″ white on all edges.

Hat: black velvet soft square cap, with black tuft.

HIGHER DOCTORS

Undress gown:

MD, DCh, DDSc, [DHy]: a black silk gown with a flap collar [d4]; the corners of the collar are cut across at 45 degrees. There is Durham doctors' pattern lace along the facings, round the collar, round the armholes up to the sleeve head, and across the base of the sleeves.

All others: as masters.

Dress robe: a scarlet cloth robe of Oxford doctors' pattern [d2], the facings and sleeves covered as follows:

DCL: white.*

DCh: rose, with 1″ palatinate along the outer edge of the facings and round the bottom of the sleeves.

DD: palatinate.*

DDS and DDSc: rose, with 1″ ivory along the outer edge of the facings and round the bottom of the sleeves.*

DEng: royal blue.

DHy: scarlet, with 5″ palatinate and 1″ white along the outer edge of the facings and round the bottom of the sleeves.*

LL.D: maroon.*

DLitt: old gold.*

MD: scarlet, with 1″ palatinate along the outer edge of the facings and round the bottom of the sleeves.*

DMus: old gold.

DSc: scarlet [was: white, with 1″ royal blue along the outer edge of the facings and round the bottom of the sleeves].

Hood: a scarlet cloth of the Durham BSc shape [f7], lined as follows:

DCL: white.*

DCh: rose, the cowl bordered inside 3″ palatinate.*

DD: palatinate.*

DDS and DDSc: rose, the cowl bordered inside 3″ ivory.*

DEng: royal blue

[DHy: scarlet, the cowl bordered inside 3″ palatinate and 1″ white.*]

LL.D: maroon.*

DLitt: old gold.*

MD: scarlet, the cowl bordered inside 3″ palatinate.*

DMus: white brocade.

DSc: white, the cowl bordered inside 3″ royal blue.

Hat: a black velvet soft square cap, with black tuft. (A white tuft for DD and DCL.)

* These hoods and robes were once part of the Durham scheme.

NOTES

1. Holders of the former Licence in Dental Surgery (LDS; a Durham diploma) wore a black gown, of London BA pattern [b4], the sleeves held by a palatinate ribbon 1″ wide, and with a palatinate cord and button on the yoke.
2. It appears that the medicine gown is no longer used, but the BA gown is supplied instead.
3. DDs wear a white silk scarf with both dress robe and undress gown.

NEWMAN UNIVERSITY COLLEGE, BIRMINGHAM
1968

Founded as a teacher training college, Newman is now a university college. It offers a number of taught and research degrees, all of which are validated by the University of Leicester. The Leicester robes are used, save that the hoods are edged with a triple twisted cord of blue, red, and gold.

UNIVERSITY OF NORTH LONDON
1992-2002

Founded as the Northern Polytechnic Institute in 1896, it merged in the early 1970s with the North Western Polytechnic which had functioned since 1929, to become the Polytechnic of North London. Under the Further and Higher Education Act 1992, the institution was granted University status. In 2002, UNL merged with Guildhall to form London Metropolitan.

UNDERGRADUATES
none specified

UNDERGRADUATE CERTIFICATES AND DIPLOMAS
Gown: as for bachelors.
Hood: a blue hood of Cambridge shape [f1], the cowl bordered 2″ bright red inside.
Hat: a black cloth square cap.

FOUNDATION DEGREES
never awarded

BACHELORS
Gown: a black stuff gown of the basic bachelor's pattern [b1].
Hood: a blue hood of Cambridge shape [f1], the cowl bordered 4″ bright red inside.
Hat: a black cloth square cap.

POSTGRADUATE CERTIFICATES AND DIPLOMAS
Gown: as for bachelors.
Hood: as for masters.
Hat: a black cloth square cap.

FIRST-DEGREE MASTERS
never awarded.

MASTERS including MASTERS OF PHILOSOPHY
Gown: a black stuff gown of the basic master's pattern [m10].
Hood: a blue hood of Cambridge shape [f1], fully lined bright red.
Hat: a black cloth square cap.

DOCTORS OF PHILOSOPHY and TAUGHT AND PROFESSIONAL DOCTORS
Undress gown: *none specified*
Dress robe: a blue robe of Cambridge pattern [d1], with bright red facings and sleeve linings.

Hood: a blue hood of Cambridge shape [f1], lined and bound 1″ bright red.
Hat: in full dress, a blue cloth bonnet with red cords and tassels.

HIGHER DOCTORS

Undress gown: *none specified*
Dress robe: a bright red robe of Cambridge pattern [d1], with blue facings and sleeve linings.
Hood: a blue hood of Cambridge shape [f1], lined and bound 2″ bright red.
Hat: in full dress, a red velvet bonnet with blue cords and tassels.

UNIVERSITY OF NORTHAMPTON
2005

In 1924, the Northampton Technical College was opened, followed by a School of Art in 1932. A teacher training college, displaced from Liverpool, opened in 1972. It amalgamated with the Technical College in 1975, as Nene College of Higher Education, awarding Leicester degrees. It absorbed several other colleges, and became University College, Northampton, in 1999, gaining full University status in 2005. This involved overturning a decree of Henry III of 1265, which said that no university was to be founded in Northampton – the result of a migration of students from Oxford, who had tried to set one up in the town: it existed from 1261 to 1265, and was closed down by Henry III as a direct act of retaliation for the students taking the part of Simon de Montfort in the civil war of 1264.

UNDERGRADUATES
none specified

UNDERGRADUATE CERTIFICATES AND DIPLOMAS
Gown: as for bachelors.
Hood: a mid-blue hood of CNAA shape [a1], lined green.
Hat: black cloth square cap.

FOUNDATION DEGREES
Gown: as for bachelors.
Hood: a black hood of Burgon shape [s2], bordered 2″ green inside the cowl.
Hat: black cloth square cap.

BACHELORS
Gown: a black stuff gown of London BA pattern [b4]
Hood: a black hood of CNAA shape [a1], lined peacock blue and tipped as follows:
BA: red embossed silk.
LL.B: green embossed silk.
BSc: white embossed silk.
Hat: black cloth square cap.

POSTGRADUATE CERTIFICATES AND DIPLOMAS
Gown: as for bachelors.
Hood: a black hood of Burgon shape [s2] lined as follows:
PGCE: lined peacock blue, the cowl bordered 1″ green inside.
All others: lined green.
Hat: a black cloth square cap.

MASTERS

Gown: a black stuff gown of Manchester Victoria MA pattern [m6].

Hood: a black hood of Cambridge shape [f1], lined peacock blue, and bordered 1″ inside the cowl as follows:

MA: red embossed silk.

MBA: yellow embossed silk.

LLM: green embossed silk.

MSc: white embossed silk.

Hat: a black cloth square cap.

MASTERS OF PHILOSOPHY

Gown: as for masters, but with blue facings.

Hood: a red hood of Cambridge shape [f1], lined blue.

Hat: a black cloth square cap.

DOCTORS OF PHILOSOPHY and TAUGHT AND PROFESSIONAL DOCTORS

Undress gown: *none specified*

Dress robe: a red robe of Cambridge pattern [d1], with blue facings and sleeve linings.

Hood: a red hood of Cambridge shape [f1], lined and bound blue.

Hat: in full dress, a black cloth bonnet with blue cords and tassels.

HIGHER DOCTORS

Undress gown: as PhD.

Dress robe: as PhD, but the facings edged 1″ gold.

Hood: as PhD, but bound 1″ gold on all edges.

Hat: in full dress, a black cloth bonnet with gold cords and tassels.

NOTES

1. As Nene College, it awarded Leicester degrees, for which it used the Leicester hoods, with the addition of a twisted cord.

NORTHUMBRIA UNIVERSITY
1992

Northumbria University has its origins in three regional colleges: Rutherford College of Technology, the College of Art and Industrial Design, and the Municipal College of Commerce. An amalgamation of these three institutions formed Newcastle Polytechnic in 1969, which gained university status in 1992.

UNDERGRADUATES
none specified

UNDERGRADUATE CERTIFICATES AND DIPLOMAS
Gown: as for bachelors.
Hood: a black hood of CNAA shape [a1], lined red embossed silk.
Hat: a black cloth square cap.

FOUNDATION DEGREES
not awarded

BACHELORS
Gown: a black stuff gown of London BA pattern [b4].
Hood: a black hood of Cambridge shape [f1], the cowl bordered inside 4″ red embossed silk, and bound 1″ gold.
Hat: a black cloth square cap.

POSTGRADUATE CERTIFICATES AND DIPLOMAS
Gown: as for masters.
Hood: a black hood of Cambridge shape [f1], the cowl bordered inside 4″ red embossed silk, and bound on cape and cowl 1″ gold.
Hat: a black cloth square cap.

MASTERS
Gown: a black stuff gown of the basic master's pattern [m10], with 2½″ facings of gold moiré silk.
Hood: a black hood of Cambridge shape [f1], lined red embossed silk, and bound on cape and cowl 1″ gold moiré silk.
Hat: a black cloth square cap.

MASTERS OF PHILOSOPHY
Gown: a royal blue gown of Cambridge doctoral pattern [d1], with 2½″ facings of gold silk; the sleeves unlined.

Hood: a royal blue hood of Cambridge shape [f1], lined red embossed silk, and bound on the cowl 1″ plain gold silk.
Hat: a black cloth square cap.

DOCTORS OF PHILOSOPHY and TAUGHT AND PROFESSIONAL DOCTORS

Undress gown: *none specified*
Dress robe: a royal blue robe of Cambridge doctoral pattern [d1], with 5″ facings and sleeve linings of gold silk
Hood: a bright blue hood of Cambridge shape [f1], lined red embossed silk, and bound on all edges 1″ plain gold silk.
Hat: in full dress, a bright blue cloth bonnet with gold cords and tassels.

HIGHER DOCTORS

Undress gown: *none specified*
Dress robe: a royal blue cloth robe of Cambridge doctoral pattern [d1], with facings and sleeve linings of gold moiré silk.
Hood: a royal blue hood of Cambridge shape [f1], lined red embossed silk, and bound on cape and cowl 1″ gold moiré silk.
Hat: in full dress, a royal blue cloth bonnet with gold cords and tassels.

NOTES

1, Masters *honoris causa* wear the same robes as MPhil, but the robe facings and hood bindings are of gold moiré silk.
2. Doctors *honoris causa* wear the same robes as the higher doctors, but the robe, hood, and bonnet are made of light blue cloth.

NORWICH UNIVERSITY COLLEGE FOR THE ARTS
2008

Founded in 1845 as the Norwich School of Design, its founders were the artists and followers of the Norwich School of Painters, the only provincial British group to establish an international reputation for landscape painting. From 1965, it awarded the degree-level DipAD of the National Council of Art and Design. NCDAD merged with the CNAA in 1975, and the School then offered CNAA degrees. In 1989 the School merged with Great Yarmouth College of Art to form the Norfolk Institute of Art and Design (NIAD). In 1991 NIAD become an Associate College of the new Anglia Polytechnic, which became Anglia Polytechnic University in 1992, and NIAD then awarded APU degrees. The first MA course was introduced in 1993 (MA Fine Art), and the first research degree student was registered in 1995. In 1994 NIAD was incorporated as a Higher Education Institution, re-named Norwich School of Art and Design. In November 2007 the School was granted the power to award its own degrees up to Master's level and took the name Norwich University College of the Arts.

The robes are a simple scheme, based on the grade-hood system. The principal differences in the hoods are the shapes and the width of the gold bindings.

UNDERGRADUATES
none specified

DIPLOMA of HIGHER EDUCATION
Gown: a black stuff gown of the basic bachelors' pattern [b1]
Hood: a pale grey hood of CNAA shape [a1], the cowl bordered inside 1½″ powder blue, and ½″ bright gold.
Hat: a black cloth square cap.

FOUNDATION DEGREES
Gown: a black stuff gown of the basic bachelors' pattern [b1]
Hood: a pale grey hood of CNAA shape [a1], lined powder blue, and the cowl bordered inside 2″ bright gold.
Hat: a black cloth square cap.

BACHELORS
Gown: a black stuff gown of the basic bachelors' pattern [b1]
Hood: a pale grey hood of CNAA shape [a1], lined powder blue, and bound on all edges 1″ bright gold.
Hat: a black cloth square cap.

POSTGRADUATE CERTIFICATES AND DIPLOMAS

Gown: as for masters.

Hood: a pale grey hood of London shape [f3], lined powder blue, and the cowl bound 1″ bright gold.

Hat: a black cloth square cap.

MASTERS

Gown: a black stuff gown of the basic master's pattern [m10].

Hood: a pale grey hood of London shape [f3], lined powder blue, and bound on all edges 1″ bright gold.

Hat: a black cloth square cap.

Research degrees (MPhil, PhD) are currently validated by the University of the Arts, London.

UNIVERSITY OF NOTTINGHAM
1948

The University of Nottingham traces its origins to the founding of an adult education school in 1798. However, the foundation stone of the original University College Nottingham on Shakespeare Street was laid in 1877. A large gift of land allowed University College Nottingham to move to a new campus in 1928. This development was supported by an endowment fund and public contributions. The transfer was made possible by the generosity of Sir Jesse Boot, who presented 35 acres to the City of Nottingham in 1921. In 1948, University College Nottingham received its Royal Charter, becoming the University of Nottingham.

The scheme of robes is partly derived from Cambridge – the gowns and hood shapes – and partly from London – the colours of hoods and robes, and method of lining hoods. The faculty bindings are its own addition. The system is simple and reasonably easy to read, although with the introduction of new levels of degrees, it has recently been overhauled. The main difference is that the PhD hood is no longer bound with faculty colour.

Faculty Colours

Architecture: orange.
Administration: salmon.
Agriculture and Horticulture: green.
Arts: cherry.
Divinity: purple.
Education: mauve.
Engineering: navy.
Nursing and Health Sciences: cream.
Laws: maroon.
Medicine: gold.
Music: pink.
Science: royal blue.
Pharmacy: grey.
Philosophy: light blue.
Veterinary Medicine: teal.

UNDERGRADUATES

Gown: a black stuff gown of London pattern [u3].
Hat: a black cloth square cap.

UNDERGRADUATE CERTIFICATES AND DIPLOMAS

Gown: as for bachelors.

Hood:

Certificates: a black hood of Belfast simple shape [s3], lined light blue.

Diplomas: a light blue hood of Edinburgh simple shape [s4], lined light blue.

Hat: black cloth square cap.

FOUNDATION DEGREES

not awarded

BACHELORS

Gown: a black stuff gown of Cambridge BA pattern [b2]. The BD wore the masters' gown.

Hood: a black silk hood of Cambridge shape [f1], bordered inside 3″ light blue silk. The cowl is bound 1″ inside and ½″ outside with faculty colour.

BArch: bound orange on the cape also.

[BD: fully lined blue, and bound purple on the cowl.]

BM, BS: bound gold on the cape also.

BPhil: bound blue on the cape also.

BVM&S: bound teal on the cape also.

Hat: black cloth square cap.

POSTGRADUATE CERTIFICATES AND DIPLOMAS

Gown: as for masters.

Hood:

Certificates, a black hood of Belfast simple shape [s3], lined Sherwood green.

Diplomas: a Sherwood green hood of Edinburgh simple shape [s4], lined Sherwood green.

Hat: black cloth square cap.

FIRST-DEGREE MASTERS

Gown: as for masters.

Hood: the relevant bachelors' hood, but bound on the cape also. (*E.g.*, the MSci wears the BSc hood with the extra binding.)

Hat: a black cloth square cap.

MASTERS including MASTERS OF PHILOSOPHY

Gown: a black stuff gown of Cambridge MA pattern [m2].

Hood: a black silk hood of Cambridge shape [f1], fully lined light blue silk. The cowl is bound 1″ inside and ½″ outside with the faculty colour.

MBA: used the MA hood until c.2005, since when it has used the old MA(Admin) hood.

MPH: is bound gold on the cape but not on the cowl.

MPhil: the same as the taught master in the same faculty, but bound with the faculty colour on the cape also.

MSW: uses the MA hood.

MTh: uses the BD hood.

Hat: black cloth square cap.

DOCTORS OF PHILOSOPHY and TAUGHT AND PROFESSIONAL DOCTORS

Undress gown: as for masters, with 4″ of Birmingham lace over the armhole.

Dress robe: a claret cloth robe of Cambridge pattern [d1], with light blue silk facings.

Hood: a claret cloth hood of Cambridge shape, lined light blue silk. The cowl is bound 1″ inside and ½″ outside as follows:

MusD: pink.

DAppPsy: royal blue.

DArch: orange.

DASS: cherry.

DBA: salmon.

EdD: mauve.

DHSc, NursD: cream.

DVM, DVS: teal.

PhD: light blue.

Hat: in undress, a black cloth square cap; in full dress, a black cloth bonnet with no cords or tassels.

HIGHER DOCTORS

Undress gown: as PhD, but the lace extends the full length of the armhole.

Dress robe: a scarlet cloth robe of Cambridge pattern [d1], with light blue silk facings.

Hood: a scarlet cloth hood of Cambridge shape [f1], lined light blue silk. The cowl is bound 1″ inside and ½″ outside with the faculty colour.

Hat: in undress, a black cloth square cap; in full dress, a black velvet bonnet with no cords or tassels.

NOTES

1. Until 1999, the PhD hood was bound with the faculty colour.

NOTTINGHAM TRENT UNIVERSITY
1992

In 1945, the Nottingham and District Technical College was designated, and opened in 1958 as the Nottingham Regional College of Technology, although it was not officially launched until 1964. Two years later, it was linked with Nottingham College of Art and Design as a Polytechnic-designate. Polytechnic status was granted, as Trent Polytechnic, in 1970. In 1975, it amalgamated with Nottingham College of Education at Clifton. The Polytechnic changed its name to Trent Polytechnic Nottingham in 1988. The following year, the Nottingham Polytechnic Higher Education Corporation was founded. University status was granted in 1992, as Nottingham Trent University.

The scheme of robes is simple and logical, using a basic hood of blue and green (red and green for doctors) bound with faculty colour.

Faculty colours

Arts: yellow.
MBA, MPA: ruby.
Education: pink.
Engineering: blue.
Laws: rust.
Philosophy: silver.
Science: orange.

UNDERGRADUATES
none specified

UNDERGRADUATE CERTIFICATES AND DIPLOMAS
Gown: as for bachelors.
Hood: a blue hood of CNAA shape [a1], lined green.
Hat: a black cloth square cap.

FOUNDATION DEGREES
Gown: a black stuff gown of the basic bachelor's pattern [b1].
Hood: a blue hood of Cambridge shape [f1], lined green, and the cowl bordered inside ½″ with the faculty colour.
Hat: a black cloth square cap.

BACHELORS
Gown: a black stuff gown of the basic bachelor's pattern [b1].
Hood: a blue hood of Cambridge shape [f1], lined green, and the cowl bordered inside 1″ with the faculty colour.
Hat: a black cloth square cap.

POSTGRADUATE CERTIFICATES AND DIPLOMAS

same as undergraduate diplomas.

MASTERS including MASTERS OF PHILOSOPHY

Gown: a black stuff gown of the basic master's pattern. For MPhil, there is 1″ silver braid on the outer edge of the facings.

Hood: a blue hood of Cambridge shape [f1], lined green, bound 2″ on all edges with the faculty colour.

Hat: a black cloth square cap.

TAUGHT AND PROFESSIONAL DOCTORS

Undress gown: *none specified*

Dress robe: a maroon robe of Cambridge pattern [d1], with green facings and sleeve linings. There is 1″ black on the outer edge of the facings.

Hood: a maroon hood of Cambridge shape [f1], lined green and bound 1″ black on all edges.

Hat: in full dress, a black cloth bonnet with green cords and tassels.

DOCTORS OF PHILOSOPHY

Undress gown: *none specified*

Dress robe: a maroon robe of Cambridge pattern [d1], with green facings and sleeve linings. There is 1″ silver braid on the outer edge of the facings.

Hood: a maroon hood of Cambridge shape [f1], lined green and bound 1″ silver on all edges.

Hat: in full dress, a black cloth bonnet with green cords and tassels.

HIGHER DOCTORS

Undress gown: *none specified*

Dress robe: a scarlet robe of Cambridge pattern [d1], with green facings and sleeve linings. There is 1″ silver braid on the outer edge of the facings.

Hood: a maroon hood of Cambridge shape [f1], lined green and bound 1″ silver on all edges. (If awarded *honoris causa*, the silver is replaced by gold.)

Hat: in full dress, a black velvet bonnet with green cords and tassels.

THE OPEN UNIVERSITY
1969

The Open University (OU) is the UK's 'open learning' university. It was established in 1969, and the first students enrolled in January 1971. The majority of students are based in the UK, but its courses can be taken anywhere in the world. The administration is based at Walton Hall in Milton Keynes, but there are regional centres in each of its thirteen regions around the UK. Since it was founded, more than 3 million students have taken its courses.

The University was asked to continue the work of the Council for National Academic Awards (CNAA, *q.v.*) when it was dissolved. This it does through the OU Validation Service (OUVS), and the old CNAA hoods are used for this (see Note 1).

The scheme is reasonably simple, and based on the University's colours of blue and gold. Three shade of blue are used (dark, light, and royal) which enables a wide range of hoods to be designed. Hoods are generally grade-specific, although the MBA and MEd have their own hoods. Hats are not worn at ceremonies, though they may be used by graduates on other occasions. The specifications for them are included below, therefore.

UNDERGRADUATES
none specified

UNDERGRADUATE CERTIFICATES AND DIPLOMAS
Gown: as for bachelors.
Hood: a dark blue stuff hood of Oxford simple shape [s1], bordered light blue inside the cowl.
Hat: a dark blue square cap.

FOUNDATION DEGREES
Gown: as for bachelors.
Hood: a light blue stuff hood of Oxford simple shape [s1], bordered dark blue inside the cowl.
Hat: a dark blue square cap.

BACHELORS
Gown: a dark blue stuff gown of OU pattern [m14]. This is like the basic masters' pattern [m10], but the sleeves are cut short to end at the hips, and there is an inverted-T armhole.
Hood: a light blue stuff hood of Oxford simple shape [s1], bordered 3″ gold silk inside the cowl.
[BPhil: a royal blue stuff hood of Oxford simple shape [s1], bordered 3″ gold silk inside the cowl (*now used for MRes*).]

Hat: a dark blue square cap.

POSTGRADUATE CERTIFICATES AND DIPLOMAS

Gown: as for masters.

Hood: a dark blue stuff hood of Oxford simple shape [s1], bordered light blue inside the cowl.

Hat: a dark blue square cap.

FIRST-DEGREE MASTERS

Gown: as for bachelors.

Hood: a gold hood of Cambridge shape [f1], lined gold and bordered 3″ light blue inside the cowl.

Hat: a dark blue square cap.

MASTERS including MASTERS OF PHILOSOPHY

Gown: a light blue stuff gown of OU pattern [m14].

Hood: of Cambridge shape [f1], except MRes, which is Oxford simple shape [s1]:

MA, MSc: dark blue, lined and bound ¼″ gold silk on all edges.

MBA, MPA: as MA, but the cowl bound inside and out 1″ light blue.

MEd: as MA, but the cowl bound inside and out 1″ white (*but see Note 3*).

MPhil: light blue, lined and bound ¼″ gold silk on all edges.

MRes: royal blue bordered inside 3″ gold silk [s1] *(the former BPhil hood)*.

MUniv: gold, lined and bound 1″ royal blue on all edges.

Hat: a dark blue square cap.

DOCTORS OF PHILOSOPHY and TAUGHT AND PROFESSIONAL DOCTORS

Undress gown: *none specified*

Dress robe: royal blue, OU pattern [m14], 3″ gold silk facings.

Hood: a hood of Cambridge shape [f1]:

PhD: royal blue, lined and bound 1″ gold silk on all edges.

DClinPsy: gold, lined and the cape bound 1″ cream brocade, the cowl bound inside and out 1″ light blue.

EdD: gold, lined, but not bound, light blue.

Hat: in full dress, a royal blue bonnet, with gold cords and tassels.

HIGHER DOCTORS

Undress gown: *none specified*

Dress robe:

DUniv: a gold robe of OU pattern [m14], with 5″ blue silk facings.

All others: a royal blue robe of OU pattern [m14], with 5″ gold silk facings.

Hood: a hood of Cambridge shape [f1]:

DLitt: gold, lined, but not bound, royal blue.

DSc: gold, lined and bound 1″ light blue on all edges.

DUniv: royal blue, lined and bound 1″ light blue on all edges.

Hat: in full dress, a gold bonnet with royal blue cords and tassels.

NOTES

1. Degrees validated by the OU Validation Service wear the bachelors' or masters' gown as appropriate, with the following hoods:
   bachelors: a gold panama hood of CNAA [a1] shape, lined turquoise taffeta.
   masters: a gold panama hood of CNAA [a1] shape, lined white taffeta.
   (These are the former CNAA bachelors' and masters' hoods.)
2. Some robemakers supply the masters' hoods made in Oxford full shape [f5], lined and bound for 2″.
3. The MEd hood appears to have recently become obsolete, and holders of this degree now wear the MA/MSc hood.

UNIVERSITY OF OXFORD

The University of Oxford is a collegiate university, with (at present) thirty-eight Colleges and six Permanent Private Halls. The exact date of foundation is unclear, but it is known that lectures were taking place as early as 1096, and the masters were recognized as a *universitas* or corporation in 1231. The oldest surviving colleges are Balliol, Merton, and University, all founded between 1249 and 1264, although the exact dates are unclear. St Edmund Hall, founded in 1225, is the only surviving mediæval Hall.

The academic robes have descended directly from those worn in the Middle Ages – at least in the faculties of Divinity, Laws, Medicine, and Arts; Music was added a little later. As new degrees have been introduced, robes have been designed which attempt to fit the existing scheme, but it is proving more difficult to do this. The latest oddity is the treatment of the DClinPsy and the EngD, which, although doctors, are not allowed any form of dress robe at all, but merely the black gown. The EngD is the first three-colour hood to be introduced in the University.

UNDERGRADUATES

Gown:

Commoners: a black stuff gown, without sleeves, but with streamers and a flap collar. It is of hip length (usually described as 'covering the normal lounge coat'). There is a 'wing' around each armhole [u5].

Graduate Students (called Advanced Students until c1993): the same gown, but of knee-length.

Scholars: a black stuff gown, of knee-length, with bell-sleeves [u2].

Hat: black cloth square cap.

UNDERGRADUATE CERTIFICATES AND DIPLOMAS

none specified

BACHELORS

Gown:

BA, BEd, BFA, BTh: a black stuff gown with open, pointed sleeves reaching the hem of the gown [b8].

BD: as for MA, in black silk or stuff, but with a black cord and button on the yoke.

BM, BCh, BMus, BPhil, BCL, [BLitt, BSc]: a black silk gown with flap collar. The sleeves are sewn shut below the armhole, which is of the inverted-T style. There is black silk gimp round the collar; round each armhole, extending to the sleeve-head; and in a five-sided figure at the base of each sleeve, and on the skirt of the gown at each side and the rear [d4].

Hood:

BD: a black hood of Oxford full shape [f5], lined fine black silk.

All others: usually of the Burgon shape [s2], but may be the simple shape [s1]. Where the simple shape is used, the fur is a 1″ binding on the cowl edge only.

BA: black silk, half-lined and bound fur.
BCL: mid-blue silk half-lined and bound fur.
BEd: black silk, bordered inside 2″ dark green silk. Between 1969 and 1980, it was fully lined and bound green.
BFA: black silk, bordered inside 2″ gold silk. Between 1978 and 198?, it was fully lined and bound gold.
[BLitt: light blue silk half-lined and bound fur.]
BM,BCh: same as BCL (*see Note 4*).
BMus: lilac silk, half-lined and bound fur.
BPhil: dark blue silk lined and bound white silk.
[BSc: same as BLitt.]
BTh: black silk, bordered inside 2″ magenta silk.

Hat: a black cloth square cap.

POSTGRADUATE CERTIFICATES AND DIPLOMAS

none specified

FIRST-DEGREE MASTERS

For the first three years from graduation, the BA robes; after that, those for the MA.

MASTERS including MASTERS OF PHILOSOPHY

Gown:

MA: a black stuff gown with long closed sleeves, with a crescent cut-out at the base [m1].
All others: the same gown as BM, *etc.*, except MCh, which has an extra gimp panel on the body of the gown at elbow level.

Hood: Burgon shape [s2]; occasionally [s1].

MA: black silk lined and bound shot silk of crimson and orange.
MBA: crimson silk lined and bound dark grey silk.
MCh: black silk lined and bound mid-blue silk.
MEd: black silk lined and bound dark green silk.
MFA: gold silk lined and bound white silk.
MJur: same as BCL.
MLitt: light blue silk lined and bound grey silk.
MPhil: dark blue silk lined and bound white silk.
MSc: same as MLitt.
MSt: dark green silk lined and bound white silk.
MTh: black silk lined and bound magenta silk.

Hat: black cloth square cap.

TAUGHT AND PROFESSIONAL DOCTORS

Undress gown: as for MCh.

Dress robe: none.

Hood: A silk hood of Burgon shape [s2], coloured as follows:

DClinPsy: a dark blue silk hood, lined and bound scarlet silk.
DEng: a red silk hood, lined and bound petrol blue silk, bordered inside the cowl 2″ grey silk.

Hat: black cloth square cap.

DOCTORS OF PHILOSOPHY and HIGHER DOCTORS

Undress gown:

DD: as for BD.

All others: as for BM, etc, but with an extra gimp panel on the body of the gown at elbow level.

Dress robe: a scarlet cloth robe of Oxford pattern [d2] (except DMus), the sleeves and facings covered as follows:

DD: black velvet.
DCL: crimson silk.
DM: crimson silk.
DLitt: grey silk.
DSc: grey silk.
DPhil: dark blue silk.
DMus: a robe of cream silk with apple-blossom damasking, with facings and sleeves of cherry silk.

Convocation habit: a sleeveless scarlet cloth robe [d5]. It is faced inside for about 6″ with silk to match the hood lining, and fastens at the top with two buttons of the same colour. It is worn over the black undress gown, the sleeves of which are pulled through the armholes of the habit. There is no habit for the DMus.

Hood: a scarlet cloth hood of Oxford full shape [f5], lined as follows:

DD: black silk.
DCL: crimson silk.
DM: crimson silk.
DLitt: grey silk.
DSc: grey silk.
DPhil: dark blue silk.
DMus: a hood of cream silk damask, lined cherry silk.

Hat:

DCL, DM, DMus: in undress, a black cloth square cap; in full dress, a black cloth bonnet with a black silk ribbon.

DD, DSc, DLitt, DPhil: in both undress and full dress, a black cloth square cap.

NOTES

1. The BLitt and BSc, introduced in the late nineteenth century, were replaced by MLitt (1977) and MSc (1975). Likewise, the BPhil became MPhil, except in the subject-field of philosophy, where it remains BPhil.
2. The MCh wore, in the early twentieth century, a black hood lined scarlet silk
3. DDs wear a black silk scarf with both dress robe and undress gown.

4. The hood for the BM and BCh is probably the BM hood alone, and the BCh, which is always awarded with the BM, does not have a hood. (*cf* Cambridge and Dublin, and later Durham/Newcastle, where it does).
5. Holders of the status of Student in Civil Law (SCL) – those reading for the BCL without first taking the BA – wore the BCL gown in black stuff, but without the gimp trim, and an unlined blue silk hood of simple shape. These robes were also used by Students in Medicine – those reading for the BM without first taking the BA. Both of these statuses were abolished in 1873.

OXFORD BROOKES UNIVERSITY
1992

Oxford Brookes University can trace its origins back to the Oxford School of Art, founded in 1865. In 1891 the School was taken over by the Oxford Technical School, which in 1956 became the Oxford College of Technology. In 1970 the College became Oxford Polytechnic, and in 1976 combined with the Lady Spencer Churchill College at Wheatley (Lady Spencer Churchill College had been founded at Bletchley Park). In 1992 the Polytechnic became Oxford Brookes University –taking its name from a distinguished principal of the Technical School, John Henry Brookes. In 2000 Oxford Brookes University merged with Westminster College, Oxford.

Throughout, 'blue' refers to the University's blue, which is a dark royal blue.

UNDERGRADUATES
No academical dress is worn.

BTEC, HNDs
Gown: a black gown of Oxford BA pattern [b8], without the tapes at the wrist.
Hood: a black stuff hood of CNAA shape [a1], partly lined cream silk, piped blue.
Hat: a black cloth square cap.

FOUNDATION DEGREES, AND CERTAIN DIPLOMAS AND CERTIFICATES
Gown: a black gown of Oxford BA pattern [b8], without the tapes at the wrist.
Hood: a black stuff hood of CNAA shape [a1], lined cream silk.
Hat: a black cloth square cap.

BACHELORS
Gown: a black gown of Oxford BA pattern [b8], without the tapes at the wrist.
Hood: a black silk hood of full shape [f1], partly lined dark blue, the cowl bound ½″ in cream. The top of the neckband is also in cream.
Hat: a black cloth square cap.

POSTGRADUATE CERTIFICATES AND DIPLOMAS
Gown: a black gown of Oxford BA pattern [b8], without the tapes at the wrist.
Hood: a black silk hood of full shape [f1], fully lined dark blue, the outside of the cowl bound ¾″ in cream. The top and bottom of the neckband is also in cream.
Hat: a black cloth square cap.

FIRST-DEGREE MASTERS
not awarded

MASTERS

Gown: a black gown of the standard pattern [m10], straight cut at the bottom of the sleeves, with facings of blue silk.

Hood: a black silk hood of full shape [f1], fully lined dark blue, edged ¾″ in cream. The neckband is black lined blue and edged ⅜″ top and bottom in cream.

Hat: a black cloth square cap.

MASTERS OF PHILOSOPHY

Gown: a black gown of the standard pattern [m10], straight cut at the bottom of the sleeves, with facings of blue silk.

Hood: a black silk hood of full shape [f1], fully lined dark blue, edged ¾″ in cream. The neckband is black lined with blue and edged ⅜″ top and bottom in cream.

Hat: a black cloth square cap.

DOCTORS OF PHILOSOPHY and TAUGHT AND PROFESSIONAL DOCTORS

Undress gown: as for masters.

Dress robe: a maroon cloth robe of Oxford doctors' pattern [d2], with blue silk facings and sleeves, embossed with the University's oak-leaf design. The facings have 1″ cream silk on the outer edge.

Hood: a maroon cloth hood of full shape [f1], fully-lined blue silk embossed with the University's oak-leaf design and bound with 1″ cream silk.

Hat: in undress, a black cloth square cap; in full dress, a black velvet bonnet with blue cord and tassels.

Professors of the University may also wear these robes.

HIGHER DOCTORS

Undress gown: *none specified*

Dress robe: a maroon cloth gown of Cambridge doctors' pattern [d1], with blue silk facings and sleeves, embossed with the University's oak-leaf design. The facings have 1¼″ cream silk on the outer edge. The cord and button on each sleeve is cream.

Hood: a maroon cloth hood of full shape [f1], fully-lined blue silk embossed with the University's oak-leaf design, and edged with 1½″ cream silk.

Hat: in full dress, a black velvet bonnet with maroon cord and tassels.

UNIVERSITY OF PAISLEY

See **University of the West of Scotland.**

PENINSULA COLLEGE OF MEDICINE AND DENTISTRY
(joint degrees of Exeter and Plymouth)
2000

The College is one of a number new medical schools established to cope with expanding numbers of medical and dental students. It consists of a Medical School, a Dental School (opened in 2006, the first for over thirty years) and a Postgraduate Health Institute.

The academic dress incorporates the grey and blue of Exeter, and the terra-cotta of Plymouth.

UNDERGRADUATES
none specified

UNDERGRADUATE CERTIFICATES AND DIPLOMAS
Gown: a black stuff gown of Cambridge BA pattern [b2].

Hood: a black hood of CNAA shape [a1], lined dove grey, tipped spectrum blue, and bordered inside the cowl edge for 1″ terra-cotta.

BACHELORS
Gown: a black stuff gown of the following pattern:

BSc: Cambridge BA pattern [b2].

BM,BS and BDS: Cambridge MA pattern [m2].

Hood: a black hood of Cambridge shape [f1], lined dove grey, and bordered inside the cowl 1″ spectrum blue and 1″ terra-cotta.

Hat: a black cloth square cap.

POSTGRADUATE CERTIFICATES AND DIPLOMAS
Gown: a black stuff gown of Cambridge MA pattern [m2].

Hood: a black hood of Cambridge shape [f1], lined spectrum blue, and bordered inside the cowl 1″ dove grey and 1″ terra-cotta.

Hat: a black cloth square cap.

MASTERS including MASTERS OF PHILOSOPHY
Gown: a black stuff gown of Cambridge MA pattern [m2].

Hood: a black hood of Cambridge shape [f1], lined terra-cotta, and bordered inside the cowl 1″ spectrum blue and 1″ dove grey.

Hat: a black cloth square cap.

ALL DOCTORS

Undress gown: as for masters.

Dress robe: a violet purple robe of Oxford pattern [d2], the facings and sleeves covered dove grey silk.

Hood: a violet purple hood of Cambridge shape [f1], lined dove grey, and bordered inside the cowl 1″ spectrum blue and 1″ terra-cotta.

Hat: in undress, a black cloth square cap; in full dress, a purple velvet bonnet with grey cords and tassels.

UNIVERSITY OF PLYMOUTH
1992

The university was originally a Polytechnic College, with its constituent bodies being Plymouth Polytechnic, Rolle College, and Seale-Hayne College. It was renamed Polytechnic South West in 1989; it remained as this until gaining university status in 1992. The new university absorbed the Plymouth School of Maritime Studies.

The robes are based round the university colours of blue and terra-cotta. The blue used is dark, and the terra-cotta is a deep orange.

UNDERGRADUATES
none specified

UNDERGRADUATE CERTIFICATES AND DIPLOMAS
Gown: as for bachelors.
Hood: a blue hood of CNAA shape [a1], lined black, tipped terra-cotta.
Hat: a black cloth square cap.

FOUNDATION DEGREES
Gown: as for bachelors.
Hood: a dark blue hood of Cambridge shape [f1], lined dark blue, the cowl bordered with a twisted cord of terra-cotta and blue.
Hat: a black cloth square cap.

BACHELORS
Gown: a black stuff gown of Oxford BA pattern [b8], but the sleeve points reach the hem of the gown.
Hood: a dark blue hood of Cambridge shape [f1], the cowl bordered inside 4″ terra-cotta.
Hat: a black cloth square cap.

POSTGRADUATE CERTIFICATES AND DIPLOMAS
Gown: as for bachelors.
Hood: a dark blue hood of Cambridge shape [f1], the cowl bordered inside 4″ terra-cotta, 1″ silver on the edge.
Hat: a black cloth square cap.

FIRST-DEGREE MASTERS
Gown: as for bachelors.
Hood: a dark blue hood of Cambridge shape [f1], the cowl bordered inside 4″ terra-cotta, ½″ black on the edge.
Hat: a black cloth square cap.

MASTERS including MASTERS OF PHILOSOPHY

Gown: a black stuff gown of Cambridge MA pattern [f2]. For MPhil, it has 3″ terra-cotta facings.

Hood: a dark blue hood of Cambridge shape [f1], lined and bound ¼″ terra-cotta.

Hat: a black cloth square cap.

DOCTORS OF PHILOSOPHY and PROFESSIONAL DOCTORS (MD, DClinPsy)

Undress gown: *none specified*

Dress robe: a terra-cotta panama robe of Cambridge pattern [d1], with 5″ facings and sleeve linings of dark blue.

Hood: a terra-cotta panama hood of Cambridge shape [f1], lined and bound 1″ dark blue.

Hat: in full dress, a black cloth bonnet with terra-cotta cords and tassels.

HIGHER DOCTORS

Undress gown: *none specified*

Dress robe: a terra-cotta panama robe of Cambridge pattern [d1], with 5″ facings and sleeve linings of dark blue, and ½″ silver oak-leaf lace along the outer edge of the facings.

Hood: a terra-cotta panama hood of Cambridge shape [f1], lined and bound 1″ dark blue, the cowl bordered ½″ silver oak-leaf lace inside.

Hat: a black velvet bonnet with terra-cotta and silver mixed cords and tassels.

UNIVERSITY COLLEGE, PLYMOUTH
(College of St Mark and St John; 'Marjon'). 1840/2007

'Marjon' has roots going back to the foundation by the National Society of the constituent colleges of St John's College, Battersea, in 1840, and St Mark's College, Chelsea, in 1841. The two colleges combined on the Chelsea site in 1923, and the College of St Mark and St John moved from London to Plymouth in 1973. It has prepared its students for degrees since 1862: from 1973 until 2007, when it gained University College status, it awarded degrees of the University of Exeter. With the new status it changed its name to 'University College Plymouth St Mark and St John', or UCP Marjon.

Until 2010, the College still awarded Exeter degrees, and the scheme below was first used in 2010.

UNDERGRADUATES
none specified

UNDERGRADUATE CERTIFICATES AND DIPLOMAS
none specified

FOUNDATION DEGREES
Gown: a black stuff gown of the basic bachelor's pattern [b1].
Hood: a black hood of CNAA shape [a1], lined black, the cowl bordered inside 2″ maroon.
Hat: a black cloth square cap.

BACHELORS and PROFESSIONAL GRADUATE CERTIFICATE IN EDUCATION
Gown: a black stuff gown of the basic bachelor's pattern [b1].
Hood: a black hood of CNAA shape [a1], lined and the cape bound 1″ maroon.
Hat: a black cloth square cap.

POSTGRADUATE CERTIFICATE IN EDUCATION
Gown: as for masters.
Hood: a black hood of London shape [f3], lined black, the cowl bordered inside 2″ maroon.
Hat: a black cloth square cap.

MASTERS
Gown: a black stuff gown of the basic masters' pattern [m10].
Hood: a black hood of London shape [f3], lined and the cape bound 1″ maroon.
Hat: a black cloth square cap.

UNIVERSITY OF PORTSMOUTH
1992

The University was founded as the Portsmouth and Gosport School of Science and the Arts in 1869. In the 1960s, following a government-sponsored expansion in Higher Education, the college was renamed Portsmouth Polytechnic. It gained university status in 1992.

The University uses a distinctive colour it calls 'blue-purple'. It is in fact a dull violet colour, and is described as such below. 'St Benet' braid is used to trim some robes. This is illustrated on page 42.

Faculty colours

Arts and Letters: white.
Architecture: lilac.
Business Administration: old gold.
Economic Sciences: old gold.
Education: hot pink.
Engineering, Technology: maroon.
Laws: light cherry.
Medicine and Surgery: deep red.
Music: cream.
Nursing: mid-blue.
Science: scarlet.

UNDERGRADUATES

none specified

UNDERGRADUATE CERTIFICATES AND DIPLOMAS

Gown: as for bachelors.

Hood:

CertHE and CertEd: no hood.

DipHE: a black hood of Burgon shape [s2], lined and bound ⅜″ violet.

University Diplomas: a black hood of Burgon shape [s2], lined and bound ⅜″ white.

Hat: black cloth square cap with a violet tassel.

FOUNDATION DEGREES

Gown: as for bachelors.

Hood: a black hood of CNAA shape [a1], lined violet.

Hat: a black cloth square cap with a violet tassel.

BACHELORS

Gown:

BArch: as masters.

All others: a black stuff gown of Oxford BA pattern [b8], with the sleeve points reaching the hem.

Hood:

BArch: a black silk hood of Cambridge shape [f1], lined and bound 1″ lilac, with 1″ silver Benet braid on the outside of the cape next to the lilac.

All others: a black silk hood of Cambridge shape [f1], lined and bound 1″ violet, with 1″ of the faculty colour on the outside of the cape next to the violet.

Hat: a black cloth square cap with a violet tassel.

POSTGRADUATE CERTIFICATES AND DIPLOMAS

Gown: as for bachelors.

Hood:

PGCE: a black silk hood of Cambridge shape [f1], lined and bound 1″ violet, with 1″ mid cherry on the outside of the cape next to the violet.

PGCert: as PGCE, but the cape is bordered outside 1″ grey.

PGDip: as PGCE, but the cape is bordered outside 1″ silver Benet braid.

Hat: a black cloth square cap with a violet tassel.

FIRST-DEGREE MASTERS (MChiro, MEng, MMath, MPharm, MPhys)

Gown: as for masters.

Hood: a violet silk hood of Cambridge shape [f1], lined and bound as follows:

MEng: lined and bound 1″ on all edges maroon.

All others: the cowl bordered inside 2″, and the cape bound 1″ scarlet.

Hat: a black cloth square cap with a violet tassel.

MASTERS

Gown: a black stuff gown of the basic master's pattern [m10].

MArch: there is ½″ silver Benet braid along the outer edge of the facings.

Hood: a violet silk hood of Cambridge shape [f1], lined and bound 1″ on all edges with the faculty colour.

MMus: lined and bound cream damask.

Hat: a black cloth square cap with a violet tassel.

MASTERS OF PHILOSOPHY and of SURGERY

Gown: a black stuff gown of the basic master's pattern [m10], with ½″ silver Benet braid along both edges of the facings, and round the armholes.

Hood: a violet silk hood of Cambridge shape [f1], lined and bound as follows:

MPhil: lined and bound grey.

ChM: lined and bound deep red.

Hat: a black cloth square cap with a violet tassel.

DOCTORS OF PHILOSOPHY, of MEDICINE, and PROFESSIONAL DOCTORS

Undress gown: *none specified*

Dress robe: a scarlet cloth robe of Cambridge MA pattern [m2]. The facings and the sleeves below the armhole are covered with violet silk, with ½″ silver Benet braid along both edges of the facings, and round the armholes.

Hood: a scarlet cloth hood of Cambridge shape [f1], lined and bound as follows:

PhD and Professional Doctors: lined and bound violet, with 1″ silver Benet braid on the outside of the cape next to the violet.

MD: as PhD, but lined deep red.

Hat: in full dress, a black cloth bonnet with violet cords and tassels.

HIGHER DOCTORS

Undress gown: *none specified*

Dress robe: a violet cloth robe of Cambridge pattern [d1], with facings and sleeve-linings of the faculty colour, and ½″ silver Benet braid along both edges of the facings. The sleeves are held by a button and cord of faculty colour.

DD: facings and sleeve linings of red-purple brocade, with purple and gold Benet braid.

DMus: the robe is of cream brocade, with violet facings and sleeve linings, and purple and gold Benet braid. The sleeves are held by a violet button and cord.

Hood: a violet silk hood of Cambridge shape [f1], lined and bound 1″ faculty colour, with 1″ silver Benet braid on the outside of the cape next to the violet.

DD: lined red-purple brocade, with purple and gold Benet braid.

DMus: the hood is of cream brocade, lined violet, with purple and gold Benet braid.

Hat: in full dress, a black velvet bonnet with violet cords and tassels.

DOCTORS OF THE UNIVERSITY

Undress gown: *none specified*

Dress robe: a violet cloth robe of Cambridge pattern [d1], with grey shot silk facings and sleeve-linings, and ½″ silver Benet braid along both edges of the facings. The sleeves are held by a silver cord and button.

Hood: a violet cloth hood of Cambridge shape [f1], lined and bound 1″ shot grey silk, and with 1″ silver Benet braid on the outside of the cape next to the violet.

Hat: in full dress, a black velvet bonnet with violet cords and tassels.

QUEEN MARGARET UNIVERSITY, EDINBURGH
2007

Queen Margaret University traces its origins to 1875, when the Edinburgh School of Cookery was established. In the 1970s, the School became a higher education institution, widening its range of degree programmes, known as Queen Margaret College. Other institutions joined and a range of degrees were developed, notably in paramedical fields such as Nursing, Physiotherapy, and Occupational Therapy. Queen Margaret was awarded University status in January 2007.

This is a good example of a 'restricted-colour' scheme, based on green, blue, and white.

UNDERGRADUATES
none specified

UNDERGRADUATE CERTIFICATES AND DIPLOMAS
Gown: as for bachelors.
Hood:
CertHE: none.
DipHE: a green hood of CNAA shape [a1], lined blue.
Hat: a black cloth square cap.

BACHELORS
Gown: a black stuff gown of Scottish bachelors' pattern [b?].
Hood: a dark blue hood of Edinburgh shape[s4], lined green, the cowl bordered inside 3½″ white.
Hat: a black cloth square cap.

POSTGRADUATE CERTIFICATES AND DIPLOMAS
Gown: a black stuff gown of Scottish bachelors' pattern [b1] with a black cord and button on the yoke.
Hood: a green hood of Edinburgh shape [s4], lined blue, the cowl bordered inside 3½″ white.
Hat: a black cloth square cap.

MASTERS including MASTERS OF PHILOSOPHY
Gown: a black stuff gown of Scottish masters' pattern. [m12]
Hood: a green hood of Edinburgh shape [s4], lined white, the cowl bordered inside 3½″ blue.
Hat: a black cloth square cap.

DOCTORS OF PHILOSOPHY
Undress gown: *none specified*

Dress robe: a dark blue robe of Scottish masters' pattern [m12], with 1″ silver on the outer edge of the facings.

Hood: a green hood of Edinburgh shape [s4], lined white, the cowl bordered 3½″ dark blue, with 1″ silver on the edge.

Hat: in full dress, a black cloth bonnet with cords and tassels.

HIGHER DOCTORS

The colour of the robe and hood is determined not by the title of the degree (DLitt or DSc), but by the field in which it is awarded.

Undress gown: *none specified*

Dress robe: a robe of Cambridge pattern [d1], with white facings and sleeve linings, the robe coloured as follows:
Arts and Business: blue.
Science: green.

Hood: a hood of Edinburgh shape [s4], lined white, bordered 1″ green set 1″ in, the hood coloured as follows:
Arts and Business: blue.
Science: green.

Hat: velvet bonnet with white cords and tassels, dark green for science, and blue for arts and business.

UNIVERSITY OF READING
1926

The University owes its origins to the Schools of Art and Science established in Reading in 1860 and 1870; these became part of an extension college of Christ Church of the University of Oxford in 1892, which was eventually renamed University College, Reading. The college first applied for a Royal Charter in 1920 but was unsuccessful. However a second petition, in 1925, was successful, and the charter was officially granted in 1926, the college thus becoming the University of Reading, the only full university to be created in England between the two world wars. In 1947 the University purchased Whiteknights Park, which has become its principal campus. In January 2008, the University announced its merger with the Henley Management College to create the university's new Henley Business School.

The robes all feature the University's colour, cream, and the system is very simple. There have been no additions to the scheme to accommodate new levels of qualification, beyond the foundation degree hood, but the original system has been adapted to do this. However, the Henley Business School has its own robes for some degrees, even though they are Reading degrees.

UNDERGRADUATES
Gown: a black stuff gown of Oxford scholars' pattern [u2], with blue facings.
Hat: a black cloth square cap.

UNDERGRADUATE CERTIFICATES AND DIPLOMAS
Gown: as for bachelors.
Hood: none.
Hat: a black cloth square cap.

FOUNDATION DEGREES
Gown: as for bachelors.
Hood: as for bachelors, but with a 2″ wide cream border.
Hat: a black cloth square cap.

BACHELORS
Gown: a black stuff gown of Cambridge BA pattern [b2], with the points of the sleeves rounded off.
Hood: a dark blue silk hood of Oxford simple shape [s1], bordered 4″ cream silk inside the cowl.
Hat: a black cloth square cap.

POSTGRADUATE CERTIFICATES AND DIPLOMAS
Gown: as for bachelors.

Hood: as for masters.
Hat: a black cloth square cap.

FIRST-DEGREE MASTERS

Gown: as for masters.
Hood: as for bachelors.
Hat: a black cloth square cap.

MASTERS including MASTERS OF PHILOSOPHY

Gown: a black stuff gown of Cambridge MA pattern [m2].
Hood: a dark blue silk hood of Cambridge full shape [f1], fully lined cream silk.
Hat: a black cloth square cap.

DOCTORS OF PHILOSOPHY and TAUGHT AND PROFESSIONAL DOCTORS

Undress gown: as for masters, but with a horizontal strip of doctors' lace along the upper edge of the arm slit.
Dress robe: a crimson cloth robe of Cambridge pattern [d2], with cream silk facings and sleeve linings.
Hood: a crimson cloth hood of Cambridge shape [f1], fully lined cream silk.
Hat: in undress, a black cloth square cap; in full dress, a black cloth bonnet without any cords and tassels.

HIGHER DOCTORS

Undress gown: as PhD.
Dress robe: a scarlet cloth robe of Cambridge pattern [d2], with cream silk facings and sleeve linings.
Hood: a scarlet cloth hood of Cambridge shape [f1], fully lined cream silk.
Hat: a black velvet bonnet with gold cords and tassels.

MPhil in Plant Breeding and Crop Improvement −Joint degree with the University of Birmingham.

Gown: a black stuff gown of Cambridge MA pattern [m2].
Hood: a dark blue silk hood of the Cambridge full shape [f1], lined and bound silver-grey watered silk.
Hat: a black cloth square cap.

HENLEY BUSINESS SCHOOL (HENLEY MANAGEMENT COLLEGE)

MASTERS OF SCIENCE

Same robes as MSc(Reading).

MASTERS OF BUSINESS ADMINISTRATION

Gown: a green gown of the basic masters' pattern [m10], the facings piped old gold on the outer edges.

Hood: a mid-dark green hood of Edinburgh shape [s4], lined mid-dark green silk brocaded with old gold oak leaves in a trefoil pattern, the cowl piped gold.

Hat: a green square cap.

DOCTORS OF BUSINESS ADMINISTRATION and of PHILOSOPHY

Same robes as PhD (Reading).

MASTERS *honoris causa*

Gown: a green gown of the basic masters' pattern [m10], with 7″ gold silk facings.

Hood: a green hood of Cambridge shape [f1], lined and bound ½″ old gold.

Hat: a green square cap.

ROBERT GORDON UNIVERSITY, ABERDEEN
1993

Robert Gordon University owes its foundation to the philanthropy of Robert Gordon, born 1668 in Aberdeen. On his death in 1731 he bequeathed his entire estate to build a residential school for educating young boys, which was to become the Robert Gordon's Hospital, later to be known as Robert Gordon's College. In 1884 the College assumed responsibility for the educational work of the Aberdeen Mechanics' Institute. In 1903 the College joined with Gray's School of Science (which had been established in the 1880s and provided training for apprentice apothecaries, chemists and druggists) and was recognised as a Central Institution in 1903. In 1965, the College assumed the name Robert Gordon's Institute of Technology. It was awarded University status in 1992.

All hoods and the doctors' robes, are lined with the University silk, which is white, with various devices embossed in it, set about two inches apart.

UNDERGRADUATES
none specified

UNDERGRADUATE CERTIFICATES AND DIPLOMAS (CertHE, DipHE)
Gown: a black gown of the basic bachelors' pattern [b1].
Hood: a black hood of simple shape [s1], bordered inside University white silk.
Hat: a black cloth square cap.

BACHELORS
Gown: a black stuff gown of the basic bachelors' pattern, [b1].
Hood: a black hood of Cambridge shape [f1], bordered inside the cowl University white silk.
Hat: a black cloth square cap.

POSTGRADUATE CERTIFICATES AND DIPLOMAS
Gown: as for masters.
Hood: a black hood of Cambridge shape [f1], lined edge-to-edge University white silk.
Hat: a black cloth square cap.

FIRST-DEGREE MASTERS (MPharm, MEng) and GRADUATE CERTIFICATE IN MANAGEMENT STUDIES
As for bachelors.

MASTERS
Gown: a black stuff gown of the basic pattern [m10].
Hood: a black hood of Cambridge shape [f1], lined and the cape bound ½″ University white silk.

Hat: a black cloth square cap.

MASTERS OF PHILOSOPHY

Gown: a black stuff gown of the basic pattern [m10], with 2½″ facings of University white silk.

Hood: a black hood of Cambridge shape [f1], lined and the cape bound ½″ University white silk.

Hat: a black cloth square cap.

DOCTORS OF PHILOSOPHY and TAUGHT AND PROFESSIONAL DOCTORS

Undress gown: *none specified*

Dress robe: a black robe of, Cambridge pattern [d1], with facings and sleeve-linings of University white silk.

Hood: a black hood of Cambridge shape [f1], lined and bound on all edges 1″ University white silk.

Hat: in full dress, a black cloth bonnet with white cords and tassels.

HIGHER DOCTORS

Undress gown: *none specified*

Dress robe: a scarlet robe of the basic masters' pattern [m10], with an inverted-T armhole, the facings covered University white silk.

Hood: a scarlet hood of Cambridge shape [f1], lined and bound on all edges 2″ University white silk.

Hat: in full dress, a black cloth bonnet with gold cords and tassels.

NOTES

1. Awards made by the Scottish Qualifications Authority (SQA) wear the SQA robes.

ROEHAMPTON UNIVERSITY
2004

In 1975, four denominational teacher-training colleges, Whitelands (1841, Anglican), Southlands (1872, Methodist), Digby Stuart (1850, Roman Catholic), and Froebel (1892), formed the Roehampton Institute of Higher Education. This awarded degrees of the University of London until 1985, then of Surrey. In 2000, it changed its name to the University of Surrey, Roehampton, with Surrey thus becoming a federal university, with two campuses – at Guildford and at Roehampton. In 2004, it became an independent university. The four colleges still operate as separate bodies within the University.

All hoods have a split lining of red and royal blue. It is divided vertically when worn, blue on the wearer's left side, and red on the right.

UNDERGRADUATES
none specified

UNDERGRADUATE CERTIFICATES AND DIPLOMAS
none specified

FOUNDATION DEGREES
Gown: as for bachelors.

Hood: a black hood of Burgon shape [s2], lined black, and the cowl bordered with a twisted cord of red, yellow, and blue.

Hat: a black cloth square cap.

BACHELORS
Gown: a black stuff gown of the basic pattern [b1].

Hood: a black hood of Cambridge shape [f1], lined red and blue, the cowl bordered inside 1″ yellow. The neckband is plain black.

Hat: a black cloth square cap.

POSTGRADUATE CERTIFICATES AND DIPLOMAS
none specified

FIRST-DEGREE MASTERS
not awarded

MASTERS including MASTERS OF PHILOSOPHY
Gown: a black stuff gown of the basic pattern [m10]. For MPhil, it has 3″ blue facings , with 1″ yellow on the outer edge.

Hood: a black hood of Cambridge shape [f1], lined red and blue, bound on all edges inside and out 2″ yellow. The neckband is bound yellow.

Hat: a black cloth square cap.

DOCTORS OF PHILOSOPHY and TAUGHT AND PROFESSIONAL DOCTORS

Undress gown: *none specified*

Dress robe: a maroon panama robe of Cambridge pattern [d1], with royal blue facings and sleeve linings. There is 1″ yellow on the outer edge of the facings, and the sleeves are held with a yellow cord and button.

Hood: a maroon panama hood of Cambridge shape [f1], lined red and blue, bound on all edges inside and out 2″ yellow. The neckband is bound yellow.

Hat: in full dress, a black velvet bonnet with red cords and tassels.

HIGHER DOCTORS

Undress gown: *none specified*

Dress robe: a scarlet panama hood of Cambridge pattern [d1], with royal blue facings and sleeve linings . There is 1″ yellow on the outer edge of the facings, and the sleeves are held with a yellow cord and button.

Hood: a scarlet panama hood of Cambridge shape [f1], lined red and blue, bound on all edges inside and out 2″ yellow. The neckband is bound yellow.

Hat: in full dress, a black velvet bonnet with gold cords and tassels.

ROYAL AGRICULTURAL COLLEGE, CIRENCESTER
1845

This was the first agricultural college to be founded in the English-speaking world, and was granted a Royal Charter in 1845. It formed the model for many other such institutions world-wide, both colleges and university departments of agriculture. It started teaching for degrees in 1911, which until 1945 were awarded by Bristol; in 1984 it offered a BSc in Rural Land Management awarded by Reading. It gained the right to award its own taught degrees in 1995.

All the hoods of the College feature its special damask. This is maroon, with the College's wheatsheaf emblem embroidered in gold. The sheaves are about 1″ long, and are very closely spaced.

UNDERGRADUATES
none specified

UNDERGRADUATE CERTIFICATES AND DIPLOMAS
Gown: black stuff, basic pattern [b1].

Hood:

Certificates: none.

Diploma: a black silk hood of Oxford simple shape [s1], bordered inside 3″ maroon College damask.

Higher Diploma: a black silk hood of Cambridge full shape, bordered inside 5″ maroon College damask.

BACHELORS
Gown: a black stuff gown of the basic pattern,[b1].

Hood: a black silk hood of CNAA shape [a1], lined as follows:

Pass degree: fully lined champagne gold, and tipped maroon College damask.

Honours degree: fully lined maroon College damask, and tipped champagne gold.

Hat: black cloth square cap.

MASTERS
Gown: a black stuff gown of the basic pattern [m10].

Hood: a black silk hood of Cambridge full shape [f1], fully lined maroon College damask, bordered on the cape edge 1″ champagne gold.

Hat: a black cloth square cap.

MASTERS of PHILOSOPHY and DOCTORS of PHILOSOPHY
These degrees are currently awarded by the University of Coventry, and wear the relevant robes of that university.

ROYAL COLLEGE OF ART
1837/1967

The RCA is the world's only wholly postgraduate art and design institution, offering the degrees of MA, MPhil, and PhD. The College is housed in a number of buildings in South Kensington and Battersea. The college was founded in 1837, and was then known as the Government School of Design. It became the National Art Training School in 1853, and in 1896 received the name The Royal College of Art. After 130 years in operation, the RCA was granted a Royal Charter in 1967, which gave it the status of an independent university with the power to grant its own degrees.

Its academic dress is noted for being the first modern scheme to break the long-standing convention that fur is the mark of a bachelor's degree

MASTERS, including MASTERS OF PHILOSOPHY

Gown: a black stuff gown of Cambridge BA shape [b2].
Hood: a hood of Oxford simple shape [s1] coloured and lined as follows::
MA: white silk, lined crimson brocade, the cowl edge bound fur.
[MDes: white silk, lined gold brocade, the cowl edge bound fur.]
MPhil: black lined purple.
Hat: black cloth square cap.

DOCTORS OF PHILOSOPHY

Undress gown: as for masters.
Dress robe: a black robe of Oxford shape [d2], the facings covered with purple silk.
Hood: a purple silk hood of Oxford simple shape [s1], lined orange silk.
Hat: in undress, a black cloth square cap; in full dress, a black cloth bonnet with gold cords and tassels.

HIGHER DOCTORS (DrRCA)

Undress gown: as PhD.
Dress robe: a vermilion cloth robe of Oxford shape [d2], the sleeves and facings covered ruby silk.
Hood: a vermilion silk hood of Oxford simple shape [s1], lined ruby velvet, the cowl edge bound fur.
Hat: in undress, a black cloth square cap; in full dress, a black cloth bonnet with gold cords and tassels.

NOTES

1. The original masters' gown was a black stuff gown of Cambridge MB pattern [b3], but with the sleeve points rounded off. The sleeve is edged with black twisted cord. Although this gown is still prescribed, the Cambridge BA gown has been used for several years.

2. The former diploma of Associate (ARCA) used the gown as specified for masters, and a hood of white silk, lined crimson brocade; the former diploma of Designer (DesRCA) used the same gown, and a hood of white silk, lined gold brocade.

ROYAL COLLEGE OF MUSIC
1883

The RCM was founded in 1883, in succession to the National Training School for Music (1873). Its Royal Charter gave it the right to award the three degrees of BMus, MMus, and DMus, although this right was unexercised until 1933, when it awarded a DMus *honoris causa* to Queen Mary. The MMus has been available by examination since 1951, initially as an external award. The College's BMus replaced the London BMus in 1995. Since 2000, the DMus has been available by examination. Before that, it was only awarded *honoris causa.*

UNDERGRADUATES
none specified

UNDERGRADUATE DIPLOMAS
Gown: a black stuff gown of the basic pattern bachelors' pattern [b1].
Hood: a royal blue hood of Oxford simple shape [s1], lined as follows:
Associates (ARCM): the cowl edge bordered inside 3″ old gold.
DipRCM: lined old gold, the cowl edge bordered inside 1″ white.
Hat: black cloth square cap.

BACHELORS of MUSIC
Gown: a black stuff gown of the basic pattern [b1]. In full dress, holders may wear this gown made in royal blue silk.
Hood: a royal blue silk hood of Durham BSc shape [f7], bound on all edges 1″ fur, with a 1″ band of old gold laid next to the fur.
Hat: a black cloth square cap.

POSTGRADUATE DIPLOMA (PGDipRCM)
Gown: a black stuff gown of the basic bachelors' pattern [b1].
Hood: a royal blue hood of Oxford simple shape [s1], bound on all edges 2″ old gold.
Hat: a black cloth square cap.

MASTERS of MUSIC
Gown: a black stuff gown of Cambridge MA pattern [m2].
Hood:
since 2000: a cream brocade hood of Burgon shape [s2], lined and bound old gold.
before 2000: a black silk hood of Cambridge full shape [f1], lined royal blue, and bound 1″ old gold on all edges.
Hat: black cloth square cap.

DOCTORS OF MUSIC
Undress gown: *none specified*

Dress robe:

until 2000: a royal blue brocade robe of the Oxford pattern [d2], the facings and sleeves covered old gold silk.

since 2000: a cream brocade robe of Cambridge pattern [d1], the sleeves lined and the facings covered royal blue silk.

Hood: a hood of the Cambridge full shape [f1], coloured and lined as follows:

before 2000: royal blue brocade, lined gold silk.

since 2000: cream brocade, lined, and the neckband bound, royal blue silk. (If awarded *honoris causa*, the neckband is bound gold silk.)

Hat: in full dress, a black velvet bonnet with gold cords and tassels.

ROYAL CONSERVATOIRE OF SCOTLAND, GLASGOW
(Royal Scottish Academy of Music and Dramatic Art)
1890

The Glasgow Athenæum School of Music was founded in 1890. It was re-named the Scottish National Academy of Music in 1930, when its Principalship was combined with the Chair of Music at Glasgow University. It was granted the prefix 'Royal' in 1944. The College of Dramatic Arts was formed in 1950, as part of the Academy, at which point the posts of Principal and Professor were separated. A re-organization in 1968 created the School of Music and the School of Drama, and the name was again changed to reflect this. It was granted degree-awarding powers in 1993, and the diploma courses were gradually upgraded to degree-level. The name was changed to the Royal Conservatoire of Scotland in September 2011 to reflect its widening curriculum.

UNDERGRADUATES
none specified

[UNDERGRADUATE CERTIFICATES AND DIPLOMAS]
Now obsolete.

Gown: a purple stuff gown of the basic pattern [b1].

Hood: a dark red hood of Edinburgh shape [s4], lined as follows:

DipDramArt: fully lined white silk.

DipStageMgt: part-lined white silk.

DipRSAMD: part-lined rose-pink silk.

Hat: a black cloth square cap.

BACHELORS
Gown: a purple stuff gown of the basic pattern [b1].

Hood: a purple hood of full shape [f1], lined as follows:

BA in Acting; Digital Film and TV; Technical and Production Arts; Contemporary Performance Practice; Modern Ballet; Music Theatre: green brocade.

BA in Scottish Music: red brocade.

BA in Performing Arts; Music Performance: ivory brocade.

BA in Music Education: red brocade, the cowl bordered inside ½″ ivory brocade.

BEd: red brocade, the cowl bordered inside ½″ ivory brocade.

BMus: ivory brocade.

Hat: a black cloth square cap.

POSTGRADUATE CERTIFICATES AND DIPLOMAS
Gown: as masters.

Hood: a purple hood of Edinburgh shape [s4], lined as follows:

Drama: lined green brocade.

Music: lined red brocade.
Hat: black cloth square cap.

MASTERS

Gown: a purple stuff gown of Scottish MA pattern [m12].
Hood: a hood of full shape [f1], coloured and lined as follows:
MA (all fields): purple lined green brocade
MDrama: green brocade lined purple silk.
MMus: red brocade lined purple silk.
MOpera: red brocade lined purple silk.
Hat: black cloth square cap.

MASTERS and DOCTORS OF PHILOSOPHY

These degrees are currently awarded by the University of St Andrews.

DOCTORS

Undress gown: *none specified*
Dress robe: a purple robe of the basic bachelors' pattern [b1], the facings and sleeves to match the hood lining.
Hood: a purple silk hood of full shape [f1], lined and bound 1″ as follows:
DDramArt: green brocade.
DMus: red brocade.
Hat: in full dress, a black cloth bonnet with cords and tassels.

NOTES

1. Until 1993, when it gained degree-awarding powers, the Academy awarded the diplomas of FRSAMD, DipMusEdRSAM, and DipRSAM. These all used the same robes: a black BA-style gown, and a maroon hood of Edinburgh simple shape [s4], part-lined 2″ caroline rose silk.

ROYAL HORTICULTURAL SOCIETY
1804

The Society was founded in 1804, and was granted a Royal Charter in 1861. This Society has the right to award one degree, the Master of Horticulture, which was instituted in 1983, replacing the former National Diploma in Horticulture (NDH). It is of 'degree equivalence', which, despite its title, implies first-degree level.

The Society also awards the RHS General (now RHS Certificate, instituted 1893), RHS Advanced Certificate, and RHS Diploma.

CERTIFICATES AND DIPLOMAS
no robes specified.

MASTERS of HORTICULTURE – MHort(RHS)
Gown: a black stuff gown of the basic masters' pattern [m10].
Hood: a black silk hood of CNAA shape [a1], lined dark green silk embossed with the RHS tree logo in black, very closely spaced.
Hat: a black cloth square cap.

ROYAL NORTHERN COLLEGE OF MUSIC
1972

The Royal Northern College of Music (RNCM) was formed in 1972 by a merger of the Royal Manchester College of Music (RMCM, founded 1893) and the Northern School of Music (NSM, founded 1920), which was also in Manchester. Students at both colleges, and after 1972 the RNCM, either sat for one of the college diplomas, or by a joint course, whereby they were awarded the Graduate Diploma and also the MusB of the University of Manchester, and this has been the norm in recent years. In 2008, the RNCM gained its own degree awarding powers.

UNDERGRADUATES
none specified

DIPLOMA of HIGHER EDUCATION (DipHE)
Gown: a black stuff gown of the basic pattern [b1].
Hood: none.
Hat: none.

GRADUATE DIPLOMAS (GRNCM; GMusRNCM)
Gown: a black stuff gown of the basic pattern [b1].
Hood: a purple hood of Manchester simple shape [s9], lined and bound as follows:
GRNCM: lined and bound gold.
GMusRNCM: lined and bound gold, piped white on all edges.
Hat: black cloth square cap.

FOUNDATION DEGREES
Gown: a black stuff gown of London BA pattern [b4], with blue and gold cords and a blue button on the sleeves and yoke.
Hood: a mid-blue hood of CNAA shape [a1], lined mid-blue, tipped champagne gold, the cape bound wine-colour.
Hat: a black cloth square cap.

BACHELORS of MUSIC
Gown: a black stuff gown of London BA pattern [b4], with blue and gold cords and a blue button on the sleeves and yoke.
Hood: a mid-blue hood of CNAA pattern [a1], lined champagne gold, the cowl and cape bound wine-colour.
Hat: a black cloth square cap.

POSTGRADUATE DIPLOMA (PGRNCM)
Gown:
before 2009: a black gown of the basic bachelors' pattern [b1].

since 2009: a black stuff gown of London BA pattern [b4], with blue and gold cords and a blue button on the sleeves and yoke.

Hood:

before 2009: a purple hood of Cambridge shape [f1], lined blue, the cowl bordered inside 3″ gold.

since 2009: a satinwood hood of CNAA shape [a1], fully lined mid-blue, the cowl and cape bound wine-colour.

Hat: black cloth square cap.

MASTERS of MUSIC

Gown: a black stuff gown of the basic pattern [m10], with a blue and gold cord and blue button on the yoke.

Hood: a satinwood hood of CNAA shape [a1], lined and the cape bound mid-blue, the cowl bordered inside gold.

Hat: a black cloth square cap.

MASTERS of PHILOSOPHY and DOCTORS of PHILOSOPHY

These degrees are currently validated by Manchester Metropolitan University.

THE ROYAL SOCIETY OF CHEMISTRY
1980

The Royal Society of Chemistry today has a global membership of over 46,000, and the longest continuous tradition of any chemical society in the world. It is the successor to four bodies:

The Chemical Society (founded in 1841)
The Society for Analytical Chemistry (founded in 1874)
The Royal Institute of Chemistry (founded in 1877)
The Faraday Society (founded in 1903)

In 1972, these four bodies took the first steps towards merger, and in 1980 they became The Royal Society of Chemistry, with a new Royal Charter and the dual role of learned society and professional body.

The Society awards the Mastership in Chemical Analysis (MChemA) which is the statutory qualification for practice as a Public Analyst and Agriculture Analyst. It also runs an MSc programme in association with the University of Strathclyde, for which Strathclyde robes are worn.

The robes were designed for use by the Royal Institute of Chemistry, and carried across to the Society.

MASTERS OF CHEMICAL ANALYSIS

Gown: a black stuff gown of the basic bachelors' pattern [b1].

Hood: a grey Russell cord hood of Oxford simple shape [s1], the cowl bordered inside 4″ gold watered silk.

Hat: a black cloth square cap.

RESEARCH DIPLOMA

Gown: a black stuff gown of the basic bachelors' pattern [b1].

Hood: a grey Russell cord hood of Oxford simple shape [s1], lined purple silk, the cowl bordered inside 4″ gold watered silk.

NOTES

1. Other qualifications awarded are status awards, dependent on the member's other qualifications and experience. These are: Associate Member (AMRSC); Member (MRSC); and Fellow (FRSC), for which no robes are worn. The former grades of membership, Licentiate and Graduate, did have robes:

   LRSC: a black stuff gown of the basic bachelors' pattern, and a grey Russell cord hood of Oxford simple shape [s1], the cowl bordered inside 4″ purple silk.

   GRSC: a black stuff gown of the basic bachelors' pattern [b1], and a grey Russell cord hood of Oxford simple shape [s1], lined purple silk.

THE ROYAL UNIVERSITY OF IRELAND
1880-1909

also the **Queen's University** (1845-1880)
and the **Catholic University** (1851-1909)

The Queen's Colleges (Ireland) Act 1845 established colleges at Belfast, Cork, and Galway, incorporated as Queen's University, with the intention that they would provide for Roman Catholic demands for university education, since they regarded Trinity College, Dublin, as Anglican, and thus schismatic. In order to appease Protestant demands, the colleges were not permitted to give instruction in theology. However, the new colleges were also seen as schismatic by the RC Church, and its members were not allowed to attend them; as a result the Catholic University of Ireland (see below) was created.

The Queen's University was superseded by a new institution, the Royal University of Ireland in 1880. It was an examining and degree-awarding university based on the model of the University of London; examinations were opened to candidates irrespective of attendance at college lectures. The Queen's University was formally dissolved on 3 February 1882. The Royal University broke with the 'godless' convention by setting examinations for, and awarding degrees to students of, colleges with a religious basis, such as Magee Presbyterian College, and the Catholic University of Ireland, which included St. Patrick's College, Maynooth, and University College, Dublin. Like the Queen's University, the Royal University was entitled to grant any degree, except degrees in Divinity (*i.e.*, BD and DD). The RUI became the first university in Ireland to grant degrees to women; the first such degree was granted on 22 October 1882. On 31 October 1909 the Royal University was dissolved; the National University of Ireland and Queen's University, Belfast, took over its functions under the Irish Universities Act 1908.

The Catholic University of Ireland (*Ollscoil Chaitliceach na hÉireann*) was founded in 1851. It was formally established in 1854 with five faculties: law, letters, medicine, philosophy, and theology. John Henry (later Cardinal) Newman was the Rector. It was neither a recognised university so far as the civil authorities were concerned, nor did it offer degrees. It went into a serious decline following Newman's departure in 1857. The situation changed in 1880 when its students were permitted to sit the examinations for, and receive the degrees of, the RUI. In 1909 it essentially came to an end with the creation of the National University of Ireland, with the Catholic University, now renamed University College Dublin, as a constituent college.

The Catholic University Medical School commenced lectures for medical students in 1855. The recognition of its graduates by chartered institutions ensured its success, unlike the associated Catholic University. This ensured that the medical school became the most successful constituent college of the Catholic University and by 1900 it had become the largest medical school in Ireland. The 1908 reforms reconstituted the Catholic University Medical School as the Faculty of Medicine of University College Dublin.

In the same way that Dublin in 1591 had adopted the common robes used by Oxford and Cambridge (though now all three have followed individual developments), the QUI and the RUI simply adopted those of Dublin, except as noted below. The Catholic University appears to have had no robes of its own.

UNDERGRADUATES

Gown: a black stuff gown, of unknown pattern.
Hat: a black cloth square cap.

BACHELORS

Gown: a black stuff gown of the basic bachelor's pattern [b1].
Hood: a hood of the Dublin full shape [f2], coloured and lined as follows:
BA: black silk, half-lined and bound fur.* (This may have been made in [s3] shape.)
BAO: black silk, lined and bound olive green silk.*
BEng: black silk, lined and bound myrtle green silk.*
LL.B: black silk, lined and bound white silk.*
MB, BCh: black silk, lined and bound scarlet silk.
MusB: light blue silk, half-lined and bound fur.*
BSc: black silk, lined and bound gold silk.
The hoods marked * are identical to the Dublin hoods.
Hat: a black cloth square cap.

MASTERS

Gown: black stuff, Dublin MA pattern [m3].
Hood: a hood of the Dublin full shape [f2].
MA: black silk, lined and bound dark blue silk.
MAO: black silk, lined and bound purple silk.
MCh: crimson lined white, bound blue.
MEng: white silk, lined and bound myrtle green silk.
All are identical to the Dublin hoods.
Hat: a black cloth square cap.

DOCTORS

Undress gown: as masters.
Dress robe: a scarlet cloth robe of Oxford pattern [d2], facings and sleeves to match the hood lining.
Hood: a hood of the Dublin full shape [f2], coloured and lined as follows:
MD: scarlet cloth, lined and bound scarlet silk.
DSc: scarlet cloth, lined and bound dark blue silk.
DLitt: scarlet cloth, lined and bound white silk.
DMus: cream brocade, lined and bound rose silk.*

LL.D: scarlet cloth, lined and bound pink silk.*

The hoods marked * are identical to the Dublin hoods.

Hat: in undress, a black cloth square cap; in full dress, a black cloth bonnet with gold cords and tassels.

UNIVERSITY OF ST ANDREWS
1410–1413

St Andrews is the oldest university in Scotland. Founded in 1410 and granted a charter by the bishop of St Andrews the following year, it was recognized as a *studium generale* by papal bull in 1413. By the middle of the sixteenth century the University had three colleges - St Salvator's (1450), St Leonard's (1511), and St Mary's (1538): the buildings of St Mary's College and St Salvator's Chapel both date from this period. In the nineteenth century the University made considerable progress in developing teaching and research in the Arts, Divinity, and the Biological and Physical Sciences. In 1897 the University was joined by a new academic centre in Dundee, known as Queen's College; it specialized in Medicine and Applied Science. This association ended in 1967 when Queen's College became the University of Dundee.

As with Glasgow and Aberdeen, the original robes fell into disuse at the Reformation, and a scheme was drawn up in the 1860s. The scheme owes much to French models, not least in the choice of faculty colours, and the design of the doctoral robes. The obsolete degrees are largely those awarded at Dundee before it became independent.

Faculty Colours

Arts: cherry red.
[Applied Science: peacock blue.]
[Dentistry: claret.]
Divinity: wood violet.
Education: primrose.
Engineering: peacock blue.
[Laws: pimento.]
Letters: saffron.
[Medicine: medici crimson.]
Music: sky blue.
Philosophy: gold (but PhD spectrum blue).
Science: purple-lilac.
Social Sciences: apple green.

UNDERGRADUATES

Gown:

United College (i.e., St Leonard's and St Salvator's): a scarlet stuff gown of the St Andrews pattern [u9], with a burgundy velvet collar.

St Mary's College: a black stuff gown of the London pattern [u3], with a violet saltire on the left facing.

Hat: a black cloth square cap, with coloured tassels depending on the year of study: First-year students wear a blue tassel, second-year students wear a crimson tassel, third-year students wear a yellow tassel, and fourth-year students wear a black tassel.

UNDERGRADUATE CERTIFICATES AND DIPLOMAS

none specified

BACHELORS

Gown: a black stuff gown of the Scottish MA pattern [m12].

Hood: a hood of the St Andrews full shape [f12] in the faculty colour, bound on all edges 2″ fur.

Hat: a black cloth square cap.

GRADUATE DIPLOMAS

Gown: as for bachelors.

Hood: a black hood of the St Andrews full shape [f12], bordered inside 3″ spectrum blue.

Hat: a black cloth square cap.

MASTERS including MASTERS OF PHILOSOPHY and FIRST-DEGREE MASTERS

Gown: as for bachelors.

Hood: a black hood of the St Andrews full shape [f12], fully lined faculty colour:

MA: cherry silk.
MLitt: saffron.
MPhil: gold.
MRes: spectrum blue.
MSc: purple-lilac.
MSci, MChem, MMath, MPhys: bordered inside the cowl 3″ purple-lilac.
MTheol: violet.

Hat: a black cloth square cap.

ALL DOCTORS

Undress gown: as for bachelors. When a doctorate is awarded *honoris causa*, the recipient wears a black gown of the same pattern as the dress robe, with 5″ cuffs of black silk. The front of a black cassock is attached behind the facings; the buttons and buttonholes are of faculty colour.

Dress robe: a robe of the St Andrews pattern, which is similar to the Cambridge MusD [d3], but with slightly narrower sleeves and a flap collar, in cloth of the faculty colour, with facings and cuffs of silk of the faculty colour.

Hood: a hood of the St Andrews full shape [f12] in the faculty colour, fully lined with white satin.

DD: violet.
DLang: dark green.
LL.D: pimento.
DLitt: saffron.
MusD: sky blue.
PhD: spectrum blue.
DSc: purple-lilac.

The hoods for DD, DLitt, LL.D, DMus, and DSc may be lined with ermine.

Hat: in undress, a black cloth square cap; in full dress, a black velvet John Knox cap.

OBSOLETE DEGREES

The following degrees have been awarded; the hoods were as follows, and may still be seen. The doctors wore robes of faculty colour, as specified above.

MA(SocSc): black lined apple green silk.
BCom: black silk lined apple green silk (but see note 3 below).
EdB: primrose silk bound fur (but see note 3 below).
MEd: black lined primrose.
BL: pimento bordered inside the cowl 3″ white satin.
BLitt: saffron bound fur.
BPhil: gold bound fur.
DPhil: black lined orange.
BSc(AppSc): peacock blue bound fur.
MSc(AppSc): black lined peacock blue.
DSc(AppSc): peacock blue lined white satin.
MB,ChB: medici crimson bound fur.
ChM: medici crimson silk, unlined.
MD: medici crimson lined white satin.
BDS: claret bound fur.
MDS: claret silk, unlined; originally claret silk, the cowl bordered inside 3″ white satin.
DDS: claret lined white satin.
LDS: no hood. A black gown, with the university arms on a claret panel on the left breast.
LLA (Lady Literate in Arts): a black gown (presumably the same as worn by MAs); an epitoge of the same red as lines the MA hood, with a silver badge with St Andrew and his cross, the letters LLA and the inscription 'University of St. Andrews, 1877'. This diploma, which was available externally worldwide as well as within the University, ran from 1877 until 1931.

NOTES

1. Under the original nineteenth-century scheme, the bachelors' hoods were of faculty colour, lined white satin and bound fur, but the white lining had disappeared by the early twentieth century. Doctors' hoods were allowed the option of an ermine lining in place of the white satin, and this still holds in case of doctors *honoris causa*.
2. The PhD colour was originally defined as 'Nanking blue'. *Athena: A Year-book of the Learned World* (1920) gives a DPhil, with a hood of 'yellow' lined white: the BPhil is also 'yellow', so this must be the gold now in use. The PhD, being a different degree, was given its own colour (as happened at Edinburgh), and the BPhil and MPhil retained theirs.

3. There is some confusion over the EdB hood. Shaw 1966 says it was black lined primrose. As it was the equivalent of the PGCE, this could have been so. Pears 1963-4 has it as black lined primrose bound fur. The same confusion arises over the BCom: some authorities have it as given above, other as apple green silk bound fur.
4. Doctors other than PhD may, if they wish, wear a black cassock under their full dress robe, with a cincture of the faculty colour.

ST MARY'S UNIVERSITY COLLEGE, TWICKENHAM
1850/2007

St Mary's College was founded in 1850 by the Catholic Poor Schools Committee to meet the need for teachers for the growing numbers of poor Catholic children. It started in Brook Green in Hammersmith. By the 1920s, the College at Brook Green was inadequate for its needs, and St Mary's was enabled to purchase Strawberry Hill, the house built by Robert Walpole at Twickenham, and to build living accommodation and classrooms for about 250 students. Strawberry Hill officially opened in 1925.

Although the college was primarily concerned with teacher training until 1975, it had offered courses leading to the University of London BA and BSc from 1920. In 1967 it became possible to stay for a fourth year to convert the Teacher's Certificate into a BEd degree. In 1979 the College changed its validation from the University of London to the University of Surrey. In September 2006, it was granted the power to award its own taught degrees by the Privy Council, and became St Mary's University College; the first students graduated in 2010.

The hoods are all of a special full shape, which is effectively the Oxford full shape [f5], but without a neckband, so the cape is pulled up onto the shoulders. The blue is a mid-blue.

UNDERGRADUATES
none specified

UNDERGRADUATE CERTIFICATES AND DIPLOMAS
none specified

FOUNDATION DEGREES
Gown: a black gown of Cambridge BA pattern [b2].
Hood: a blue hood of special full shape, lined blue and piped on all edges white cord.
Hat: a black cloth square cap.

BACHELORS
Gown: a black gown of Cambridge BA pattern [b2].
Hood: a blue hood of special full shape, lined and bound 1″ 'St Aidan' pattern white brocade.
Hat: a black cloth square cap.

POSTGRADUATE CERTIFICATES AND DIPLOMAS
Gown: as for masters.

Hood: a blue hood of special full shape, lined blue. The cowl bordered 3″ pink inside, and the cape 1″ outside white 'St Aidan' pattern brocade.

Hat: a black cloth square cap.

FIRST-DEGREE MASTERS

not awarded

MASTERS

Gown: a black stuff gown of basic pattern [m10].

Hood: a blue hood of special full shape, lined and bound on all edges 1″ pink.

Hat: a black cloth square cap.

MASTERS OF PHILOSOPHY, DOCTORS OF PHILOSOPHY, TAUGHT AND PROFESSIONAL DOCTORS and HIGHER DOCTORS

These are still awarded by the University of Surrey.

UNIVERSITY OF SALFORD
1967

In 1896 Salford Working Men's College joined with Pendleton Mechanics Institute to form Salford Technical Institute, later called the Royal Technical Institute Salford. In 1921 the Institute was renamed the Royal Technical College, Salford, but in 1958 it divided. One part, the Royal College of Advanced Technology, became the University of Salford in 1967. The other part, Peel Park Technical College, changed its name first to Salford Technical Institute (in 1961), then to Salford College of Technology (in 1970), and finally to University College Salford (in 1992). In 1996 both organisations reunited to form the University of Salford as it is today.

The scheme is based on the colours of blue and gold. It was initially faculty-based, but a recent overhaul has produced a grade-specific system. The original specification is at the end of this entry.

UNDERGRADUATES
none specified

UNDERGRADUATE CERTIFICATES and DIPLOMAS
Gown: as for bachelors.
Hood: a mid-blue hood of CNAA shape [a1], bordered as follows:
Certificates: cowl edge bordered inside 2″ gold satin.
Diplomas: cowl edge bordered inside 3″ gold satin.
Hat: a black cloth square cap.

FOUNDATION DEGREES
Gown: as for bachelors.
Hood: a mid-blue silk hood of CNAA shape [a1], lined blue silk, tipped gold satin.
Hat: a black cloth square cap.

LICENTIATE DIPLOMA IN BANDMASTERSHIP
Gown: as for bachelors.
Hood: a mid-blue silk hood of CNAA shape [a1], the cowl edge bordered inside 3″ cream brocade.
Hat: a black cloth square cap.

BACHELORS
Gown: a black stuff gown of the basic pattern [b1].
Hood: a mid-blue silk hood of CNAA shape [a1], lined as follows:
ordinary degrees: lined gold satin, the cowl edge bordered inside 2″ light blue silk.
honours degrees: lined gold satin, the cowl edge bordered inside 2″ grey silk.
Hat: a black cloth square cap.

GRADUATE CERTIFICATES and DIPLOMAS

Gown: as for bachelors.

Hood: a mid blue silk hood of CNAA shape [a1], fully lined gold satin, the cowl edge bordered inside 2″ pale blue silk.

Hat: a black cloth square cap.

FIRST-DEGREE MASTERS (MChem, MEng, MEnv, MPhys)

Gown: a black stuff gown of London MA pattern [m5].

Hood: a mid blue silk hood of CNAA shape [a1], fully lined gold satin, the cowl edge bordered inside 3″ and bound ⅜″ light blue silk.

Hat: a black cloth square cap.

POSTGRADUATE CERTIFICATES and DIPLOMAS (PgCert; PgDip)

Gown: a black stuff gown of London MA pattern [m5].

Hood: a mid-blue silk hood of CNAA shape [a1], lined as follows:

PgCert: lined gold satin, the cowl edge bordered inside 2″ pale green silk.

PgDip: lined and the cape edge bound ⅜″ gold satin, and the cowl edge bordered inside 3″ dark green silk.

Hat: a black cloth square cap.

MASTERS (taught course: MA, MSc, LLM, MBA, MRes)

Gown: a black stuff gown of London MA pattern [m5].

Hood: a mid blue silk hood of CNAA shape [a1], fully lined and the cape edge bound ⅜″ gold satin, and the cowl edge bordered inside 3″ grey silk.

Hat: a black cloth square cap.

MASTERS (by research: MRes, MPhil, LLM, MSc)

Gown a black stuff gown of London MA pattern [m5].

Hood a mid blue silk hood of CNAA shape [a1], fully lined and the cape edge bound ⅜″ gold satin, and the cowl edge bordered inside 3″ scarlet satin.

Hat a black cloth square cap.

DOCTORS OF PHILOSOPHY and TAUGHT AND PROFESSIONAL DOCTORS

Undress gown: as for masters.

Dress robe: a black stuff gown of London MA pattern [m5] with 3″ facings of mid-blue silk.

Hood: a mid blue silk hood of CNAA shape [a1], lined and bound ⅜″ scarlet satin.

Hat: a black cloth bonnet with scarlet cord and tassels.

HIGHER DOCTORS

Undress gown: as for masters.

Dress robe: a scarlet cloth of the Cambridge pattern [d1], with 5″ facings and sleeve linings of gold satin.
Hood: a dark blue silk hood of CNAA shape [a1], lined and bound ⅜″ gold satin.
Hat: a black velvet bonnet with gold cord and tassels.

NOTES

1. In 1994, the scheme underwent considerable revision, to produce the one specified above. The main differences are in the hoods, which originally had a faculty colour system. They were:
   BA: blue lined gold, the cowl bordered inside bordered 2″ light blue.
   BSc: blue lined gold, the cowl bordered inside bordered 2″ grey.
   BEng: blue lined gold, the cowl bordered inside bordered 2″ dark blue.
   DipEng: blue lined gold, the cowl bordered inside bordered 3″ grey and 1″ light blue.
   MMath, MPhys, MChem: blue lined gold, the cowl bordered inside 3″ grey.
   MEng: blue lined gold, the cowl bordered inside bordered 3″ dark blue.
   MA: blue lined and bound gold, the cowl bordered inside bordered 3″ light blue.
   MSc: blue lined and bound gold, the cowl bordered inside bordered 3″ grey.
   MBA: blue lined and bound gold, the cowl bordered inside bordered 3″ maroon.
   MPhil: blue lined and bound gold, the cowl bordered inside 3″ and the cape bound 1″ scarlet.
   Doctors and diplomas: *as above.*

UNIVERSITY OF SHEFFIELD
1905

The University of Sheffield was originally formed by the merger of three colleges. The first two were the Sheffield School of Medicine (1828), and Firth College (1879) for arts and science subjects. Firth College then helped to fund the opening of the third college, the Sheffield Technical School in 1884, to teach applied science. The three institutions merged in 1897 to form the University College of Sheffield. It was originally envisaged that the University College would join Manchester, Liverpool, and Leeds as the fourth member of the federal Victoria University. However, the Victoria University began to split up before this could happen, so the University College of Sheffield received its own Royal Charter in 1905 as the University of Sheffield.

The hood system seems to be based on Cambridge, but the bachelors' hoods are bound with faculty silk on the cape instead of fur. The bachelors' and masters' hoods are noted for being green. The dark green cloth used for the bachelors' hoods is so dark as to appear black in some circumstances, while the dark green silk of the master's hoods can approach olive green. The doctors are unusual in that their hoods are indeed red, and not scarlet to match their dress robes. The distinguishing colours of the hoods are partly degree-specific, and partly faculty-specific.

Faculty Colours.

Arts:

BMus, MMus, DMus: cream brocade.

All other degrees: crushed strawberry.

Architectural Studies:

All degrees: old gold (includes MPlan).

Board of Collegiate Studies:

All degrees: saxon blue (includes the BMin, MMin, and DMin).

[**Education:**

All degrees: pearl.]

Engineering:

BSc(Tech): lilac.

All other degrees: purple.

Laws

BA(Law), MA(Law): olive green.

All other degrees: pale green.

Medicine:

MB,ChB, ChM, MD: red.

BDS, MDS: pale rose pink.

All other degrees: cerise.

[**Metallurgy:**

All degrees: steel grey.]

Science:

All degrees: apricot.

Social Science and Economics:

All degrees: lemon yellow.

UNDERGRADUATES

Gown: a black stuff gown of the Oxford scholars' pattern [u1].

Hat: a black cloth square cap.

UNDERGRADUATE CERTIFICATES AND DIPLOMAS

Gown: A black stuff gown of basic pattern [b1], with a ribbon of faculty colour along the outer edge of each facing. The ribbon is 1″ wide for certificates, and 2″ wide for diplomas.

FOUNDATION DEGREES

not awarded

BACHELORS

Gown: a black stuff gown of basic pattern [b1].

Hood: a dark green cloth hood of the Cambridge shape [f1], the cowl part-lined 6″white fur, the cape bound 2″ with silk of the faculty colour, and the neckband entirely of the faculty colour.

Hat: a black cloth square cap.

POSTGRADUATE CERTIFICATES AND DIPLOMAS

Gown: as for bachelors.

Hood: a dark green silk hood of the Cambridge shape [f1], as the bachelors' hoods, but without the fur.

Hat: a black cloth square cap.

FIRST-DEGREE MASTERS

Gown: as for bachelors.

Hood: a dark green silk hood of the Cambridge shape [f1], lined as follows:

MArch: old gold.
MChem: apricot.
MEnvSc: apricot.
MLA: old gold.
MMath: apricot.
MPhys: apricot.

Hat: a black cloth square cap.

MASTERS including MASTERS OF PHILOSOPHY

Gown: a black stuff gown of Oxford MA pattern [m1].

Hood: a dark green silk hood of the Cambridge shape [f1], lined with silk of the faculty colour.
MPhil: lined dark green.
Hat: a black cloth square cap.

DOCTORS OF PHILOSOPHY and TAUGHT AND PROFESSIONAL DOCTORS

Undress gown: a black silk gown of flap-collar pattern [d4], with Oxford gimp arranged as on the Oxford DPhil undress gown, save that the pentagons on the skirt have concave sides.
Dress robe: a scarlet cloth robe of the Oxford pattern [d2], with facings (but not the sleeves) covered with dark green silk.
Hood: a red silk hood of the Cambridge shape [f1], lined as follows:
DBA: lemon yellow.
DClinPsy: apricot.
DDS: pale rose pink.
DEcon: lemon yellow.
EdD: pearl.
DMedSc: cerise.
DMin: saxon blue.
MD: red.
PhD: dark green.
Hat: a black velvet square cap.

HIGHER DOCTORS

Undress gown: as PhD.
Dress robe: a scarlet cloth robe of the Cambridge pattern [d1], with facings of dark green and sleeve-linings of scarlet silk, with a green cord and button.
Hood: a red silk hood of the Cambridge shape [f1], lined with silk of the faculty colour.
Hat: a black velvet square cap.

NOTES

1. The University awarded a number of now-defunct diplomas, which had gowns, but not hoods. The gowns were of London BA pattern [b4], in black stuff, with coloured cords and buttons on the sleeves as follows:
   DipArch: old gold.
   LDS: pale rose pink.
   AEng: purple.
   AMet: steel grey.
   AMD (Art Masters' Diploma): crushed strawberry. There was a crushed strawberry cord along the facings, also.

2. The masters' degrees awarded jointly by Sheffield and Hallam wear the MA gown, and a hood of Cambridge shape [f1], in gold silk, lined and bound with dark blue silk.
3. The MD was originally classed as a higher doctorate but has since been reclassified as a professional doctorate.
4. Obsolete hoods:
   BMus: as BA, but bound also ½″ white watered silk on the cape.
   DMus: as DLitt, but bound 1″ white watered silk on all edges.
   ChM: green, lined red, bound ½″ white silk on all edges.

SHEFFIELD HALLAM UNIVERSITY
1992

In 1843 the Sheffield School of Design was founded, followed in 1905 by the City of Sheffield Training College. In 1969 the Sheffield School of Design merged with the city's College of Technology to form Sheffield Polytechnic, which in 1976 became Sheffield City Polytechnic when it absorbed the city's two teacher training colleges. In 1992 it became a university with the right to award its own degrees, and was named Sheffield Hallam University.

The scheme of dress is simple, and based on black, maroon, and silver-grey.

UNDERGRADUATES
none specified

UNDERGRADUATE CERTIFICATES AND DIPLOMAS and FOUNDATION DEGREES
Gown: as for bachelors.
Hood: a black silk hood of the CNAA shape [a1], lined maroon silk, tipped silver-grey silk.
Hat: a black cloth square cap.

BACHELORS
Gown: a black stuff gown of Wales BA pattern [b6].
Hood: a black silk hood of the Cambridge shape [f1], the cowl bordered inside with 4″ maroon silk, and 1″ silver-grey on the edge.
Hat: a black cloth square cap.

POSTGRADUATE CERTIFICATES AND DIPLOMAS
Gown: as for masters.
Hood: a black silk hood of the Cambridge shape [f1], lined silver-grey silk, the cowl bordered inside with 1″ maroon silk.
Hat: a black cloth square cap.

FIRST-DEGREE MASTERS
Gown: as for masters.
Hood: as for bachelors.
Hat: a black cloth square cap.

MASTERS including MASTERS OF PHILOSOPHY
Gown: a black stuff gown of basic pattern [m10]. For MPhil it has maroon facings.
Hood: a black silk hood of the Cambridge shape [f1], lined maroon silk, the cowl bordered inside with 1½″ silver-grey silk.

Hat: a black cloth square cap.

DOCTORS OF PHILOSOPHY and TAUGHT AND PROFESSIONAL DOCTORS

Undress gown: as for masters.

Dress robe: a maroon cloth robe of the Cambridge pattern [d1], with facings and sleeve linings of silver-grey silk, and ½″ black silk along the outer edge of the facings.

Hood: a maroon cloth hood of the Cambridge shape [f1], lined silver-grey silk, the cowl bordered inside with ½″ black silk.

Hat: in undress, a black cloth square cap; in full dress, a black cloth bonnet with maroon cords and tassels.

HIGHER DOCTORS

Undress gown: as PhD.

Dress robe: a maroon cloth hood of the Cambridge pattern [d1], with facings and sleeve linings of black silk, and ½″ silver lace along the outer edge of the facings.

Hood: a maroon cloth hood of the Cambridge shape [f1], lined black silk, the cowl bordered inside with ½″ silver lace.

Hat: in undress, a black cloth square cap; in full dress, a black velvet bonnet with maroon cords and tassels.

NOTES

1. Jointly-awarded masters' degrees:

   Sheffield and Hallam: an Oxford MA gown [m1], and a gold silk hood of Cambridge shape [f1], lined and bound dark blue silk.

   Hull and Hallam: an Oxford MA gown [m1], and a black hood of Cambridge shape [f1], lined maroon, and bordered inside the cowl with 2 ½″ Hull turquoise (currently not awarded).

SOUTH BANK UNIVERSITY, LONDON
1992

In June 1888 the South London Polytechnics Committee, approved 'a Scheme for the establishment in South London of Polytechnic Institutes'. In May 1890 of that year, the South London Polytechnics Institutes Act was passed, and in 1892 the Borough Polytechnic Institute opened with a remit to educate the local community in a range of practical skills and was thus nicknamed 'The People's Palace'. In 1970 the Borough Polytechnic Institute changed its name to the Polytechnic of the South Bank. 1976 saw the merger of Battersea College of Education and Battersea Training College with the Polytechnic. In 1992 the Polytechnic became South Bank University.

All hoods and doctors' robes are trimmed with a specially-woven silk, which is ultramarine blue, with the University arms embroidered into it in black outline.

UNDERGRADUATES
none specified

UNDERGRADUATE CERTIFICATES AND DIPLOMAS
Gown: as for bachelors.
Hood: a black hood of the CNAA shape [a1], lined with University silk.
Hat: a black cloth square cap.

FOUNDATION DEGREES
Gown: as for bachelors.
Hood: a black hood of the CNAA shape [a1], lined with University silk, the cowl bordered with 1″ silver.
Hat: a black cloth square cap.

BACHELORS
Gown: a black stuff gown of basic pattern [b1].
Hood: a black hood of the Cambridge shape [f1], the cowl bordered inside with 4″ University silk.
Hat: a black cloth square cap.

POSTGRADUATE CERTIFICATES AND DIPLOMAS
Gown: as for masters.
Hood: a black hood of the Cambridge shape [f1], lined as follows:
PGCE: the cowl bordered inside with 4″ University silk, with 1″ silver set in the middle.
All others: the cowl bordered inside with 4″ University silk, with 1″ silver set on the edge.
Hat: a black cloth square cap.

FIRST-DEGREE MASTERS

Gown: as for bachelors.
Hood: as for masters.
Hat: a black cloth square cap.

MASTERS

Gown: a black stuff gown of basic pattern [m10].
Hood: a black hood of the Cambridge shape [f1], fully lined with University silk.
Hat: a black cloth square cap.

MASTERS OF PHILOSOPHY

Gown: a black stuff gown of basic pattern [m10], with facings of University silk.
Hood: a black hood of the Cambridge shape [f1], fully lined with University silk, and bound 1″ silver on all edges.
Hat: a black cloth square cap.

DOCTORS OF PHILOSOPHY and TAUGHT AND PROFESSIONAL DOCTORS

Undress gown: *none specified*
Dress robe: a royal blue robe of the Cambridge pattern [d1], the facings and sleeve-linings of University silk.
Hood: a royal blue hood of the Cambridge shape [f1], fully lined with University silk.
Hat: in full dress, a black cloth bonnet with dark blue cords and tassels.

HIGHER DOCTORS

Undress gown: *none specified*
Dress robe: as for PhD, but the sleeves held by a blue cord and button.
Hood: a bright blue hood of the Cambridge shape [f1], fully lined and bound 1″ with University silk.
Hat: in full dress, a black cloth bonnet with dark blue cords and tassels.

UNIVERSITY OF SOUTHAMPTON
1952

The University of Southampton has its origin as the Hartley Institution, which was formed in 1862 from a benefaction by Henry Robertson Hartley (1777–1850), who bequeathed £103,000 to the Southampton Corporation on condition that it was invested 'in such manner as might best promote the study and advancement of the sciences of Natural History, Astronomy, Antiquities, Classical and Oriental Literature in the town, such as by forming a Public Library, Botanic Gardens, Observatory, and collections of objects with the above sciences'. The city officials housed Hartley's books in a building in Southampton's High Street, in the city centre. The Hartley Institution was born out of this, and became a university college in 1902. In 1919 it was renamed Hartley University College, and subsequently University College Southampton. It gained full university status in 1952.

The robes were designed by Charles Franklyn, and include his various signatures: the London BA gown, the Burgon and London shape hoods, and the use of a shade of light blue. As originally designed, the faculty was indicated by coloured cords on the sleeves and yoke of the bachelors gowns, and on the yoke of masters', doctors' undress and dress robes. These were abolished in 1993, and replaced by blue ones for bachelors, and claret for the PhD dress robe, although the higher doctors retain their degree colour ones. An illogicality is that none of the doctors' hoods are bound with degree colour.

Faculty colours

Arts and Letters: mid-cerise.
[Business Administration: petrol blue.]
[Education: white.]
Engineering: primrose.
[Engineering Science: orange.]
Laws: blue (same as lining).
Medicine: crimson.
Medical Science: rich gold piped crimson.
[Music: ivory.]
Nursing, Midwifery: powder blue.
Philosophy: claret.
Science: rich gold.
Science in Medicine, Health, Biological Science, Occupational and Physiotherapy: pale turquoise.
Social Sciences: light green.
Theology: violet.

UNDERGRADUATES

Gown: a black gown of the London undergraduate pattern [u3].

Hat: a black cloth square cap.

UNDERGRADUATE CERTIFICATES AND DIPLOMAS

Gown: as for bachelors.

Hood: a black hood of the CNAA shape [a1], lined black, the cowl bordered inside ³⁄₈″ peacock blue silk.

Hat: a black cloth square cap.

FOUNDATION DEGREES

Gown: a black gown of the London BA pattern [b4], with peacock blue cords and buttons on the sleeves and yoke.

Hood: a black hood of the CNAA shape [a1], bordered 3″ peacock blue silk.

Hat: a black cloth square cap.

BACHELORS

Gown: a black gown of the London BA pattern [b4], but with peacock blue cords and buttons on the sleeves, and on the yoke.

Hood: a black silk hood of Burgon shape [s2], lined with peacock blue silk, the cowl bound ³⁄₈″ degree colour silk.

LL.B: the lining is bound over the cowl edge to form the faculty binding.

BMus: until 2004, had a dark blue shell.

Hat: a black cloth square cap.

POSTGRADUATE CERTIFICATES AND DIPLOMAS

Gown: as for bachelors.

Hood: a black hood of the London shape [f3], lined black, the cowl bound ³⁄₈″ peacock blue silk.

Hat: a black cloth square cap.

FIRST-DEGREE MASTERS

Gown: a black gown of the London BA pattern [b4], but with peacock blue cords and buttons on the sleeves, and on the yoke.

Hood: a black silk hood of Burgon shape [s2], lined with peacock blue silk, and the cowl bound 1″ degree colour silk.

MChem, MMath, MPhys: bound rich gold.

MEng: bound primrose.

[MSW: bound light green.]

Hat: a black cloth square cap.

MASTERS including MASTERS OF PHILOSOPHY

Gown: a black gown of Oxford MA pattern [m1], with a blue cord and button on the yoke.

Hood: a black silk hood of London shape [f3], lined and the cape bound ³⁄₈″ peacock blue silk, the cowl bound ³⁄₈″ degree colour silk.

LL.M: the lining is bound over the cowl edge to form the faculty binding.

MCh: a black cloth hood of Oxford full shape [f5], lined and the cape bound ⅜″ peacock blue silk, the cowl bound ⅜″ crimson silk.

MBA: the cowl bound ⅜″ light green silk.

Hat: a black cloth square cap.

DOCTORS OF PHILOSOPHY and TAUGHT AND PROFESSIONAL DOCTORS

Undress gown: as for masters, but with a single row of black Southampton lace round the armhole.

Dress robe: a claret cloth robe of Oxford pattern [d2], the sleeves and facings covered with peacock blue silk, and a claret cord and button on the yoke.

Hood: a claret cloth hood of Oxford full shape [f5], lined peacock blue silk.

Hat: in undress, a black cloth square cap; in full dress, a black cloth bonnet with claret cords and tassels.

HIGHER DOCTORS

Undress gown: as for masters, but with a double row of black Southampton lace round the armhole.

Dress robe: a scarlet cloth robe of Oxford pattern [d2], the sleeves and facings covered with peacock blue silk, and a cord and button on the yoke in faculty colour.

Hood: a claret cloth hood of Oxford full shape [f5], lined peacock blue silk.

Hat: in undress, a black cloth square cap; in full dress, a black velvet bonnet with cords and tassels of degree colour.

SOUTHAMPTON SOLENT UNIVERSITY
2005

The university's origins can be traced back to a private School of Art founded in 1856, which eventually became the Southampton College of Art. Mergers with the Southampton College of Technology, and later the College of Nautical Studies, led to the establishment of the Southampton Institute of Higher Education in 1984. It became a university in 2005, adopting the name Southampton Solent. Before then, its degrees were validated by Nottingham Trent University, and the research degrees (MPhil, PhD) continue to be awarded by Trent, although robes have been designed for these degrees. It is possibly unique among British universities in awarding the honorary degree of Doctor of Sport.

The scheme of academic dress is simple, and is based round three shades of a single colour, in this case purple, although the doctoral ones introduce the colour cream. The undergraduate awards hood is the old Southampton Institute hood, and thus does not fit the new scheme.

UNDERGRADUATES
none specified

UNDERGRADUATE CERTIFICATES AND DIPLOMAS
Gown: a black stuff gown of basic bachelors' pattern [b1].
Hood: a mid-blue hood of the Oxford simple shape [s1], the cowl bordered 4″ white inside.
Hat: a black cloth square cap.

FOUNDATION DEGREES
Gown: as for bachelors.
Hood: a dark purple ribbed polyester hood of the CNAA shape [a1], lined mid-purple.
Hat: a black cloth square cap.

BACHELORS
Gown: a black stuff gown of the basic pattern [b1].
Hood: a dark purple ribbed polyester hood of the CNAA shape [a1], lined mid-purple stuff, and bound on all edges ½″ light purple.
Hat: a black cloth square cap.

POSTGRADUATE CERTIFICATES AND DIPLOMAS
Gown: a black stuff gown of basic masters' pattern [m10], with 2½″ facings of purple stuff.

Hood: as for masters, but the neckband is not bound.
Hat: a black cloth square cap.

FIRST-DEGREE MASTERS

not awarded

MASTERS including MASTERS OF PHILOSOPHY

Gown: a black stuff gown of basic pattern [m10], with 2½″ facings of purple stuff, which are bound on the outer edge with the same purple ribbon as binds the hood.
Hood: a dark purple ribbed polyester hood of the Cambridge shape [a1], lined mid-purple stuff, and bound on all edges (including neckband) ½″ light purple.
Hat: a black cloth square cap.

DOCTORS OF PHILOSOPHY and TAUGHT AND PROFESSIONAL DOCTORS

Undress gown: *none specified*
Dress robe: a maroon robe of the Cambridge pattern [d1], with cream facings and sleeve linings. There is 1″ purple on the outer edge of the facings, and the sleeves are held by purple cords and buttons.
Hood: a maroon hood of the Cambridge shape [f1], lined cream, and bound on all edges ½″ purple.
Hat: in full dress, a black cloth bonnet with purple cords and tassels.

HIGHER DOCTORS

Undress gown: *none specified*
Dress robe: a scarlet cloth robe of the Cambridge pattern [d1], with cream facings and sleeve linings. The facings have 1″ purple on the outer edge, and the sleeves have a purple cord and button.
Hood: a scarlet hood of the Cambridge shape [f1], lined cream, and bound on all edges ½″ purple.
Hat: in full dress, a black velvet bonnet with purple cords and tassels.

STAFFORDSHIRE UNIVERSITY
1992

North Staffordshire Polytechnic was formed in 1971 from the merger of Stoke-on-Trent College of Art and North Staffordshire College of Technology, both based in Stoke-on-Trent, with the Staffordshire College of Technology, in Stafford. In 1977 it absorbed a teacher training facility in Madeley. In September 1988 the institution changed its name to Staffordshire Polytechnic, and in 1992 it became Staffordshire University.

The scheme of dress is simple, but has some unusual features, such as the use of doctoral-pattern gowns for the masters, and the PhD gown, while of doctoral pattern, does not have the usual sleeve linings and facings. It is difficult to see a logical progression in the hoods. The red is a very bright vermilion, the blue a dark navy.

UNDERGRADUATES
none specified

UNDERGRADUATE CERTIFICATES AND DIPLOMAS
Gown: as for bachelors.
Hood: a black hood of the Burgon shape [s2], lined, bound, and the neckband faced as follows:
Certificates: dark grey.
Diplomas: white.
Hat: a black cloth square cap.

FOUNDATION DEGREES
Gown: as for bachelors.
Hood: of the Burgon shape [s2], in grey, lined red and the cowl bound white; the neckband is faced white.
Hat: a black cloth square cap.

BACHELORS
Gown: a black stuff gown of London BA pattern [b4].
Hood: a grey hood of the Burgon shape [s2], lined and bound red; the neckband faced red.
Hat: a black cloth square cap.

POSTGRADUATE CERTIFICATES AND DIPLOMAS
Gown: as for bachelors.
Hood: a black hood of the London shape [f3], lined and bound blue.
Hat: a black cloth square cap.

FIRST-DEGREE MASTERS

Gown: as for bachelors.

Hood: a grey hood of the Burgon shape [s2], lined red, the cowl bound blue and the neckband is faced blue.

Hat: a black cloth square cap.

MASTERS including MASTERS OF PHILOSOPHY

Gown: a grey stuff gown of Cambridge doctors' pattern [d1], with unlined sleeves.

Hood: a grey hood of the London shape [f3], lined and bound 1″ blue on all edges.

Hat: a grey cloth square cap.

DOCTORS OF PHILOSOPHY and TAUGHT AND PROFESSIONAL DOCTORS

Undress gown: *none specified*

Dress robe: a scarlet panama hood of the Cambridge pattern [d1], with unlined sleeves and uncovered facings.

Hood: a scarlet hood of the London shape [f3], lined and bound ⅜″ blue on all edges.

Hat: in full dress, a scarlet velvet bonnet with blue cords and tassels.

HIGHER DOCTORS

Undress gown: *none specified*

Dress robe: as for PhD, but with scarlet taffeta facings and sleeve linings.

Hood: a gold panama hood of the London shape [f3], lined and bound ⅜″ white.

Hat: in full dress, a scarlet velvet bonnet with gold cords and tassels.

UNIVERSITY OF STIRLING
1967

The University of Stirling was founded on a greenfield site in 1967 as a result of the 1963 Robbins Report on the Future of Higher Education in the United Kingdom. As well as the main campus in Stirling, the University also has campuses in Inverness and Stornoway, Isle of Lewis, which specialise in Nursing and Midwifery.

Stirling caused a certain amount of controversy among previous writers on academic dress by using fur on the masters' hoods, and not the bachelors', but this has several mediæval precedents. It should also be noted that the degree of MA – uniquely among British universities – cannot be earned, but is solely an honorary award.

UNDERGRADUATES
none specified

UNDERGRADUATE CERTIFICATES AND DIPLOMAS
Gown: as for bachelors.
Hood: a black hood of Edinburgh shape [s4], bordered 3″ azure blue inside the cowl.

BACHELORS
Gown: a black stuff gown of Scottish masters' pattern [m12].
Hood: of the Edinburgh shape [s4], in black, lined as follows:
BA: dove grey.
BAcc: calamine blue.
BEd: bunting azure blue.
BEdStud: sapphire blue.
LL.B: dove grey, bordered inside the cowl with 3″ maroon.
BM and BN: dove grey, bordered inside the cowl with 3″ bunting azure blue.
BSc: : dove grey, bordered inside on all edges with 1″ malachite green.
BSW: dove grey, bordered inside the cowl with 3″ crocus (mauve).

POSTGRADUATE CERTIFICATES AND DIPLOMAS
Gown: as for bachelors.
Hood: a black hood of Edinburgh shape [s4], bordered 3″ dove grey inside the cowl.

MASTERS including MASTERS OF PHILOSOPHY
Gown: as for bachelors.
Hood: a black hood of Edinburgh shape [s4], lined as follows. In all cases the cowl edge is bound fur:
MBA: maroon.
MEd: bunting azure blue.
LL.M: dove grey, bordered inside the cowl with 3″ maroon.

MLitt: malachite green, bordered inside the cowl with 3″ stone white.
MM, MN: dove grey, bordered inside the cowl with 3″ bunting azure blue.
MPhil: stone white, bordered inside the cowl with 3″ malachite green.
MRes: malachite green, bordered inside the cowl with 3″ dove grey.
MSc: malachite green.

DOCTORS OF PHILOSOPHY and TAUGHT AND PROFESSIONAL DOCTORS

Undress gown: *none specified*
Dress robe: as for bachelors, but faced 3″ dove grey.
Hood: a dove grey hood of the Edinburgh shape [s4], lined as follows:
PhD: malachite green.
DBA: maroon.
EdD: bunting azure blue.
DMid and DN: dove grey, bordered inside the cowl with 3″ bunting azure blue.

HIGHER DOCTORS

Undress gown: *none specified*
Dress robe: a dove grey robe of the same pattern as the bachelors, with facings to match the lining of the hood.
Hood: a dove grey hood of the Cambridge full shape [f1], lined as follows:
DLitt: violet.
DSc: crocus (mauve).

MASTERS OF ARTS

Gown: as for other masters, but faced 2″ medici crimson.
Hood: a black hood of the Cambridge full shape [f1], lined medici crimson.

DOCTOR OF THE UNIVERSITY

Dress robe: a dove grey robe of the Oxford pattern [d2], with a powder blue flap collar and facings.
Hood: a malachite green hood of the Cambridge full shape [f1], lined powder blue.

NOTES

1. The published regulations say the DLitt and DSc hoods are made in Cambridge shape, but all examples to date have been made in Edinburgh [s4] shape.
2. Hats have never been part of the Stirling scheme.

STOCKTON: JOINT UNIVERSITY COLLEGE ON TEESSIDE (JUCOT)
1992-1994

This college was founded in 1992 as a joint enterprise of the Universities of Durham and of Teesside, and it was to award certificates, diplomas, and BA and BSc degrees validated by both universities. However, Teesside was unable to fulfil its part in the undertaking, and in 1994 Durham took sole control, and it became part of Durham as University College Stockton, awarding Durham degrees. Since then the campus has been developed, originally as the University of Durham Stockton Campus, and now as Queen's Campus. The original college was split into two full colleges of the University, in 2001: John Snow and Stephenson.

The joint academic dress thus had a short life only, from 1992 until 1994, and it is unclear whether it was ever used. The grey gown for non-degree awards is from the Teesside robes, as is the hood, but with its grey binding replaced by palatinate purple.

UNDERGRADUATES
none specified

UNDERGRADUATE CERTIFICATES AND DIPLOMAS
Gown: a grey gown of Durham BA pattern [b5].
Hood:
Certificates: no hood.
Diplomas: as bachelors.
Hat: a black cloth square cap.

BACHELORS
Gown: a black stuff gown of Durham BA pattern [b5].
Hood: a black hood of CNAA shape [a1], lined red silk, and bound on all edges 1″ palatinate purple.

UNIVERSITY OF STRATHCLYDE
1964

The University of Strathclyde can trace its origins to the philanthropy of John Anderson, who died in 1796 leaving a bequest for 'a place of useful learning,' a university open to everyone, regardless of gender or class. By the 1890s, Anderson's university had become a major technological institution with a wide reputation for research and learning. In 1910, the institution was renamed the Royal Technical College and continued to earn a reputation in technical education and research. In the early 1960s, the College merged with the Scottish College of Commerce, which offered a wide range of business and arts subjects. Shortly afterwards, in 1964, the enlarged Royal Technical College was granted a Royal Charter and became the University of Strathclyde.

This is an unusual system in that the doctors in any faculty (including the PhD) revert to the bachelor's hood – thus there is no difference between the hood used for BSc, DSc, and PhD in Science. The system is based on a split between Arts (lined white) and Science (lined gold), with various cord bindings added to whichever is more appropriate for other degrees. This has started to break down with the use of the blue lining for MRes, and the green one for MEnvSt, and two hoods (MEd and MPhil) have borders rather than cord piping. 'Saltire blue' is a light blue, almost sky blue.

UNDERGRADUATES

Gown: a black stuff gown of the Oxford scholars' pattern [u2], except that the facings taper off at breast level, forming lapels. The yoke is trimmed with a blue cord, with a blue button on each shoulder.

Hat: a black cloth square cap.

UNDERGRADUATE CERTIFICATES AND DIPLOMAS

Gown: as for bachelors.

Hood: none. Holders of the DipHE wear a 'collar' of blue edged with red.

Hat: a black cloth square cap.

BACHELORS

Gown: a black stuff gown of basic pattern [b1], with a black cord and button on the yoke.

Hood: a saltire blue hood of the Cambridge full shape [f1], lined as follows. Where there is a cord binding, it is on the cowl only.

BA: white.
BArch: gold, bound scarlet cord.
BCom: white, bound green cord.
BEd: white, bound gold cord.
BEng: gold, bound fur on the cape.
LL.B: white, bound scarlet cord.

BSc: gold.
BTech: gold, bound white cord.

Hat: a black cloth square cap.

POSTGRADUATE DIPLOMAS

Gown: as for bachelors.

Hood: a saltire blue hood of the Edinburgh shape [s4], lined gold, bordered 3″ saltire blue inside the cowl.

Hat: a black cloth square cap.

FIRST-DEGREE MASTERS

Gown: as for masters.

Hood: a saltire blue hood of the Edinburgh shape [s4], lined and bound as follows:
MPharm: lined gold and bound on the cowl with green cord.

Hat: a black cloth square cap.

MASTERS including MASTERS OF PHILOSOPHY

Gown: a black stuff gown of Oxford MA pattern. [m1].

Hood: a saltire blue hood of the Cambridge full shape [f1], lined as follows; in all cases the lining is brought out to form a 1″ edging. Where there is a cord binding, it is on the cowl only.
MA: lined and bound white.
MArch: lined and bound gold, bound scarlet cord.
MBA: lined and bound white, bound black cord.
MCom: lined and bound white, bound green cord.
MCM: lined and bound gold, bound black cord.
MEng: lined and bound gold, bound fur on the cape.
MEnvSt: lined and bound green.
LL.M: lined and bound white, bound scarlet cord.
MLitt: lined and bound white, bound blue cord.
MRes: lined and bound saltire blue.
MSc: lined and bound gold.
MSci: lined and bound gold, bound blue cord.
MTM: lined and bound gold, bound white cord.

The following do not conform to the pattern:
MEd: lined white, bordered 1″ gold on the outside of cape and cowl.
MPhil: lined gold, bordered 1″ white on the outside of cape and cowl.

Hat: a black cloth square cap.

DOCTORS OF PHILOSOPHY and TAUGHT AND PROFESSIONAL DOCTORS

Undress gown: a black gown of the Oxford pattern [d2], with a flap collar.
Dress robe: a saltire blue robe of the St Andrews dress robe pattern [d3].
Hood:
PhD: as for the bachelor in the relevant faculty.
DBA: same as MBA.
EdD: same as MEd.
Hat: a black cloth square cap.

HIGHER DOCTORS

Undress gown: as PhD.
Dress robe: a scarlet cloth robe of the Cambridge pattern [d1], with blue facings.
Hood: as the bachelor in the relevant faculty.
DLitt: lined white.
DUniv: lined saltire blue.
Hat: a black velvet modified John Knox cap.

UNIVERSITY CAMPUS SUFFOLK (joint degrees of East Anglia and Essex) 2007

This institution was set up in 2007, comprising several colleges. Until then, Suffolk was one of the four English counties that had no university. The main campus is in Ipswich, with subsidiary ones in Bury St Edmunds, Lowestoft, Otley, and Great Yarmouth, which are now designated 'UCS Lowestoft', etc. Graduates have their degrees awarded jointly by the University of East Anglia and the University of Essex – designated 'BA(UEA & Essex)' – but separate robes have been designed. The blue lining is a mid-dark blue.

UNDERGRADUATES

none specified

UNDERGRADUATE CERTIFICATES AND DIPLOMAS and FOUNDATION DEGREES

Gown: as for bachelors.

Hood: a red hood of the CNAA shape [a1], lined blue, bordered ½″ old gold inside the cowl.

Hat: a black cloth square cap.

BACHELORS

Gown: a black stuff gown of Wales pattern [b6].

Hood: a red hood of the CNAA shape [a1], lined blue, the cowl bound 1″ old gold inside and out.

Hat: a black cloth square cap.

PROFESSIONAL GRADUATE CERTIFICATE IN EDUCATION

Gown: as for bachelors.

Hood: a red hood of the London shape [f3], lined blue, the cowl bound ¾″ old gold inside and out.

Hat: a black cloth square cap.

POSTGRADUATE CERTIFICATES AND DIPLOMAS

Gown: as for masters.

Hood: a red hood of the London shape [f3], lined blue, the cowl bound ¾″ old gold inside and out.

Hat: a black cloth square cap.

MASTERS

Gown: a black stuff gown of London MA pattern [m5].

Hood: a red hood of the London shape, lined and the cape bound ½″ blue, the cowl bound 1″ old gold inside and out.

Hat: a black cloth square cap.

DOCTORS OF PHILOSOPHY and TAUGHT AND PROFESSIONAL DOCTORS

not yet awarded

HONORARY DOCTORS

Dress robe: a red robe of the Cambridge pattern [d1], the facings covered and the sleeves lined blue, with 1″ old gold on the outer edge of the facings, and an old gold cord and button on the sleeve.

Hood: a red hood of London shape [f3], lined blue, bound 1″ old gold on all edges.

Hat: in full dress, a black velvet bonnet with blue cords and tassels.

UNIVERSITY OF SUNDERLAND
1992

The University's roots can be traced back to 1901, when Sunderland Technical College was established as a municipal training college on Green Terrace (the site of the current Priestman Building). It was the first to offer sandwich courses. Naval architecture and pharmacy were introduced between the two World Wars. Sunderland Polytechnic was established in 1969, incorporating the Technical College, the School of Art (which was also established in 1901) and the Sunderland Teacher Training College (established in 1908). In 1992 the Polytechnic gained University status.

The system of robes is simple and grade-specific; the hoods use some unusual shades. 'Nasturtium' is used in all hoods and the doctors' robes. It is a bright orange colour.

UNDERGRADUATES
none specified

UNDERGRADUATE CERTIFICATES AND DIPLOMAS
Gown: as for bachelors.
Hood: a dark blue hood of the CNAA shape [a1], lined mauve, tipped nasturtium.
Hat: a black cloth square cap.

FOUNDATION DEGREES
not awarded

BACHELORS
Gown: a black stuff gown of basic pattern [b1].
Hood: a dark blue hood of the CNAA shape [a1], lined nasturtium.
Hat: a black cloth square cap.

POSTGRADUATE CERTIFICATES AND DIPLOMAS
Gown: a black stuff gown of basic pattern [b1].
Hood: a dark blue hood of the Edinburgh shape [s4], lined nasturtium.
Hat: a black cloth square cap.

FIRST-DEGREE MASTERS
Gown: as for bachelors.
Hood: a dark blue hood of the CNAA shape [a1], lined nasturtium, the cowl bordered 1½″ gold.
Hat: a black cloth square cap.

MASTERS including MASTERS OF PHILOSOPHY
Gown: a black stuff gown of basic pattern [m10], with black silk facings.

Hood: a dark blue hood of the Cambridge shape [f1], lined as follows:
MPhil: lined Wedgwood blue, bound 1″ nasturtium on all edges.
All others: lined gold, bound 1″ nasturtium on all edges.
Hat: a black cloth square cap.

DOCTORS OF PHILOSOPHY and TAUGHT AND PROFESSIONAL DOCTORS

Undress gown: *none specified*
Dress robe: a dark blue panama robe of the masters' pattern [m10], with blue silk facings.
Hood: a dark blue hood of the Cambridge shape [f1], lined jade green, bound 1″ nasturtium on all edges.
Hat: in full dress, a dark blue panama bonnet with gold cords and tassels.

HIGHER DOCTORS

Undress gown: *none specified*
Dress robe: a nasturtium cloth robe of the masters' pattern [m10], with the facings covered and the sleeve slits lined dark blue damask.
Hood: a nasturtium hood of the CNAA shape [a1], lined jade green, bound dark blue damask on all edges.
Hat: in full dress, a nasturtium panama bonnet with blue cords and tassels.

UNIVERSITY OF SURREY
1966

The University of Surrey was preceded by the Battersea Polytechnic Institute which was founded in 1891, and admitted its first students in 1894. In 1956 the Institute was among the first to become a College of Advanced Technology, and was renamed Battersea College of Technology. By the beginning of the nineteen-sixties the College had outgrown its building in Battersea and had decided to move to Guildford. The Robbins Report of 1963 had proposed that the Colleges of Advanced Technology, including Battersea, should expand and become degree-awarding universities. In 1965 the university-designate acquired a greenfield site in Guildford from Guildford Cathedral, Guildford Borough Council and the Onslow Village Trust. The following year the University of Surrey was established by Royal Charter, and by 1970 the move from Battersea to Guildford was complete.

Surrey was the first university to use brocade linings for its hoods. The brocade used is St Aidan. Initially, the only hoods with an extra border were the BMus and MMus, but faculty borders were later introduced for other degrees, leaving the BSc and MSc with the original unbordered hoods. The bachelors' hoods are of a modified simple shape – effectively the Oxford simple with the liripipe cut off – and all others use a version of the CNAA pattern. The degrees of BUniv, MUniv, and DUniv are honorary awards.

Faculty colours:

Arts: red.
Business Administration: gold.
Education: green.
Engineering: grey.
Laws: purple.
Medicine: burnt orange.
Music: white brocade.
Research: apricot.
Science: not bordered.
Theology: claret.

UNDERGRADUATES

none specified

UNDERGRADUATE CERTIFICATES AND DIPLOMAS

Gown: as for bachelors.
Hood: a black hood of the Surrey shape [s10], the cowl bordered 1″ mid-blue brocade inside, and ½″ white on the edge.
Hat: a black cloth square cap.

FOUNDATION DEGREES

Gown: as for bachelors.

Hood: a black hood of the Surrey shape [s10], the cowl bordered 1″ mid-blue brocade inside, and ½″ faculty colour in the edge. (For Science, the brocade is 1½″ wide.)

Hat: a black cloth square cap.

BACHELORS

Gown: a black stuff gown of London BA pattern [b4].

Hood: a black hood of the Surrey shape [s10], lined mid-blue brocade, bordered 1″ degree colour inside the cowl edge.

Hat: a black cloth square cap.

BACHELOR of the UNIVERSITY

Gown: as for masters.

Hood: a black hood of the Surrey shape [s10], lined mid-blue brocade, bordered 1″ gold satin inside the cowl.

Hat: a black cloth square cap.

POSTGRADUATE CERTIFICATES AND DIPLOMAS

Gown: as for masters.

Hood: a black hood of the CNAA shape [a1], lined mid-blue brocade, bordered 1″ white inside the cowl edge.

Hat: a black cloth square cap.

FIRST-DEGREE MASTERS

Gown: as for bachelors.

Hood: a black hood of the Surrey shape [s10], lined mid-blue brocade, bordered 2½″ degree colour inside the cowl edge.
MEng: grey.
MMath, MChem, MPhys, [MSci]: light blue.

Hat: a black cloth square cap.

MASTERS including MASTERS OF PHILOSOPHY

Gown: a black stuff gown of the basic pattern [m10].

Hood: a black hood of the CNAA shape [a1], lined mid-blue brocade, bordered 2½″ degree colour inside the cowl edge.
MRes: apricot.
MPhil: lined and the cape bound ½″ blue brocade; no faculty border.
MTeach: magenta.

Hat: a black cloth square cap.

MASTER of the UNIVERSITY

Gown: as for other masters.

Hood: as for other masters, but bordered 2½″ gold satin.

Hat: a black cloth square cap.

DOCTORS OF PHILOSOPHY and TAUGHT AND PROFESSIONAL DOCTORS

Undress gown: as for masters.

Dress robe: a cardinal red cloth robe of the same shape as the masters' gown, with blue brocade facings

Hood: a cardinal red hood of the CNAA shape [a1], lined blue brocade, bordered inside the cowl for 1″ with degree colour, set 1″ in:

PhD: no border.
DBA: gold.
DClinPrac: turquoise.
EngD: grey.
PsychD: light blue.
EdD: green.
MD: burnt orange.

Hat: in undress, a black cloth square cap; in full dress, a black cloth bonnet with red cords and tassels.

HIGHER DOCTORS

Undress gown: as PhD.

Dress robe: a cardinal red cloth robe of the Oxford pattern [d2], the facings and lower 8″ of the sleeves covered with blue brocade.

Hood: a cardinal red hood of the CNAA shape [a1], lined and bound 2″ blue brocade, and bordered inside the cowl for 1″ with degree colour, set 1″ in:

DLitt: red.
DSc: not bordered.

Hat: in undress, a black cloth square cap; in full dress, a black cloth bonnet with gold cords and tassels.

DOCTOR OF THE UNIVERSITY

Dress robe: as higher doctors.

Hood: a gold cloth hood of the CNAA shape [a1], lined blue brocade.

Hat: in full dress, a black velvet bonnet with gold cords and tassels.

NOTES

1. Until 1998, the PhD dress robe was the black masters' gown with blue brocade facings.

UNIVERSITY OF SUSSEX
1961

The University of Sussex began as an idea for the construction of a university to serve Brighton, and in December 1911 a public meeting was held to discover ways in which to fund the construction of a university, but the project was halted by the First World War. The idea was revived in the 1950s, and in June 1958, the government approved the corporation's scheme for a university at Brighton, the first of a new generation of universities which came to be known as 'plate glass universities'. The University was established as a company in 1959, with a Royal Charter granted in 1961.

The University rapidly gained a reputation for radicalism, and this is expressed in the style of its academic dress, universally execrated by all previous writers on the subject. As with many other universities of similar date (notably East Anglia) the robes were never intended for everyday wear, and thus incorporate a number of impractical features. The bachelors' hood was particularly famous, with its grey nylon fur arranged in squares. A number of names have been linked with the scheme, notably those of John Piper, who seems to have been responsible for the doctors' robes at least, and of W. N. Hargreaves-Mawdsley, a writer on academic dress, who is supposed to have made some unidentified contribution.

The bachelors' hoods were revised in 2004, and again in 2010. Also in 2010, the robes for DPhil, EdD and DSW were redesigned.

UNDERGRADUATES

No dress is currently specified, but originally they wore a black gown sleeveless gown of special pattern [u6]. It is not known when it fell into disuse. There was no hat.

UNDERGRADUATE CERTIFICATES AND DIPLOMAS and FOUNDATION DEGREES

Gown: the bachelors' gown.

Hood: a black alpaca hood of the Sussex shape [s8], the cowl bordered inside with 3″ scarlet satin. The reversing neckband is black lined black.

Hat: a black cloth square cap.

BACHELORS and FIRST-DEGREE MASTERS

Gown: a black stuff gown of basic pattern, but the back of the sleeve is shorter, and the sleeve-opening is sewn shut. There is a scalloped vertical slit for the arms at elbow level in the forearm seam. The yoke is semi-circular, and the gown is pleated into it in flat pleats [b12].

Hood:

until 2004: a black alpaca hood of the Sussex shape [s8], lined grey nylon fur arranged in 5″ squares so that ¼″ black shows between them. (As made, ¼″

black tape was sewn over a single piece of fur to give the effect.) The reversing neckband is black lined black.

2004-2010: a black alpaca hood of the Sussex shape [s8], the cowl bordered inside with 6″ of the school colour. The reversing neckband is black lined black.

Humanities: orange.

Life Sciences: emerald green.

Science and Technology: purple.

Sussex Institute: cerise.

Social Sciences and Cultural Studies: buttercup yellow.

Science and Policy Research Unit: bright red.

Validated degrees: grey nylon fur in squares (the original bachelors' hood).

since 2010: a black alpaca hood of the Sussex shape [s8], lined scarlet satin. The reversing neckband is black lined black.

Hat: a black cloth square cap.

POSTGRADUATE CERTIFICATES AND DIPLOMAS

Gown: the bachelors' gown.

Hood: a black alpaca hood of the Sussex shape [s8], the cowl bordered inside with 3″dove grey silk. The reversing neckband is black lined black.

Hat: a black cloth square cap.

MASTERS including MASTERS OF PHILOSOPHY

Gown: a black stuff gown of Sussex pattern. The yoke is in the form of a double bracket, and the facings are of black grosgrain.

Hood: a black alpaca hood of the Sussex shape [s8], lined dove grey silk. The reversing neckband is black lined black.

MPhil: there is also a 1″ band of scarlet set ¼″ in on the opposite side from the cowl edge.

Hat: a black cloth square cap.

MASTERS OF THE UNIVERSITY

Gown: the doctors' robe in black, with a red collar which continues down to form lapels.

Hood: a black hood of the Cambridge shape [f1], lined red.

Hat: a black velvet bonnet, with gold cords and tassels.

MASTERS honoris causa

Gown: the doctors' robe in gamboge, but without the shoulder ribbon.

Hood: a gamboge hood of the Cambridge shape [f1], lined gamboge.

Hat: a black velvet bonnet, with gold cords and tassels.

DOCTORS OF PHILOSOPHY and TAUGHT AND PROFESSIONAL DOCTORS

until 2010:

Undress gown: as for masters, but the lower edge of the sleeve is scalloped, and there is a single row of braid on each shoulder.

Dress robe: a deep royal blue robe of the same pattern as the undress gown, but with a stand-up collar. On the right shoulder is a wide ribbon, hanging down before and behind, and held by a button of the same colour:

PhD: scarlet.

EdD: grey.

Hood: a royal blue hood of the Cambridge shape [f1], lined as follows:

PhD: scarlet.

EdD: grey.

Hat: in undress, a black square cloth cap; in full dress, a black velvet pileus with a royal blue button.

since 2010:

Undress gown: *none specified*

Dress robe: a scarlet panama robe of the Cambridge pattern [d1], with a scalloped yoke as for masters, with royal blue silk facings and sleeve linings. The sleeves are held by scarlet cords and buttons.

Hood: a scarlet panama hood of the Sussex shape [s8], lined with royal blue silk. The reversing neckband is scarlet lined scarlet.

Hat: in full dress, a black velvet bonnet with scarlet cords and tassels.

HIGHER DOCTORS

Undress gown: as PhD, but with two rows of braid on each shoulder.

Dress robe: a gamboge robe of the same pattern as the PhD. The shoulder ribbons are coloured as follows:

LL.D: red.

DLitt: blue.

DMus: oyster white.

DSc: green.

Hood: a gamboge hood of the Cambridge shape [f1], lined as follows:

LL.D: red.

DLitt: blue.

DMus: oyster white.

DSc: green.

Hat:

if earned: a black cloth square cap.

if honorary: a black velvet pileus with a gamboge button.

DOCTORS OF THE UNIVERSITY

Dress robe: the doctors' robe in red. The collar is blue, which continues down to form lapels.

Hood: a red hood of the Cambridge shape [f1], lined blue.

Hat: in full dress, a black velvet bonnet, with gold cords and tassels.

JOINT MASTER'S DEGREE WITH BRIGHTON

Gown: as for masters.

Hood: a black alpaca hood of the Sussex shape [s8], lined dove grey silk, and bordered gold and red.

Hat: a black cloth square cap.

BRIGHTON-SUSSEX MEDICAL SCHOOL

see separate entry.

NOTES

1. In the 1966 first edition, Shaw said that the bachelors' and masters' hoods had a binding of school colour, and that the gowns had a piece of cord at the top of each sleeve, also of school colour, although it appears that this never happened. The school colours he listed, for the sake of comparison with those given above, were:
   English and American Studies: white.
   Social Studies: muscat green.
   European Studies: old rose.
   African and Asian Studies: eggshell blue.
   Education and Social Work: chartreuse yellow.
   Physical sciences: amethyst.
   Biological Sciences: marina green.
   Applied Sciences: lilac.

SWANSEA METROPOLITAN UNIVERSITY
2008

Swansea Metropolitan University was formed in 1976 from three separate colleges in the town: Swansea College of Art (f 1853), Swansea College of Education (f 1872), and Swansea Technical College (f 1897). They united in 1976 to form the West Glamorgan Institute of Higher Education, which was renamed Swansea Institute of Higher Education in 1992. In 2008, it was permitted to assume its current title. It awards degrees of the University of Wales, and thus uses those robes.

Late in 2010, a merger with the University of Wales Trinity St David was announced.

SWANSEA UNIVERSITY
1920/2005

The College was founded in 1920 as University College, Swansea, and at once became a constituent college of the University of Wales. In 2005, it was granted its own degree awarding powers, and has been exercising them since then; Wales degrees are gradually being phased out.

UNDERGRADUATES
none specified

DipHE (see Note)
Gown: as for bachelors.
Hood: none.
Hat: a black cloth square cap.

FOUNDATION DEGREES
not awarded

BACHELORS and GRADUATE DIPLOMA IN LAW (GDL)
Gown: a black stuff gown of the Wales pattern [b6].
Hood: a black hood of the Oxford simple shape [s1], lined maroon, the cowl bordered inside 1″ silver. The neckband is faced maroon, bound silver.
Hat: a black cloth square cap.

POSTGRADUATE CERTIFICATES and DIPLOMAS
Gown: as for masters.
Hood: a black hood of the London shape [f3], the cowl bordered inside 6″ maroon, with 1″ silver on the edge. The neckband is faced maroon, bound silver.
Hat: a black cloth square cap.

FIRST-DEGREE MASTERS
Gown: as for bachelors.
Hood: a black hood of the Oxford simple shape [s1], lined maroon, the cowl bordered inside 1″ silver and 1″ black. The neckband is faced maroon, bound silver.
Hat: a black cloth square cap.

MASTERS
Gown: a black stuff gown of the basic pattern [m10].
Hood: a black hood of the London shape [f1], lined maroon, and the cowl bordered inside 1″ silver. The neckband is faced maroon, bound silver.

Hat: a black cloth square cap.

MASTERS OF PHILOSOPHY and of RESEARCH

Gown: as for masters, but with facings of maroon, 1″ silver on the outer edge.

Hood: a black hood of the London shape [f3], lined maroon, and bound on all edges 1″ silver.

Hat: a black cloth square cap.

DOCTORS OF PHILOSOPHY and TAUGHT and PROFESSIONAL DOCTORS

Undress gown: *none specified*

Dress robe: a maroon robe of the Cambridge pattern [d1], facings and sleeve linings of silver. The facings and sleeves have 1″ black on their outer edges, and the sleeves are held with a silver cord and button.

Hood: a maroon hood of the London shape [f3], lined silver, bound on all edges ½″ black.

Hat: in full dress, a black velvet bonnet with silver cords and tassels.

HIGHER DOCTORS

Undress gown: *none specified*

Dress robe: a scarlet robe of the Cambridge pattern [d1], facings and sleeve linings of silver. The facings and sleeve have 1″ black on their outer edges, and the sleeves are held with a silver cord and button.

Hood: a scarlet hood of the London shape [f3], lined silver, bound on all edges ½″ black.

Hat: in full dress, a black velvet bonnet with silver cords and tassels.

NOTES

1. Between 2005 and 2009 the following robes were used for sub-degree awards:
   Gown: as for bachelors.
   Hood: a black hood of the Oxford simple shape [s1]:
   Certificates: the cowl bordered 3″ blue, the neckband faced blue and bound white.
   Diplomas: the cowl bordered 3″ blue and ½″ white, the neckband faced blue and bound white.

Hat: a black cloth square cap.

UNIVERSITY OF TEESSIDE
1992

The Middlesbrough-based Mechanics' Institute was opened in 1844, and succeeded by Constantine Technical College, opened in 1930. Constantine was both a further and a higher education college. The College briefly restyled itself as Constantine College of Technology, before becoming Teesside Polytechnic in 1969. It gained university status in 1992.

Only one hood is used at Teesside. This is black and of CNAA shape [a1], lined and bound bright red, the cowl bordered inside 1″ grey. The difference in degree is marked by the gowns.

UNDERGRADUATE CERTIFICATES and DIPLOMAS
Gown: as for bachelors, but in grey.
Hood: the University hood.
Hat: a black cloth square cap.

FOUNDATION DEGREES
Gown:
Hood: the University hood.
Hat: a black cloth square cap.

BACHELORS
Gown: a black stuff gown of basic pattern [b1].
Hood: the University hood.
Hat: a black cloth square cap.

POSTGRADUATE CERTIFICATES and DIPLOMAS
Gown: a black stuff gown of basic bachelor's pattern [b1].
Hood: the University hood.
Hat: a black cloth square cap.

MASTERS including MASTERS OF PHILOSOPHY
Gown: a red stuff gown of Cambridge MA pattern [m2], but with a narrower boot.
Hood: the University hood.
Hat: a black cloth square cap.

DOCTORS OF PHILOSOPHY and TAUGHT and PROFESSIONAL DOCTORS
Undress gown: *none specified*

Dress robe: a red robe of the Cambridge pattern [d1], with grey facings and sleeve linings, edged black.
Hood: the University hood.
Hat: in full dress, a black cloth bonnet, with red cords and tassels.

HIGHER DOCTORS

Undress gown: *none specified*
Dress robe: as for PhD.
Hood: the University hood, but with silver lace on all edges.
Hat: a black velvet bonnet, with red cords and tassels.

THAMES VALLEY UNIVERSITY

see University of West London

UNIVERSITY OF ULSTER
1984

The University of Ulster is a multi-centre university and is the largest single university in Ireland, discounting the federal National University of Ireland. The University was created in 1984 by the merger of the New University of Ulster (founded 1968, at Coleraine) and Ulster Polytechnic (founded 1971, at Jordanstown).

The system used is very simple and was designed by Charles Franklyn. All hoods are fully lined 'University green', which is a mid-dark shade. This is put inside a black shell for bachelors, a burgundy one for masters, and a scarlet one for doctors. They are then further bound with faculty colour. The robes are basically those used by the New University of Ulster (see Note 1).

UNDERGRADUATES
none specified

UNDERGRADUATE CERTIFICATES and DIPLOMAS and ASSOCIATE BACHELORS
Gown: as for bachelors.
Hood: black hood of the Cambridge shape [f1], lined university green, bound ¾″ on all edges apple green.
Hat: a black cloth square cap.

FOUNDATION DEGREES (FdA, FdSc, FdEng)
as for the corresponding bachelor's degree

BACHELORS
Gown: a black stuff gown of basic pattern [b1].
Hood: black hood of the Cambridge shape [f1], lined university green, bound ¾″ on all edges as follows:
BA: royal blue.
BDes: cherry.
BEng: rose tyrien.
BEd: cobalt violet
LL.B: pale burgundy.
BLitt: light blue.
BMus: white.
BPhil: gold.
BSc: Shannon green.
BTech: chestnut.
Hat: a black cloth square cap.

POSTGRADUATE CERTIFICATES and DIPLOMAS

Gown: as for bachelors.

Hood: black hood of the Cambridge shape [f1], lined university green, bound ¾″ on all edges apple green.

Hat: a black cloth square cap.

MASTERS including MASTERS OF PHILOSOPHY and FIRST-DEGREE MASTERS

Gown: a black stuff gown of Oxford MA pattern [m1].

Hood: burgundy silk hood of the Cambridge shape, lined university green, bound ¾″ on all edges as follows:

MA: royal blue.
MBA and MPA: spectrum yellow.
MBS: pale grey.
MDes: cherry.
MEd: cobalt violet.
MEng: scarlet.
MFA: mint green.
LL.M: pale burgundy.
MMedSc: lime green.
MRes and MClinRes: pale gold.
MPhil: gold.
MSc: Shannon green.
MUniv: bright blue.

Hat: a black cloth square cap.

ALL DOCTORS

Undress gown: as for masters.

Dress robe: scarlet cloth of the Oxford pattern [d2], facings of scarlet silk.

Hood: burgundy silk of the Cambridge shape, lined university green, bound ¾″ on all edges as follows:

DPhil: gold.
Professional Doctors: gold.
DLitt: royal blue.
DSc: Shannon green.
DUniv: bright blue.

Hat: in undress, a black square cap; in full dress, a black cloth bonnet, with gold cords and tassels.

NOTES

1. As the New University of Ulster, 1968-84, the hoods were bound on the cape only.
2. The former CertEd wore a bachelor's gown, with the yoke covered in turquoise silk.

VICTORIA UNIVERSITY (1880-1903); VICTORIA UNIVERSITY OF MANCHESTER (1903-2004).

The Victoria University was a federal university. It consisted of colleges in Manchester, Leeds, and Liverpool. Owens College, Manchester, (named after John Owens, a textile merchant) was founded in 1851, and prepared its students for the degrees of London. It moved to its current location in 1873, and was granted a Royal Charter in 1880, becoming the first institution of the federal Victoria University. In 1884, University College Liverpool joined the University, followed in 1887 by Yorkshire College in Leeds.

In 1903, University College, Liverpool, left the Victoria University to become independent, chartered as the University of Liverpool; Leeds followed in 1904. The remaining Manchester site was renamed the Victoria University of Manchester, but was commonly known as the University of Manchester. Manchester retained the robes of the Victoria University.

In March 2003 it was announced that the University was to merge with UMIST. The new institution is simply called The University of Manchester. In legal terms both the Victoria University of Manchester and UMIST ceased to exist when the University of Manchester came into existence on 1 October 2004.

UNDERGRADUATES

Gown: a black stuff gown of knee length, with false sleeves, pressed into permanent accordion pleats. (This gown was in use *c.*1902 to 1919, since when there has been no prescribed gown.)

Hat: a black cloth square cap.

UNDERGRADUATE CERTIFICATES and DIPLOMAS

none specified

FOUNDATION DEGREES

not awarded

BACHELORS

Gown:

BArch, BD, BDS, BLD, BLing, MB,ChB, BPl, BTCP: as for masters.

All others: a black stuff gown of Cambridge BA pattern [b2].

Hood: a black silk hood of the Manchester simple shape [s9]. The following hoods are bound 1″ silk on all edges, with 1″ fur next to the silk binding on the inside:

BA: pale blue.

BA(Th), BA(RelSt): 'heliotrope' (mauve).
BA(Com), BA(Econ), BA(Adm): orange.
BA(Accg & Law): violet.
BA (*under the Board of Part-time Studies, 1988-1999*): silver.
BA(Ed): pale blue, and 1″ of blue-green inside the fur.
BDS: fawn.
BEd: blue-green.
BNurs: red.
BSc: salmon pink.
BSc(Ed): salmon pink, and 1″ of blue-green inside the fur.
BSc(Tech): terra-cotta.
BSc (*under the Board of Part-time Studies, 1988-1999*): silver.
BSocSc: orange.

The following hoods are bound 1″ silk, without fur:
BMedSc: red.
BMedSc(Dent): fawn.

The following hoods are bordered silk 2″ inside and ¼″ outside, without fur:
LL.B: violet.
MB, ChB: red.
BArch, BLD, BLing, BTP, BTCP: pale blue.

The following hood is lined fully, with a 1″ border of fur set 1″ in:
BD, BTh: heliotrope.

The following hood is of dark blue silk, bound 2″ inside and out:
MusB: pale blue.

Hat: a black cloth square cap.

POSTGRADUATE CERTIFICATES and DIPLOMAS

none specified

FIRST-DEGREE MASTERS

Gown: as for other masters.

Hood: black silk hood of the Manchester simple shape [s9], bordered silk 2″ inside and ¼″ outside:
MEng(Sc): salmon pink.
MEng(Tech): terra-cotta silk.
MTP: fully lined pale blue, a 1″ border of fur set 1″ in.

Hat: a black cloth square cap.

MASTERS including MASTERS OF PHILOSOPHY

Gown: a black stuff gown of Manchester pattern [m6].

Hood: black silk hood of the Manchester shape [s9], lined and bound ¼″ as follows (those marked * were used for the MPhil in the relevant faculties):
*MA: pale blue.
MA(Econ), MA(Com): orange.

MA(Ed): blue green, and bordered inside 2″ pale blue.
*MA(Theol): heliotrope.
MA (*under the Board of Part-time Studies, 1988-1999*): silver.
MArch: pale blue.
*MBA, MBSc: gold.
ChM: red.
MDS: fawn.
*MEd: blue green.
MLing: pale blue.
*LL.M, MJur: violet.
*MMus: dark blue.
MMus(Perf): dark blue, bordered inside 1″ gold.
*MSc: salmon pink.
MSc(Ed): blue green, and bordered inside 2″ salmon pink.
*MSc(Med), MHSc, MRes: red, and bordered inside 2″ salmon pink.
MSc(Tech): terra-cotta.
MSc (*under the Board of Part-time Studies, 1988-1999*): silver.
MTCP: pale blue.
MLD: pale blue.

Hat: a black cloth square cap.

ALL DOCTORS

Undress gown: as for masters

Dress robe: a scarlet cloth robe of the masters' pattern [m6]. The facings and the sleeves below the armhole are covered with pale gold silk.

Hood: a gold velvet hood of the Manchester shape [s9], lined and bound ½″ pale gold silk.

Hat: in undress, a black square cap; in full dress, a black velvet bonnet, with a black silk ribbon.

NOTES

1. At one point, the BA(Accg & Law) wore a black hood, lined violet, and bound orange.
2. From 1880 until 1901, the BA and BSc hoods had no fur border, but merely a 1″ binding of faculty colour. This makes sense of the higher bachelors (LL.B, MB) having a 2″ border, although they never gained fur.

THE UNIVERSITY OF WALES
1893

The University of Wales was composed of colleges in various locations, and was intended to be the sole national university for Wales. Aberystwyth (1872), Cardiff (1883) and Bangor (1884) were the original colleges; they were joined by Swansea in 1921, the School of Medicine in 1931, UWIST in 1967, and Lampeter in 1971. Recent additions have been Newport; Trinity College, Carmarthen; the North-East Wales Institute at Wrexham (NEWI, now Glyndŵr University, *q.v.*); and Swansea Metropolitan University (until 2008, Swansea Institute of Higher Education). The Royal Welsh College of Music and Drama awarded Wales degrees until 2007, since when it has awarded those of Glamorgan. The University also validates degrees for a large number of institutions world-wide.

Cardiff and UWIST merged in 1988, and in 2004 formed, with the College of Medicine, Cardiff University *(q.v.)*, with its own degree-awarding powers. In 2007, the colleges at Aberystwyth, Swansea, and Bangor gained degree-awarding powers (see separate entries), and adopted the title 'University' (in the form Aberystwyth University, *etc*), and now award their own degrees. In 2010 Lampeter and Trinity Carmarthen united as the University of Wales Trinity St David, which will continue to award Wales degrees.

Late in 2011, the University of Wales underwent a number of major alterations, ultimately resulting in the demise of the federal University. The entries for it in this book, and for those institutions which awarded Wales degrees, reflect matters as they stood early in 2011, at the time of compilation. Future editions will incorporate any changes made.

The University's academic dress is noted for the use of shot silks for its faculty colours, which give a very beautiful effect inside the black, scarlet, and crimson hoods. The use of shot silks has been traced back to a suggestion of Lady Verney, as all the 'ordinary colours' had been taken by existing universities. Closely related degrees are differenced with bindings. Unfortunately, the choice of colours for these bindings seems to have been random, and so they are less intelligible than they might be. However, as more colleges attain university status in their own right, some of the faculties and their silks are becoming obsolescent; principal among these is the Faculty of Music.

FACULTY SILKS

(degrees in [square brackets] are no longer awarded)

Arts and Letters: mazarin blue shot green (BA, MA, MPhil, PhD, DLitt).
Architecture: scarlet shot red (BArch, MArch, MPhil, PhD).
Business Administration: red shot yellow, bound pale blue (MBA, DBA).
Dentistry: saxe blue shot white, bound purple (BDS, [MChD], MScD, MPhil, PhD, [DChD], DScD).
Divinity: mazarin blue shot red (BD, MTh, MPhil, PhD, DD).
mazarin blue shot red, bound white (BTh, MMin, DMin).

Economic and Social Studies: red shot yellow (BScEcon, MScEcon, MPhil, PhD, DScEcon).
Education: green shot white (BEd, MEd, MPhil, EdD, PhD).
Engineering: red shot green (BEng, MEng, MPhil, EngD, PhD, DEng).
Laws: purple shot red (LL.B, LL.M, MPhil, PhD, LL.D).
Librarianship: mazarin blue shot green, bound white ([BLib], [MLib]).
Medicine: green shot black, bound white (MB,BCh, MCh, MPhil, PhD, MD).
Medical Science: bronze colour, bound green shot black (BMedSc).
Nursing: green shot white, bound red (BN, BMid, MN, MPhil, DNursSci, PhD).
Music: pearl colour (a shot silk of yellow, orange and pale blue), (BMus, MMus, MPhil, PhD, DMus).
Pharmacy: saxe blue shot white (BPharm, MPharm).
Philosophy: as for the faculty in which the degree was registered. (MPhil, PhD).
Repro: green shot black, bound dark blue (MScRepro).
Sciences: bronze colour (yellow shot black) (BSc, MSc, MPhil, PhD, DSc).
Public Health: green shot black, bound emerald green (MPH).
[Technology: bronze colour, bound white (BScTech); red shot green, bound white (BEngTech).]

Other degrees

BSD (Bachelor of Science in Dentistry): bordered 3″ saxe blue shot white, and bound ½″ purple on the cowl edge.
BScMidwifery: bordered 3″ green shot black, and bound ½″ light blue on the cowl edge.
MMath, MESc, MChem, MPhys: the BSc gown with the MSc hood.
EMBS (European Master of Business Studies): same as MBA.
MBL (Master of Business and Law): lined red shot yellow, and bound red.
MFA (Master of Fine Art): same as MA.
MRes: as the relevant taught master's hood.
DBMS (Doctor of Biomedical Science): *t.b.c.*
DBA: crimson, lined red shot yellow, and bound pale blue.
DClinPsy, DCompSci, DCounsPsy, DInfoSys, DEdPsy: same as PhD in Science.
EdD: same as PhD in Education.
EngD: same as PhD in Engineering.
DNursSci: same as PhD in Nursing.
DSW: same as PhD in Economic and Social Studies.
DTourism: *t.b.c.*

UNDERGRADUATES

Gown: a black gown of the Oxford scholars' pattern [u2].
Hat: a black cloth square cap.

FOUNDATION DEGREES and certain DIPLOMAS and CERTIFICATES

(Postgraduate Diplomas and Certificates; Diplomas and Certificates of Higher Education; Postgraduate Certificate in Education; Postgraduate Certificate in Higher Education)

Gown: as for bachelors.

Hood: black stuff, of the Wales simple shape [s5], bordered inside 3″ black, and bound on the cowl edge with triple twisted cord of dark blue, crimson, and gold.

Hat: a black cloth square cap.

Holders of all other diplomas and certificates wear the bachelors' gown and square cap.

BACHELORS

Gown: a black stuff or silk gown of the pattern [b6]: *i.e.* an Oxford BA gown with the forearm sleeve slit for 4″ from the wrist; the two flaps are turned back, and secured by black buttons. There is a third button on the mid-seam, level with them, from which a ½″ black silk ribbon runs to the upper end of the slit. The effect is a tri-form fold intended to emulate the Prince of Wales feathers.

A *first variant* has black velvet ribbon and buttons, and black velvet ribbon along the edges of the turned-back flaps.

A *second variant* is the same as the first variant, but with black twisted cords instead of velvet ribbon.

There is no significance attached to these variants, beyond the whim of robe makers.

Hood: a black stuff or silk hood in the Wales simple shape [s5]: *i.e.* the Oxford simple shape with the end of the cowl rounded off. The neckband is cut to reverse and shews the lining when worn. Hoods are bordered inside for 3 or 4 inches faculty silk, which is brought over the edge for ¼ inch. Separate bindings are ½″ wide on either side, and are placed on the cowl edge only, continuing along the neckband.

BMus: the shell is of dark blue silk.

MB,BCh and BDS: the hoods are fully lined, and the white or purple binding is placed on both edges.

Hat: a black cloth square cap.

FIRST-DEGREE MASTERS

Gown: as for bachelors.

Hood: as for masters in the same faculty.

Hat: a black cloth square cap.

MASTERS

Gown: a black stuff or silk gown of the Wales pattern [m4]: *i.e.* an Oxford MA gown, but the lower point of the boot is removed to form a right angle; it has an inverted-T armhole.

Hood: a black silk hood (dark blue for MMus) of Cambridge shape [f1], but with a reversed neckband. The hoods are lined faculty silk, which is brought out for ¼″ on all edges. Separate bindings are ½″ wide on either side, and are placed on all edges.

MMus: the shell is of dark blue silk.

MRes: the master's hood appropriate to the faculty (MA, MSc, etc).

Hat: a black cloth square cap.

MASTERS OF PHILOSOPHY

Gown: as for other masters.

Hood: the relevant master's hood (MA, MSc, etc), bound on all edges for 1″ on each side crimson silk. If the MPhil is awarded in a faculty for which the hood is already bound – *e.g.*, Medicine –the original binding is omitted:

MPhil in Medicine: lined green shot black, bound crimson.

MPhil in Dentistry: lined saxe blue shot, bound crimson (same as MPhil in Pharmacy).

MPhil in Nursing: lined green shot white, bound crimson (same as MPhil in Education).

Hat: a black cloth square cap.

DOCTORS OF PHILOSOPHY and PROFESSIONAL DOCTORS

Undress: the master's gown.

Full dress: a crimson cloth robe of the Cambridge doctor's [d1] pattern (see Note 1). It has facings and sleeve-linings to match the lining of the hood. Where the hood has a separate binding, this is applied also to the outer edge of the facings of the robe, and also round the edge of the sleeves.

Hood: a crimson cloth hood of the Cambridge shape [f1], but with a reversed neckband, and lined and bound for ¼″ on all edges with faculty silk. Separate bindings are ½″ wide on either side, and are placed on all edges.

Hat: a black velvet square cap.

HIGHER DOCTORS

Undress: the master's gown.

Full dress: a scarlet cloth robe of the Cambridge doctor's [d1] pattern, with facings and sleeve-linings to match the lining of the hood. Where the hood has a separate binding, it is applied also to the outer edge of the facings of the robe.

Hood: a scarlet cloth hood of the Cambridge shape [f1], but with a reversed neckband, lined and bound for ¼″ on all edges with faculty silk. Separate bindings are ½″ wide on either side, on all edges.

Hat: in undress, a black square cap; in full dress, a black velvet square cap.

DOCTOR OF THE UNIVERSITY

Gown: the master's black gown; there is no full-dress robe.

Hood: a scarlet cloth hood of the same shape as other doctors, lined navy blue silk, and bound on all edges with a triple twisted cord of dark blue, crimson, and gold.

Hat: a black velvet square cap.

NOTES:

1. The published regulations imply that the PhD alone wears a crimson robe and hood, but this is because they have not been updated since the introduction of the EdD, *etc.*
2. The PhD and DLitt were originally regarded as the same degree, and both wore the scarlet robes with the Arts lining, until 1921, when the PhD was given its crimson robes.
3. The MMus had a black shell until 1918. It may then have gained the blue one by being aligned with the BMus.
4. The BMus may have been fully lined originally.
5. The Laws silk is specified as red shot purple, but what is used (and has been for many years) is magenta shot blue.
6. Degrees in Economics and Social Studies (BScEcon, *etc*) were originally designated 'Economic and Social Sciences', hence the form of the degree abbreviation.
7. Professional doctors are currently wearing the robes of the equivalent PhD, but a special robe and hood for them is under consideration.
8. The Science silk is called 'bronze', and is yellow shot black. This is different from the bronze shot silk of Liverpool Laws, which is red shot green.

THE UNIVERSITY OF WALES: TRINITY SAINT DAVID
2010

This institution was formed in 2010 by a merger of St David's College, Lampeter (the University of Wales Lampeter) and Trinity University College, Carmarthen. Although both colleges have degree-awarding powers, those of Lampeter have been in abeyance since 1971, and those of Trinity (granted 2007) have never been exercised. For the time being, this new university will continue to award University of Wales degrees.

UNIVERSITY OF WARWICK
1964

The idea for a university in Coventry was mooted shortly after the conclusion of the Second World War. A partnership of the City and the County Councils brought the University into being on a 400-acre site jointly granted by the two authorities. There was some discussion between local sponsors over whether it should be named after Coventry or Warwickshire. The name 'University of Warwick' was adopted, even though the county town of Warwick itself lies some 8 miles to the southwest and Coventry city centre lies only 3½ miles northeast of the campus. The establishment of the University of Warwick was given approval by the government in 1961 and received its Royal Charter of Incorporation in 1965.

The scheme of academic dress is simple, and based on a faculty colour system:

Arts and Letters: cerise.
Education: mid-green.
Engineering : navy blue.
Laws: purple.
Medicine and Surgery: scarlet.
Philosophy: red shot green.
Science: mid-blue.

UNDERGRADUATES
none specified

UNDERGRADUATE CERTIFICATES and DIPLOMAS
none specified

FOUNDATION DEGREES
Gown: as for bachelors.
Hood: a black hood of the Burgon shape [s2], lined and bound on the cowl edge white silk.
Hat: a black cloth square cap.

BACHELORS
Gown: a black stuff gown of basic pattern [b1].
Hood: a black hood of the Burgon shape [s2], lined and bound on the cowl edge in faculty colour.
BEng: lined light blue.
BMedSci: lined scarlet, bound mid-blue.
BPhil(Ed): lined light green.
Hat: a black cloth square cap.

POSTGRADUATE CERTIFICATES and DIPLOMAS
none specified

FIRST-DEGREE MASTERS (MChem, MMath, MMathPhys, MMathStat, MMORSE, MPhys)

Gown: as for other masters.
Hood: a black hood of the Burgon shape [s2], lined and bound on the cowl edge:
MEng: navy blue.
All others: royal blue.
Hat: a black cloth square cap.

MASTERS including MASTERS OF PHILOSOPHY

Gown: a black stuff gown of Warwick pattern [m15].
Hood: a black hood of the CNAA shape [a1], lined and bound on all edges in faculty colour.
MBA: lined and bound gold.
MClinSci: scarlet (*i.e.*, same as MS).
MMedEd: scarlet (*i.e.*, same as MS).
MMedSci: lined scarlet, bound blue.
MPA: lined and bound lilac.
MPH: lined and bound scarlet (*i.e.*, same as MS).
MRes: lined and bound peacock blue.
MTL: mid-green (*i.e.*, same as MEd).
Hat: a black cloth square cap.

DOCTORS OF PHILOSOPHY and TAUGHT and PROFESSIONAL DOCTORS (MD, EngD, EdD)

Undress gown: as for masters.
Dress robe: a black gown as for masters, with facings of faculty colour.
Hood: a crimson hood of the CNAA shape [a1], lined and bound on all edges for 2″ in faculty colour.
Hat: in undress, a black square cap; in full dress, a black cloth bonnet, with cords and tassels coloured as follows:
PhD: mixed green and red;
EngD: navy blue;
EdD: green;
MD: scarlet.

HIGHER DOCTORS

Undress gown: as PhD.
Dress robe: a red cloth robe of the Oxford pattern [d2], facings and 5″ cuffs of faculty colour.
Hood: a red hood of the CNAA shape [a1], lined and bound on all edges for 2″ in faculty colour.

Hat: in undress, a black square cap; in full dress,a black cloth bonnet, with gold cords and tassels.

DOCTOR OF CLINICAL PSYCHOLOGY (DClinPsych – joint degree with Coventry University)

Undress gown: *none specified*

Dress robe: a black gown of Cambridge doctor's shape [d1], 3″ silk facings (1½″ scarlet on the inner edge and 1½″ royal blue on the outer edge), the sleeves lined royal blue silk, bordered inside 2″ scarlet silk and gathered at the elbows with dark blue cord and buttons.

Hood: a scarlet hood of the CNAA shape [a1], lined royal blue.

Hat: a black bonnet, with scarlet and blue cords and tassels.

OBSOLETE DEGREES AND HOODS

MHist (awarded 1989-98): hood lined and bound dull red.

MEng: from its inception in 1985 until 1997, the hood was made in CNAA shape [a1], and lined and bound navy blue.

UNIVERSITY OF WEST LONDON
1992

The university was based on campuses in Slough, Reading, and Ealing. It traces its roots back to 1860, when the Lady Byron School was founded at what is now the Ealing campus; it later became Ealing College of Higher Education. The Slough campus was founded in 1907 as an elementary school. By the 1940s, it had become a technical institute, and in the 1970s it became Thames Valley College of Higher Education. In 1990, it joined with Ealing College of Higher Education, Queen Charlotte's College of Health Care Studies, and the London College of Music to become the Polytechnic of West London. Two years later, the polytechnic became a university and adopted the name Thames Valley University. In 2004, the university merged with Reading College and School of Arts and Design, whose premises became TVU's Reading campus. In 2011, the Reading campus was transferred to a new partnership, and the Slough campus was closed: to reflect the university's resulting geographical focus, the name University of West London was adopted. The university focuses entirely on vocational courses and the needs of industry, offering qualifications in business, computing, forensic science, health, hospitality, law, media, psychology, and technology, as well as in music, art, and design.

The University's robes feature its colours of purple and gold. The gold is a very vivid shade – nearer saffron than gold.

UNDERGRADUATES
none specified

UNDERGRADUATE CERTIFICATES, DIPLOMAS, and FOUNDATION DEGREES
Gown: as for bachelors.
Hood: a black hood of the CNAA shape [a1], lined purple, tipped gold.
Hat: a black cloth square cap.

BACHELORS
Gown: a black stuff gown of basic pattern [b1].
Hood: a purple hood of the Cambridge shape [f1], the cowl bordered inside 4″ gold.
Hat: a black cloth square cap.

POSTGRADUATE CERTIFICATES and DIPLOMAS
Gown: as for masters.
Hood: a black hood of the Cambridge shape [f1], lined purple, with a gold neckband.
Hat: a black cloth square cap.

FIRST-DEGREE MASTERS

not awarded

MASTERS including MASTERS OF PHILOSOPHY

Gown: a black stuff gown of basic pattern [m10]; MPhil gown has gold facings.

Hood: a purple hood of the Cambridge shape [f1], lined gold.

Hat: a black cloth square cap.

DOCTORS OF PHILOSOPHY and TAUGHT and PROFESSIONAL DOCTORS

Undress gown: as for masters.

Dress robe: a purple robe of the Cambridge pattern [d1], facings and sleeve linings of gold.

Hood: a purple hood of the Cambridge shape [f1], lined gold.

Hat: in undress, a black square cap; in full dress, a black cloth bonnet, with purple cords and tassels.

HIGHER DOCTORS

Undress gown: as PhD.

Dress robe: as for PhD, but with a gold cord and button on the yoke and each sleeve.

Hood: a purple hood of the Cambridge shape [f1], lined and bound 1½″ gold.

Hat: in undress, a black square cap; in full dress, a black cloth bonnet, with gold cords and tassels.

NOTES

1. The London College of Music, which is part of the University, awards diplomas under its own name. The robes for these are:

   Gown: a black gown of London BA pattern [b4], the sleeves gathered by three light blue cords without buttons.

   Hood:

   FLCM: a black hood of the Cambridge shape [f1], lined light blue, and bordered inside the cowl 3″ lemon yellow.

   LLCM: as FLCM, without the lemon border.

   ALCM: no hood.

   Hat: a black cloth square cap, with light blue tassel.

UNIVERSITY OF THE WEST OF ENGLAND, BRISTOL
1992

The roots of UWE are held to go back to the foundation of the Merchant Venturers' Navigation School in 1595. Part of this institution (to which the Universities of Bristol and Bath also partly owe their origins) became a technical college which, after merger with various other colleges, became Bristol Polytechnic in 1970. The Polytechnic gained university status in 1992.

The robes feature a maroon-red 'cloister' pattern brocade lining to the hoods.

UNDERGRADUATES
none specified

UNDERGRADUATE CERTIFICATES and DIPLOMAS
Gown: as for bachelors.
Hood: a black hood of the CNAA shape [a1], lined black, tipped red taffeta.
Hat: a black cloth square cap.

BACHELORS
Gown: a black stuff gown of London BA pattern [b4].
Hood: a black hood of the CNAA shape [a1], lined red brocade.
Hat: a black cloth square cap.

POSTGRADUATE CERTIFICATES and DIPLOMAS
Gown: a black stuff gown of London BA pattern [b4].
Hood: a black hood of the CNAA shape [a1], lined and bound red brocade.
Hat: a black cloth square cap.

MASTERS including MASTERS OF PHILOSOPHY
Gown: a black stuff gown of basic pattern [m10], with red brocade facings.
Hood: a red hood of the CNAA shape [a1], lined red brocade.
Hat: a black cloth square cap.

DOCTORS OF PHILOSOPHY and TAUGHT AND PROFESSIONAL DOCTORS
Undress gown: as for masters.
Dress robe: a red robe of the Cambridge pattern [d1], with grey facings and sleeve linings.
Hood: a red hood of the CNAA shape [a1], lined grey silk.
Hat: in undress, a black cloth square cap; in full dress, a black cloth bonnet, with red cords and tassels.

HIGHER DOCTORS

Undress gown: as PhD.

Dress robe: a red robe of the Cambridge pattern [d1], with grey facings and sleeve linings of red brocade.

Hood: a grey panama hood of the CNAA shape [a1], lined red brocade.

Hat: in undress, a black cloth square cap; in full dress, a black velvet bonnet, with grey cords and tassels.

UNIVERSITY OF THE WEST OF SCOTLAND
2007

The University of the West of Scotland was formed in 2007 through the merger of University of Paisley (1992) and Bell College. The University of Paisley was the successor of several institutions in the south-west of Scotland, including the Philosophical Institution, (1808) and the School of Arts, (1836), which was succeeded by the School of Design (1846) and Paisley College of Design (1897). The College was a centre for teaching the London University external degree programme. In 1950, it became a Central Institution, known as Paisley Technical College. It was granted university status in 1992.

Bell College was created in 1972, and was initially known as Bell College of Technology. It operated in co-operation with the University of Strathclyde between 1993 and 2007. In 1995, the Lanarkshire and Dumfries and Galloway Colleges of Nursing and Midwifery were amalgamated into Bell College.

All hoods and the doctors' robes are trimmed red brocade with a paisley design.

UNDERGRADUATES
none specified

UNDERGRADUATE CERTIFICATES and DIPLOMAS
Gown: a black stuff gown of basic pattern [b1], with a cord and button on the yoke.
Hood: a black hood of the Burgon shape [s2], the cowl bordered inside 2″ red Paisley brocade.
Hat: a black cloth square cap.

BACHELORS
Gown: a black stuff gown of basic pattern [b1], with a cord and button on the yoke.
Hood: a black hood of the Cambridge full shape [f1], the cowl bordered inside 4″ red Paisley brocade. The neckband does not reverse, but is faced with red brocade.
Hat: a black cloth square cap.

POSTGRADUATE CERTIFICATES and DIPLOMAS
Gown: as for bachelors.
Hood: a black hood of the Burgon shape [s2], lined as follows:
PGCE: lined red Paisley brocade.
All others: lined and bound red Paisley brocade.
Hat: a black cloth square cap.

MASTERS including MASTERS OF PHILOSOPHY
Gown: a black stuff gown of basic pattern [m10], with a cord and button on the yoke.

Hood: a black hood of the Cambridge full shape [f1], lined red Paisley brocade. The neckband does not reverse, but is faced red brocade.

Hat: a black cloth square cap.

DOCTORS OF PHILOSOPHY and TAUGHT and PROFESSIONAL DOCTORS

Undress gown: *none specified*

Dress robe: a black robe of the Cambridge pattern [d1], facings and sleeve linings of red Paisley brocade.

Hood: a black hood of the Cambridge full shape [f1], lined and bound on all edges with red Paisley brocade. The neckband does not reverse, but is faced red brocade.

Hat: a black cloth bonnet with cords and tassels.

HIGHER DOCTORS

Undress gown: *none specified*

Dress robe: a red Paisley brocade robe of the Cambridge pattern [d1], the facings and sleeve linings of red Paisley brocade.

Hood: as for PhD.

Hat: a black cloth bonnet, with gold cords and tassels.

HONORARY DEGREES

Masters: as for other masters, but the gown is of silver grey, facings of red paisley brocade, hood body silver grey.

Doctors: as for higher doctors.

UNIVERSITY OF WESTMINSTER
1992

In 1838, the Polytechnic Institution opened to the public at 309 Regent Street. Its aim was to demonstrate new technologies and inventions to the public, and it played a significant role in the popularisation of science and engineering, The name was changed to The Royal Polytechnic Institution when Prince Albert, the Prince Consort, became Patron in 1841. The Royal Polytechnic closed in 1881. In 1881 the Regent Street Polytechnic was founded by Quintin Hogg; it was known in full as The Polytechnic Young Men's Christian Institute, Regent Street. It became the Polytechnic of Central London (PCL) in 1970, and gained university status in 1992.

The robes are based on a dual split between Arts (claret) and Science (silver-grey), with additional borders for other faculties. The music degrees are awarded through Trinity College of Music, and hoods feature the College's mauve lining.

UNDERGRADUATES
none specified

UNDERGRADUATE CERTIFICATES and DIPLOMAS
none specified

FOUNDATION DEGREES
Gown: as for bachelors.
Hood: a black hood of the Burgon shape [s2], the cowl bordered inside:
FdA: 2″ claret.
FdSc: 2″ silver-grey.
Hat: a black cloth square cap.

BACHELORS
Gown: a black stuff gown of basic pattern [b1].
Hood: a black hood of the Burgon shape [s2], lined as follows:
BA: lined claret.
BSc: lined silver-grey.
LL.B: lined claret, the cowl bordered inside 2″ purple.
BEng: lined silver-grey, the cowl bordered inside 2″ dark blue.
BA(Mus): lined mauve, the cowl bound 2″ fur.
Hat: a black cloth square cap.

POSTGRADUATE CERTIFICATES and DIPLOMAS
Gown: as for bachelors.
Hood: a light blue hood of the CNAA shape [a1], lined silver-grey, tipped claret.
Hat: a black cloth square cap.

MASTERS including MASTERS OF PHILOSOPHY

Gown: a black stuff gown of basic pattern [m10].

Hood: of the Burgon shape [s2], coloured and lined as follows:

MA: maroon hood, lined claret.
MSc: dark grey hood, lined silver-grey.
LL.M: maroon hood , lined purple.
MEng: dark grey hood , lined dark blue.
MBA: dark blue hood, lined claret.
[MA(Mus): maroon hood, lined mauve.]
MPhil: maroon hood, lined silver-grey.

Hat: a black cloth square cap.

DOCTORS OF PHILOSOPHY and TAUGHT and PROFESSIONAL DOCTORS

Undress gown: as for masters, with 1″ black velvet over the armhole.

Dress robe: a maroon robe of the Oxford pattern [d2], facings and 8″ cuffs of silver grey.

Hood: a maroon hood of the Oxford full shape [f5], lined silver-grey.

Hat: in undress, a black square cap; in full dress, a maroon velvet bonnet, with silver cords and tassels.

HIGHER DOCTORS

Undress gown: as PhD, but with two bands of velvet.

Dress robe: a scarlet cloth robe of the Oxford pattern [d2], facings and 8″ cuffs as follows:

DLitt: claret.
DSc, DTech: silver-grey.
LL.D: purple.
DMus: mauve.

Hood: a scarlet cloth hood of the Oxford full shape [f5], and lined as follows:

DLitt: claret.
DSc, DTech: silver-grey.
LL.D: purple.
DMus: mauve.

Hat: in undress, a black square cap; in full dress, a maroon velvet bonnet, with silver cords and tassels.

UNIVERSITY OF WINCHESTER
2007

Formed in 1840 as a College for training teachers, King Alfred's College, Winchester, moved to its main campus in West Hill, Winchester in 1862. The scope of the syllabus widened from the 1970s, and it awarded Southampton degrees. It became University College, Winchester, in 2004, when it gained taught degree-awarding powers, attaining full university status in 2005. It was granted research degree-awarding powers in 2008.

The shells of all hoods are of violet 'St Aidan' pattern brocade, but 'Winchester' pattern is used for the higher doctors.

UNDERGRADUATES
none specified

UNDERGRADUATE CERTIFICATES and DIPLOMAS and FOUNDATION DEGREES
Gown: as for bachelors.
Hood: a violet brocade hood of the CNAA shape [a1], lined ivory.
Hat: a black cloth square cap.

BACHELORS
Gown: a black stuff gown of London BA pattern [b4].
Hood: a violet brocade hood of the CNAA shape [a1], lined and the cape bound ½″ ivory.
Hat: a black cloth square cap.

POSTGRADUATE CERTIFICATES and DIPLOMAS
Gown: as for bachelors.
Hood: a violet brocade hood of the CNAA shape [a1], lined and the cape bound 1″ ivory.
Hat: a black cloth square cap.

FIRST-DEGREE MASTERS
not awarded

MASTERS
Gown: a black stuff gown of London MA pattern [m5]; there is a cord of violet and ivory and a button of violet on the yoke.
Hood: a violet brocade hood of the London shape [f3], lined ivory; the neckband is violet brocade lined and bound ivory.
Hat: a black cloth square cap.

MASTERS OF PHILOSOPHY

Gown: a black stuff gown of London MA pattern [m5], the facings covered in violet brocade. There is a cord of violet and ivory and a button of violet on the yoke.

Hood: as for other masters.

Hat: a black cloth square cap.

DOCTORS OF PHILOSOPHY

Undress gown: *none specified*

Robe: a scarlet robe of the Oxford pattern [d2], with 4″ facings and 4″ cuffs of violet brocade.

Hood: a scarlet hood of the Oxford full shape [f5], lined violet brocade.

Hat: a black cloth bonnet, with violet cords and tassels.

HIGHER DOCTORS

Robe: a scarlet robe of the Oxford pattern [d2], with 4″ cuffs of violet brocade ('Winchester' pattern). The 4″ facings are 3″ violet brocade, 1″ ivory on the outer edge.

Hood: a scarlet hood of the Oxford full shape [f5], lined violet brocade. ('Winchester' pattern).

Hat: a black velvet bonnet, with violet cords and tassels.

UNIVERSITY OF WOLVERHAMPTON
1992

The Polytechnic was granted full university status in 1992.

The robes are grade-specific, and all hoods are lined red and gold brocade ('Cloister' pattern).

UNDERGRADUATES
none specified

UNDERGRADUATE CERTIFICATES and DIPLOMAS
Gown: as for bachelors.
Hood: a black hood of the CNAA shape [a1], lined plain red, tipped plain gold.
Hat: a black cloth square cap.

FOUNDATION DEGREES
Gown: as for bachelors.
Hood: as for bachelors, but the hood linings are of plain silk, not brocade.
Hat: a black cloth square cap.

BACHELORS
Gown: a black stuff gown of Oxford BA pattern [b8].
Hood: a black hood of the CNAA shape [a1], lined red brocade, the cowl bordered inside 1″ gold brocade.
Hat: a black cloth square cap.

POSTGRADUATE CERTIFICATES and DIPLOMAS
Gown: as for bachelors.
Hood: of the CNAA shape [a1], in black, lined gold taffeta, and tipped red.
Hat: a black cloth square cap.

MASTERS including MASTERS OF PHILOSOPHY and POST-MASTER DIPLOMA IN SCIENCE
Gown: a black stuff gown of basic pattern [m10], with an inverted-T armhole.
Hood: a black hood of the CNAA shape [a1], lined gold brocade, the cowl bordered inside 1″ red brocade.
Hat: a black cloth square cap.

DOCTORS OF PHILOSOPHY and TAUGHT and PROFESSIONAL DOCTORS
Undress gown: as for masters.

Dress robe: a crimson cloth robe of the Oxford pattern [d2], the facings and 4″ cuffs of gold brocade.

Hood: a crimson hood of the CNAA shape [a1], lined gold brocade.

Hat: in undress, a black square cap; in full dress, a black cloth bonnet, with gold cords and tassels.

HIGHER DOCTORS

Undress gown: as PhD.

Dress robe: a scarlet cloth robe of the Oxford pattern [d2], the facings and 4″ cuffs of gold brocade.

Hood: a scarlet hood of the CNAA shape [a1], lined gold brocade.

Hat: in undress, a black square cap; in full dress, a black velvet bonnet, with gold cords and tassels.

UNIVERSITY OF WORCESTER
2005

In 1947 an Emergency Teacher Training College was opened at Worcester, as part of the University of Birmingham Department of Education, eventually becoming the Worcester College of Higher Education. In 1997 the Privy Council gave the institution degree-awarding powers and it subsequently became known as University College Worcester (UCW). In 2005 it gained full university status.

All hoods and robes feature a colour called 'Worcester blue'; this in fact a teal colour, and is noted as such below.

UNDERGRADUATES
none specified

UNDERGRADUATE CERTIFICATES and DIPLOMAS
Gown: a black stuff gown of the basic pattern [b1].
Hood: a black hood of the CNAA shape [a1], the cowl bordered inside 2″ teal.

FOUNDATION DEGREES
Gown: a black stuff gown of the basic pattern [b1].
Hood: a black hood of the CNAA shape [a1], lined silver, and tipped teal.
Hat: a black cloth square cap.

BACHELORS
Gown: a black stuff gown of the basic pattern [b1].
Hood: a black hood of the CNAA shape [a1], lined teal, the cowl bordered inside 1″ silver silk.
Hat: a black cloth square cap.

POSTGRADUATE CERTIFICATES and DIPLOMAS
Gown: a black stuff gown of the basic pattern [b1].
Hood: a black hood of the CNAA shape [a1], lined and bound 1″ teal, the cowl bordered inside 1″ silver silk.
Hat: a black cloth square cap.

FIRST-DEGREE MASTERS
not awarded

MASTERS including MASTERS OF PHILOSOPHY
Gown:
MPhil: a black stuff gown of the basic pattern [m10], with 2½″ facings of teal.

All others: a black stuff gown of basic pattern [m10].

Hood: a black hood of the Cambridge shape, lined and bound 1″ teal, the cowl bordered inside 1″ silver silk. If awarded *honoris causa*, the silver is set 1″ in.

Hat: a black cloth square cap.

DOCTORS OF PHILOSOPHY and TAUGHT and PROFESSIONAL DOCTORS

Undress gown: *none specified*

Dress robe: a black stuff robe of the basic masters' pattern [m10], faced 2½″ teal and ¾″ silver braid.

Hood: a black hood of the Cambridge shape, lined and bound 1″ teal, the cowl ordered inside 1″ silver braid.

Hat: a black cloth bonnet, with teal cords and tassels.

HIGHER DOCTORS

Undress gown: *none specified*

Dress robe: as for PhD, but the whole gown made in teal panama, faced 1″ silver braid.

Hood: a teal panama hood of the Cambridge shape, lined and bound teal silk, the cowl bordered inside 1″ silver braid.

Hat: a teal cloth bonnet, with silver cords and tassels.

UNIVERSITY OF YORK
1963

The first petition for the establishment of a university in York was presented to King James I in 1617. In 1903 a 'Victoria University of Yorkshire' was proposed. The University of York was opened in 1963, as part of the expansion of higher education, admitting 200 students. It is collegiate, with eight colleges, of which one is for postgraduates only; the others accept undergraduate and postgraduate students.

The academic dress is noted for the use of grey – which appears in the gowns and hats as well as the hoods. The PhD (originally designated DPhil) has possibly the least 'showy' set of robes of any, as the dress robe is the MA gown with the addition of a red cord and button on the sleeves. Faculty colours are in part-use – for example, all science degrees have light blue – but in other cases they do not: the BA is grey bordered white, while the MA is grey lined red, the white lining going to the MSW. The original degrees were BA, BPhil, MPhil, DPhil, DLitt, DSc, and DUniv. Originally, all graduates were awarded a BA, and the BSc was not introduced until c.1980.

UNDERGRADUATES
none specified

UNDERGRADUATE CERTIFICATES and DIPLOMAS
Gown: as bachelors.
Hood:
DipHE: of the CNAA shape [a1], grey cloth, bound on all edges ½″ pale blue.

FOUNDATION DEGREES
not awarded

BACHELORS
Gown: a grey stuff gown of basic pattern [b1].
Hood: a grey cloth hood of the CNAA shape [a1], lined grey silk, and bordered 3″ inside as follows:
BA: white silk.
BEng: dark blue silk.
[BPhil: red silk.]
BSc: light blue silk.
Hat: a grey cloth square cap.

POSTGRADUATE CERTIFICATES and DIPLOMAS
none specified

FIRST-DEGREE MASTERS (MChem, MEng, MMath, MPhys)

Gown: as for bachelors.

Hood: a grey cloth hood of the CNAA shape [a1], lined dark blue silk.

Hat: a grey cloth square cap.

MASTERS including MASTERS OF PHILOSOPHY

Gown: a black stuff gown of basic pattern [m10], with an inverted-T armhole.

Hood: a grey cloth hood (except MPhil) of the CNAA shape, fully lined:

MA: red.
MRes: gold.
[MSW: white.]
MPA: red (same hood as MA).
MUniv [*was BPhil*]: bordered inside 3″ red silk.
MPhil: a red hood, lined red, bordered inside the cowl 3″ grey silk.

Hat: a grey cloth square cap.

DOCTORS OF PHILOSOPHY and TAUGHT and PROFESSIONAL DOCTORS

Undress gown: as for masters.

Dress robe: as for masters, but with a 4″ red cord at the top of the vertical slit, and a red button at its top.

Hood: a red hood of the CNAA shape [a1], lined grey silk.

Hat: in undress, a grey square cap; in full dress, a grey cloth bonnet, with grey cords and tassels.

HIGHER DOCTORS

Undress gown: as PhD.

Dress robe: as for masters, but the facings and the sleeves below the armhole covered in red silk.

Hood:

DUniv: a red hood of the CNAA shape [a1], lined grey.
DLitt, DSc, DMus: a red hood of the CNAA shape [a1], lined and bound 1″ grey.

Hat: in undress, a grey cloth square cap; in full dress, a grey cloth bonnet, with grey cords and tassels.

NOTES

1. The obsolete diploma of EngDip had the bachelors' gown and a red hood bordered inside 3″ dark blue silk.
2. Originally, higher doctors had red hoods of the CNAA shape [a1], lined and bound as follows:
   DLitt: grey.
   DSc: light blue.
   DMus: white.
   DUniv: lined but not bound grey.

YORK ST JOHN UNIVERSITY
2007

The university descends from two Anglican teacher training colleges, which were founded in York in 1841 (for men) and in 1846 (for women). In 1862, the women's college relocated to Ripon. Over the next century, the colleges gradually diversified their education programmes. The colleges merged in 1974 to form the College of Ripon and York St John. In 1990 the combined institution formally became a college of the University of Leeds; this arrangement allowed it to award degrees in the name of the latter, while remaining in practice largely autonomous. Between 1999 and 2001, all activities were transferred to York, the Ripon campus closed, and the college received the name York St John College. In February 2006, the College was granted the right to award degrees in its own name and became the University College of York St John. In 2006 the Privy Council approved a request from the college to become a University, and the name was changed to York St John University.

The scheme is simple and grade-specific. The damask used to line all hoods is a special design, based on the rose window of York Minster. The green is mint green.

UNDERGRADUATES
none specified

UNDERGRADUATE CERTIFICATES and DIPLOMAS
Gown: as for bachelors.
Hood: a dark blue hood of the CNAA shape, the cowl bordered inside 2½″ mint green damask, and bound ½″ gold.
Hat: a black cloth square cap.

FOUNDATION DEGREES
Gown: as for bachelors.
Hood: a dark blue hood of the CNAA shape, the cowl bordered inside 4½″ mint green damask, and bound ½″ gold.
Hat: a black cloth square cap.

BACHELORS
Gown: a black stuff gown of basic pattern [b1].
Hood: a dark blue hood of the CNAA shape, lined mint green damask, and bound on all edges ½″ gold.
Hat: a black cloth square cap.

POSTGRADUATE CERTIFICATES and DIPLOMAS
Gown: as for masters.

Hood: a dark blue hood of the Cambridge shape, lined mint green damask, and the cowl bound ½″ gold.
Hat: a black cloth square cap.

FIRST-DEGREE MASTERS
not awarded

MASTERS
Gown: a black stuff gown of basic pattern [m10].
Hood: a dark blue hood of the Cambridge shape [f1], lined mint green damask, and bound on all edges ½″ gold.
Hat: a black cloth square cap.

DOCTORS OF PHILOSOPHY and TAUGHT and PROFESSIONAL DOCTORS
not yet awarded

HIGHER DOCTORS
Undress gown: *none specified*
Dress robe: a dark blue robe of the Oxford pattern [d2], with 5″ facings and 12″ sleeve cuffs of mint green damask and 1″ gold on the outer edge of the facings and on the lower edge of the sleeves.
Hood: of the Cambridge shape [f1], lined mint green damask, and bound on all edges 1″ gold.
Hat: a dark blue cloth bonnet, with gold cords and tassels.

BIBLIOGRAPHY

This covers the more immediately accessible works. Others, including articles in journals, are to be found in the exhaustive Bibliography on the Burgon Society's website (www.burgon.org.uk/society/library/biblio.php).

HISTORICAL WORKS

Franklyn, C A H, *Academical Dress from the Middle Ages to the present day, including Lambeth degrees*, Lewes, 1970.

Hargreaves-Mawdsley, W N , *A History of Academical Dress in Europe until the end of the Eighteenth Century*; Oxford, 1963.

CATALOGUES

Shaw, G W, *Academical Dress of British Universities*; Cambridge, 1966. ('Shaw 1')

Shaw, G W, *Academical Dress of British and Irish Universities*; Chichester, 1995 ('Shaw 2')

Baty, T, *Academic Colours*, Tokyo, 1934

Ealand, C A (ed.), *Athena – A Year-book of the Learned World. Vol. 1: The English-Speaking Nations*, London, A&C Black, 1920

Groves, N W , *Key to the Identification of Academic hoods of the British Isles*, Burgon Society, 2002 (second edition, 2003; third, 2008; fourth 2010).

Gutch, J W G, *University Hoods*, Notes & Queries (second series) 6 (1858) pp. 211–212

Haycraft, F W , *The Degrees and Hoods of the World's Universities and Colleges*
first edition, Ware, 1923.
second edition, Cheshunt, 1924.
third edition, Cheshunt,1927.
fourth edition, Cheshunt, 1948, revised by E W S Stringer.
fifth edition, Lewes 1972, revised by F R S Rogers, C A H Franklyn, G W Shaw, and H A Boyd.

Smith, H H, and Sheard, K, *Academic Dress and Insignia of the World: Gowns, Hats, Chains of Office, Hoods, Rings, Medals and Other Degree Insignia of Universities and Other Institutions of Learning*, 3 volumes, Cape Town, 1970.

Vincent, W D F, *The Cutter's Practical Guide to the Cutting and Making All Kinds of Garments, part 9*, London, John Williamson, 1898.

Wood, T W, *Ecclesiastical and Academical Colours*, London, Bemrose & Sons, 1875.

Wood, T W, *Degrees, Gowns and Hoods of the British, Colonial, Indian and American Universities and Colleges*, London, c.1882 (revised 1887).

ORKS ON INDIVIDUAL UNIVERSITIES

ond, A G, *College Gowns*, London, 1926.

d, A G, *Cambridge Robes for Doctors and Graduates*, Cambridge, 1909 (second edition eprinted with revisions, 1959).

B, *Academic Dress in the University of Hertfordshire*, 2nd edition, Hatfield, 2006.

lachite and Silver: Academic Dress of the University of Stirling, Burgon Society,

ty of London Academic Dress, London, 1999.

Groves, N W, *The Academical Robes of St David's College, Lampeter (1822-1971)*, Lampeter, 2001.

Groves, N W, and Kersey, J, *Academical Dress of Music Colleges and Societies of Musicians in the United Kingdom*, Burgon Society, 2002.

Groves, N W, *Theological Colleges, their hoods and histories*, Burgon Society, 2004.

Groves, N W, *The Academical Dress of the University of East Anglia*, Burgon Society, 2005.

Lowe, P J, *Manchester Academic Dress: the origins and development of Academical Dress at the Victoria University of Manchester from 1880 to the present day*. Manchester, 2002 (privately printed).

Shaw, G W, *Cambridge University Academical Dress*, Cambridge, 1992.

Venables, D R and Clifford, R E, *Academic Dress of the University of Oxford*, 1957 (second edition, 1966; third 1972; fourth, 1975; fifth, 1979; sixth, 1985; seventh, 1993; eighth, 1998; ninth, 2009).

PERIODICALS

Transactions of the Burgon Society, annually. The first four issues (2001–2004) were called *The Burgon Society Annual*. Electronic copies of older issues may be downloaded from the society's website (www.burgon.org.uk/society/library/trans/index.php).

Scanned copies of some of the older texts listed above can be found online via the Internet Archive (www.archive.org)

THE BURGON SOCIETY

The Burgon Society was founded in 2000 in response to a growing interest in the subject of academical dress. It is named after John Burgon (1813–1888), sometime Dean of Chichester Cathedral, fellow of Oriel College, Oxford, and the only person to have a shape of academical hood named after him.

The aims of the Society are:

- to co-ordinate the study of academical dress in all its aspects - design, history and practice;
- to preserve details of the past and present practices of institutions regarding academical dress;
- to act in an advisory capacity to film and television companies, and to those who wish to ensure correctness in the usage of academical dress.

Membership of the Society is open to anybody who is interested in academical dress. Fellowship of the Society is awarded to members on the successful submission of a suitable piece of original work.

The Society meets several times a year to receive newly submitted fellowship papers and to discuss other matters related to academical dress. It publishes a scholarly journal, *Transactions of the Burgon Society*, containing research papers submitted during the year; and organizes exhibitions of academical dress and study visits. The Society also possesses a substantial collection of robes, and an archive of books and papers which are open, by prior arrangement with the Archivist, to anyone interested in undertaking research on academic dress.

If you would like to join the Burgon Society, please visit the website www.burgon.org.uk and download a membership form.

For further information, please email registrar@burgon.org.uk.

The Burgon Society is a registered charity in England and Wales (no. 1137522).

L - #0137 - 120620 - C0 - 246/189/24 - PB - DID2849810